Strategic Relationship Marketing

Springer
Berlin
Heidelberg
New York
Hong Kong
London
Milan
Paris
Tokyo

Søren Hougaard
Mogens Bjerre

Strategic Relationship Marketing

Springer

Søren Hougaard
Loevvaenget 3
2960 Rungsted Kyst
Denmark
shougaard@amsgroup.dk

Mogens Bjerre
Skovlodden 24
2840 Holte
Denmark
mb.marktg@cbs.dk

Co-publication by Springer-Verlag, Heidelberg, Germany
and Samfundslitteratur, Frederiksberg, Denmark.

ISBN 3-540-01870-0 Springer-Verlag Berlin Heidelberg New York

Cataloging-in-Publication Data applied for
A catalog record for this book is available from the Library of Congress.
Bibliographic information published by Die Deutsche Bibliothek
Die Deutsche Bibliothek lists this publication in the Deutsche Nationalbibliografie; detailed bibliographic data is available in the Internet at <http://dnb.ddb.de>.

Springer-Verlag Berlin Heidelberg New York
a member of BertelsmannSpringer Science+Business Media GmbH

http://www.springer.de

Printed in Denmark

Softcover-Design: Erich Kirchner, Heidelberg

SPIN 10925881 42/3130/DK-5 4 3 2 1 0 – Printed on acid-free paper

Tabel of Content

Part III – Relationship Marketing Strategies

Preface

Our Vision

Welcome to the fantastic universe of relationships and strategic relationship marketing!

Our vision is to take you, our reader, on an exciting journey into the frontier of marketing management via relationship-oriented understanding of business life. This is quite a challenge as we intend to present and develop a marketing philosophy that is innovative and focuses unconditionally on relationships. Furthermore, our goal is to present a relationship approach to strategy that is both theoretically founded as well as applicable in real world situations.

Many well-established management theories, we believe, need to be reformulated as the network economy sweeps through business life and permeates all areas of society. Individuals and groups will behave in new ways; organisations become reconfigured and will have to develop new cooperative and adaptive mechanisms to stay competitive. *All that can think must link.*

The importance of strategic marketing excellence in reaching a level of superior market performance remains unchanged. But a great many aspects of strategic marketing management have changed and are changing.

The Dawn of New Marketing Thinking

Therefore, the demand for a relationship based marketing framework is growing. Structures and conditions of markets have changed. Competition moves away from inter-firm rivalry to competition among value chains leading us in a direction of dyadic[1] or triadic marketing management. Any company must therefore pay attention to the supply chain as a vertical system and try to create

1. Dyadic referes to two organisations acting as one, triadic refers to three, etc. See also footnote 2 in chapter 2.

relationship benefits for customers and suppliers, not just for the company itself. This applies to both physical and virtual relationships.

Industries, where relationships between trade parties are a critical success factor, such as within service-based industries, information technology, new media and telecommunication are gaining momentum in the global economy at a tremendous speed. In many situations time-to-market, capacity, trust and stability are a competitive necessity, whereas the issue of price seems to be much less important. Partnership, not arms' length business practice, is on the marketing agenda.

At all levels of society BtB[2], as well as BtC[3], interactivity is a fact. Before the age of interactivity and the unlimited access to information, marketing decisions were governed by the *economics of things.*[4] Management faced a great many trade-offs, e.g. one-way mass communication versus richness in terms of personal communication. These days, high reach is no longer a barrier for interactivity. And lack of face-to-face contact does not prevent richness in communication and purchasing processes. We are moving in the direction of economics of informations and knowledge.

Market Leadership – Old Economic Rationales under Pressure?

Marketing is a management discipline, meaning that it is a set of values supporting certain company culture characteristics. Marketing is also a technique decision-makers use for allocating resources in order to reach specific goals in the best possible way under dynamic market and competitive conditions. Marketing deals with understanding and application of business economic rationales. And the questions about "why", "where", "how" and "when" to allocate resources will certainly not disappear in the future.

But there is more and more evidence that economic effectiveness and quality in customer relationships must be viewed as a separate strategic issue in marketing. Who says that market leadership means dominance, gorilla thinking and the highest market share? What happens when economies of scale are

2. BtB is used throughout the book as an abbreviation for business-to business.
3. BtC is used throughout the book as an abbreviation for business-to-consumer.
4. Evans and Wurster (2000).

linked more to network economics than to accumulated experiences? In that case agility and fast movers might eventually break the marketing codes of former market leaders. The thunder flies will win.

Consequently the idea arises that the attributes of exchange, i.e. reciprocity, interdependence, partnership and transparency vis-à-vis every single customer, create more profit and value for the company than negotiating power or market dominance. New paths to market leadership are becoming more attractive.

Future Marketing Paradigm

A new, dynamic paradigm for marketing management based on relationships will gradually emerge and work its way into boardrooms, graduate schools and consulting firms. It is fed by an exponential increase in the amount of new research in this field. It gets further stimulation from more and more best practise cases, where a growing number of customers design their marketing strategies, organisational structures and business models along a relationship perspective. Just think about great companies like Cisco, Southwest Airlines or Dell Computers.

The market for Customer Relationship Management (CRM) systems and concepts is among the fastest growing industries. This growth reflects the need for companies to strengthen their relationship marketing competencies.

Traditional strategy and marketing textbooks treat customer-supplier relationships as an adjunct, an extra dimension within the existing theoretical frames of reference. The relationship perspective has been viewed as a modification of accepted marketing theories, a new parameter among others to consider.

What we need, however, is a new marketing paradigm *founded* on relationships. Why? Because relationships are becoming the backbone to any competitive business and are the key to market success. Customers now pool their bargaining power in virtual associations and value chains that require a holistic perspective where competitors can also be partners!

Objectives

When we began writing Strategic Relationship Marketing we had a very clear objective in mind. We wanted to demonstrate that a relationship approach to marketing could and should be developed into a discipline of its own. In our view, this would require the design of a completely new relationship-marketing framework. A framework that is based on business economics and integrates the best of the existing marketing management thinking. A framework that is derived from basic and esteemed theories on relationship behaviour and business strategy. A framework that gives the reader conceptual insight as well as inspiration and applicable techniques for strategic marketing purposes.

Research in relationship behaviour and relationship marketing has presented a lot of strong evidence that supports the hypothesis that the relationship aspect plays a central role in the understanding of markets and company behaviour in real life. This research not only draws such conclusions from empirical evidence, but also from theoretical models of behaviour and marketing systems that can actually describe and explain relationship patterns and market structures.

Our objective is to structure, integrate and synthesise what we know about strategic relationship marketing across research boundaries into one framework of analysis and strategy formulation. Based on this framework the reader should not only get a complete overview of the why's, what's and how's of strategic relationship marketing, but also a series of logical links between traditional marketing thinking and definitions on the one hand and relationship marketing models on the other.

Target Audience

As a textbook writer one must be careful defining the target audience. First, Strategic Relationship Marketing is not a handbook or a checklist like "how-to" book, although Chapter 11 does present a series of recent relationship marketing cases across a variety of industries, countries and marketing situations. Second, our clear goal is to give our reader a mental roadmap to relationship marketing in terms of definitions, models, archetypes, parametric overviews and analytical templates and methodologies. Nothing is more practical than a reliable theory, by the way!

Both authors have long professional backgrounds both in business and academia. We are convinced that practitioners do seek frameworks for conceptual understanding and mental landscapes for decision-making, and that relationship marketing in particular is considered to be a crucial matter in most companies.

We also believe that students in marketing management, business administration and economics can benefit from a textbook that presents a holistic and applicable approach to relationship management connecting relationship-marketing theories to business economics, traditional marketing strategy and organisational behaviour.

In summary, we therefore have graduate students, scholars, management consultants and marketing practitioners as our target audience as they all demand a new relationship marketing framework.

It does not require any specific prerequisites to benefit from reading Strategic Relationship Marketing, just time and dedication. However, some parts of our the book do assume that the reader has insight into general marketing management and mainstream strategy models as well as basic business economic theories. Therefore we recommend our reader to first become acquainted with the basic principles of strategic marketing management.

Outline of the Book

Strategic Relationship Marketing does not quite follow the traditional outline of a marketing textbook, which typically is organised along the marketing process: First market and competitor analysis, then the formulation of marketing goals and strategies and finally tactical issues going through the marketing mix parameters one by one.

We have replaced the step-by-step planning textbook logic with a principle of progression based on what we think is a more pedagogical approach. The book is divided into three parts.

In Part I we ask and answer the following question: "*What is the value of relationships*"? Part I is the "why strategic relationship marketing?" portion of the book.

Part II – Preconditions for Building Successful Relationships explores and discusses the building blocks in terms of drivers, levels and contexts for successful relationship marketing. Where Part I answers the "why" question, Part II elaborates on the "where, what and who".

Part III – Relationship Marketing Strategies synthesises the previous discussions into a framework of generic marketing relationship strategies, the "how" aspect of a relationship managerial approach to the marketing task.

A graphical overview of the book is illustrated in the following:

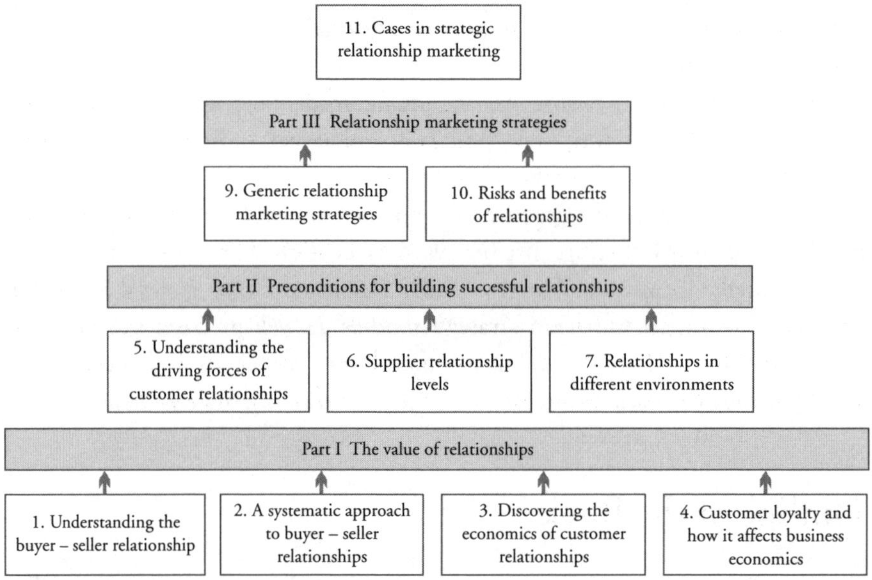

Figure 1: An overview of the book.

Although the pyramid structure of the book reflects a principle of progression and vertical synthesis, it is possible to only read parts of the book or specific chapters that are of special interest. Admittedly, this is in conflict with the physical nature of the pyramid, where each part is crucial for stability.

Part I – The Value of Relationships

In *Chapter 1* we focus on the *Understanding of the buyer-seller relationship – the roots of relationship marketing.* Our thesis that the value of relationships > the value of exchanges leads to a presentation and discussion of a new marketing definitions that is centred on relationships. The structural attributes of buyer-seller relationships are outlined and described in a dynamic context, as well as typologies regarding relationship categories and purchasing and selling strategies, cooperation, competition or command and the outcome in terms of the degree of mutual dependence.

Chapter 1 lays our foundation, the roadmap of understanding so to speak, of what brings value to relationships and hence to marketing. One of the distinctions outlined is whether relationships are exchange, interactive or integration centric.

We conclude chapter 1 with an overview of the main research directions that have contributed to the formulation of theories in relationship marketing.

The political economy paradigm is now introduced as an overall framework for analysing and influencing relationships. *Chapter 2*, which covers this topic, has been given the title: *A systematic approach to the buyer-seller relationship.* What we expand upon here is the concept of marketing as a system of exchanges. The introduction of the exchange perspective in marketing leads to a complete reorientation of our view on marketing management and on the role of marketing in a supply chain context. We describe the different types of exchange and their implications: Restricted, generalised and complex exchanges that contain the how and who dimensions are discussed and compared with the more utalitarian, symbolic and mixed exchanges that contain the what dimension.

The political economy paradigm should be considered as a framework of relationship understanding and analysis. It includes three different spaces – (I) internal, (II) inner environment and (III) outer environment of the business entity and combines this with a political (power, dependence, control...) perspective combined with the sets of economic laws such as markets and competition. We use the political economy paradigm throughout the book to gain insight into different archetypes of relationship strategies and behavioural patterns of business. The paradigm (not to be confused with a theory) represents a holistic approach to the understanding of relationships, markets and supply chains covering their complexities and different levels of influence. The concepts of dyadic and triadic structures and relationship philosophies are touched upon as well.

Approaching a parametric view on marketing in *Chapter 2* we are now able to fit the 30R typology developed by Gummesson[5] and the referral market framework[6] into the political economy paradigm of strategic relationship management. This offers a new perception of these former stand-alone typologies.

Traditional business economics is episode centric in the sense that it does not include relationship economic rationales and terminologies. If relationships are considered to be the *purpose* of strategic marketing, which we to some degree are claiming, then we must *uncover the economics of customer relationships.*

This central topic is covered in *Chapter 3*. In this chapter we develop the basic principles and concepts of relationship economics as opposed to exchange economics. We rely heavily on transaction cost theory and the underlying forces of that theory such as risk, opportunism, idiosyncrasy, regulating mechanisms and customisation of assets. The relationship is a hybrid activity form as compared with the hierarchy and the classical market contract. The relationship marketing

5. Gummesson (1996).
6. Christopher, Payne and Ballantyne (1999).

philosophy follows its own rules and business economic laws. The three cornerstone principles in relationship economics are (1) customisation of assets as compared with complete resource mobility, (2) costs of friction versus the concept of smooth exchanges and (3) the customer life cycle versus the periodic view.

Relationship economic laws become visible and measurable in the pattern and level of transaction costs in terms of the 3 C's: Contact, Contract and Contract costs representing the different "stages" of an exchange.

Customer loyalty is usually considered to be the most precise and ultimate expression of the value of relationships. Therefore, *Chapter 4 – Customer loyalty and how it affects business economics* describes loyalty as phenomenon and goes behind and beyond the prevailing perceptions of what loyalty is about.

Here we separate the value elements of customer loyalty into three very different basic relationship economic effects: (1) lifetime economy, (2) efficiency economy and (3) value adding economy. Loyalty can in many situations be used as prime segmentation criteria based on the common notion of attractiveness and position. Not only the level of loyalty, but also its origin and fit with business strategies.

It is crucial for the marketer to identify loyalty and the factors that enhance loyalty within a business economic and strategic frame of reference. Therefore *Chapter 4* concludes by presenting a range of loyalty measurement techniques. We view loyalty within the notion of relationship economics and discuss why and where it pays off for customers (and suppliers) to actually become loyal. The consumer marketing kind of emotional or one-way brand loyalty is also included, and it is demonstrated that it makes a lot of relationship economic sense to become dedicated buyers of brands.

Part II Preconditions for Building Successful Relationships

What are the key drivers behind customer relationships? Which structural elements are at play when reinforcing or discontinuing any customer relationship at any time – why and when? How difficult are these forces to understand, control or adjust for a marketer? When do the forces offer opportunities or represent threats? *Chapter 5* takes a closer look at these crucial strategic matters under the heading: *Understanding the driving forces of customer relationships.*

Like the competitive climate in an industry, customer relationships are influenced by, or even a product of, a set of driving forces. These driving forces become the scope of analysis as an integral part of formulating a relationship marketing strategy leading to sustainable competitive advantage. We have chosen an actor-based framework as the independent driving forces of customer relationships.

External driving forces comprise the relationship participants – seller, buyer and competitors plus a range of influents – who have the intention of disturbing or conquering the relationship, be it invaders or innovators. The bargaining power of each incumbent depends on a multiple of factors that can be derived from basic constitutional factor analysis such as opportunism, risk, regulating mechanisms, asset customisation and barriers to entry and exit. Our idea is that all the triadic players and their "plays" have a huge impact on the relationship, and we show how to analyse the atmosphere.

The internal driving forces are embedded in the relationship and its basic structures; they comprise the relationship form, the exchange form and the customer life cycle. The internal driving forces co-exist and they may or may not pull in the same direction and with the same strength.

The driving force model attempts to separate the customer relationship influences into distinctly different sources and areas of impact. Understanding the driving forces of customer relationships is a precondition for the formulation of a sustainable relationship marketing strategy and hence a key element in the relationship marketing process. If customer loyalty is the achievement, and if the relationship economic principles are the rules, then the driving forces are the landscape that must be navigated in, interpreted and capitalised on.

Proceeding with *Chapter 6 – Supplier relationship levels* and *Chapter 7 – Relationships in different environments* we combine the relationship value principles in Part I and the driving force model in *Chapter 5* with specific strategic environments and situations, in which relationships exist and are governed by marketing management.

Chapter 6 goes into detail with regard to the genuine types of customer relationships, with special concern for the "degree" of relationship orientation among buyers and sellers. We work on the idea that there are significant differences between low level relationships and relationships at the top of the relationship ladder, also with regard to the strength and direction of the driving forces.

In BtB markets, key account management is a concrete relationship marketing arrangement stemming from certain business and marketing axioms and development stages. Key account management is one among the many different parametric decisions, and organisational forms, that can be used to implement a dyadic marketing strategy in a company.

The four classes, or roles, of key account management reflect at which relationship level the selling organisation wishes to run its business with customers.

They are (1) contact, (2) passive coordinator, (3) proactive coordinator and (4) integrator. These very different customer relationship levels represent individual relationship approaches with different relationship economic scope and consequences. The higher the relationship level, the better relationship economy, although frequently combined with investments in customised assets, there is also a high level of risk involved as well as a high propensity of opportunistic behaviour.

Some authors treat the specific sales organisational design, and hence also key account management, as a tactical solution of minor importance as seen from a theoretical perspective. We do not share this view. The flesh and blood of purchasing and selling strategies and of loyalty development consists of behavioural preconditions, where the profile of a company's customer organisation is of central importance.

Industry characteristics differ and so do customer relationships. In *Chapter 7* we define an analytical technique that enables marketing management to better realise the relationship-based opportunities. The analytical process goes through three steps: (1) industry attractiveness analysis, (2) business system analysis and (3) competitor analysis. This analysis should both be carried out with specific emphasis on relationships and with the purpose of actually identifying the main drivers behind these three factors. This approach does not conflict with the driving forces presented in *Chapter 5* but rather supplement them.

Chapter 7 also deals with relationships in different industry contexts, across the industry life cycle and focuses on the contents of relationships. Among others, the digital value chain represents one such unique and different industrial structure where business systems and behaviours of suppliers and buyers have very different constraints, levers and relationship economic rationales. The migration of intelligence leads to a different composition of driving forces, which are presented and debated. In digital value chains both buyers and sellers within a relationship will try to capitalise on migration in terms of "arbitrage", "aggregation", "rewiring" and "reassembly".

Part III – Relationship Marketing Strategies

Part III focuses on marketing planning in terms of relationship marketing strategies, their risks and benefits. You will find two very different approaches to relationship strategies, which we have combined. *The individualised approach to relationship* in *Chapter 8* geared towards for BtB markets assumes that each customer (or partner) has a different relationship behaviour or purchasing strategy, if you will, and that these behavioural patterns can be divided into role models or typologies. The marketer must tailor the relationship strategy to each customer.

Chapter 9 presents overall *generic relationship marketing strategies.* In this chapter we ask: What does it take to develop sustainable competitive relationship advantage for a company or a business unit? And: Which generic strategies can possibly lead in that direction?

Companies do not adapt to external changes in the same manner; their "adaptive circles" differ. Hence, for a supplier to become a successful relationship partner, he must take the individual approach. Based on empirical evidence Miles and Snow[7] have identified four main types of such organisational relationship behaviour in terms of: (1) The defender, (2) the prospector, (3) the analyser and (4) the reactor. They exhibit very different patterns of behaviour, when it comes to their motives for engaging in relationships, the content, contractual mechanisms, attitude to risk, adoption to partnerships etc. Based on a detailed description of the four relationship behavioural styles, we have been able to identify areas where individualised approaches imply opportunities for relationship-based transactions, why and when. The four-type classification can give a supplier a deeper understanding of the explicit strategy and/or the de facto behaviour of customers and can therefore lead to relationship alignment superior to competitors.

The basic thesis underlying the generic relationship marketing strategies presented and discussed in *Chapter 9* is that above average profitability in an industry assumes extraordinary customer satisfaction and loyalty. It is the top step on the loyalty ladder that makes the difference. Extraordinary customer satisfaction is what separates the excellent from the mediocre. Therefore the loyalty-satisfaction paradox explains why even satisfied customers (but no more than satisfied) very often do not behave with affection, but are more or less indifferent.

A relationship based marketing strategy is not always the most obvious source of competitive advantage, but in many contexts it is the most successful. Through careful analysis of relationship economic structures and impacts, the buyer experience life cycle, identification of hidden segments demanding different relational features etc. a company will very often face a whole new world of strategic opportunities based on relationship marketing principles.

Here, we introduce the customer relationship benefit grid combining the

7. Miles and Snow (1978).

stages of the customer life cycle with *relationship economic levers* (contact, contract and control costs) and *relationship quality levers* (customisation, convenience and comfort) as a technique to discover structural relationship opportunities.

Detecting the potential market and the potential sources for relationship based competitive advantages the marketer can either: (a) develop sustainable relationship benefits on the total market as opposed to part of the market or (b) focus on relationship economic levers as opposed to relationship quality features.

We identify four generic relationship marketing strategies. We present them, highlight which elements will stimulate them, define which means will point in this specific direction and how a relationship based market leadership can be defended from presumed attacks from competitors and other driving forces in the relationship universe.

Transaction cost leadership is a generic relationship strategy targeting the total market with the purpose of developing and defending a unique relationship economic position. *The relationship differentiator strives* for overall leadership through relationship quality attributes highly appreciated by the total market and difficult for others to imitate or with compete.

The relationship quality segment specialist successfully reaches a relationship based leadership position in specific segments with a differentiated set of preferences and relationship priorities. Whereas *the transaction cost niche explorer* attempts to capitalise in certain well-defined segments which have distinctly different, but for them very important, relationship economic demands either across the customer life cycle or in some stages.

Most researchers agree and many studies have shown a very strong and indeed a very surprising correlation between profitability and aspects of relationships as outlined earlier. For any manager of a market activity on either BtB or BtC markets the strategic perspectives of the relationship view should definitely not be overlooked.

We conclude Part III by discussing *risks and benefits of relationships* in *Chapter 10.* We do not unilaterally focus on customer benefits, but look at the supplier benefits as well and the relationship in itself. We combine the archetypes of individual organisational relationship behaviour outlined in *Chapter 8* with the generic relationship marketing strategies and ask: Based on our insight into the relationship response profiles of the different archetypes, how and when will each of the generic relationship marketing strategies be viable, risky or prohibitive? And why? The political economy paradigm and the exchange systems view on relationship marketing *(Chapter 2)* are included in the analysis.

Standardisation and *individualisation* represent two distinctly different relationship directions, both being potentially beneficial and each accompanied by embedded and situational risks as well. The discussion of standardisation versus individualisation touches relationship economics, the pros and cons of specifying assets to customer needs, and match and mismatch in regulating mechanisms between parties depending on their more or less monadic strategies versus dyadic philosophies etc.

This book is packed with examples, small cases and documentations from real life business situations in very different industries and geographical regions. We have deliberately tried to inspire our readers not only by developing applicable models and frameworks, but also through the presentation of exciting situations, where relationship-marketing strategies really matter and make a difference.

As a digestive, *Chapter 11* is dedicated to relationship marketing cases. The cases cover (and demonstrate) many of the central topics from the previous ten chapters and the difficult dilemmas the marketer is confronted with when deciding between different marketing strategic directions. In retrospect, successful relationship marketing strategies seem so obvious. Please read each case in chapter 11 carefully and you will probably agree that the strategic diagnosis and the trade offs can be rather difficult to make. Try and get into the relationship nervous system of Ikea. Discuss all the built-in conflicts in frequent bonus schemes, the most successful loyalty programme ever. Analyse why the flames died for Firestone and Ford after generations of strategic cooperation. And consider your view of the economics of customer relationship in e-business: benefits, traps, and opportunities, etc.

We wish you a pleasant journey to the land of customer relationship marketing!

Acknowledgements

Writing a book doesn't come easily, even though it seems to when the process is undertaken and the table of contents gradually emerges during the first phase.

Gradually the process turns into a project and if managed as such, the result will actually be a complete work. However, this cannot be done without support and understanding from the surroundings, sources of information, and interested case-firms.

We would therefore specifically dedicate our acknowledgements to our families, our colleagues who have commented and discussed ideas with us – Associate Professor Eskild Lyngholm, Århus Business School, Associate Professor Henrik Johannsen Duus, and Professor Deo Sharma, both Copenhagen Business School. The case-firms deserve a special note of gratitude, as they are the reason why we undertook this project and have been a continuous source of encouragement.

References

Evans, P. and Wurster, T. (2000) *Blown to Bits.* Harvard Business School Press.

Christopher, M., Payne, A. and Ballantyne, D. (1999) *Relationship Marketing,* Butterworth-Heinemann.

Gummesson, E. (1996) *Towards a Theoretical Framework of Relationship Marketing,* Proceedings of the International Conference on Relationship Marketing, Berlin, pp. 5-18.

Miles, R.E. and Snow, C.C. (1978) *Organizational Strategy, Structure, and Process,* McGraw-Hill.

PART I

The Value of Relationships

CHAPTER 1

Understanding Buyer-Seller Relationships

The concept of strategic relationship marketing is an innovative approach to marketing in the new economy. This book organises these concepts into basic analytical and managerial tools. The narrow focus on strategic positioning and tactical marketing planning has become obsolete. Similarly outdated is the categorical idea of supplier superiority and dominance over consumers. The underlying assumption that the buyer and the seller shall never meet is gone forever.

In relationship marketing, the focus is on the overall rapport between customer and supplier, not just on the individual exchange between them. Maintaining relationships is the real value driver behind competitive market advantage and outstanding performance. Relationship marketing is the art of building and maintaining profitable relationships, turning prospects into customers and customers into friends.

Strategic relationship marketing concepts are the basis for analysing relationship markets and developing viable customer strategies. Presented here are fresh approaches to market understanding, as well as an outline of the main economic principles of customer relationships, the nuts and bolts of developing a successful relationship marketing strategy.

1.1 Introduction – the Power of Relationships

Consider the following situation: Two competing construction companies make a bid for a major, prestigious contract. One of the two companies has maintained a long, close relationship with the buyer. The two competing offers are almost identical in price, quality, delivery and service. Who do you think will get the account? Now, what do you think would happen if the proposed budget presented by the supplier with the long-standing buyer relationship costs 5% more with the quality and other terms still being identical? What if the price difference is 9%? Or even 24 %?

The outcome depends on many variables. It depends on the cultural context of the relationship, the managerial policies within the organisation and a multitude of other factors. Generally however, the buyer will be influenced by the previous relationship experiences.

There is conclusive evidence that the supplier/customer relationship is a critical part of today's business life reality. This relationship mentality differs from that of pure exchange, as it is an intangible commodity that must be maintained over time. This fact of business life reflects the following fundamental assumptions:

The value of relationships > The value of exchanges

This assumption makes it necessary for us to alter our understanding of marketing as a discipline and of what marketing management as a company philosophy should be. Similarly, the intrinsic value of relationships in business is a strong stimulus for researchers to establish a new paradigm of marketing strategies.

The purpose of this book is not only to formulate a new marketing paradigm, but also to offer the reader these theories in a structured accessible way so that they can be applied to everyday business life. Theories based on fundamental relationship behavioural models integrated with marketing strategy techniques have never been organised into a comprehensive and accessible framework for students and practitioners, until now.

Taking the above example from the construction industry to the next level, it can also be argued that there is a distinct correlation between the long-term profitability of a company and its customer relationships. Relationships must then be considered an intangible asset and a resource base, possibly on the fringe of or even beyond managerial control. It could then be said that since the quality of a company's relationships is directly linked to its revenue stream, its relationships are more important than its market share.

In the virtual network economy of today, competitors are only a click away. So, it is easy for customers to control the communication and purchasing process. This creates a fertile environment for what is called *permission marketing*. In the permission-driven, consumer network economy, market share without relationship quality does not have much value. Recent examples of this phenomenon are markets for toys, books, music, travel and securities trading among others.

As shall be demonstrated later, outstanding customer relationships, long-standing consumer loyalty and competitive advantage in the marketplace are not just results from generally satisfying customers. What it requires is much more than that. It requires extremely satisfied customers. This highest rung on the customer satisfaction ladder can be difficult and risky to reach.

Systematic analysis of relationships as well as the economics of such relationships can in fact help companies increase their marketing skills and improve their overall market performance. The customer with the building project mentioned above might very well end up saving money by choosing the project with the highest proposed budget. Why? It is due to the fact that existing relationships often are combined with more effective regulating mechanisms, e.g. the perception of smooth cooperation, trust and partnership and hence they are less costly to administer. Therefore, buyers must consider the cost of maintaining the relationship as part of the total budget before deciding which supplier to use. Consequently marketing professionals must also take this into consideration.

1.2 What Business is Marketing Really In?

It has been suggested that relationship marketing is taking marketing back to its roots. It has also been claimed that the relationship approach to marketing represents a paradigm shift in marketing.[1] Throughout the history of marketing the leading marketing management theories have focussed on fast moving consumer good industry. The main thrust of marketing strategies in the past was set in the belief that how, when and where to position your product to make consumers buy was the optimal marketing approach. This is not necessarily a bad managerial approach, but does it express what business marketing really is in today?

Initially two quite different approaches to marketing are introduced, see figure 1-1.

1. Grönroos (1990;1992), Morgan and Hunt (1994), Gummesson (1996).

MARKETING IS:

"Marketing is the process of planning and executing the conception, pricing promotion and distribution of ideas, goods and services to create exchange and satisfy individual and organisational goals"

MARKETING IS:

"Marketing means to establish, maintain and enhance relationships with customers in a profitable way in order to accomplish the objectives of both parties through the reciprocal interchange and keeping of promises"

Figure 1-1: What business is marketing really in? Source: American Marketing Association, AMA (1985), Grönroos (1990; 1992)

These two definitions draw on distinctly different theoretical sources. The classical definition (left) underscores business success through careful planning made and executed by specialists under straight managerial control. The marketing mix in terms of product, price, place and promotion is what is going to conquer the consumer and create market dominance. The consumer's only possible response is.... to buy or not to buy! Any business success formula should be derived from the marketing concept: "Satisfy the needs of the consumers better and/or at a lower cost than your competitors while allowing you to make an above average profit". John Egan has expressed this view in this way:

> Despite the obvious problems, little was changing in marketing education. Marketing theory remained mired in a futile search for laws, regularities and predictability. The marketing mix was (is) still the dominant marketing model, although it was seen as offering a too seductive sense of simplicity.... The toolbox approach of science-oriented marketing was criticised as a neglect of process in favour of structure leading to a consequent lack of study into other key variables....[2]
>
> So it appeared that marketing, the leading department of the first three-quarters of the century, was loosing its primacy.... Marketers were so busy attending to the practise of marketing that they may not have

---

2. Egan (2001, p. 12).

noticed that it was, for all practical purposes, dead. If not dead, it was certainly in crisis.

Companies like Procter and Gamble, Coca Cola, Lego or Disney would never have become so huge had their core competence not been within exchange based marketing. But is that all? What about Disney? Some of Disney's new electronic products allow kids to create their own figures and scripts while using the product. They have become interactive. And what about Lego Mindstorm? With Lego Mindstorm, children from all over the world play together on-line in Cyberspace. And what do you think about the producer of sanitary towels having created a web service site through which young girls can actually chat with boys. Not to mention book publishers now printing personalised books on demand: "Do you want a happy ending or..."

The relationship-based approach to marketing – the definition in figure 1.1 (right) – does not deny the exchange as *the moment of truth*. But it relies on a different assumption. Marketing is about relationships. How they are established, develop, become consolidated and terminate. How they work, how expectations are created and promises kept. This definition recognises the voice of each individual customer. The marketing process does not stop after the purchase. "If the purchase is the courtesy then the relationship is the marriage".[3]

A well-known founder of a great company more than 70 years ago said it this way: "Your customers are your fortune".[4]

Even in traditional exchange oriented business-to-consumer industries such as retail, insurance, financial services, IT, automobiles etc. it becomes increasingly clear that the heart of marketing lies in the relationship. Consumers have always been searching for positive relationships with suppliers and emotional associations to brands, because it makes buying easier. Not at any price, but within the range of tolerable cost differences. This however is nothing new.

What **is** new to marketing as a discipline is that it must revitalise itself by moving from "left to right" and get a piece of the relationship business, so to speak.

In the first stages of the networks economy from 1994 and onward we have witnessed a series of tough and extremely costly battles about customer relationships. Mobile network providers' financial support of mobile phones is a good example. In some countries consumers would receive a top of the line

3. Levitt (1960).
4. Børge Olsen – the former M.D. of the Danish retail chain IRMA.

mobile phone for free – assuming they signed a subscription contract with the operator. The relationship is the purpose and the exchange only the means.

Two completely identical mobile phones can be sold at very different prices in the same outlet at the same time depending on which mobile network carrier the customer decides to subscribe to. Sales reps in the trade of mobile phones have even developed creative ways of "arbitrage" designed for obtaining the maximum network carrier discount and at the same time advising the customer about the best and fastest way to neutralise the contract.

In the US, the telecommunications sector headed by warrior enterprises such as AT&T have been willing to pay sky-high prices for cable networks subscribers. The capitalisation of digital access to customers is dramatic. Customer loyalty is the name of the game. Relationship marketing is what the market demands!

1.3 The Classical Buyer-Seller Relationship

When is it reasonable to conclude that a relationship between two parties has evolved? The nice young person giving you a smile from the cash register at the supermarket? The local taxi company that your secretary calls whenever a cab is needed? The employment agency you used only once to hire an IT person with very specific skills? The accounting firm re-elected each year at the general assembly? When does a relationship become meaningful in this context?

One possible definition is presented in figure 1-2.

> A SUPPLIER/CUSTOMER RELATIONSHIP IS:
>
> A relationship is composed of the sum of exchanges and contacts between supplier and customer over time via the regulating mechanisms in work and the parties' intensions for the future based on mutual understanding.

Figure 1-2: One definition of a relationship.

The depth of understanding between the parties, the type of regulating mechanisms and the motives and goals for future exchanges differs greatly. In industrial markets, relationships are generally reciprocal or *one-to-one*. In most consumer markets, it can to some extent seem artificial to use the term "relationship", as the supplier only communicates one way with the end customers or *one-to-many*. But things are changing. The electronic media (i.e. the Internet) has become highly integrated into customer communication and the business nervous system as a whole.

A company's portfolio of relationships is not only comprised of its customers, but of all its stakeholders such as suppliers, financial institutions, competitors, alliance partners etc. The exchange balance between inducements to and contributions from each stakeholder must still be kept competitive in order to maintain stakeholders' interest in doing business with the company. The relationship factor however, can play an important role in the stakeholder "balance score"; and the relationship dimension can easily influence the relative balances as a consequence of intangibles such as trust and experience.

1.4 Classifying the Buyer-Seller Relationships

The simplified model in figure 1-3 illustrates the components of a relationship in a vertical supply structure.

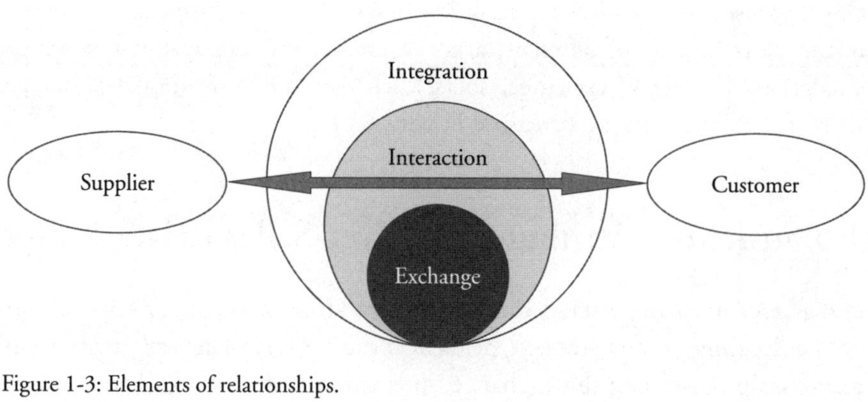

Figure 1-3: Elements of relationships.

When a company buys a commodity or a standard raw material with a transparent price structure, the procurement manager will typically act on a pure market basis. He will focus on the exchange. He will ask several suppliers for a bid and compare quality, price, delivery time etc. He will act within the constraints of an exchange contract framework. He may eventually purchase through a dealer, broker or trader and has no interest in further interaction with the specific supplier. The supplier will ask for a payment guarantee or trust the broker. Pure market contracts are *exchange-centric.*

At the opposite end of the spectrum, consider a car manufacturer working with a series of strategic subcontracted partners within a closed supply chain network based on just-in-time and joint R&D. The production plan for the upcoming week must be perfectly coordinated backwards within the supply chain taking into account subcontractors and their supplies. In this case, the market mechanisms have been removed and do not function at the exchange level just described. The relationship is integrated into a hierarchical, cooperative structure where the actors actively try to eliminate the friction between them. Therefore, network contracts are *integration-centric.*

In between we find thousands of different relationship hybrids. Many types of interactions require direct two-way communication between supplier and customer – often in the form of mutual interactions in operational or strategic problem solving. This enhanced interaction between the parties develops over time and often at different organisational levels, either under managerial control or as bottom-up initiatives.

The *interactive-centric* relationships carry some elements of arms length control like in the pure exchange perspective. But they are quite frequently inclined to also adopt integrative qualities. In a slightly different interpretation, a relationship consists of different layers or circles: Product-against-finance exchange, informational exchange, social exchange and institutional exchange, where the associations are structural in nature.

1.5 Structural Attributes of Buyer-Seller Relationships

A marketer must understand the internal workings of customer relationships before deciding on any strategic or tactical move. The structural attributes of relationships governing this exchange, interaction and/or integration are composed of four distinctly different elements as shown in figure 1-4.

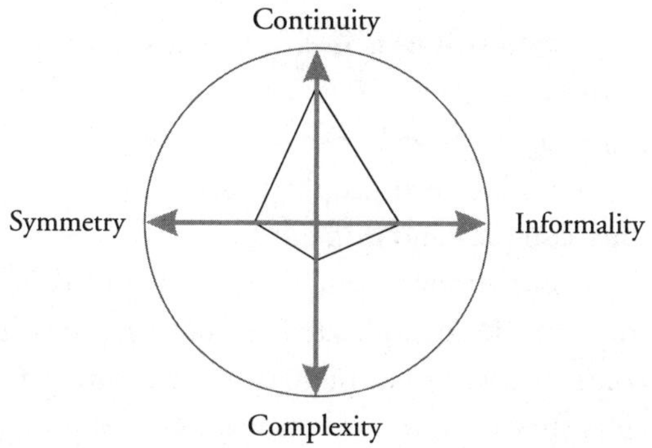

Figure 1-4: Structural attributes of relationships.

Continuity means that the buyer and the seller have reached a stage of stability and repetition in their relationship. Rivalry still exists between the two parties and win-lose situations do happen during the ongoing trade between them.

Many types of business relationships possess a high degree of embedded continuity. This is the case in most OEM product-markets, where a company designs a component, a module or other features into an end product. In this situation continuity is a result of product uniqueness. Another example of this is in the area of accounting services. Accounting firms typically retain their clients for decades. This is due to the fact that all accounting firms have almost identical service packages governed by legislation and professional standards. Here, continuity is in fact rooted in anti-uniqueness, which has created a "no-reason-to-change" market. In both cases the arguments behind continuity are relatively straightforward.

As shall be clearly demonstrated later, continuity in customer relationships represents substantial value in terms of retention economics and is one of the key elements in all relationship marketing programs and investments.

Relationships differ in their degree of *complexity*. Relationships with high levels of complexity can be not only difficult to manage but difficult to break as well. This can lead to a breakdown in communication, redundancy, high control costs and just mistakes in general. Complexity can be caused by:

- *The exchange*: High involvement durable goods and services such as buying a house or a new car means that there is a very complex relationship between the individual and "the market". The same will be the case for companies seeking a sole distributor in a new market with a different culture and different terms of trade.

- *The interaction*: Social contact in the context of extensive networks of personal communication between people in organisations makes industrial relationships rather complex and difficult to change.
- *The integration*: Contracts and regulating mechanisms in business-to-business relationships can be complicated, incomplete and inconsistent. Very rarely does a contract cover all possible issues that can come up between two parties. Therefore they must rely on some kind of common problem solving strategy. This can also complicate the process.

Whereas continuity in relationships strengthens a business's ability to remain competitive, complexity can become a double-edged sword. Some companies follow a strategy that has a maximum level of complication in order to create an atmosphere of perceived dependence. In insurance and financial services suppliers consciously try to deliver packages – bundles of products that are tied together in complex "all or nothing" relationship contracts.

A counter-strategy to this would be to reduce the level of complexity through unbundling – i.e. offering transparent, understandable ranges of products, where the customer can choose exactly what he or she wants.

Symmetry is the third structural characteristic of the buyer-seller relationship. Symmetry is a question of relative distribution of influence and information within the relationship. Asymmetry in relationship can be a powerful motive for individuals as well as companies.

The superior party will tend to capitalise on the cost and effort his counterpart will have to absorb in order to overcome the gap in knowledge or bargaining power. In some situations, however, this approach would not be optimal. When the asymmetry is recognised by both parties, defensive measures such as lower quality, less knowledge sharing, and more control tend to be adopted by the weaker party.

Several studies[5] have demonstrated that a relationship between companies often continues despite top management's decision to dissolve it. This is due to the *informality factor*. The real institutionalisation of a business relationship is what goes on between people. They view the employees and their counterparts as colleagues and management as the enemy.

5. Hedaa (1991).

1.6 Classifying the Pattern of Interaction within the Standard Buyer-Seller Relationship

Whereas the basic attributes of the traditional market relationship are both external as well as within the company's control and used as part of a marketing strategy, it is also interesting to consider how effective a set of marketing actions will be in a dynamic perspective as a function of the customer's purchasing strategy. This can be illustrated in the following classification of supplier-customer relationships, see figure 1-5.

		Marketing strategies		
		Competitive	Co-operative	Command
Purchasing strategies	Competitive	1 Independent	2 Mismatch	3 Independent
	Co-operative	4 Mismatch	5 Interdependent	6 Dependent
	Command	7 Independent	8 Dependent	9 Mismatch

Figure 1-5: Generic classification of supplier-customer relationships.
Source: Based on Sørensen (1997)

The relationship behaviour of a supplier in terms of exchange, interaction and integration can be based on any of the three marketing management philosophies:

- *Competitive:* A give and take zero sum attitude. What the customer gains we lose. The regulating mechanism will be based on arm's length and extensive control.
- *Co-operative*: Assuming that the customer will enter into a win-win relationship and will work together to the benefit of both parties. In this case frictions are minimised and interdependence between the parties will be the end result.
- *Command* relationship behaviour relies on opportunism and is based on a

pure dominance ideology. The philosophy is that a supplier can earn above normal profits by making the customer dependent on the offering. The core of the relationship, i.e. the product has unique features that influence the customer into entering into a command relationship in order to attain the product. The end result is the dominant supplier and the dependent customer.

The generic purchasing strategies can be classified into the same categories:

Independent relationships are characterised by intense rivalry between supplier and customer. The relationship can have a high degree of continuity and complexity. Independence does not necessarily mean that there is a constant threat of the relationship breaking down. But none of the parties are interested in testing the benefits of a closer co-operative structure. Independence means that both parties consciously evaluate alternatives and keep switching costs down.

A Mismatch Scenario is the result when a cooperative oriented supplier or purchaser is confronted with a counterpart who has a competitive strategic approach. A co-operative style seeks joint optimisation through the utilisation of the different capabilities in organisations. Mismatch occurs because the competitive reaction is not commensurate with advantage of the invitation to co-operate. When suspicion is present regarding motives, control, lack of commitment, focus on formal contractual arrangements etc. and even the potential for a win-lose situation is what meets a peacemaker, then the chances of reaching a positive result are minimal.

As shall be demonstrated later, *interdependence* assumes mutual trust and the inclination to optimise the relationship. This requires a co-operative marketing philosophy as well as a co-operative purchasing attitude. Both parties give up some of their autonomy, impose switching costs on themselves and assume the risk of trusting the other party. But even a mutually co-operative relationship needs regulating mechanisms in terms of control and outside pressure from competing relationships.

In reality only a few relationships are truly "generic" in the sense that a marketing strategy is solely based on a command relationship. Typically, it is a combination of different types relationships and strategies. Furthermore, relationships are dynamic; they change over time and adapt to the actions of both parties. The typology of buyer/seller strategies can be useful as a frame of reference used for analysing existing relationships and for creating relationship marketing strategies. It is necessary to ask and answer the following questions when analysing existing as well as creating new relationship marketing strategies:

- Which marketing strategy or behaviour do we follow as a supplier and why?
- Which purchasing policy or practice does the customer x, y and z follow and why?
- Within the relationship typology how can a certain customer relationship or portfolio of customer relationships be evaluated and classified. What are the main courses?
- What actions can a supplier take in order to prevent mismatch or move a relationship in a certain direction?

In recent years, most companies have made radical changes in the structure and perception of their relationships to become an integral part of the implementation of new business models. There is a rapidly growing interest in relationship management as a key success factor, and huge IT investments have been made in order to organise, integrate and interpret relationship data. Value chains have become atomised and company roles more focused on core competencies. At the same time inter company values chains have had to develop and become more integrated, which enables each company to remain competitive. In this combined focus-integration perspective the relationship as such has become an even more important factor and hence also relationship strategies.

1.7 Defining Relationship Marketing

Kotler et al. has attempted to adapt the traditional framework of marketing in a relationship-oriented direction. He agrees with Grönroos that the marketing mix represents the seller's view of marketing. Hence, they suggest that marketers should view the 4P's from a customer-oriented perspective as demonstrated by the 4C's in figure 1-6.

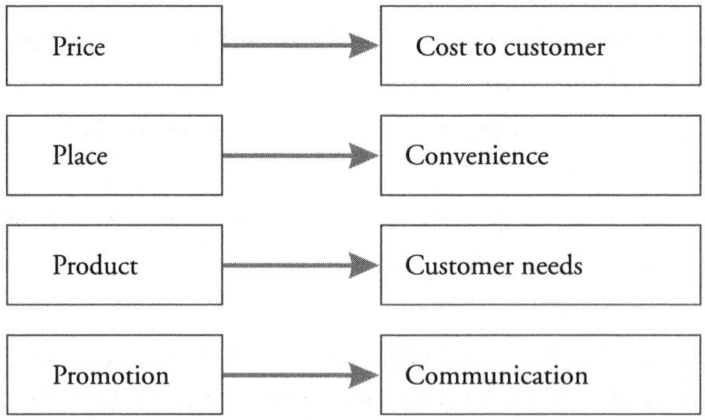

Figure 1-6: From 4P's to 4C's. Source: Kotler et al. (1999)

This contribution is valuable for some marketers, but it does not represent a paradigm shift or a new relationship based marketing definition. It is an attempt to update the marketing mix, but it stills sticks to the toolbox view of marketing. Although there are many aspects to marketing management, the relationship aspect appears to have a substantial impact on long-term business success. We will define relationship marketing as in figure 1-7.

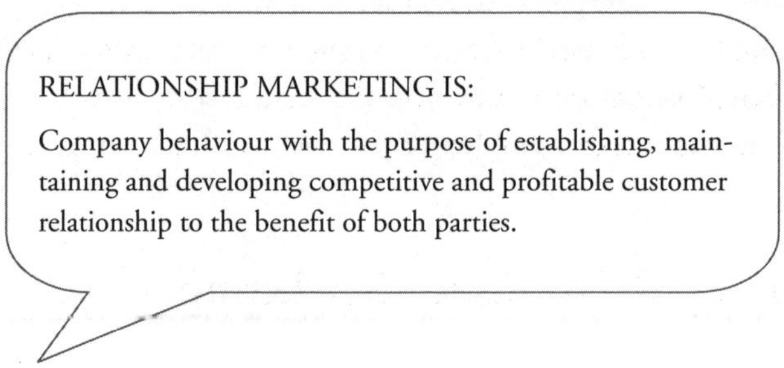

Figure 1-7: Defining relationship marketing.[6]

---

6. One important aspect of the relationship marketing definition requires attention. The seeming philanthropy of the altruistic sentiments implied by relationship marketing (mutuality, equality...) might seem to contradict the fact that that profit motive is still the a principal business driver. The difference between relationship marketing and traditional marketing is that relationship marketing to some extent replaces the idea of manipulation with the idea of cooperation, subject however to differences in regulating mechanisms. Terminating relationships that are not profitable is an underlying assumption behind the above definition.

We do not consider marketing to be strictly a parametric, program-oriented function but as a pattern of total organisational behaviour. Additionally, we consider interdependence, mutual cooperation and commitment between supplier and customer to be absolutely crucial to relationship marketing.

This definition has no ethical basis. Neither does it reflect "good will" per se. The basic notion "for the benefit of both parties" introduces the idea of optimising relationships because it is the most profitable long-term strategy. No more – No less. The bottom line is still the bottom line. The relationship as a whole is considered to be the key to competitive advantage.

Relationship marketing principles do not exist in opposition to traditional segmentation/positioning marketing with regard to techniques and marketing mix decisions. Likewise, it would be a mistake to look at the relationship dimension as one tactical approach among others. Relationship marketing is a fundamental managerial approach to business. The basic belief is that reduction of frictions in networks of trade is a prime source of profitability.

The definition above indicates that not all relationships are profitable. Relationships that are profitable on a lifetime basis may create loss in some stages during the lifetime. The recognition of potential loss making relationships suggests that marketing management must pay attention to three different objectives in terms of:

- The management of the initiation of customer relationships.
- The maintenance and enhancement of existing relationships.
- The handling of relationship termination.

Marketing management introduces two new aspects to the marketing process: *Customer deselection* and *management of different stages of the relationship*. Both elements play key roles in profitability.

1.8 The Relationship Marketing Context – Categorising Relationships

Marketing is context driven. As the context changes, so does the marketing task. Context varies across industries and over time. Some basic relationship elements of a more structural kind may remain unchanged, but focus often shifts.

One such contextual dimension in the relationship between a supplier and a customer refers to the level of investment that the buyer and seller are each willing to commit to the relationship. The level and the type of dependencies and regulating mechanisms as described earlier represent one such classification based on a contextual perception.

The motivational investment the buyers and the sellers are prepared to make is another framework for understanding the relationship-marketing context as illustrated in figure 1-8 below.

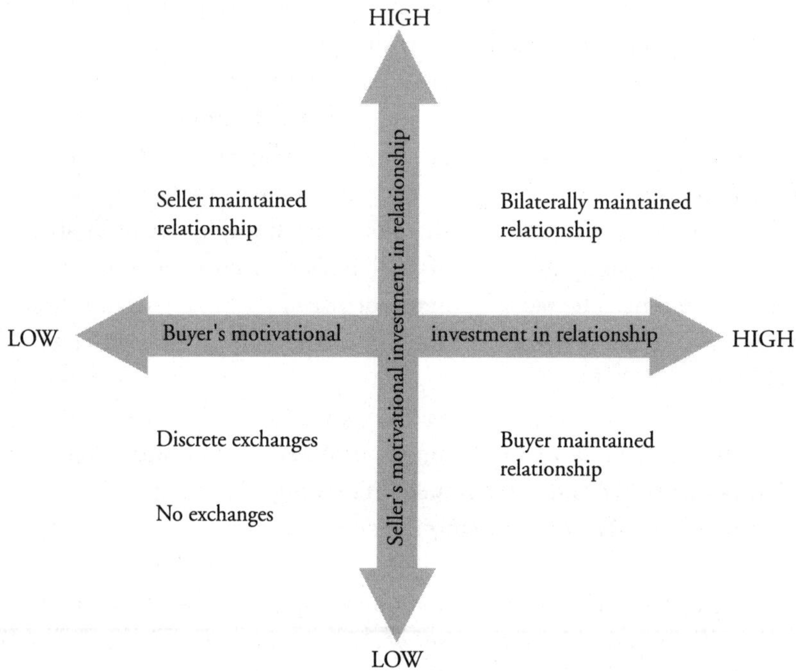

Figure 1-8: The relationship categories and relationship marketing contexts.
Source: Egan (2001) based on Dwyer (1987)

Figure 1-8 classifies supplier-customer relationships into different segments according to the motivation of the parties to committing resources to the relationship. The bilaterally maintained relationships will in many situations be cooperative and lead to interdependence between the parties as mentioned earlier. The high motivation for both parties to commit themselves to the specific one-to-one relationship is most apparent in business-to-business situations.

The context of discrete exchanges exists where neither party has any interest in establishing a relational bond of any kind to the counterpart. In situations where the importance of the core product is high and the service requirements are low, discrete exchanges are likely to develop as the dominant terms of trade context, as none of the parties have a strong enough motivation to commit resources of strategic importance to a relationship approach.

The context drivers affecting a relational versus a more exchange oriented marketing approach can be summarised as illustrated in figure 1-9.

Context drivers in favour of relationship marketing	**Context drivers in favour of exchange marketing**
High acquisition costs relative to retention costs	Acquisition/retention cost difference minimal
High exit barriers	Low exit barriers
Core product dominant dimension	Service dominant dimension
Repeat behaviour benefits	No negative consequences of switching

Figure 1-9: Context drivers and relationship marketing approach. Source: Based on Egan (2001)

The context drivers most often are a continuum, and not all drivers necessarily point in the same direction. Hence marketing in many situations requires a hybrid managerial approach.

1.9 Relationships in a Broader Perspective with Impact on Relationship Marketing

The approach to relationship marketing has traditionally followed two very different paths. Relationship marketing on *BtC markets* by nature is based in a context characterised by one-to-many marketing model. Hence the theoretical approach to relationship marketing on this type of market tends to be focussed on *marketing tools* as opposed to *interaction orientation.* This is not to say that the relationship perspective is less important on BtC markets, but most of the elements and governing rules that can be observed in the exchanges between two or more organisations – such that buying and selling strategies in dynamic interplay have no relevance.

Moreover, consumer behaviour, which plays an important role in the understanding of consumer markets, is most often perceived as something quite different from industrial buying behaviour. Not only the difference between emotional vs. rationale decision making elements, but also regarding the number of steps involved in the buying process.

BtB markets in many situations are also one-to-many markets, and it would be wrong to assume that humans are irrational when they are consumers, yet they are completely rational economic men and women while on the job. We do not intend to go into the details of the subtle and very complex exploration of the similarities and differences between BtB and BtC markets. Most of the literature on strategic relationship marketing is oriented towards BtB situations, where the concept of "real" relationships seems to be a more common term of trade, whereas true – as in equal – relationships at first glance appear to be a somewhat artificial construct in BtC. As shall be demonstrated later, we will not take this traditional and to some extent limiting direction[7]. By basing the concept of relationship marketing on a relationship economic foundation, many of the principles work in BtC markets as well.

Another way to look upon these relationships is to distinguish between *external versus internal relationships* and *formal relationships in contrast to informal ones* as shown in this model.

	External relationships	**Internal relationships**
Formal relationships	Exchange relationship contracts	Hierarchical Relationships
Informal relationships	Social networks	Informal groups

Figure 1-10: Different types of relationships within a relationship marketing context.

The classic buyer-seller relationship falls into the external-formal category. The

7. See chapter 2.

scope of relationship strategies tends to focus on the external or formal type of relationship. There is comprehensive evidence[8] that customer relationships have an informal dimension in the form of social networks between individuals and groups of individuals. Social networks are not a part of the "marketing plan" as such but are nevertheless of great importance in understanding what goes on between buying and selling organisations. Social networks can support the relationship and create value for the parties involved or have the opposite effect, i.e. reduce productivity and deteriorate value. From a strict parametric marketing point of view, social relationships are difficult to control.

Understanding and accepting the potential benefits of social networks represents a transition from a specialist, clinical view of the marketing process within a company to a phenomenon covering the overall organisational behaviour,[9] symbolised by the conception of the *part time marketer.*

Likewise, internal relationships within organisations can be arranged into formalised structured hierarchies as opposed to informal groupings, which either complement and support formal structures or try to tear them apart by circumventing crucial information processes. The internal relationships within a company tend to be the source of its values and norms or corporate culture, and it is this image the company presents its customers and suppliers. In the 1980's, internal marketing became a very popular mode of steering firms in a more service-oriented direction. Hence, the understanding of the dynamic interplay between internal and external relationships is one of the cornerstones of strategic relationship marketing.

1.10 Different Theoretical Directions in Relationship Marketing

Relationship marketing is a relatively new discipline still in search of its roots. Various sciences have contributed to the systematisation of marketing into a viable research and teaching discipline: Economics, psychology, sociology, political science and mathematics. Relationship marketing draws upon these sources as well.

Today, there is no commonly accepted theoretical foundation, no commonly accepted paradigm of relationship marketing. Different research ap-

8. Hedaa (1991), and research done by IMP, see note 10 below.
9. Grönroos (1990; 1992) and Gummeson (1990).

proaches come into play here.[10] Their origins, the complexity of problems studied and their research methodologies differ widely. The main approaches to relationship marketing are shown below.

	The marketing management approach	**Transaction cost approach**	**Political economy approach**	**Network interaction approach**
Contributors	Borden, Kotler	Williamson	Arndt, Skytte	Hedaa, Håkansson, Gummesson
Focus	The marketer	Buying and selling parties	Systems of exchanges	Complex social processes
Relationship view	A tactical tool to build customer loyalty	A Balance of economic risc/ return calculations	A mix of dyadic forces	Mutually interdependent clusters
Marketing scope	Segmentation/ positioning	Contractual dominance	Single partner perspective	Total value chain
Intent	Normative: planning and plan	Normative: activity structuring	Descriptive: analytical framework	Descriptive: system behaviour

Figure 1-11: Overview of main relationship marketing approaches.

The four main academic approaches to relationship marketing do not represent a process of evolution. They have developed exclusive of each other.

The new marketing concept is to a large extent inspired by the network interaction approach and a foundation of promises, mutuality and confidence. Whereas traditional marketing paradigms are clearly derived from the marketing management approach.

The *marketing management approach*, which in fact covers a rather heterogeneous amount of literature, does not consider relationships to be the most im-

10. Payne (1988) e.g. identifies four different research schools within relationship marketing: (1) The Scandinavian School identified by the Swedish School of Economics and Business Administration, (2) The Anglo Australian School, (3) the Northern American School and (4) the IMP Group (Industrial Marketing and Purchasing Group) based in Sweden.

portant aspect in marketing. Through the marketing mix (the 4P's) the intention of marketing is to position the offering of the company or the business unit vis a vis target groups identified and prioritised through careful market segmentation and competitor analyses. The relationship dimension is an "extra", a tactical tool among many others that a marketer can use. Marketing management has its primary focus on consumer goods.

Institutional economics (transactions costs) is a theoretical field that can be used within a relationship marketing framework but it was not developed as such. The thrust of institutional economics is basically that the transactional system, i.e. the relationship, has a huge impact as a driver of costs and benefits. Markets, buying and selling strategies and the contractual terms under which supply and demand meet can not be explained without understanding all potential obstacles, all the pro's and con's and all the in-between arrangements between two parties. That is, the complex and challenging trade-offs between arm's length and deep partnership. Institutional thinking assumes a kind of Darwinist world order in which own-interests orientation is the key to understanding market behaviour. One of the main discussions under the institutional economic paradigm is activity structuring, i.e. the optimal composition of internal activities ("make") versus externalisation of activities ("buy"), and which marketing management challenges arising from different activity structures.

The *political economy paradigm*, which will be described in much more detail in chapter 2, discusses the comprehension and articulation of organisational behaviour and hence relationship marketing in more depth than institutional economics. This approach offers a holistic framework for analysing how and why exchanges take place, how two or more customer-supplier parties interact and relate. It outlines different profiles or archetypes of strategic behaviour, which can be used to create and execute single partner strategies; the ultimate relationship marketing solution.

The most famous and genuine attempt to create a new relationship oriented marketing paradigm is the IMP[11] group. Their starting-point was an amazing curiosity with regard to relationships and markets. For reasons of simplicity all

11. The IMP-school refers to the "Industrial Marketing and Purchasing Group" or "International Marketing and Purchasing Group" – depending on the audience (Ford, 1995, p. 2). See also note 11.

the descriptive, social oriented approaches to relationship marketing are labelled the *network interaction approach.* This was not done with the intention of giving the marketer or the market analyst any specific methodologies or techniques to create substantial competitive advantages. But the network approach has indeed made a substantial contribution to the study of vertical supply chains. It has been able to explain how clusters of companies act and where obstacles and limitations may arise and why. In does not pretend to judge what is good or less good marketing, but it has inspired us to create more application-oriented models in particular on business-to-business markets.

In the following chapters all four approaches to strategic relationship marketing will be utilized, not just the one of them. It is necessary to present all of them as they all work together to make a comprehensive set relationship marketing rules and principles and therefore none should be excluded.

Another way to classify relationship-marketing research was made by Palmer[12] who introduced the three level approach:

Level 1

- At the tactical level where relationship marketing is used as a sales promotion tool, e.g. loyalty schemes.

Level 2

- At the strategic level where long-term relationships with customers and other stakeholders are created by detention rather than retention with the aid of legal, economic, technological, geographical and other barriers to exit.

Level 3

- At the philosophical level where relationship marketing is perceived to be the heart and soul of marketing philosophy by refocusing marketing away from products and their life cycles towards customer relationship life cycles and the integration of customer orientation with inter-functional coordination.

In this book we will deliberately be dealing with relationship marketing at levels 2 and 3, not as a smoke screen for traditional promotional measures.

---

12. Palmer (1996).

References

AMA (1985) *Board Approves New Marketing Definition,* Marketing News.

Arndt J. (1979) *Toward a Concept of Domesticated Markets,* Journal of Marketing.

Berry, L. L. (1983) *Relationship Marketing: Perspectives on Services Marketing,* American Marketing Association.

Blois, K. (1995) *Relationship Marketing – is it always appropriate?,* Management Research Papers.

Blomqvist, R., Dahl, J. and Haeger, T.(1993) *Relationsmarknadsföring – strategier og metoder i Servicekonkurrens,* Göteborg.

Christopher, M., Payne, A. and Ballantyne, D. (1991) *Relationship Marketing for Competitive Advantage – Winning and Keeping Customer,* Butterworth-Heinemann.

Coase, R. (1937) *The Nature of the Firm,* Economica.

Cyert, R.M. and March, J.G. (1963) *A Behavioural Theory of the Firm,* Prentice Hall Englewood Cliffs.

Dietrich, M. (1994) *Transaction Cost Economics and Beyond,* Routledge.

Duus, H. J. (1994) *Economic Foundations for an Entrepreneurial Marketing Concept,* Handelshøjskolen i København.

Dwyer, F.R.; Schurr, P.H. and Oh, S. (1987) *Developing buyer-seller relationships,* Journal of Marketing.

Egan, J. (2001) *Relationship Marketing – exploring relational strategies in marketing,* Pearson

Ford, D. (1980) *The Development of Buyer-Seller Relations in Industrial Markets,* European Journal of Marketing.

Ford, D. (1990) *Understanding Business Markets: Interaction, Relationships and Networks.* Academic Press London.

Ford, D.; Håkansson, H. and Johanson, J. (1986) *How do companies interact?,* Industrial Marketing and Purchasing.

Freytag, P. V. (1991) *Leverandørsamarbejde –Koncipering af en referencemodel Bind I og II,* Samfundslitteratur, 1991.

Groenewegen, J. (ed) (1996) *GRASP: Conference Report Transaction Cost and Beyond*

Groenewegen, J. (ed.) (1996) *Transaction Cost Economics and Beyond,* Kluwer Academic Publishers.

Grönroos, C. (1992) *Facing the challenge of service: The economic of service,* Swedish School of Economics and Business Administration in Helsinki.

Grönroos, C. (1993) *From Marketing Mix to relationship Marketing: Toward a Paradigm Shift in Marketing,* Swedish School of Economics and Business Administration in Helsinki.

Grönroos, C. (1994) *Quo vadis, marketing? Toward a relationship marketing paradigm,* Journal of Marketing Management.

Grönroos, C. (1990) *Relationship approach to the marketing function in service contexts: the marketing and organization behaviour interface,* Journal of Business Research.

Grönroos, C. (1995) *The Rebirth of Modern Marketing,* Meddelande från svenka Handelshöskolan i Helsinki.

Gummesson, E. (1996) *Relationsmarkedsføring. Fra 4P til 30R,* KOLLE Forlag.

Gummesson, E. (1987) *The new marketing – developing long-term interactive relationships*, Long Range Planning.

Gummesson, E. (1990) *The part-time marketer*, University of Karlstad.

Hedaa, L. (1991) *On Interorganizational Relationships in Industrial Marketing*, Samfundslitteratur.

Heskett, J.L.; Sasser, W. et al. (1990) *Service Breakthroughs – Changing the Rules of the Game*, Free Press.

Hougaard, S. (1994) *Den Markedsorienterede Virksomhed: En diagnostisk indkredsning af begrebet markedsorientering og dets praktiske anvendelse*, Handelshøjskolen i København.

Håkansson, H. and Snehota, I.(1995) *Developing Relationships in Business Networks*, Routledge.

Koehn, N. (2001) *Brand New: How Entrepreneurs earned Consumers Trust from Wedgwood to Dell*, Harvard Business School Press.

Kohli, A.K. and Jaworski, B.J.(1990) *Market Orientation: The construct, research, propositions and managerial implications*, Journal of Marketing.

Kohli, A.K.and Jaworski, B..J. (1993) *Market orientation: Antecedents and consequences.* Journal of Marketing.

Kotler, P., Armstrong, G., Saunders J.,and Wong V. (1999) *Principals of Marketing*, Prentice Hall.

Larreché, J.C. and Gatignon, H. (1990) *Markstrat – A Marketing Management Simulation*, The Scientific Press.

Levitt, T. (1960) *Marketing Myopia*, Harvard Business Review.

Lippert-Rasmussen, M. and Mols, N. P. (1993) *Transaktionsomkostningsteori – en introduktion til Williamson*, Institute of Management University of Aarhus.

Macneil, I. (1980) *The New Social Contract, An inquiry into Modern Contractual Relations*, Yale University Press.

Mattson, L. G. (1994) *An Application of Network Approach to Marketing: Defending and Changing Market Positions*, JAI Press Greenwich CT 1985. American Marketing Association.

McKenna, R.(1992) *Relationship marketing – win the market through strategic customer relationship*, Century Business.

Morgan, R. M. and Hunt, S. D. (1994) *The Commitment-Trust Theory of Relationship Marketing*, Journal of Marketing.

Möller, K. K.E. (1992) *Interorganizational Marketing Exchange: Metatheoretical Analysis of Dominant Research Approaches*, ELASM.

Owusu, R. (1997) *Relationship Marketing and the Interactioninetwork Approach*, Svenska Handelshögskolan i Helsinki.

Palmer A. J. (1996) *Relationship Marketing: A universal Paradigm or Marketing Fad?*, The Learning Organisation.

Parvatiyar, A. and Sheth, J. (1995) *Contemporary Knowledge of Relationship Marketing*, Emory University.

Parvatiyar, A. and Sheth, J. (1995) *Relationship Marketing in Consumer Markets: Antecendents and Consequenses*, Emory University.

Parvatiyar, A. and Sheth, J. (1995) *Toward a Theory of Relational Partnering Governance*, Presentation Materials Emory University.

Parvatiyar, A. (1995) *Evolution of Relational Marketing*, Presentation Paper Emory University for Handelshøjskolen i København.

Payne, A. F. (1988) *Developing a Marketing-Oriented Organization*, Business Horizons.

Penrose, E. (1959) *The Theory of The Growth of the Firm*, Basil Blackwell.

Reve, T. (1990) *The Firm as Nexus of Internal and External Contracts from The Firm as a Nexus of Treaties*, in Gustafsson, A. and Williamson, O. E. (eds). Sage Publications.

Stenvinkel Nilsson, O. and Olsen, J. K. (1969) *En adfærdsteoretisk model til beregning af kunders levetid og værdi*, Handelshøjskolen i København.

Storbacka, K. (1993) *Customer Relationship in Retail Banking*, Helsinki.

Sørensen, C. (1997) *Transaktionsomkostningsteori versus Relationship marketing som paradigme på business-to-business markedet*, IAØ, Handelshøjskolen i København.

Turnbull, P.W and Valla, J.P. (1986) *Strategies for International Industrial Marketing: the Management of Customer Relationships in European Industrial Markets*, Crom Helm.

Turnbull, P.W. and Valla, J.P. (1992) *Strategies for International Industrial Marketing*, Croom Helm.

Williamson, O. E. (1985) *The Economic Institutions of Capitalism – Firms, Markets, Relational Contracting*, Free Press.

Williamson, O.E. (1975) *Markets and Hierarchies, Analysis and Antitrust Implications*, Free Press.

CHAPTER 2

A Systematic Approach to Buyer-Seller Relationships

The previous chapter outlined some of the cornerstones of customer relationships and relationship marketing. This chapter takes it a step further by posing the questions: "How can the fantastic universe of relationships be described in more detail? And do these relationships influence business models?

Looking at marketing as mutually beneficial exchanges as opposed to marketing as a one-sided tool managed by the seller requires no less than a completely new theoretical framework. This is because in the past traditional marketing has focussed predominantly on meeting customer demands and fulfilling them as a one-off situation, and not as a continuous exchange process. In this chapter the political economy paradigm will be introduced as the one such new approach to strategy and marketing. This paradigm will be applied using different analytical models in an attempt to better understand the concept of a "relationship marketing mix". The result of this exercise is the conclusion that the existing relationship marketing frameworks may be used only as analytical tools or check lists, in order to ensure that potentially relevant influencing relationships are included.

The political economy paradigm will be utilised in order to illuminate the various layers of influential relationships and their potential impact on the relationship in focus.

The factors that influence the dyadic type of relationship between two parties will also be discussed, as well as layers or variables surrounding a relationship such as environmental factors. One conclusion is that the exchange view will inevitably support the idea of marketing as a system of exchanges encompassing width and depth at the same time.

2.1 Marketing as Mutual Exchange

During the past 20 to 30 years the concept of markets and consequently also the concept of marketing has changed considerably.[1] Marketing as exchange

1. Skytte (1990).

and exchange relationships has served as the foundation for new theoretical developments. It may also be regarded as a further development of the senior "one-way exchange view" which refers to the exchanges in dyadic[2] relationships.[3]

That marketing should be regarded as exchanges within dyadic relationships is not a recent observation.[4] However, as it is still new to many marketers we will focus on the outcome for both parties involved in the exchange as the foundation of the strategic relationship marketing and the theories presented. One of the most significant differences between relationship marketing and traditional marketing is that when using relationship marketing strategies it is necessary to identify the needs and demands of the customer's customers in order to satisfy the customer's demands. This requires not just a clear understanding of the customer's demands, but also the motivations the customers have for formulating their demands in the way they have. This is comparable to the change of focus when selling a product because of its features to focus on the customer's benefit from using the product.

In other words, an exchange takes place if there is perceived value by at least one of the parties. The important implication of this comment is that the relationship will benefit in total, if at least one of the parties is better off. Therefore the focus is not merely on the individual party, but on both parties simultaneously and holistically. An example of this would be that if you could inform your airline operator of your travel needs in advance, they would be able to plan ahead thereby optimising the capacity necessary and giving you a lower price on the ticket.

We have to go back to Kotler[5] to find the first time the term "relationship marketing" was added to the definition of marketing as exchange. Kotler saw relationship marketing as the way in which suppliers try to:

2. A dyad exists when two organisations, typically a selling and a buying organisation, can be regarded as one because they act as one. This is possible due to joint coordination, planning and execution
3. Enis & Mokwa (1979, p. 486): "Both marketer and buyer play interactive roles in the process. This view is in sharp contrast to the older view of exchange as a set of producer-to-consumer flows, in which the seller performed all exchange activities while the buyer only responded."
4. Alderson (1957).
5. Kotler, (1988, p. 8).

> ... build up long-term, trusting, "win-win" relationships with customers, distributors, dealers and suppliers.

Kotler further argued that organisations would be able to lower the transaction costs as they build trust and develop an interest in cooperating with one another. It is important to note that this definition is still a "one-way" understanding of relationships, i.e. it is the initiating organisations that build relationships.

This is in line with the IMP-school and their focus on trust.[6] Another parallel is the introduction of the "marketing network" concept introduced by Kotler to further explain the concept of marketing.[7]

> A marketing network consists of the company and the firms with which it has built a solid, dependable business relationship and thereby has built good relationships and profitable transactions will follow.

Thus, the marketing concept has gradually changed its focus towards processes and a more long-term perspective. However, relationships are still perceived as a result of activities managed by the initiating organisation, i.e. the "one-way" perspective. Strategic relationship marketing challenges this type of thinking, as it regards mutual exchange to be a basis for building mutual beneficial relationships.

The introduction of marketing systems has however, altered this one-way perception considerably and this was where the introduction of the "two-way" marketing concept came into play.

2.2 Marketing as Systems

Exchange is the most basic[8] activity in marketing, but exchange needs to be linked to the parties responsible for the exchange and variables affecting them.[9] Therefore exchange is described as part of a marketing system or exchange system:

---

6. Håkansson and Snehota (1995).
7. Kotler (1988, p. 9).
8. See figure 1-3 in chapter 1.
9. Bagozzi, (1974, p. 78).

> In essence, the exchange system may be defined as a set of social actors, their relationships to each other, and the endogenous and exogenous variables affecting the behaviour of the social actors in those relationships.[10]

Examples of *endogenous* (internal as seen from the relationship's point of view) variables could be benefits from previous exchanges, evaluations of know how and expertise of the other part, and expected benefits from future exchanges. The endogenous variables highlight the principle that all transactions must be regarded as part of a greater entity and that a transaction cannot be evaluated on its own.

Examples of *exogenous* (external as seen from the relationship's point of view) variables are competitive situations, competitive limitations and laws regulating the area of transaction. The central comment related to these variables is that it is the interplay between the endogenous and exogenous variables will determine the volume of the exchange.

The relationship must therefore be seen as a result of past experiences[11] combined with the expectation of positive interaction in the future. Furthermore, the importance of internal factors, as well as external factors, is stressed as they influence the exchange and the content of the exchange.

2.2.1 Three Types of Exchanges

The system approach also leads to three different forms of exchange,[12] based on the notion that marketing is about understanding why people and organisations engage in exchange relationships and how exchanges are created, resolved or avoided:

- Restricted Exchange
- Generalised Exchange
- Complex Exchange

Restricted exchange, or dyadic exchange takes place between two parties and only two (this is why it's called *restricted*), A and B. The relationship between A

10. In chapter 5 the driving forces of relationships are examined in further detail.
11. This is also referred to as "path dependency". The implication of this is that the future of a relation will, at least to some extent, be dependent on exchanges in the past, the way conflicts have been resolved etc.
12. Bagozzi (1975, p. 32).

and B can be described as follows: A ⇔ B. These parties could be end-users, retailers, salesmen, manufacturers etc., and the "⇔" symbolises that A and B simultaneously are supplying and receiving. The continuous existence of the dyad is based on mutually beneficial exchanges as seen from both parties' point of view where both parties contribute and benefit. Such relationships are often seen for example between men and the florist from whom they buy flowers for their wives. In short these are exchanges involving only two parties, and the exchanges flows in both directions.

Generalised exchange takes place between, at least, three parties, A, B, and C. Generalised exchange, in principle, covers all one-way exchanges taking place between more than two parties, hence the label *generalised.* The relationship between A, B, and C can be described as follows: A ⇒ B ⇒ C ⇒ A. The "⇒" symbolises that it is a one-way direct exchange. The exchange takes place directly between the parties, and an example could be the FMCG-sector with A as the supplier, B the retailer and C the end-user. In short, these exchanges involve more than two parties, but the exchange flow is only one way.

Complex exchange takes place between at least three parties, A, B, and C. Complex exchange, in principle, covers all two-way exchanges that take place between more than two parties and is therefore *complex.* The relationship between A, B, and C can be described as follows: A ⇔ B ⇔ C. The exchange is direct between A and B, or B and C – and indirect between A and C. A wholesaler is a good example of complex exchanges, as the ability to transform the offer from the supplier (A) to the end customer (C), and vice versa. To summarise, these exchanges involve more than two parties, and exchanges are flowing both ways.

The type of exchange will provide you with a description of the number of participants, whether the exchange is direct or indirect, and whether exchanges are happening one-way or two-ways. In other words it is merely a way to describe the direction and complexity of the exchange in question.

However, it is one thing to define the direction and complexity of exchange, but crucial to consider is *what* is being exchanged. The content of an exchange can be categorised in two ways.[13]

---

13. Bagozzi (1975, p. 36).

2.2.2 Two Approaches to Exchanges

The first category, *Utilitarian Exchange* is more or less based on the concept of "Economic Man" and rational behaviour, maximisation, complete information and no external influence. The utilitarian exchange is the exchange of goods and services and is widely described in distribution channel literature.[14] In the distribution channel literature the seller develops relationships in order to handle exchanges with buyers who serve two purposes; they are buyers of the products and they are at the same time handling the distribution task for the seller.

This form of exchange is based on the rational approach, which is that one will participate in an exchange because it is in itself beneficial. This approach to exchange is actually taken into further detail later in this chapter; see section 2.5.1 – The 30 R's.

The second group *Symbolic Exchange* is based on the psychological, social and other non-physical transformations between two or more parties. This form of exchange may be described as adding the perception of what a product or service means to an individual, and not just focussing on what the product or service can do. This form is based on the expectation of the exchange; one will participate in an exchange because it feels right. This approach to exchange is only mentioned indirectly by other authors; perhaps it belongs to the physiological and sociological sphere. It is however clearly used as a marketing tool especially with regards to perception of status, culture or fitness and therefore is extremely relevant in this context.

Most exchanges cannot be identified as either or but often carry elements of both forms of exchange. Therefore, the two groups of exchange are combined in what is called *Mixed Exchange.*[15] Mixed exchange means that the exchange can be characterised by utilitarian and symbolic elements simultaneously. However, combining the two forms of exchange makes it difficult to separate the physical from the psychological. The consequence of this is that it is difficult to distinguish between the individuals involved in handling exchanges between organisations and the processes and perceptions supporting these exchanges. Which elements of exchange were involved in your last exchange? Can you tell them apart are they interdependent? An overview is introduced in figure 2-1.

14. We use the term distribution literature to refer to physical distribution of goods and services, as defined by Stern and El-Ansary (1992).
15. Bagozzi (1975).

	Utilitarian	Symbolic	Mixed
Restricted	2 parties involved in exchanging both ways due to mutual benefits Hard- and software	2 parties involved in exchanging both ways because it feels right Love	2 parties involved in exchanging both ways because they expect benefits Marriage
Generalised	More than 2 parties involved in one-way exchanges because of mutual benefits Assembly line	More than 2 parties involved in one-way exchanges because it feels right	More than 2 parties involved in one-way exchanges because they expect benefits
Complex	More than 2 parties involved in exchanging both ways because of mutual benefits Auditing	More than 2 parties involved in exchanging both ways because it feels right Sponsoring	More than 2 parties involved in exchanging both ways because they expect benefits FMCG-sector

Figure 2-1: Combining types of exchange and approaches to exchange.

Furthermore, relationships must be understood in terms of both *individual (personal)* and *institutional (organisational)* relationships. This distinction may also help the reader to recognise that the individual is often the vehicle around which organisational relationships are developed and maintained. Some of the original studies of relationships[16] were actually based on industries where standardised products were sold. They found that relationships were primarily between individuals, not between organisations.

Other studies of relationships are closely related to the concept of brands, and the relationships that may grow around a relationship between a consumer and the brand. Some strong examples of consumer identification with brands are; Nike, Harley-Davidson, Marlboro, Coca-Cola, etc.

Describing exchanges must include time, partly because *how* exchanges take place develop over time, and partly because *what* is exchanged may change over

16. Grönroos (1990).

time. Time was introduced as an important dimension[17] influencing the relationship and the exchange processes. Time seems especially important when understanding the reasons and background the development of relationships. Why is it that some relationships take off in one direction and other relationships tend to go in other directions? Why don't they develop in the same manner, in the same speed and in the same way? And why is it some exchanges are close and intimate while others are distant and formal?

To answer this we have to introduce a framework to describe relationships, their content and their environment in order to identify potential influencing factors. The answers to these questions lie in the Political Economy Paradigm.

2.3 Introduction to the Political Economy Paradigm

When theories change they often do so by building on top of already developed insights. However, once in a while new theories do not merely build on existing and acknowledged insights, but actually break with tradition and are based on fundamentally different assumptions. This is where the issue of paradigm shifts comes into play.[18] Paradigms tend to be identified when authors suggest alternatives to or the shortcomings of existing paradigms. The concept of marketing as a network of exchanges and systems as described earlier is the basis of a new marketing paradigm.

Paradigms suggest units of analysis, constructs, and similar necessary elements to form evaluation techniques within a specific discipline. Basically, that is the reason why they are so relevant. Yet paradigms fall short of advancing propositions, axioms, law-like generalisations, and testable hypotheses. Paradigms are not theories.

The political economy paradigm serves as the frame of reference for strate-

---

17. Dwyer, Schurr and Oh (1987) list four important reasons for focusing on exchange processes in marketing in their article: "Developing Buyer-Seller Relationships" (p. 11):
    a) First, exchange serves as a focal event between two or more parties.
    b) Second, exchange provides an important frame of reference for identifying the social network of individuals and institutions that participate in its formation and execution.
    c) Third, it affords the opportunity to examine the domain of objects or physic entities that get transferred.
    d) Finally, and most important, as a critical event in the marketplace it allows the careful study of antecedent and processes for buyer-seller exchange.
18. Kuhn (1970).

gic relationship marketing basically because this paradigm has much in common with relationship marketing principles. These similarities include:

The analytical unit is an organisation or a group of organisations. The paradigm deals with interactions and transactions between organisations, groups of individuals and individuals. Constructs are used to describe a system in relation to:

- The goal of the system.
- The environment and constraints within which the system exists.
- The resources of these entities.
- The functions these units perform.
- The management and control mechanism for the system, including why and how conflicts are resolved.
- The developments over time.
- The ability to distinguish between behavioural systems and mechanical systems.
- The inclusion to power and mutual dependency, which legitimises discussions of structures (and organisation), economic aspects of relationships.

The political economy paradigm breaks with other paradigms in various ways as listed below:

- *The Microeconomic Paradigm* focuses on market perfection and resource allocation[19] through market mechanisms (production and demand) and at the same time, has cost reduction as the main objective. In this paradigm, relationships are not regarded as beneficial; on the contrary, the market is more efficient to handle exchanges.
- *The Persuasion/Attitude Paradigm* is rather narrow by aiming exclusively at the communication part of the marketing mix. Furthermore this paradigm has a single actor perspective. The relationship will merely be considered from one point of view, often the initiator of the relationship.

The paradigm thus serves as a tool for analysing important components within strategic relationships as well as a structure in which it is possible to locate existing theoretical contributions to relationship marketing, network theory, and other recent contributions.

---

19. As mentioned in chapter 1.

2.4 The Political Economy Paradigm

This paradigm is built around two central issues, *politics* and *economics* both *internally* and *externally*. This structure makes it possible to work with the concept of power, internally and externally, as well as the concept of economic structures, also internally and externally. Internally and externally encompasses different things, depending on the unit of analysis. The unit of analysis may be the relationship, the dyad or a number of dyadic relationships.

- The *internal politics* and the *internal economics* of the entity in question, typically based on the dyad
- *Political relationship* to the environment and *economic relationship* to the environment of the entity placing the dyad in a context
- *The environment* relating to factors beyond the immediate context

As mentioned above, the political economy paradigm regards marketing as the execution of a series transactions and exchange processes. Another way of looking at it is that the paradigm uses the concept of social systems as a way to understand interaction within the dyad and between the dyad and its environment. The paradigm will be presented further below.[20] This framework is useful for analysing organisations as social systems and covers a variety of areas:[21]

> Political economy is fairly general, as the paradigm may be applied in theory construction in a wide range of marketing areas. It is integrative through offering a unifying framework by incorporating major economic and socio-political constructs in the comparative analysis of marketing relationships.

Furthermore, a major advantage of using the political economy paradigm is that it also provides the opportunity to utilise a wide range of theories. As this paradigm not only operates in the context of national economy, but also in the fields of organisational theory, political science, sociology, transactional cost theory, contractual regulation theory, and social psychology. It therefore allows for the combining of a number of areas into comparative organisational studies.

The conceptual framework of the paradigm encompasses internal structures

---

20. As described by Arndt (1983), as he has refined the work carried out by Stern & Reve (1980) and later supplemented by Skytte (1990).
21. Arndt (1983, p. 44).

and processes, connecting them with the variables characterising the environment. These variables are called relationship variables. This group of variables is the connection between the social unit and the environment. The groups of components in the political economy paradigm are illustrated in figure 2-2.

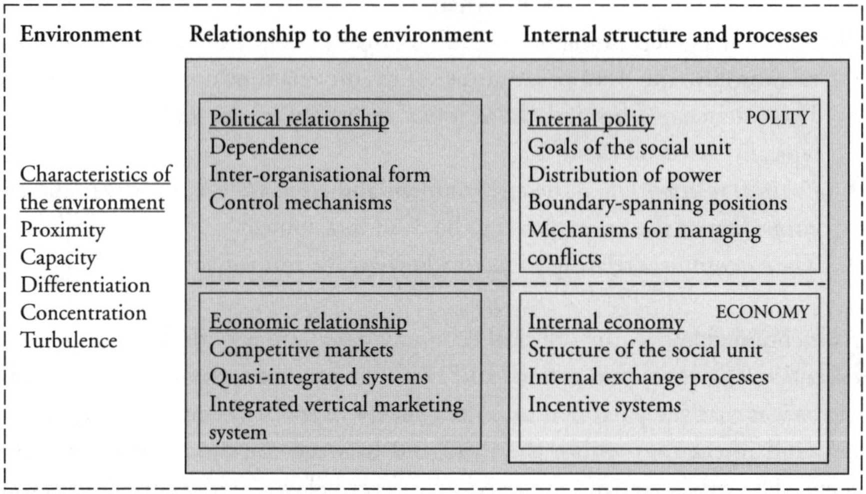

Figure 2-2: Major component groups of the political economy paradigm. Source: Based on Skytte, 1990, p. 33

Relationships are based on the rational arguments and emotional symbolism as introduced in figure 2-1. In figure 2-2 the argument is made that the analytical view of economy and power is useful for identifying and describing how a relationship is influenced by these variables. Furthermore, it must be emphasised that the relationship is part of the environment whether in close or distant proximity. The point being that relationships cannot be understood as isolated entities as they are but part of a larger mechanism and the relationships both effect and are affected by this mechanism.

The basic idea behind this conceptual framework is that the unit of analysis (the inner box) is connected through relationship variables (the middle box), which depends on the environment (the outer box). In other words, all relationships must be understood and analysed within a context. That context may be the immediate surroundings, the middle box, or the environment, the outer box. This will reflect that the relationship cannot be understood or analysed merely unto itself. We have to look at potential influencing factors in the political and economic sense.[22]

This implies that searching for explanations within the unit of analysis should not only focus on the unit itself but should simultaneously focus on the interaction between internal economic and political structures, processes and their interaction with external variables such as relationship variables or strategy variables. Thus, we are combining the analysis of the relationship with analysis of the environment.

The boundaries and external variables of the unit of analysis will depend on how the analytical unit is chosen and defined and of course later analysed. The analytical unit could be a network; for example the Nissan car dealers in the UK, a distribution channel; for example the Internet, a market sector; for example the pig farmers in Holland, relationships within an organisation; could be between the sales and logistics department or the classical dyad; for example the supplier and customer, etc.

Naturally, the choice of analytical unit will be a decisive factor with regard to the content of the internal and external variables. The implication of this is that this framework can be used in many different situations and is able to encompass small as well as large parts of a marketing system. See figure 2-3 for details.

When determining the most suitable variables to use when describing the external environment in relation to theory development, a compromise was reached between detailed raw data and aggregated abstraction.[23] The first one could be a list of various interest groups and the second could be a classification of the external environment according to various dimensions or forces. In the political economy framework these two methods are combined.[24] To illustrate the flexibility of the framework figure 2-3 lists a number of typical units of analysis. The have been labelled in accordance with the units included in the unit of analysis.

22. See also chapter 5 for description of driving forces of relations.
23. Achrol et al. (1983); Arndt (1983).
24. Pfeffer et al. (1978).

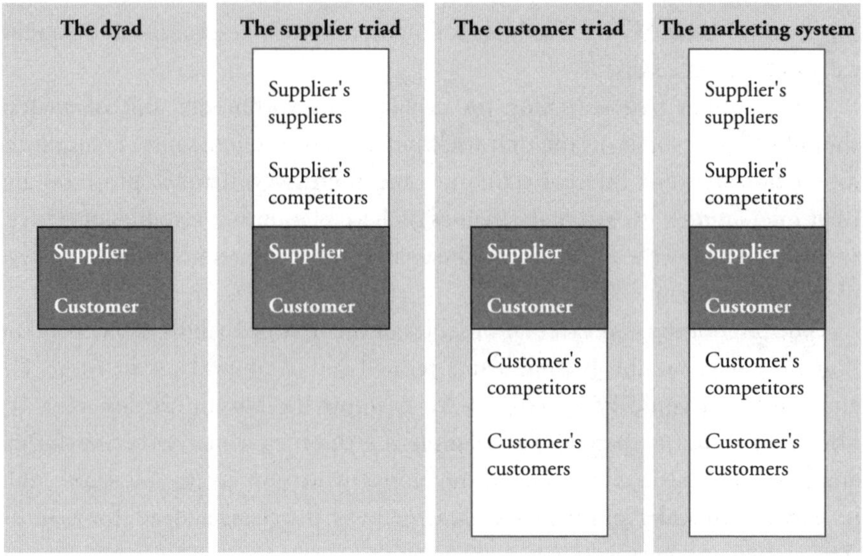

Figure 2-3: Different units of analysis in the political economy paradigm.

The important point in figure 2-3 is that the unit of analysis may vary depending on the need, in other words, relationships can be analysed no matter whether it is a dyadic relationship, a triadic relationship or a system of relationships. Thus, figure 2-3 highlights the flexibility of the political economy paradigm, as all four examples may be defined as the unit of analysis.

Relationships with the environment itself allow for the possibility of including the context of the classic dyadic relationship, either supplier's or customer's competitors and furthermore to include either their suppliers or customers. In the marketing system all these elements are taken into account.

The five variables used in the paradigm to characterise the *environment* are: distance, capacity, differentiation, concentration, and turbulence.

The first variable, *distance*, describes the distance between the unit of analysis and the number of levels between the unit and the organisation or other external factors influencing the social unit. The distance variable is divided into three levels:

- The first level is the primary organisational environment and contains suppliers and customers directly related to the social unit of analysis.

- The second level is the secondary organisational environment and contains suppliers' suppliers and customers' customers.
- The third level is the tertiary organisational environment or the macro environment.

This environmental framework made up of a national economic, political, and legislative elements influences the social unit indirectly via the primary and secondary organisational environment.

The second variable, *capacity*, is related to the social unit's potential of acquiring production factors and the question of whether or not there is sufficient demand for the output(s).

The third variable, *differentiation*, is related to the homogeneity or heterogeneity of organisations, individuals, and socio-political factors that influence the social unit and its possibility of acquiring resources. This will directly influence the level of required information for decision-making.

The fourth variable, *concentration*, is related to whether the degree of resource concentration is high or low, i.e. whether resources are concentrated in a few organisations or individuals or dispersed to many organisations or individuals. This variable is also related to geographic concentration.

The fifth variable, *turbulence*, is related to the pace of change and the dependency between the change processes in the input and output markets of the social unit and other environmental factors. Turbulence is often caused by changes related to external forces or resources and is therefore difficult to identify for the social unit. Hence, it may be difficult to obtain sufficient information for planning purposes and decision-making.

Focusing on the concept of exchange highlights the dyad as the central object. The dyadic approach is an important theoretical contribution to the understanding of relationship marketing, as the existing literature neglects the importance of the dyadic relationships between the supplier and the customer. Therefore, the dyadic focus provides a theoretical structure for describing the relationship between a supplier and a customer. As mentioned earlier, the paradigm is a framework for analysing relationships, and in figure 2-4 there are suggestions regarding what to look for where, i.e. what type of questions should be asked in relation to what part of the paradigm.

Environment	Relationship to the environment	Internal structure and processes
Characteristics of the environment Industry analysis Relation to other industries Concentration Speed of change "Paradigm shifts"	Political relationships Who is dependent on whom? Are there any relationships to organisations outside the unit of analysis? Type of strategic behaviour How are these relationships monitored?	Internal polity Vision, mission and strategic goals in the unit of analysis Are they congruent or conflicting? How are conflicts resolved? What power bases exist? Strategic behaviour Personal relationships
	Economic relationship Business system analysis "Paradigm for who does what" Kind of integration in the business systems Generic strategies in the business Competitors/Suppliers	Internal economy Legal structure(s) in the unit of analysis Exchange processes within the unit What incentive systems exist How performance is measured Business model and key success factors Profit and cost distribution

Figure 2-4: Type of questions that may be answered. Source: Based on Skytte (1990), Hunt and Morgan (1994), and Gummesson (1996, 1999)

Furthermore, several suggestions have been presented regarding the ways in which this paradigm may be supplemented. Two of these suggestions will be analysed more closely, one based on the IMP-school and network approach and another one the Cranfield relationship marketing approach. Both are part of the Network Interaction Approach.[25]

2.5 Supplementing the Political Economy Paradigm

Since the political economy paradigm only provides a framework, several authors have attempted to supplement the paradigm by formulating a relationship marketing mix. Most of these authors began with the opinion that the original marketing mix[26] was far too narrow.

25. See figure 1-11 in chapter 1.
26. Borden (1964).

Setting out to define a relationship marketing mix, the most distinctive and widely accepted contribution has been the introduction of the 30 different relationships.[27] It is presented in the following text and represents not a marketing mix but rather an overview of the many very different relationship types one may be able to identify. Please refer to the appendix to chapter 2 for more details.

We have linked the 30 relationship types to the five groups of components that operate within the political economy paradigm to illustrate where each of the 30 may be placed. Placing the 30 R's within the framework we can transform the typology of the 30 R's into an analytical tool, as it is now possible to link all 30 relationships to a location within the framework. This will provide a map of relationships between the unit of analysis and its environment. Furthermore, the map will provide suggestions for relationship development in the areas where relationship types are missing.

In essence, the 30 R's cover a variety of elements in the political economy paradigm and they represent a systematic approach for opportunity seeking rather than a marketing mix approach. Therefore the 30 R's come in as a useful checklist when mapping relationships.

Several authors[28] have stressed the need to go beyond the basic customer-supplier dyad by supplementing the dyad with a series of stakeholders or markets. Using the concept of markets[29] within a framework has been developing over the past decade and has formulated *internal* markets – i.e. consider your colleagues as customers, markets related to *relationships to the environment* – i.e. the competition between alternative relationships, and markets related to *the environment* – i.e. the market the dyad is serving. The aim of this framework is to combine the market concept (and thus the externally oriented analytical components) and yet to ensure the dyad (the internally oriented analytical components) is the foundation.

2.5.1 The 30 R's Framework

Gummesson's 30 R's can be seen as the most provocative attempt at grasping the complexity of relationship marketing and was originally a contribution pointing

27. Gummeson (1996).
28. Christopher, Payne and Ballantyne (1991); Kotler (1992); Hunt and Morgan (1994); Egan (2001).
29. Christopher, Payne and Ballantyne (1991; 1999).

out that the marketing mix concept was far too narrow.[30] Going through the list of R's it becomes quite clear that all of them might impact the dyadic relationship in some way. Although some of the R's are more obvious than others.

If the relationships are linked to the political economy paradigm the following illustration will appear – see figure 2-5. It should be noted that the "R's" are placed in the same line as the component of the political economy paradigm if there is a close or identical description of contents. The "R's" are placed in between the groups of components (could be "Relationships to the environment") if the content of the "R" is related to the group.

Furthermore, it is worth noting that the R's actually *can be related to all parts* of the political economy paradigm, meaning that they can serve as a checklist covering important elements of the major groups of the paradigm. As will be seen later however, is that the R's are primarily descriptive and not in any way normative or prescriptive.

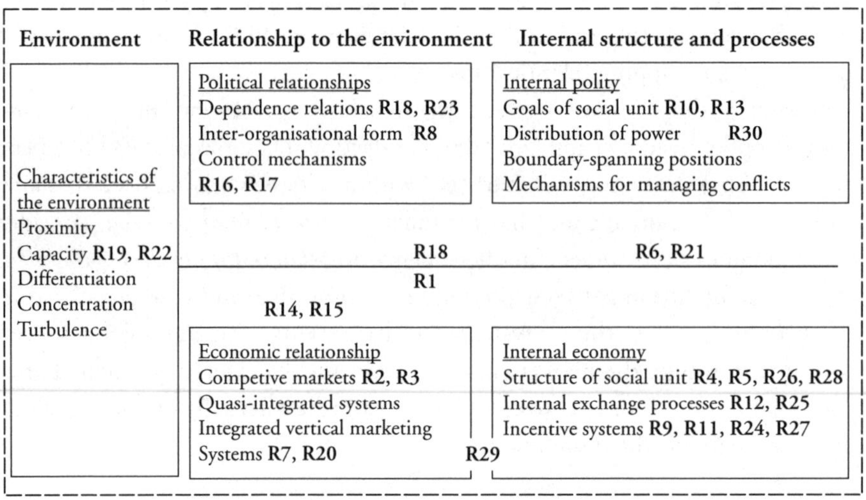

Figure 2-5: 30 R's framework linked to the political economy paradigm.

30. Borden (1964) introduced the marketing mix concept, whereas McCarthy (1960) had conceptualised the 4 P's – Product, Price, Promotion, and Place as part of the marketing mix. Later descriptions also include a 5th P – People. Christopher, Payne and Ballantyne (1991) further added two P's – Processes and Physical evidence.

Gummesson divides the 30 R's into 4 groups: *Classical* market relationships, *Special* market relationships, *Mega* relationships, and *Nano* relationships. These labels are explained below. The 30 R's are presented below and are supplemented by examples and explanations where necessary.

Classical Market Relationships
This group of relationships is concerned only with the core components of these relationships as well as the dyad and its relation to other partners.

Special Market Relationships
Special market relationships are concerned with the relationship elements beyond the narrow description of relationships presented in the classical relationships. This group of relationships therefore covers a wide range, including customers, enablers (IT and organisational structures, brands, and power bases) and even criminal networks.

Mega Relationships
Mega relationships are oriented towards the individual (personal) and cultural settings of a relationship (closely linked to the discussion earlier about importance of physical relationships) and the need for identifying the decision making unit(s) of the partner. These relationships are also concerned with limitations to competition, either in terms of alliances between organisations within the marketing system or supranational structures that provide the setting for developing relationships.

Nano Relationships
Nano relationships are internally oriented as they are concerned with resource allocation and the ability to attract resources. They also deal with internal power bases and the discussion of planning principles, incentive systems (for example profit centre principles) as well as monitoring principles.

One of the crucial points of the 30 R framework is the necessity of managing them all, or at least that the management must be conscious about their existence and relevance. Not all R's will be relevant to all organisations and therefore the individual entity or group of entities must analyse and decide which R's have the most impact on their business. One task would be to prioritise all 30 R's from the most important to the least important then adding the time element that is short term vs. long term. If there are differences these are expected to be of strategic interest.

The framework also stresses that the basic dyad should never be regarded as an entity in itself, but an entity that is highly influenced by many different types of relationships. Furthermore, the diversity covered by the 30 R's may provide the inspiration to look beyond the obvious relationship types.

2.5.2 The 6 Markets Framework

Using the market metaphor to describe relationships and the environment in which they exist is often used to highlight the so-called professional aspects of relationships and exchanges, i.e. exchanges that take place in a commercial setting. This metaphor also reflects the competitive aspects of relationships, namely that the parties involved in a relationship often have other options.

The 6 markets framework[31] may be used to supplement the 30 R's framework. This framework has been chosen as it attempts to provide an operational framework for analysing relationships using a simple structure and it focuses on marketing as exchange. The framework thus reflects groups of components that are critical to building and maintaining relationships.

The 6 markets model addresses relationship marketing at the organisational level as it presents 6 role-related market domains or "markets". Each of these markets represents dimensions of relationships as well as relationships with a number of organisations or individuals that may influence the marketing performance of the organisation in question. The 6 markets are: customer markets, referral markets, internal markets, employee markets, influence markets and supplier markets.

Initially, this model placed internal markets in the centre in order to highlight the importance of marketing's role as an integrator and facilitator between the other markets while supporting the management of these relationships at the same time. As illustrated in figure 2-6, one can see that this framework has evolved and customer markets are now prioritised higher than internal markets. This change reflects the gradual change of marketing's role in the organisation, from being a central component to being one of several. Marketing's perception of marketing has found a new balance!

31. Christopher, Payne and Ballantyne (1991).

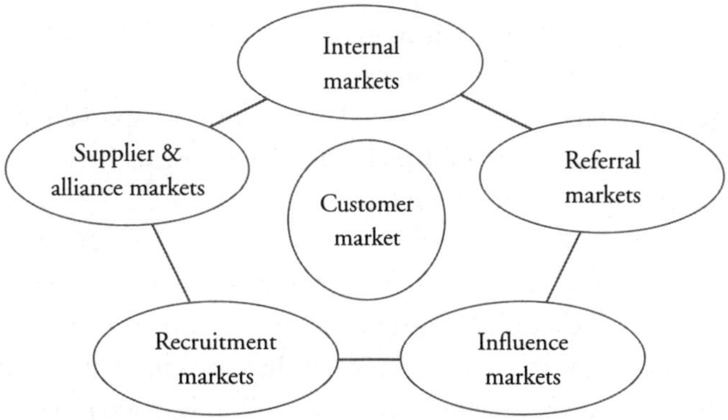

Figure 2-6: The 6 markets framework. Source: Christopher, Payne and Ballantyne (1999)

In essence, this framework maintains that customer markets are, although it is placed in the centre of the figure, not the only market of importance in terms of relationship marketing, the other markets can be just as influential as customer markets depending on the situation and context.

Customer Markets

Whether the customer is the end user of a product or service does of course depend on the position the supplier occupies in that particular supply chain. Many organisations market both to trade customers (intermediaries, distributors or retailers) and consumers (end purchasers, users and consumers) but their relative power within the supply chain is likely to determine which relationships are in focus and which are not.

A point not to be overlooked, however, is that relationship marketing is not a universal recipe. There are situations such as low-involvement or commodity products, where a swift and simple transaction approach is most appropriate and preferred by the customer.

Referral Markets

Referral markets are characterised by their credibility towards the environment of the relationship, or as endorsers of one of the parties involved. It is important to note that these markets sometimes have a "logic of their own" in which referrals and endorsements are decided on a personal level and therefore these decisions are not necessarily rational or economically sound.

Referrals can be a decisive element, as they possess a high credibility factor, i.e. the individuals or organisations that contribute the referrals are typically not gaining from publishing their point of view. Therefore their credibility is usually high and not easily compromised.

Often referral markets can be treated as customers, especially if the parties involved enter into formal or informal referral agreements between themselves and suppliers of complementary products or services.

Independent individuals, government institutions, customers, or competitors may give referrals, depending on the recipient in question. Developing relationships in referral markets calls for great caution, as those who are the "referrers" will not accept the risk of being intimidated by even the slightest suspicion of concealed relationships. Therefore relationships in this market require complete openness, fairness as well as clear definition of areas of interest and activity.

Internal Markets

A popular quote states, "Marketing and sales is too important to be left to a single department as it concerns all". This quote also indicates that every person within an organisation directly or indirectly provides value to customers. The internal focus of relationship marketing is partly a reaction to the traditional outside-in perspective of marketing that is assessing market opportunities based on external factors. An inside-out perspective of marketing assesses opportunities as being based on internal factors such as competencies, resources and asset specificity.[32]

Among the internal factors is employee retention, which ensures continuity of the individuals involved in handling relationships. This factor is considered important in the promotion of smoothness of relationships as well as the individual exchanges taking place within the relationship.

Sharing knowledge and partner insights is necessary if several individuals are involved in the relationship, as everyone must be able to access necessary information to handle his or her part of the exchange. One of the ways to do this is by developing networks within one's own organisation. Focusing on the same goals is often considered to be a precondition for developing relationships, but what is just as important is that there is a shared set of goals and values within each organisation as a whole. In profit centre organisations however, this precondition may be difficult to fulfil.

32. Penrose (1959); Barney (1991); Nelson and Winter (1982); Williamson (1975); etc.

Employee Markets (Recruitment)

Recruiting individuals to become part of an organisation is gradually becoming a marketing related task that calls for relationships with recruitment partners, educational institutions and labour unions. The potential employee will assess the organisation in terms of its attractiveness as a basis for a career and will therefore judge the company based on internal qualitative factors that go far beyond its products and services.

Thus, the boundaries of the organisation are vital, especially when the organisation is engaged in the outsourcing of functions, activities or processes.

Influence Markets

Influence markets are markets that may or may not influence a relationship, however they share the potential to influence relationships regardless of whether they are internal or external. Therefore, influence markets are closely related to the concept of the decision-making unit within an organisation.[33]

To analyse influence markets it is necessary to identify all the functions and individuals that may be able to say "No" or who have the ability to prolong negotiations etc. Furthermore, the internal market challenges the traditional sales approach that is selling to one individual as opposed to relationship sales based on selling to a group of individuals sharing a strategic goal but rarely sharing operational goals.

One of the consequences of the internal market is the need for developing networks within the partner's organisation in order to avoid being dependent on single individuals. Furthermore, future members of the decision-making unit should be identified in order to maintain the relationship.

Supplier Markets

The marketing system approach involves downstream as well as upstream activities, which implies that suppliers should be included as relationship partners. This understanding coincides with the developments within SCM – Supply Chain Management where the whole marketing system is considered the unit of analysis. This match is not surprising when the originators[34] of the 6 Markets framework are kept in mind.

Furthermore, one of the consequences of close relationships with suppliers

---

33. Nielsen and Wilke (1999).
34. M. Christopher is a well known author of articles and books on logistics, supply chain management and marketing logistics.

may be competing marketing systems, as relationships becomes mutually exclusive, i.e. developing relationships with one organisation will exclude relationships with competitors of that organisation.

We have linked the 6 markets framework to the political economy paradigm to illustrate the focal areas of the framework. Please refer to footnote for supplemental information.[35] As can be seen in figure 2-7 it is the *internal components* that dominate the 6 markets framework.

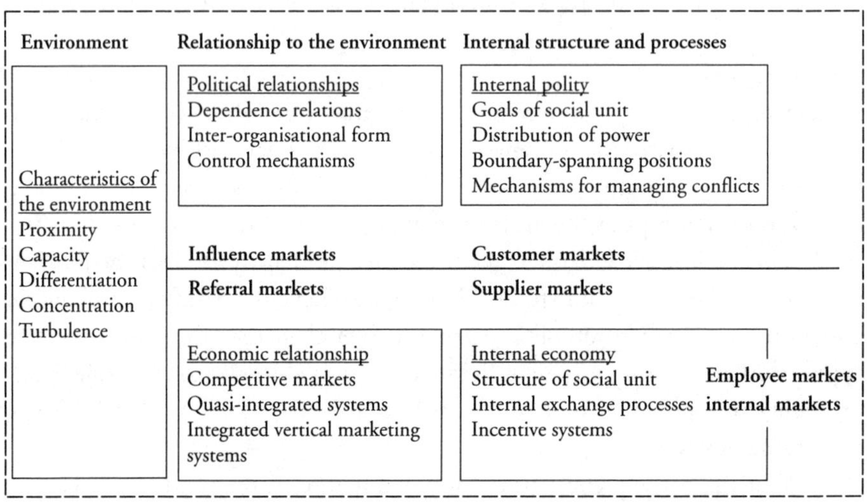

Figure 2-7: The 6 markets framework linked to the political economy paradigm.
Source: Hougaard and Bjerre

Figure 2-7 illustrates, as did figure 2-6, where there are linkages between the paradigm and the model. The illustration indicates that the 6 markets framework is focused primarily on the internal parts of the paradigm, especially internal economics, and secondly on the relationships to the environment, but

35. As a supplement to the 6 markets framework we also point to the contributions from Doyle (1995) – describing the core firm and its partnerships, Morgan and Hunt (1994) – describing the relational exchanges of the focal firm, and Kotler (1992) – describing the ten players in the organisation's immediate and macro environment. These authors all share the perspective that the organisation (a supplier) is the focal point of departure and that relationships should be regarded from this centre and development of relationships takes place from this centre.

not the environment itself. In other words, one might say that the 6 markets framework highlights the inner parts of the political economy paradigm, whereas the 30 R's framework also highlights the outer parts of the political economy paradigm.

The central contribution of the political economy paradigm and the two supplemental frameworks presented is that we no longer identify other members of a marketing system as being merely suppliers or customers but include them when relationships are analysed. The central contribution of chapter 2 is therefore:

> When analysing relationships, we no longer consider just the relationship itself, but also include the connection between the relationship and its environment, as well as the conditions within that environment.

References

Achrol, R. S., Reve, T. and Stern, L. W. (1983) *The Environment of Marketing Channel Dyads: A Frame Work for Comparative Analysis*, Journal of Marketing, vol. 47 (fall), pp. 55-67.

Alderson, W. (1957) *Marketing behaviour and Executive Action*, Richard D. Irwin

Arndt, J. (1983) *The Political Economy Paradigm: Foundation for Theory Building in Marketing*, Journal of Marketing, vol. 47 (fall), pp. 44-54.

Bagozzi, R. P. (1974) *Marketing as an Organized Behavioral System of Exchange*, Journal of Marketing, vol. 38, pp. 77-81.

Bagozzi, R. P. (1975) *Marketing as Exchange*, Journal of Marketing, vol. 39, pp. 32-39.

Barney, J. B. (1991) *Firm Resources and Sustained Competitive Advantage*, Journal of Management, vol. 17, pp. 99-120.

Borden, N. H. (1964) *The Concept of the Marketing Mix*, Journal of Advertising Research, vol. June, pp. 2-7.

Brinberg, D. and McGrath, J. E. (1985) *Validity and the Research Process*, Sage Publications.

Carman, J. M. (1980) *Paradigms for Marketing Theory*, Research in Marketing, vol. 3, pp. 1-36.

Christopher, M. (1997) *Marketing Logistics*, Butterworth-Heinemann

Christopher, M., Payne, A. and Ballantyne, D (1991) *Relationship Marketing*, Butterworth-Heinemann

Christopher, M., Payne, A. and Ballantyne, D (1999) *Relationship Marketing*, Butterworth-Heinemann

Doyle, P. (1995) *Marketing in the new millennium*, European Journal of Marketing, vol. 29, pp. 23-41.

Dwyer, R. F., Schurr, P. H. and Oh, S. (1987) *Developing Buyer-Seller Relationships*, Journal of Marketing, vol. 51, pp. 11-27.

Egan, J. (2001) *Relationship Marketing – Exploring relational strategies in marketing*, Pearson Education.

Enis, B. M. and Mokwa, M. P. (1979) *The Marketing Management Matrix: A Taxonomy for Strategy Comprehension*, in Ferrell, O. C., Brown, S. W. and Lamb, C. W. Jr. (eds.), Conceptual and Theoretical Developments in Marketing, Proceedings Series, AMA.

Ford, D. (1995) *Understanding Business Markets*, International Thomson Business Press.

Gummesson, E. (1996) *Towards a Theoretical Framework of Relationship Marketing*, Proceedings of the International Conference on Relationship Marketing, Berlin, pp. 5-18.

Hunt, S. D. and Morgan, R. M. (1994) *Relationship marketing in the era of network competition*, Journal of Marketing Management, vol. 5 (5), pp. 18-28.

Håkansson, H. and Snehota, I. (1995) *Developing Relationships in Business Networks*, Routledge.

Kotler, P. (1988) *Marketing Management*, Prentice Hall

Kotler, P. (1992) *Total Marketing*, Business Week, Advance Executive Brief no. 2.

Kuhn, T. S. (1970) *The Structure of Scientific Revolutions*, University of Chicago Press.

Morgan, R. M. and Hunt, S. D. (1994) *The Commitment-Trust Theory of Relationship Marketing*, Journal of Marketing.

Nelson, R. R. and Winter, S. (1982) *An Evolutionary Theory of Economic Change*, Harvard University Press.

Nielsen, O. and Wilke, R. (1999) *Organisationers købsadfærd i grundtræk*, Samfundslitteratur.

Norman, R. and Ramirez, R. (1983) *From Value Chain to Value Constellation; Designing Interactive Strategy*, Harvard Business Review

Penrose, E. T. (1959) *The Theory of the Growth of the Firm*, Oxford University Press

Pfeffer, J. and Salancik, G. R. (1978) *The External Control of Organizations: A Resource Dependence Perspective*, Harper & Row.

Pickton, D. and Broderick, A. (2001) *Integrated Marketing Communication*, Pearson Education.

Skytte, H. (1990) *Interorganisatoriske relationer i vertikale markedsføringssystemer*, Ph.D. dissertation, HHÅ.

Stern, L. W. and El-Ansary, A. I. (1992) *Marketing Channels*, Fifth Edition, Prentice Hall.

Stern, L. W. and Reve, T. (1980) *Distribution Channels as Political Economies: A Framework for Comparative Analysis*, Journal of Marketing, vol. 44, pp. 52-64.

Williamson, O. E. (1975) *Markets and Hierarchies – Analysis and Antitrust Implications*, The Free Press.

Appendix: Gummesson's 30 R Framework Presented in Detail

Gummesson has divided the 30 R's into 4 groups: *Classical* market relationships, *Special* market relationships, *Mega* relationships, and *Nano* relationships. These labels are explained below. The 30 R's are presented in the following, and supplemented by examples and supplementary explanations where this has been found to be necessary.

Classical Market Relationships

This group of relationships is concerned with the core components of relationships, the dyad and it's relationships with other partners.

1. The classic dyad: the relationship between the supplier and the customer. This is the parent relationship of marketing, the ultimate exchange of value, which constitutes the basis all business transactions.
R1 is in essence covering all aspects of the internal politics and economics.

2. The classic triad: the drama of the customer-supplier-competitor triangle. Competition is a central ingredient of market economy. Within the dynamics of competition there are relationships between three parties: between the customer and the current supplier, between the customer and the supplier's competitors, and between competitors.

R2 is focused on the dyad's relationship to the external environment, specifically related to competitors of the supplier as well as the buyer. In essence this is focused on the dyad as an entity in the industry.

3. The classic multidimensional network: physical distribution. The physical distribution consists of a network of relationships, which can be a decisive factor for marketing success.

R3 takes R2 further to include all parties interacting with the dyad. In principle this also includes the supplier's supplier, the customer's customer etc.

Special Market Relationships

Special market relationships are concerned with the relationship elements beyond the narrow description of relationships presented in the classical relationships section. This group of relationships therefore covers a wide range, including customers, enablers (IT and organisational structures, brands, and power bases) and even criminal networks.

4. Relationships via full-time marketers (FTMs) and part-time marketers (PTMs). Those who work in marketing and sales departments – the FTMs – are professional relationship-makers. All others, who perform other main functions yet influence customer relationships directly or indirectly, are PTMs. There are also contributing FTMs and PTMs outside the organisation.

R4 points out that all individuals in an organisation are important to the relationships with other organisations, and underlines that even those without any formal external responsibility are also contributing to relationships.

5. The service encounter: interaction between the customer and front line personnel. Production and delivery of services involves the customer in an interactive relationship with the service provider's personnel, often referred to as the moment of truth[36].

R5 highlights the unique exchange in service industries because when the exchange takes place, the production and consumption also take place simultaneously.

6. The many-headed customer and the many-headed supplier. Marketing to other organisations, i.e. industrial marketing or business-to-business marketing, often means contact between many individuals from the supplier's and the customer's organisation.

R6 underlines that relationships are not the doing of one individual, but principally everyone in the organisation. In other words: relationships are too complex (and important) to be left in the hands of single individuals or departments.

7. The relationship to the customer's customer. A condition for success is often the understanding of the customer's customer, and what suppliers can do to help their customers become successful.

---

36. See also chapter 1.

R7 takes the dyad one step further to the customer triad illustrated in figure 2-3. Furthermore this also points to a shift in focus for sales organisations: know your customer's business and market in order to understand why you may develop the relationship.

8. The mental and physical proximity to customers vs. the distant relationship. In mass marketing, the closeness to the customer is lost and the relationship becomes distant and is based on surveys, statistics and written reports.

R8 states that to know your customer you need to be close.

9. The relationship to the dissatisfied customer. The dissatisfied customer perceives a special type of relationship, more intense than the normal situation, and often badly managed by the provider. The way of handling a complaint, the recovery, can determine the quality of the future relationship.

R9 touches on one of the aspects of path dependency is the resolution of conflicts. We know that in some service industries that just about 10 % of customers complain, while the other 90 % simply leave without providing a reason.[37]

10. The monopoly relationship: the customer or supplier as prisoner. When competition is inhibited, the customer may be at the mercy of the provider – or the other way around. One of them becomes prisoner.

R10 describes what we later define as a "one-sided" relationship, a relationship that exists only because one part forces the other into the relationship. In this type of relationship, as soon as an alternative presents itself the customer leaves. In other words, this is not a positive foundation for a lasting relationship.

11. The customer as "member". In order to create a long term sustaining relationship, it has become increasingly frequent to enlist customers as members of various marketing programmes.

R11 is linked to the development of loyalty programs, see chapter on customer loyalty.

12. The electronic relationship. A significant amount of marketing today takes place networks via IT. This volume is expected only to grow in significance.

37. Normann, R. and Ramirez, R. (1983).

13. Parasocial relationships: relationships to symbols and objects. Relationships do not only exist between people and physical phenomena, but also with mental images and symbols such as brand names and corporate identities.

R13 suggests a link between relationships and branding as relationships are influenced by the image of the partner. It's important to note that this is not just the individual's own image of the partner but the other individuals' image of the partner as well.

14. The non-commercial relationship. This is a relationship between the public sector and citizens/customers. It also includes voluntary organisations and other activities outside of the profit-based or monetarised economy, such as those performed in families.

R14 could also be seen as a recognition of the importance of NGOs – Non Government Organisations and their membership of the organisation's interest sphere.

15. The green relationship. The environmental and health issues have slowly but gradually increased in importance and are creating a new type of customer relationship through legislation, the voice of opinion leading consumers, changing behaviour of consumers and an extension of the customer-supplier relationship to encompass a recycling process.

R15 is important and was discovered by Shell when it was decided to dump the Brent Spar platform in the North Atlantic. Many organisations now have developed formal relationships with "green organisations" and use these relationships to avoid Shell's experience.

16. The law-based relationship. A relationship to a customer is sometimes founded primarily on legal contracts and the threat of litigation.

R16 relates to R10 in the sense that this relationship is partly forced onto one of the partners.

17. The criminal network. Organised crime is built on tight and often impermeable networks guided by an illegal business mission. They exist around the world and are apparently growing but are not observed in marketing theory. These networks can disturb the functioning of a whole market or industry.

R17 is rarely studied academically but undeniably set the scene in some sectors (such as gambling, prostitution).

Mega Relationships

Mega relationships are oriented towards the individual (personal) and cultural settings of a relationships (closely linked to the discussion earlier about importance of physical relationships) and the need for identifying the decision making unit(s) of the partner. These relationships are also concerned with limitations to competition, either in terms of alliances between organisations within the marketing system or supranational structures providing the setting for developing relationships.

18. Personal and social networks. The personal and social networks often determine the business networks. In some cultures, business can be conducted exclusively between friends and friends-of-friends.

R18 touches on the environment in which relationships reside, and this is especially important for internationally operating companies as differences between national traditions may vary considerably, i.e. consider differences between the Japanese, German, Arab, American and Scandinavian cultures.

19. Megamarketing: the real "customer" is not always found in the marketplace. In certain instances, relationships must be sought with governments, legislators, influential individuals, and others in order to make marketing feasible on an operational basis.

R19 is focused on the relationships needed for developing the focal relationships of the organisation. Some of these relationships include registrations, permits, regular audits, authorisations etc.

20. Alliances change the market mechanisms. Alliances mean closer relationships and collaboration between companies. Thus, competition is partly curbed, but collaboration is necessary to make a market economy function.

R20 could aim at limiting competition or to dividing the market into cartels etc.

21. The knowledge relationship. Knowledge can be the most strategic and critical resource and knowledge acquisition is often the rationale for alliances.

R21 was clearly the case when BMW and Honda developed their relationship to ensure BMW's access to Honda's patents and quality assurance systems.

22. Mega alliances. EU (The European Union) and NAFTA (The North America Free Trade Agreement) are examples of alliances above the single company and industry. They exist on government and supranational levels.

R22 confirms that relationships can be found at any level of the global economy.

23. The mass media relationship. The media can be supportive or damaging to the marketing and they are particularly influential in forming public opinion. The way of handling the media relationships is often crucial for success or failure.

R23 is also by some described as Public Relations, which in itself has developed into a separate industry. This can be seen at the personal level (spin-doctors handling this together with politicians) and at the organisational level (PR-agencies) and the emergence of the Integrated Marketing Communication concept.[38]

Nano Relationships

Nano relationships are internally oriented and they are concerned with resource allocation and the ability to attract resources. They also deal with internal power bases and the discussion of planning principles, incentive systems (for example profit centre principles) and monitoring principles.

24. Market mechanisms are brought inside the company. By introducing profit centres in an organisation, a market inside the company is created and internal as well as external relationships of a new kind emerge.

R24 often describes the situation where existing internal exchanges are no longer limited by relationships of the type R10, but internal exchanges are forced to respect market conditions and terms as the basis for future exchanges.

25. Inter-functional and inter-hierarchical dependency: the relationship between internal customers and internal suppliers. The dependency between the different tiers and departments in a company is seen as a process consisting of relationships between internal customer and internal providers.

R25 may link to the concept of transaction cost theory,[39] in which the hierarchy is seen as the most efficient governance structure.[40]

---

38. See for example Pickton and Broderick (2001).
39. See chapter 3 for elaboration on this.
40. See Williamson (1975).

26. Quality providing a relationship between operations management and marketing. The modern quality concept has built a bridge between design, manufacturing and other technology-based activities and marketing. It considers the company's internal relationships as well as its relationships to the customers.

R26 reflects the development of the TQM or Total Quality Management concept, highlighting the need for regarding the receiver of your output as a customer, and that you haven't delivered satisfactorily until your customer is satisfied.

27. Internal marketing: relationships with the "employee market". Internal marketing can be seen as part of relationship marketing as it gives indirect and necessary support to the relationships with external customers.

28. The two-dimensional matrix relationship. Organisational matrices are frequent in large corporations, above all in the relationships between product management and sales.

R28 reflects the need for keeping internal focus as well as partner focus. Therefore, "double reporting systems" are introduced to ensure two focuses at one time.

29. The relationship to external providers of marketing services. External providers reinforce the marketing function by supplying a series of services, such as those offered by advertising agencies and market research institutes, but also in the area of sales and distribution.

R29 could also be labelled "outsourcing" as organisations focus on their core competencies and look to external suppliers to handle tasks and processes handled internally in the past. This could encompass sales representatives, marketing planning and execution, customer service (i.e. call centres) or even customer complaints.

30. The owner and financier relationship. Owners and other financiers can sometimes determine the conditions under which marketing works. The relationship to them may influence the marketing strategy.

R30 is the stakeholder approach also reflected in the emergence of "Shareholder Value".

One of the critical points of the 30 R framework is the necessity of managing them all, or at least that the management must be conscious about their existence and importance. Not all R's will be applicable to all organisations and therefore each individual entity or group of entities may analyse and decide which R's have the most impact on their business. One constructive task might be to prioritise all 30 R's from the most important to the least important factoring in the time element, i.e. short term vs. long term benefits. If there are differences then these are expected to be of strategic interest.

This framework also stresses that the basic dyad should never be regarded as an entity in itself, but an entity that is highly influenced by many different types of relationships. Furthermore, the diversity covered by the 30 R's may provide inspiration to look beyond the obvious relationship types.

CHAPTER 3

Discovering the Economics of Customer Relationships

An exchange between a seller and a buyer can have vastly different economic ramifications for either party depending on the specific relationship context it takes place in. Defining the basic contextual elements of relationships and their rules as well as explaining the specific economic behaviours of each player is the focus of customer relationship economics.

Strategic relationship marketing deals with the formation of sustainable competitive advantages through establishing, expanding and maintaining profitable, strong customer relationships. Understanding the economics of customer relationships has become a precondition for market leadership. Therefore, it is necessary to formulate a concrete framework for understanding and analysing relationship economics.

In this chapter, the key concepts of relationship economics from a business perspective will be discussed. They are bounded rationality, transaction costs, opportunism, customer life cycle and asset specificity, i.e. customisation of assets. Understanding and controlling these variables is the key to developing competitive power and generating greater earnings through precise relationship marketing strategies.

3.1 Replacing Traditional Economic Cornerstones

In the imaginary world of complete resource mobility, the relationship as phenomenon is in fact meaningless to discuss, because relationship considerations are not considered to have any impact on the behaviour of market participants.

If, on the other hand, a buyer and a seller who do business with each on a regular basis eventually and gradually adjust to the needs and wants of the other party, then the situation might change significantly. For example, if a supplier adapts his machinery, products, organisation, systems, staff or other assets in order to meet the requirements of individual customers or segments, then the resources are no longer completely mobile. Assets adapted or even tailor-made to certain relationships will presumably lose some, or maybe all their productivity, if the relationship breaks and the resources must then find new "employment" in- or outside of the company.

Traditional market economy postulates are based on the concept of a world without the kind of disturbances that relationships tend to create. These cornerstones are like a false mirror, as it does not reflect what goes on in everyday business life. These two marketing concepts present opposite points of view; on the one hand, the well accepted market economic rationale and on the other hand, the real world that is made up of relationships. It is easy to see the difference between the two paradigms, traditional marketing vs. relationship marketing when expressed in these terms.

	Traditionally based marketing concept	**Relationship based marketing concept**
Resource mobility	Complete – no asset specificity	Incomplete – asset specificity
Exchange friction	No friction between parties	Friction causing costs
Time frame dimension	The periodic view	Customer life cycle view

Figure 3-1: Foundation of traditional market economics versus relationship marketing economics.

Consider slogans like "the customer comes first" or "customers make paydays possible" or "we try harder". These catch phrases are not just clichés but are expressions that reflect the vision, values and corporate identity of a company. They express a customer relationship philosophy and not on a pure exchange perspective.

3.1.1 The Principle of Complete Resource Mobility

As briefly mentioned earlier, complete mobility of resources means that a company can adjust its capacities and resources from one area of application or one type of customer to new purposes and other customers without any loss of return on such assets. The behaviour of the supplier and the customer is therefore not supposed to be influenced by resource mobility considerations such as: a customer trying to unilaterally improve their bargaining power because of the supplier's specified assets or a supplier wishing to impose control and compensation mechanisms in contractual agreements due to customisation.

Additionally, it can be assumed that any company can acquire identical bundles of resources on the factor market, which then means that competitive advantages are stimulated by unique resource combinations or core competencies that in principle can be excluded from the range of available strategic options.

The classic, well accepted framework for marketing tasks maintains that sustainable competitive advantages are created by the capability of a firm to exploit market opportunities better, cheaper, faster or more focused than its competitors, sometimes called the *s-c-p axiom* for structure (opportunities), conduct (exploitation), and performance.

Market leadership based on the unique ability to build and defend long-term, mutually beneficial customer relationships more effectively than the competition rests on the idea that the competencies that have created the leading position can neither be copied nor acquired on the factor market.

Relationship based market leadership may impose a risk of dependence to the extent that the relationship competencies rely on customisation of assets to satisfy individual customer demands. Specific assets are less valuable for other customers and hence they require protection via contract mechanisms.

Relationship economic thinking weighs the economic value of an investment in customer specific assets against the risks, which follow. The classic marketing concept does not address this dilemma as being of central importance.

3.1.2 The Principle of Frictionless Transactions

In traditional business economics it is assumed that the total cost of a good or a service equals the sum of production costs. Therefore, the total costs are not influenced by the relational context of the production process as such. This is usually called the make-buy trade-off and it looks only at the cost of goods alone. It does not consider whether the way of organising an activity i.e. producing or purchasing, is the key to potential differences in the cost structure.

This opinion reflects the principle of no friction as the eventual costs and in particular the cost differences, arise as a result of the basic interaction between a customer and an external supplier. Transaction costs between an internal supplier or sister department are considered non existent or of minor importance only.

Implicitly, the principle of no friction assumes that the alternative to internal activity (the "make" solution) and thus use of the hierarchy as command structure in the regulation of the interaction between supplier and user is the classic market contract. According to the idea of the classical market contract, any buyer can eliminate risk, get the lowest price and obtain full transparency by a contractual arrangement, such as a bill of lading in maritime transportation.

But the real world is far from frictionless where relational structures are primary cost drivers. The relationship is a hybrid, in between the perfect world of the classic market contract and *the hierarchy*. The hierarchy assumes mutual confidence between parties who are all members of the same organisation and under the same governing structure. Hence, the frictions are supposed to be at a minimum, although realities are often very different from this ideal depending on factors such as reward mechanisms, corporate policies etc. Frictions are not only minimised when using the market construct as a regulating mechanism, but even more so when the parties agree on an arrangement beforehand and thereby regulating every possible situation.

Most economic activity does not live up to the *frictionless ideal*. Modifying the market mechanisms in the form of relationships also introduces the costs of friction between two economic spheres. Managing the costs and benefits arising from frictions between a buyer and a seller more efficiently than competitors then becomes a crucial marketing strategic issue.

3.1.3 The Principle of Focusing on the Period

For obvious reasons the period (year, quarter, month) is the key measurement interval in financial management. The time period can, however, only to some extent include the dynamics and the cause-effect mechanisms in market oriented problems.

The Attention-Interest-Desire-Action effect hierarchy communications model (AIDA) is a good example. Costs of communication (creating attention) are paid in period x, whereas the outcome in terms of revenues materialises in period x++.

Relationships between supplier and customer go through different stages over its lifetime. The most and maybe the only relevant economic approach to marketing management from a relationship perspective is the principle of lifetime value of relationships and how it can be influenced by whom or what.

In recent years, interest in measuring relationship value has increased dramatically. An outstanding study in this field concluded that every new pizza customer on average represented a net present value of 5,000 USD. Amazing but true.

As discussed earlier, vast amounts are being invested in building fixed line cable networks. The valuation of such infrastructure is determined by the total value of user relationships that will develop into future cash flow. What is calculated is life cycles and effect hierarchies, not specific periods.

This is not a revolutionary discovery. Most businesspeople would agree regarding the economic importance of relationship elasticities such as volume, price, and lifetime. What people must find perplexing is that there is a desperate need for reliable theories and measurement tools in this area that do not yet exist.

In the following sections there will be an overview of the core points in the business economics of customer relationships.

3.2 Risk and Opportunism of Customer Relationships

Research has demonstrated that mere planning and execution of transactions drive 25% of costs in an average company between suppliers and customers, the price of "running the economic system".[1] Furthermore, several case studies have documented a significant positive correlation between the durability of customer relationships and profitability. One of these studies[2] concluded that a company, depending on the industry, could potentially increase the net present value of the customer relationship by 35-95% by reducing the turnover rate to 5%. This clearly indicates the value of retention elasticity.

The phrase which says it "costs ten times less to sell more to existing customers than to sell the same amount to new customers" is true in most situations, revealing the *acquisition economics* versus the *retention economics* dichotomy.

The following real life case illustrates the importance of customer relationship economics.

3.2.1 Case – Skanska and Rockwool[3]

Skanska is an international construction company with offices worldwide and is one of the leading companies in Sweden. Skanska is managed according to decentralised principles. Therefore, local managers, including the purchasing manager make all decisions. And it does not matter whether it is management in charge of a department, an individual project or a site.

Rockwool produces insulation materials of mineral wool, and Skanska is one of Rockwool's biggest and most important customers.

1. Williamson (1975; 1985).
2. Reichheld (1996).
3. Heikkila (1996).

Both Skanska and Rockwool operate on extremely competitive markets characterised by low margins and constant price pressure, where even minor deviations, delays or miscalculations can eliminate all profits from a given project. Recently Skanska and Rockwool entered into a cooperative contract with each other with the explicit purpose of optimising the economics of the trade between them. In other words, Skanska and Rockwool aimed at replacing traditional business economic thinking with relationship market economics.

The managerial motives for a switch from exchange to relationship economies are illustrated in figure 3-2.

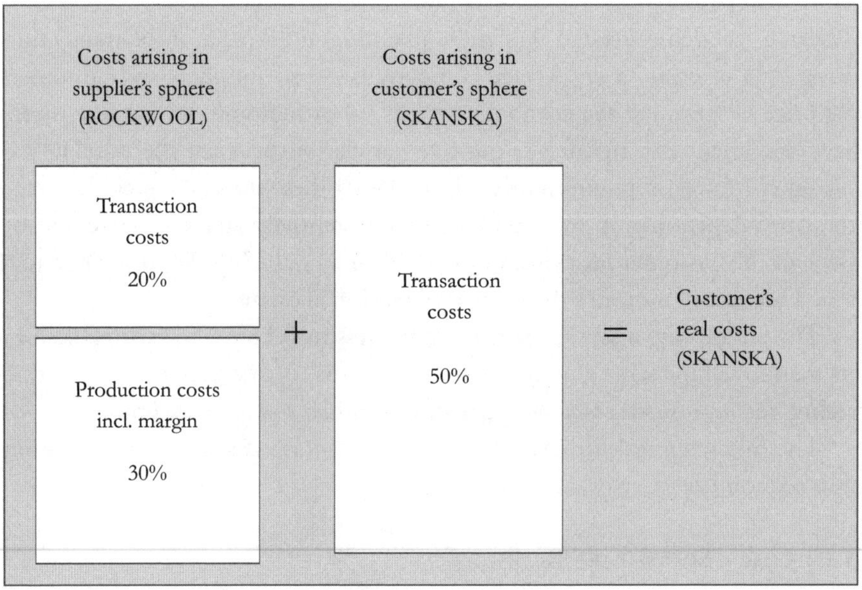

Figure 3-2: Skanska and Rockwool in the before-situation: The true costs of mineral wool at the arrival to the site. Source: Heikkila (1996)

Before the relationship contract between the parties purchasing at Skanska was taken care of at a decentralised level within the Skanska organisation. The supplier of insulation materials was chosen from project to project, most often in bid rounds where the suppliers of insulation, being a quite homogenous commodity, were played out against each other.

These terms of trade led to the cost structure shown in figure 3-2 above. The total costs arising in the supplier's, i.e. Rockwool's sphere, amounted to no more than 50% of the total price Skanska really paid. A series of hidden costs, such as inventory costs, loading and unloading, transportation, waste, loss, delays of deliveries and administration should be added to get a true picture of the business economic price.

More than half of Rockwool's internal costs derived from delivering to Skanska's building sites likewise then consisted of the same type of transaction costs. The core production and administrative expenses amounted to less than 25% of total costs, whereas the higher costs originated from frictions between the counterparts.

In the pre-relationship situation, both parties pursued a monadic, sub-optimising objective, making use of the classical market contract. The outcome was opposite of the intention of both parties, that is a dramatic rise in the price of insulation materials for the seller as well as for the buyer in terms of extremely high transaction costs, a subtle kind of prisoners' game, where the outcome is lose-lose.

The Skanska-Rockwool case demonstrates that the relationship economic rationale not only has an academic interest, but also is a strong influential factor in the generation of profits.

3.2.2 What are the True Product Costs – Introducing Risk and Opportunism

Even when a supplier and a customer develop an interdependent relationship based on cooperation, the rivalry within the relationship will not disappear all together. Conflicts of interest are imbedded in any buyer-seller relationship, despite the strategic match because each party wants the biggest slice of the cake. Therefore, the probability of conflict arises in any case.

The Skanska-Rockwool case shows the true costs of a sales or purchase exchange in business economic terms and not from an accounting angle. Which is:

$$\textit{Total costs} = \textit{Product price} + \textit{Transaction costs}$$

In hindsight, it appears to be sound business logic for Rockwool to promote a relationship economic, co-operative marketing approach, as the end result happened to be a win-win situation. Although it seemed obvious and in the interest of both parties to mutually drive down the exorbitant friction costs, due to idiosyncratic reactions, buyers and sellers rarely agree to "open the books" with the idea of chasing joint optimisation and deepening the relationship. Instead, management most often prefers to stick to a pure or slightly modified market contract, as this regulating mechanism is considered to offer a maximum safeguard of self-interest, transparency and bargaining position.

As soon as the market contract is replaced by the hybrid relational contract elements of risk and insecurity arise. The relationship contract contains a consciously chosen risk element, where the parties agree on a certain level of manoeuvrability, where confidence plays a key role. Risk is the cost, whereas saved transaction costs is the benefit.

Risk is revealed via *opportunism*, which is the other basic element in any relationship. Opportunism means that a party, buyer or seller, will exploit a situation to gain unilateral benefits at the expense of the counterpart. Opportunism can even move into what can be called legal swindling in a great many bargaining processes.

The opportunity of developing mutual benefit, which is an integral part of our relationship marketing definition does not rest on idealism, but on a concrete business self interest calculation. What are the pros and con's of relationship contracts, balancing the benefits against the risks of counterpart or perhaps one's own opportunism? Additionally, no decision-maker is completely rational or in possession of all the information regarding alternatives and consequences. *Bounded rationality* means that risk cannot be eliminated through contracts and control.

Two kinds of risk are at play in any relationship. *External insecurity* is caused by disturbances outside the relationship. *Opportunism between parties in the relationship or expected opportunism can also cause internal risk.* Opportunism and insecurity as well as idiosyncrasy are cost drivers, as they stimulate protection mechanisms. Ultimately, these protection mechanisms threaten the competitiveness of the relationship. For either party there is also the trade off between cost of risk and cost of insurance through safeguard mechanisms.

The Internet has created interesting innovations aiming at dampening opportunism and insecurity among buyers and sellers. Consumers unite in mega communities bringing reverse buying to life. Consumers bid together for all kinds of goods and service with the purpose of increasing bargaining power, their anonymously and through an infomediary as intermediate. This innovation has led to a fundamental change in the relationship contract between suppliers and private customers. Now, the buyer is an infomediary representing a lot of consumers. Consumers presumably get more favourable prices and a lower perceived risk for two different reasons: First, the infomediary screens the market for alternative suppliers saving time for the individual. Secondly, the consumer will tend to think that the risk of being "cheated" in terms of price is much lower.

3.2.3 Types of Decision Scenarios within Relationships

In a simplified way, the different kinds of decision scenarios with respect to risk and opportunism can be categorised as described in figure 3-3.

		Risk	
		High	**Low**
Opportunism	**High**	Type 1	Type 3
	Low	Type 2	Type 4

Figure 3-3: Risk and opportunism matrix.

Type 1 relationships are characterised by high risk and a high level of opportunism. In type 1 consider situations such as buying real estate or purchasing raw materials from a remote overseas supplier. In both situations the buyer will tend to believe that the exchange risk is significant due to factors like geographical distance, complexity, the very low exchange frequency or just the expected morality of the seller. Both the buyer and the seller will be tempted to exploit the situation to gain unilateral advantages, e.g. provide the counterpart with incorrect information or just not paying the invoice. In cases like this both parties will not work within the framework of fairness. Control is considered to be a more effective tactic than trust.

Type 2 relationships may be found between a supplier and a new distributor. Both parties will tend not to trust the motives of the other party, but the inclination towards opportunism is much less obvious as the intention of both is to build a long-term relationship. For this reason, both the buyer and the seller will pay attention to the interests of the other party.

In certain industries like insurance, IT or telecommunications, suppliers will attempt to create situations where customer relationships can be "milked". The customer has accepted an elimination of market mechanisms and does not control prices or terms. The customer finds it difficult and time consuming to change insurance companies, IT suppliers or Internet service providers.

In *type 3 relationships* it is rather tempting for the supplier to tighten the screw and gradually increase prices, a sign of unilateral dependence.

Relationships characterised by combining low risk and low opportunism are *type 4 relationships* which develop in more extreme situations. One such situation could be when both parties are dedicated to a cooperative style, as is the case with key components, security services, partner-like arrangements etc. At the other extreme, switching costs are low and the relationship has none or only marginal importance, therefore it does not pay to exploit the situation.

The risk and opportunism factors have a considerable economic impact on relationship economics, as they are cost drivers of risk management, extra inventory, information gathering, control and managerial costs, administration etc. On the other hand, opportunism also represents the potential of increasing revenues and saving costs.

The case of Skanska-Rockwool illustrates exactly how the perception of risk, control, rationality and prevention of opportunism combined with conflict solving mechanisms has a tremendous negative influence on profitability of the relationship.

The *dyadic motive* as opposed to the *monadic motive* means that the buyer and the seller make systematic attempts to optimise the relationship by taking the interests of the other party into consideration as well. The basic concept behind the dyadic approach is that a marketer should plan and execute such actions that minimise the customer's total costs, including the savings following managed frictional reductions. As demonstrated, this is not only a pricing issue. The contractual form of the relationship and the governing principles are equally important. Dyadic marketing deals with the overall relationship economic cost-benefit balance within a competitive perspective. The ability to understand the game and the way cards are distributed in that game enables you to define the best possible strategy for yourself.

The triad situation[4] includes the threats and opportunities stemming from the present or the potential relationships between a company's customers and its competitors.[5]

4. See also figure 2-3 in chapter 2.
5. As described in detail in sub-section 2.2.

Risk and opportunism are guidelines for understanding and navigating through the mechanisms that are the basic concepts behind relationship marketing. The key economic expression is the transaction costs arising from the relationship parameters.

3.3 Customisation of Assets, Frictions and the Life Cycle

Customised assets or asset specificity[6] refers to the extent to which an asset represents a lower economic value for a company in alternative employments than for the actual customer(s). Assets, which have been adapted to only one individual customer, have a positive impact on the relationship economy in that specific customer relationship. Customisation must be considered a focal point and a crucial parameter in strategic relationship marketing. Customisation of assets in that respect is in contrast to the idea of complete resource mobility in traditional business economics.

3.3.1 Customisation of Assets versus Complete Resource Mobility

Asset customisation can ultimately bring supplier and customer closer together. Consider the manufacturing company that invests in dozens of manufacturing plants all working as subcontractors for only one customer. This is often the situation in consumer goods, where leading firms like Coca-Cola, McDonalds and Marks & Spencer create a one-to-one sole supplier relationship with subcontractors or partners.

The same level of *symbiotic relationships* can also be found in the relationship between airlines and handling agents and airline caterers or between newspapers and printing houses.

Dedicated, customised resources contribute to rationalise and reduce the cost of the buyer-seller interaction; they create profitability for both sides and impose entry barriers for competitors and substitutes. Imagine what would happen, if McDonalds decided to buy potatoes on the spot market instead of contracting with farmers or preferred to use short-term arrangements with manufacturers processing the potatoes. Any manufacturer that would offer an attractive price to McDonalds for a short-term deal would hardly succeed in breaking into the existing relationships.

6. Williamson (1975).

Asset specificity, "a better product", is a convincing marketing tool, but it also induces high risk and opportunism. Large companies very often have one sole or preferred supplier plus a second source. The idea is that the second source absorbs above peak capacity situations from the prime source, while at the same time safeguarding the customer against supplier opportunism or bankruptcy. If assets like equipment, staff, sites or intellectual property rights are tailor-made to this specific important customer, the supplier is potentially vulnerable if the customer has a nearby alternative solution available.

Some of Coca-Cola's sole regional partners, such as anchor bottling plants, have been granted the exclusive licence rights to bottle and distribute Coca-Cola products. They claim that the whole business to business line gives a negative profit because of the exorbitant price of the concentrate delivered by Coca-Cola Company. The heavy investments in brewery and logistic capacity, however, leave the anchor bottling plants in a somewhat difficult position.

Not all products or services that are perceived as customised within a certain range of features are individualised. Mass customisation does not imply the same level of risk and opportunism as previously described. Restaurants prepare the meal according to the taste of the guest without customising any asset. Car manufactures do the same when the customers choose an individual mix of design, colour and accessories.

Digitalisation adds completely new dimensions to the idea of customisation. The computer on your desk becomes fully individualised in its patterns of response to your movements. Traditional portals and intelligent Customer Relationship Management (CRM) concepts recognise every user and has a strong built in artificial intelligence about every single visitor coming up with proposals and menus in accordance with personal needs and wants.

3.3.2 Cost of Frictions versus the Concept of Smooth Exchanges

The Skanska-Rockwool case illustrates how buying behaviour based on a market contract paradigm can lead to frictions in the physical and in the administrative system and hence also becomes the generator of considerable and unnecessary costs. Frictions are derived from idiosyncratic reactions. The rational buyer assumes that optimal buying behaviour means using the market for each exchange because any special preference for a supplier will be exploited by that supplier. Competitive pressure is what prevents a supplier from excess pricing and term twisting. Therefore, both parties must live with the frictional costs. The costs of idiosyncrasy are expected to be more than offset by lower prices.

In BtB relationships, it has become quite usual to distinguish between the *phase of negotiation* and the *phase of delivery*. During the purchasing phase the market mechanisms are active. Existing relationship contracts are being stalled. Both parties act, and react, idiosyncratically; they distrust the motives, statements and calculations of counterparts. When an agreement has been reached, the parties enter into the phase of implementation. Both the seller and the buyer have an interest in minimising the frictions in processes like order flow, documentation, quality control, exchange of information and corrective actions if requested by the other party. The relationship is an in-between, hybrid, regulating structure and in many respects more complex to manage than the market contract or the hierarchy. Competition forces companies to concentrate on core skills only. This has created a demand for new management qualities, because the patterns of relationships change and become much more important. Whereas the idea of identifying and nursing a company's core competencies has become strategic mantra, the business economic discipline derived from that, i.e. to establish and administer customer and supplier relationships with a minimum of frictional costs, then becomes the key to competitive advantage.

3.3.3 Customer Life Cycle versus the Periodic View

The product life cycle and its underlying diffusion of innovation curve is the ancestor of most conventional marketing strategy models from the BCG[7] matrix to Porterian thinking. The composition of a company's marketing programs, in the form the 4 P's, changes over the product life cycle because of market segments attractiveness and competition.

All products, product categories and industries tend follow the bell formed development curve from birth to death. The same pattern can be observed for customer relationships as well. In that respect, the customer life cycle or CLC becomes the framework for the formulation of marketing program prescriptions and of understanding the business economics of relationships. In contrast to the period as the time interval in program formulation and in impact measurement, the CLC relies on a much more dynamic, cause-effect and customer oriented view of economics and marketing management. One possible representation of the CLC concept is shown in figure 3-4.[8]

7. Boston Consulting Group – BCG.
8. Described as different types in figure 4-1 in chapter 4.

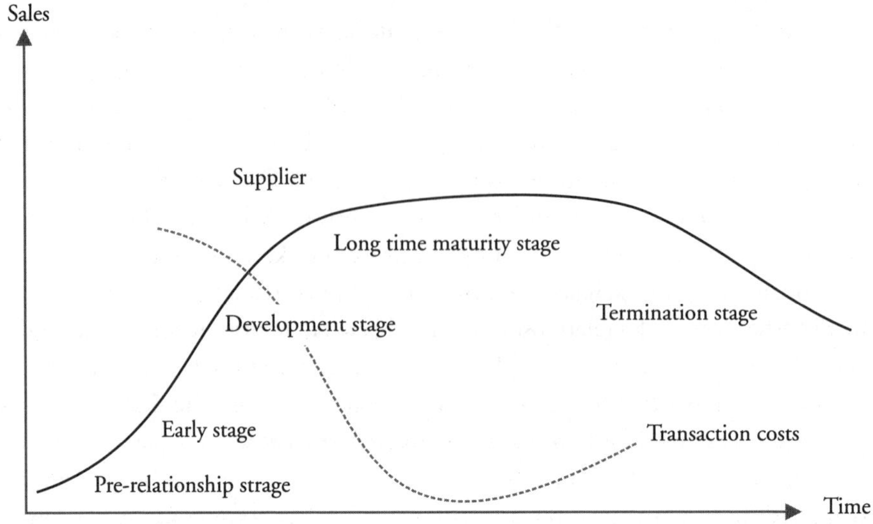

Figure 3-4: The customer life cycle – CLC.

The customer life cycle matrix illustrates four different areas of business economics:

- Acquisition economics in the pre-relationship stage.
- Penetration economics in the early- and the development stage.
- Retention economics in the long-term/maturity stage.
- Termination economics at the end of the customer life cycle.

The business economics and the marketing tasks are quite different in the five distinct generic stages of the customer life cycle. In the pre-relationship stage a company must e.g. invest time and effort to convince the customer to make a trial purchase, change supplier, take in a second source or buy a project.

It is reasonable to believe that the margin of profitability will increase and that transaction costs will decline over the customer life cycle as a function of time, experience and eventually adaptation of assets. Some of the main factors supporting the idea of increasing returns over the customer life cycle can be summarised in a few headlines:

- High transaction costs at the beginning of the life cycle ("bargaining/pre-relationship") where monadic motives still dominate.
- Anticipation of opportunism and high costs of control as the market mechanisms still regulate the trade between seller and buyer. Hence prices are also lower.

- Higher cost of service, administration and mistakes in the earlier stages.
- Add-on revenues in terms of cross-selling, increase in volume, product line extension assumes mutual confidence.

The customer relationship-profitability curve reflects a similar path.

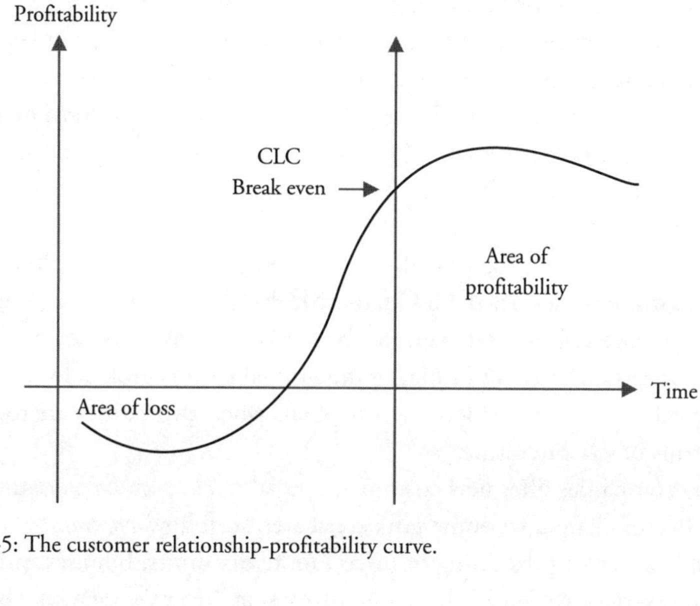

Figure 3-5: The customer relationship-profitability curve.

A company may get stuck if for some reason the customer breaks off the relationship before or just after the CLC break-even point. *Retention economics* in terms of extending of the life cycle and other kinds of add-on revenue streams then become a key factor to understanding and improving overall performance.

Customer life cycle and relationship economic coherence varies across industries. Some experience driven, order-producing industries have extremely high entrance costs to relationships in terms of customised assets. This is the case with shipbuilding, heavy construction and in great many subcontractor industries, e.g. components to aircraft manufacturers etc. In such industries suppliers must practise marketing based on a customer life cycle orientation. Often the CLC break-even point will be passed in a relatively late stage, and profitability depends entirely on the marketing efficiency of the customer, e.g. the numbers of aircraft of a given type being sold over the lifetime of the specific model. The same will be the case in industries with high customer acquisition costs such as in banking, insurance or asset management, where suppliers must invest in order to gain customer trust.

In other industries which are also characterised by made-to-order and asset customisation, there will be no or at least very low expectations of continuity and life cycle. The marketing strategy must therefore be exchange oriented and deliver profitability on the first order and on every order thereafter. In industries such as home construction, travel or some segments of consulting, this will be the case.

The business economics of customer relationships is about understanding and influencing the benefits across stages of the CLC. It is in the pre-relationship stage that the primary marketing objective is to motivate consumers to try the product or service. If a company can minimise the waste of resources on prospects that never turn into customers via creative marketing tactics this will increase profitability.

The transition from the growth to the maturity stage also implies a risk of loosing customers, so-called CLC-fads. Maybe there is a fundamental mismatch in buying-selling strategies; maybe customers have a policy of changing suppliers at certain intervals or maybe the mutual trust is broken by accident or systematically over time, which often happens when two parties are too different in terms of size or culture.

Many companies offer new customers special *start-up advantages:* discounts, services free of charge, welcome gifts etc. Later on follow *relationship enhancement packages:* cross subsidising of prices, more discounts, bonuses, simplification or just service packages. In the maturity stage *retention programs* based on prestige, "member-get-member", core customer advantages etc. flourish (this will be described in detail further ahead).

3.4 Transaction Costs – Bridging Economics and Relationship Marketing

Customised assets, the existence of frictions and the life cycle in the physical system are the drivers of transaction costs in the economic system. Perceptions of risk and opportunism determine how far two parties will go in order to reduce frictions and develop a relationship that is based on interdependence. Relationship marketing develops competitive advantage by reducing transaction costs and creating transaction benefits.

A transaction cost is the amount the buyer and the seller must pay in addition to the cost of the core service in order to participate in the exchange. There are three distinguishable types of transaction costs: Pre-exchange costs in terms of information gathering, negotiation and decision costs and post-exchange or control costs. These are the 3 C's of transaction costs: Contact, Contract and Control costs. How the underlying mechanisms in a physical system are the drivers of transaction costs is summarised in figure 3-6.

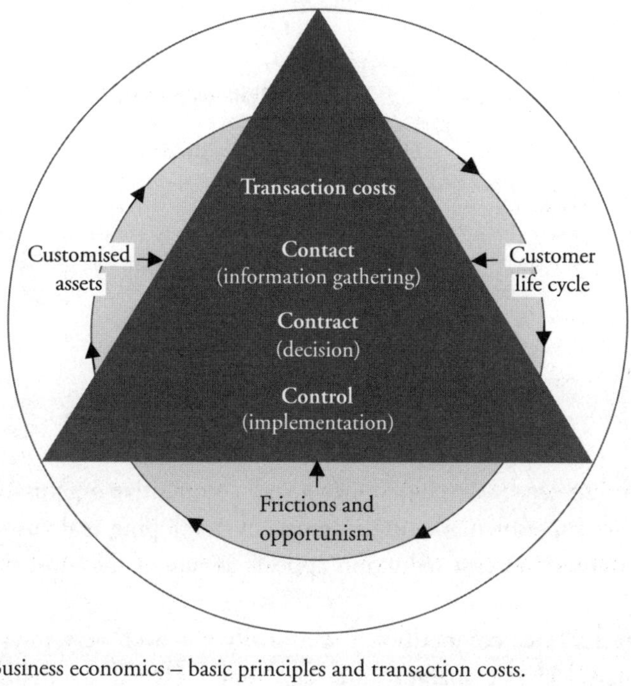

Figure 3-6: Business economics – basic principles and transaction costs.

The total transaction costs of any exchange are the sum of contact, contract and control costs within both the seller and the buyer organisations. This is not the same as saying that these costs and the bargaining power are symmetrically distributed. Usually suppliers will be open to a relationship contract arrangement. One of the main purposes of relationship marketing therefore is to motivate customers to move from market contractual behaviour in the direction of the relationship. But why should a buyer give up the pure market contract in favour of the riskier relationship contract?

First of all, the buyer saves transaction costs as the market mechanisms become excited or modified. Secondly, dyadic oriented supplier behaviour might eventually reduce frictions and be beneficial to both parties. And finally, a buyer who demands customisation of assets must accept some kind of relationship ties.

The trade-offs facing a buyer can be simplistically expressed in the following way as illustrated in figure 3-7.

		Transaction Costs		
		High	**Middle**	**Low**
Production Costs	**High**			Hierarchy
	Middle		Relationship Contract	
	Low	Market Contract		

Figure 3-7: The buyer's transaction cost trade-off.

The relationship can be developed into a very competitive organisational form, but it requires superior marketing in terms of developing real customer benefits, where transaction cost reduction appears as one of the most powerful instruments.

BtB parcel service competition traditionally has been very intense. Service profiles of parcel service operators are very similar. Hence, the market contract used to be the most common terms of trade. Detailed market segmentation studies showed that certain attractive customers would prefer to have one supplier of parcel services, even though transaction costs in parcel transportation are relatively low. These customers however, were concerned that a relationship contract was likely to lead to price increases and a reduced service level. As the profitability in the parcel service industry was extremely low, it would be tempting for a sole supplier who is not being checked by competition to actually increase margins.

In order to be competitive in terms of production costs, a parcel transportation supplier must have a critical mass of business in any geographical area where it is represented. In order to keep its promises to relationship-oriented customers, most of whom demanded full geographical coverage and short delivery time, the supplier had to either have a high global market share, a clear segment focus or relationship oriented agreements with competitors. The relationship method of marketing parcel transportation services turned out to be a difficult but successful path.

3.4.1 The Reach and Richness Trade-Off of Transaction Costs

The breakthrough of the digital information age has had a tremendous impact on the level and structure of transaction costs and has consequently also influenced the relationship economics. Before the Internet a marketer had to carefully pay attention to the two factors: reach and richness. High reach communication means mass communication, i.e. advertising in print media, on television, promotions etc. High reach one-way communication reaches many consumers. It is pushed, sequentially and standardised. High reach means low richness, as there is no interaction or adaptation to the needs and wants of the consumer.

High richness communication on the other hand, offers interactivity, time, accessibility and adaptation. A typical example is personal sales. The contact costs per customer are high, but so is the communication richness.

Before the Internet, a marketer would have to plan a marketing mix that took into consideration which contact cost structure would give the highest return. Maintaining richness in customer contact required sacrifices on the reach side due to financial constraints. The Internet has effectively eliminated the line between reach and richness as illustrated in figure 3-8.

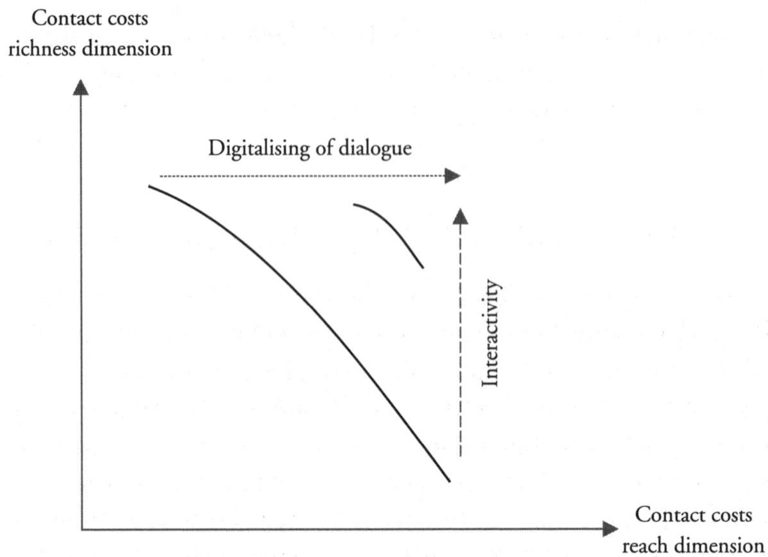

Figure 3-8: The contact cost dilemma.

The new digital market economy has decreased or eliminated many of the former transaction cost barriers. Today, a company has every opportunity of having a rich, close interaction with existing customers, prospective customers and suppliers regardless of geography. The technological opportunity has caused a dramatic reduction in contact costs. This reduction is clearly in favour of the pure market contract, but at the same time it allows a company to reach more prospects and to establish a two-way communication with end users.

If we assume the following about communication and implicitly also then about the contact costs:

1. Information is by nature neither precise nor secure
2. Information gathering is costly
3. Communication is a dynamic development process over time

Under these assumptions the cyclical process of communication between supplier and customer will tend to create a mutual understanding that did not exist before. This means that transparency and just-a-click-away capabilities on the one hand, bring new freedom to customers, as transaction costs were a barrier to exit for customers. And on the other hand, the sharing of information between A and B is a step towards establishing a relationship. Rogers and Kincaid stated this back in 1981:

Communication is a process in which participants create and share information with one another in order to reach mutual understanding. This cyclical process involves giving meaning to information that is exchanged between two or more individuals as the move toward *convergence.*

3.5 The Business Economics of Customer Relationships and Competitive Advantage

One way of reaching a position of competitive advantage is to develop a relationship economic competence that is superior to the competitors. In this case, the following questions are crucial to marketing management superiority: When and how will a customer enter into a market modification contract? What does it take to maintain and develop the relationship? How should the dyad be administered?

The overall framework that links business economics of customer relationships together with marketing strategy is presented in figure 3-9.

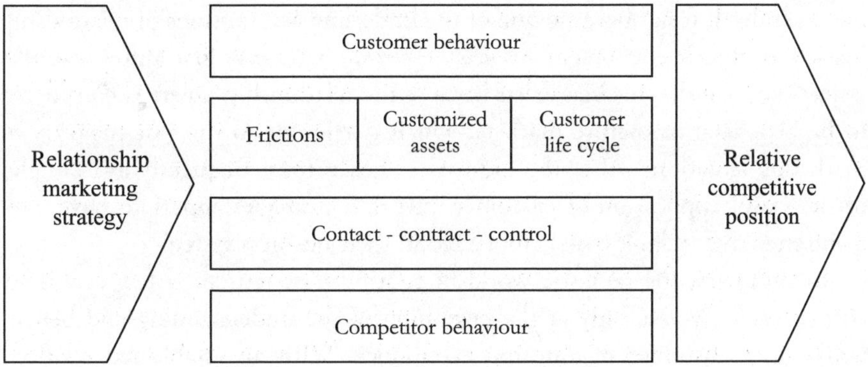

Figure 3-9: Framework for Analysing Relationship Economic Link to Strategic Marketing.

Via relationship marketing strategies and programmes, the purpose is to reach a strong, profitable competitive position. Improving the relative position of the specific dyad means creating perceived relationship economic advantages or eventually relationship quality advantages that can not be imitated by competitors. Investing in customised assets, reducing the frictions and understanding the critical paths of the CLC become the key ingredients in the strategic marketing mix.

Strategy is created and executed under the influence of competition. The triadic motive must of course be included in the strategic considerations.

Sustainable competitive advantages appear via a unique relationship economic value or low transaction costs. *Value focus* and *cost focus* represent two very different and simple ways to market success.

When Microsoft introduced DOS operating systems several decades ago in close co-operation with IBM, the company decided to almost give the product away. Subsequently, DOS was viewed as an integrated part of a certain piece of PC hardware. At that time, there was a fierce competition on the market for standards and platforms to serve the booming market of personal computers. Microsoft later replaced DOS with Windows. In the beginning, when the frictions were high, Microsoft created its strong position not only by minimising the price of its core service but also by reducing transaction costs by integrating DOS into IBM computers. In the later stages of the customer life cycle Microsoft changed its focus to a relational value proposition.

Although relationship marketing has a dual focus on both acquisition and retention strategies, the element of retention value is often given more prominence. Indeed, it has become one of the underling assumptions of relationship marketing that it encourages *retention economic rationales* first and *acquisition marketing* second. This bias exists because the relationship aspect is considered to be beneficial in mature markets, which is relevant to the vast majority of marketing situations. Also, the industries chosen most frequently as examples of successful application of customer retention strategies appear to have high front-end costs (selling costs) embedded in their business system.

In summary, the fantastic world of relationships rests on a few economic cornerstones. We are only at the beginning of the understanding and benchmarking of customer relationship economics. With an established relationship-marketing framework there is a greater opportunity to formulate effective marketing programmes.

References

Arnerup, B. & Edvardson, B. (1992) *Marknadsföring av tjänste*, Studenterlitteratur.

Coase, R. (1937) *The Nature of the Firm*, Economica.

Council on Financial Competition (1995) *Perfecting Customer Retention and Recovery – Overview of Economics and Proven Strategies*, Advisory Board.

Dietrich, M. (1994) *Transaction Cost Economics and Beyond*, Routledge.

Groenewegen, J. (ed) (1996) *GRASP: Conference Report Transaction Cost and Beyond.*

Groenewegen, J. (ed.) (1996) *Transaction Cost Economics and Beyond*, Kluwer Academic Publishers.

Grönroos, C. (1990) *Relationship approach to the marketing function in service contexts: the marketing and organization behaviour interface*, Journal of Business Research.

Hedaa, L. (1993) *Distrust, Uncertainties and Disconfirmed Expectations in Supplier-Customer Relationships*, International Business Review.

Heikkila, J. (1996) Skanska & Rockwool: *Making the supply chain partnership work*, Case IMD.

Lippert-Rasmussen, M. & Mols, N. P. (1993) *Transaktionsomkostningsteori – en introduktion til Williamson*, Institute of Management University of Aarhus.

Menard, C. (ed.) (1997) *Transaction Cost Economics – Recent Developments*, Elgar.

Monthoux de Guillet, P. B.L. (1975) *Organizational Mating and Industrial Marketing Conservatism – some Reasons why Industrial Marketing Managers resist Marketing Global Theory*, Industrial Marketing Management.

Penrose, E. (1959) *The Theory of The Growth of the Firm*, Basil Blackwell.

Peter, J.P and Olson, J.C. (1990) *Consumer Behaviour and Marketing Strategy*, Irwin.

Porter, M. E. (1982) *Competitive Strategy: Techniques for Analyzing Industries and Competitors*, Free Press.

Porter, M. E. (1985) *Competitive Advantage: Creating and Sustaining Superior Performance*, Free Press.

Porter, M. E. (1990) *The Competitive Advantage of Nations*, Macmillia Press.

Prahalad, C.K. and Hamel, G. (1990) *The Core Competence of the Corporation*, Harvard Business Review.

Prahalad, C.K. and Hamel, G. (1994) *Competing for the Future*, Harvard Business School Press.

Reichheld, F. (1993) *Loyalty-Based Management.* Harvard Business Review.

Reichheld, F. (1996) *The Quest for Loyalty – Creating Value through Partnership*, Harvard.

Reilly, M. and Parkinson, T. (1985) *Individual and Product Correlates of Evoked Set Size*, Advances in Consumer Research.

Rogers, E. M. and Kincaid, D. L. (1981) *Communication Networks – towards a new paradigm for Research*, The Free Press.

Turnbull, P.W and Valla, J.P. (1986) *Strategies for International Industrial Marketing: the Management of Customer Relationships in European Industrial Markets.* Crom Helm.

Turnbull, P.W. and Valla, J.P. (1992) *Strategies for International Industrial Marketing.* Croom Helm.

Williamson, O.E. (1975) *Markets and Hierarchies, Analysis and Antitrust Implications*, Free Press.

Williamson, O. E. (1985) *The Economic Institutions of Capitalism – Firms, Markets, Relational Contracting.* Free Press.

CHAPTER 4

Customer Loyalty and the Effect on Business Economics

It has always been the conventional wisdom that customer loyalty is a key success factor in the development of superior market performance. What is remarkable is that the research in strategy and marketing only recently has recognised the huge impact customer loyalty in fact has on long-term profitability. Traditional marketing paradigms more or less consider the relationship aspect to be an adjunct to the core marketing theories rather than an integrated element of central importance.

In this chapter the following questions will be posed: What is customer loyalty? How does loyalty influence the overall business economics of customer relationships and hence the bottom-line of the company? And how can a company incorporate customer loyalty into the marketing process? Detecting the accelerating and impeding mechanisms that drive loyalty needs to be added to the list of marketing skills in order to work out viable relationship marketing strategies.

Also, new typologies for relationship segments will be introduced and the causes and effects of customer loyalty within the framework of relationship economics will be discussed.

4.1 Defining and Describing Customer Loyalty

The quest for loyalty has always been a basic rule in organisational life. In a hierarchical power structure, members of an organisation accept the necessity of obeying leadership figures. In ancient times, participants even swore their loyalty as an entry ceremony. In modern organisations however, loyalty is implicitly assumed and the reward-punishment system has loyalty as a central decisive factor. In hierarchies market forces are eliminated. As long as you are a member of this organisational hierarchy you must stick to our rules.

Customers do not react as organisational members. Loyalty is something a company strives to attain, not something that can just be asked for. It must be earned.

Customer loyalty conceptually implies both an *attitude ("think") dimension* and a *behavioural ("do") dimension,* neither one acts exclusively of the other. A few of the many well-known definitions of loyalty highlights this assertion:

> Customer loyalty is the seller's perception of the consumer's positive attitude to the product manifested by rebuying.[1]

The loyalty creating company is

> A company where the entire organisation carries out conscious, ongoing and effective efforts with the purpose of securing an optimal development of satisfied, loyal and hence profitable customers.[2]

A buyer making a straight rebuy with no information gathering at all about alternatives experiences very low transaction costs compared with the buyer who uses the pure market contract to plan, decide and execute the exchange. This is also the case for the supplier side. Loyal customers means minimal transaction costs in terms of sales and marketing expenses compared with a situation where only a small fraction of customers repurchase.

We will work with the distinction between instrumental and motivational loyalty. *Instrumental loyalty is the kind of loyalty more often found in BtB relationships. It is related to the objective, functional dimensions of the product or service vis a vis a usage situation. Motivational loyalty* is the predisposition coming out of a more affective pattern of reaction typically expected in consumer markets. The rationale/cognitive and the affect driven reasons for loyalty do not act exclusive each other and are often mixed.[3]

There are many ways of classifying loyal and non-loyal customer behaviour. One such example proposes three ways of considering customer repurchase behaviour:

- *Switching behaviour*: where purchasing is seen as an either/or decision – either the customer stays with you (loyalty) or turns against you (switching).
- *Promiscuous behaviour*: Also an either/or situation in the sense that either the customer is loyal to you or flirts with many and various alternatives (promiscuous).
- *Polygamous behaviour*: Again, the customer makes a stream of purchases,

1. Kunøe (1994).
2. Svanholmer (1996).
3. See also sub-section 2.2.1 on different exchange types.

but her loyalty is divided among a number of products. She may be more or less loyal to your brand or solution than any other.

Consumer research tends to support the view that most customers[4] (consumer market) are multibrand buyers and that only one out of ten is 100% loyal. Consumers are therefore searching for products and services matching their specific needs. There is also some doubt as to whether loyal customers are more profitable than promiscuous and polygamous buyers are. Loyalists are often more light users, whereas multibrand buyers are more heavy users within a specific product category.

4.1.1 Customer Life Cycle as Reflection of Various Loyalty Patterns

The shape of the customer life cycle is a clear indication of the level and sources of customer loyalty. There are several variations as illustrated in figure 4-1.

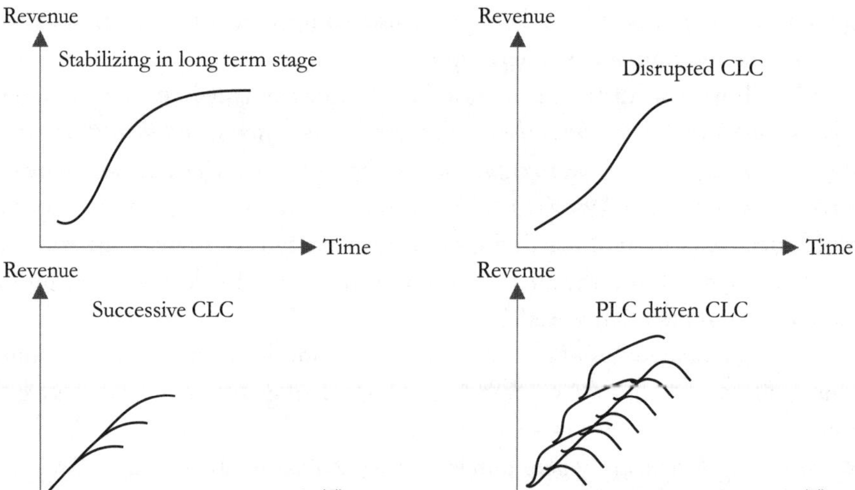

Figure 4-1: Different customer life cycles.

Customer relationships that *stabilise in the long-term stage* will typically be dyadic in their structure and mutually beneficial for both parties, assuming that customers have nearby alternatives. The dyadic balance will come from

4. Barnard and Ehrenberg (1997).

customised assets, co-operative relationship style, close proximity of the parties, security, mutual commitment and probably also strong contractual agreements.

Almost all relationships are exposed to opposing pressures: Partly in direction of deepening involvement, adaptation and repurchase and partly in the direction of increased control and dissolution to neutralise dependency and dampen idiosyncrasy.

In this battlefield of contrasting forces, astonishingly many relationships do manage to stabilise. Just as many consumer brands have been able to defend leading positions throughout generations such as: Kodak, Gillette, Colgate, Coca-Cola, Del Monte, etc.[5]

Some relationships are *cut off suddenly and abruptly* illustrated by the disrupted CLC. In strongly knowledge-based industries there is a high risk of relationship brake up if a supplier begins cooperating with the customer's competitors, the reverse triadic situation. In trade arrangements where the supplier invests in highly specialised customisation of assets, he will idiosyncratically tend to cut off the customer relationship in the early stages (before investing) if it turns out that the customer is taking unilateral advantage of the situation.

In relationships with *several successive mini CLCs* the parties ride on the wave of good experiences. This will often be the case in project-oriented industries, where each project is a CLC in itself. The customer either tends to have preferences for the supplier in the next bid round or she will bring new competencies into the relationship.

Customer loyalty should not only be viewed as a relationship economic phenomenon. In some instances the CLC is driven by frequent product innovations or renewals. We then talk about *Product Life Cycle (PLC) driven CLCs.* In the software industry, new product generations appear regularly. The same is the case in the automotive industry. Whether driven by technology, fashion or other factors the competitiveness of the core product or service is always a precondition for loyalty.

In some industries it is necessary to distinguish between *lost-for-good-customers* and *always-a-share-customers,* each reflecting very different CLCs. In the retail sector consumers make use of most of the supermarket chains within their geographical area depending on the buying motivation, special offers or products etc. It is interesting also to observe that the supermarket chains do not attempt to invest in customer loyalty through a more focused or differentiated chain profile. This is a typical always-a-share market.

---

5. Aaker (1991).

Lost-for-good customers are most often found in relationships with a high level of loyalty that is driven by confidence. If your doctor prescribes the wrong medicine or less dramatically, if your supplier of R&D consulting services becomes engaged with a major competitor, the relationship will often close down forever.

The digital network economy does not only affect transaction costs, it also changes the balance of power between customer and supplier. The key to this is information mastering leading to the invitation economic rationale mentioned earlier. Before the Internet, suppliers typically had much more power to manage the flow of information. In this *push economy* a supplier can more easily control the exposure of information to well defined target groups, using separate media forms, at any given time. You could force your message through a mix of channels in order to get consumers' attention by using TV spots, print ads, promotions or sales rep visits. You could also control the content of information. The consumer can just turn it off therefore participation is voluntary.

In the *pull economy* the consumer is much more in control. The customer decides the type, level, length and content of exposure and clicks away. Pay per view, micro payment and interactive TV represent steps in this direction. E-books, where the reader defines his or her individual book based on needs and wants is another example. An example of interactive TV is sporting events where the individual decides among a large number of camera angles and highlights. Consumers create their own TV program and interface. Virtual and individual reality is taking over.

Somebody once said: "If we compare the development of the invitation economy with a trip from London around the globe, we have not reached Birmingham yet"! So it is impossible to forecast the future importance of customer relationships. In this fierce global economy, the central point has moved from inter-company rivalry to a competition between clusters of companies that operate within total value chains. The CLC economy still has so much untapped potential that the future will belong to relationship thinking.

4.2 The Value of Customer Loyalty

Customer loyalty as a concept creates a strange paradox. Almost anyone will agree that true customer loyalty is a substantial intangible asset for a company, for branded products the most valuable asset of all, because it is the ultimate indicator of future sales and profits. Despite that, there are virtually no companies that have any factual based knowledge about their customer's loyalty and the value of such loyalty (loyalty is not the same as customer satisfaction, as shall be discussed later). Why? Could it be that we are lacking clear value definitions and reliable measurement techniques?

It is necessary to separate the value of customer loyalty into a number of value categories that can be analysed collectively and separately as well as be applied to the marketing mix. We have developed the following typology regarding loyalty economy:

- Lifetime economy – the ability of retaining the customer for a longer period of time.
- Efficiency economy – the ability to create dyadic cost advantages to the benefit of both parties throughout the CLC.
- Value adding economy – customer participation in the supplier's value generation.

In many cases all the effects are active at the same time but they do not necessarily pull in the same direction, and it requires careful analysis to separate each of the loyalty value drivers.

4.2.1 Lifetime Economy and Customer Retention

A loyal Cadillac customer is worth $ 332,000 over his or her lifetime.[6]

In a great many industries profitability is heavily dependant on the lifespan of customer relationships, as already discussed in the previous section 4.1.1. This is the case when contact or contract costs are high compared with the rate of contribution per exchange or if investments in customised assets are substantial or if the experience effects are extraordinary. In such cases the relationship contribution is negative until rather late in the CLC. Therefore the total unit costs decrease as a function of the cumulative sales to the customer.

On markets where lifetime economy is a critical factor, marketing must concentrate on giving the customer continuous motivations and arguments to keep coming back to do business. This will typically consist of positive inducements that confirm the value of the relationship for the customer stimulating repeat business e.g. annual bonuses or progressive discounts. A subtle way is to establish exit barriers is through fees or non-refundable prepayments, administrative simplifications or integration.

6. Gummeson (1996).

The value of lifetime economics consists of three distinctly different elements:

> *Basic profits over a longer time span* obviously increase the net present value of the customer relationship. In industries like IT, support and service contracts are common and in markets where revenues depend on subscription, licenses, spare part sales etc. increasing lifetime is an essential marketing task.
>
> *Add on sales based on confidence.* In the maturity stage of the relationship the customer often tends to trust the supplier and will be positively inclined to cross-selling initiatives. When commercial banks begin selling insurance or when Amazon.com extends the product line from books to all sorts of consumer goods, it is clearly a way of capitalising on customer trust.
>
> *Price premium.* Loyal customers to a certain extent have neutralised the market forces to harvest on the advantages of low transaction costs. Loyal customers trusting the supplier will hence not pay attention to price increases; they become price inelastic. Loyal customers become the cash cow.

Loyalty schemes have become widespread and popular as retainer tools. What some loyalty pioneers such as American Airlines and Tesco have experienced is that loyalty programs were effective and gave additional business in the short-term. But the incentives rapidly became sector norms that customers would expect. All to quickly early benefits were turned into unavoidable costs of doing business. Furthermore, once loyalty schemes become an expected award, it can be costly and damaging to rattle the loyalty ladder. The question is whether customer bribery of this kind in fact leads to a consolidation of loyalty or the opposite in terms of promiscuity.

4.2.2 Efficiency Economy – The Positive Dyadic Effect

Suppliers gain insight into their customers' reaction patterns and thereby define the do's and the don'ts for each specific marketing case. This marketing knowledge can be useful and can lead to efficient economic profitability. Often the customer contributes actively to produce efficiency driven profitability. This can be in terms of communicating needs and wants like volume forecasts, service level indications, engaging in smoothing the administrative procedures such as automatic reordering or EDI, correction of errors etc.

Reducing the supplier's quality costs like waste, redoing, more precise points of delivery, insight into habits, routines and service requirements are valuable contributions to improved relationship economy.

Chasing efficiency advantages is an ongoing process that takes place over time. Both parties will struggle to attain as great a proportion of the efficiency benefits as possible.

The commercial banking sector's introduction of private customer net-banking solutions in 1998-2000 is an interesting case. Many of the banks decided to charge their customers for using their net-banking facilities. In fact, the banks requested to get a share of their customers' efficiency advantages. In opposition to this policy, the customers could argue that the bank would profit on net-banking because of the electronic self service, which will lead to substantially lower transaction costs for the bank compared with traditional banking in terms of personal service. The customers' view was that the bank should credit the customer through lower interests rates or bonuses.

4.2.3 Value Adding Economy – Value for the Customer's Money

Sometimes customers participate in, or even take responsibility for, a portion of the relationship value generation. By doing so, the supplier obtains a price premium, larger volume, lower costs, less friction and risk as well as reduced transaction costs.

A company like Cisco has network aggregation as one of its core competencies. Cisco utilises relationship contracts as a strategic tool. Cisco, while sitting in the customer's seat, presents ideas and opportunities to preferred suppliers and contributes innovatively and directly to build values for suppliers and hence for the overall value chain placing Cisco in the centre of a vast web relationship contracts. Adding value to Cisco's suppliers is exactly what Cisco's own customers find extremely attractive.

For some companies it is an integrated element of a relationship marketing strategy that the customer contributes to the value creating processes. In consumer markets, active customer involvement can be one of the primary keys to fulfilment of needs, as is the case with do-it-yourself-products, where the feeling of creating something is part of the overall experience and is an effective motivation. Electronic 3D interior design, where the consumer can simulate alternative use of space, furnishing plans and test various decorations in the virtual landscape, offers the same type of value adding economic benefits.

At the other extreme, there are situations or scenarios where loyalty based behaviour leads to substantial disadvantages for either the customer or the supplier. The contrast in which loyalty is disadvantageous are illustrated in figure 4-2.

Disadvantages for the customer	Disadvantages for the supplier
When it is not likely that the buyer will again purchase from the supplier.	When there is no reason why a seller should ever see a buyer again.
When there is an obvious risk of dependency, and where competitive alternatives exist.	When the seller seeks to avoid dependency of a buyer, and where alternatives exist.
When the buying process is governed by non-relationship oriented processes.	When the selling process is governed by non-relationship oriented processes.
When the purchase is low risk and reversible.	When industry ethics makes relationship building inappropriate.

Figure 4-2: Non loyalty oriented scenarios. Source: Based on Egan (2001).

4.3 Loyalty in a Market Segmentation Perspective

Loyalty is not a question of either-or, black or white. There are grey areas and complicated, minute differences. Loyalty reflects the different degrees of belonging, preferences and decision criteria among customers and target groups. As customer loyalty is a key success factor and therefore a catalyst for competitive superiority, the loyalty factor should be considered the most relevant market segmentation criteria.

Some basic notions that stress the overall relevance of loyalty as segmentation variable are:

1. When first identified, loyalty segments can be analysed and compared with respect to their attraction: Size in $, volume or numbers, growth rates, accessibility etc.
2. The company's relative competitive strengths and weaknesses can be analysed vis-à-vis each segment identified.

3. Marketing targets concerning positioning can be formulated.
4. Marketing programmes geared towards specific loyalty segments can be formulated aiming at specific goals such as attracting, retaining and growing through means affecting lifetime efficiency value economics.

Segmentation based on loyalty levels has led some companies to separate customers in the following four groups: hard-core loyalists, soft-core loyalists, shifting loyalists and switchers.[7] An almost identical segmentation model came up with these six loyalty segments: ambassador, core customer, customer, trial customer, prospect and suspect.[8]

A third approach takes into account the degree of loyalty and more affective motivational elements. It categorises customers in loyalists/apostles versus defectors/terrorists, mercenaries and hostages.[9] Some industries have succeeded in formulating very beneficial loyalty segmentation definitions. The fine-tuned, graduated loyalty program practices of airline companies seem rather sophisticated. Typically they run at least three "mileage card levels", bonus, silver and gold. Each category gives the customer access to various, alternative peripheral services and prestige levels like quick check-in, gate services, VIP lounges, baggage handling, etc.

4.3.1 The Loyalty Pyramid as Segmentation Variable

The loyalty pyramid[10] is a simple yet convincing behavioural model illustrating loyalty segmentation. (see figure 4-3)

7. Kotler (1992).
8. Svanholmer (1996).
9. Reichheld (1993; 1996).
10. Alternative approaches to this is presented in chapter 6, sub section 6.1 The Relationship Ladder.

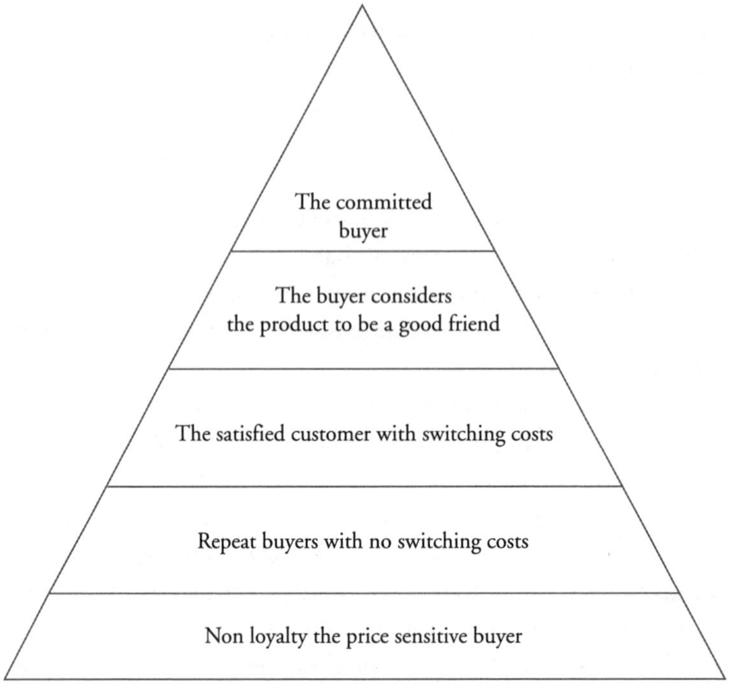

Figure 4-3: Market segmentation based on the loyalty pyramid. Source: Aaker (1991)

The relationship economy is strongest at the higher levels of the pyramid, because market mechanisms are modified and eliminated at the top. Hence, one of the purposes of relationship marketing is to move customers up the loyalty pyramid. So simple, and yet so difficult. Any product market and any existing customer portfolio will consist of different loyalty segments or groups, however not necessarily at all the levels of the pyramid. Take motorbikes or cars, where the perceived position and key benefits for the customer ranges from transportation, fashion or prestige. The same brand, Harley Davidson, attracts customers at the upper end of the loyalty scale, but covers several of the other high involvement segments as well.

In BtB markets loyalty is supposed to be less effective and more instrumental. Still, the loyalty pyramid can be observed in markets like accounting, consulting, IT, office supplies or company cars. Such industrial markets are composed of very different, vertical loyalty segments, and any supplier must cope with the different segments in their marketing operations. When the dot.com wave was at its hottest in 1998-2000, high-prestige firms such as McKinsey & Company and Accenture introduced incubation centres, joint ventures with e-business start ups, quite a different loyalty segment than the blue chip corporate segment.

Paradoxically, it can in some situations be a disadvantage to have extremely loyal customers. The famous Royal Copenhagen porcelain manufacturer used to have many, extremely loyal and committed customers. The problem was that these loyalists did not require any renewals in design, functionality, colour etc. On the contrary, innovations and product development were considered a threat against the prestige image of Royal Copenhagen and hence the main argument for the customers to buy, to own and to decorate with Royal began to disintegrate. Royal Copenhagen became stuck with their existing, loyal customer base. During the years, the loyal customers grew older, and practically no women in the domestic market aged below 55 would appreciate Royal Copenhagen porcelain as a gift. Royal Copenhagen porcelain was perceived to be clumsy and old fashioned. Great brands like Laura Ashley and Marks & Spencer are also potential victims of this.

Another loyalty paradox is attached to *diffusion of innovation*. Penetration of any innovation goes through innovators, early adopters, early majority, late majority and finally the laggers. An innovation will not completely disappear, but will fade away unless this pattern of adoption and loyalty is obtained.

Some years ago Great Greenland relaunched seal furs as a fashion-designed, trendy product. Sale of the Greenland seal furs stopped completely 20 years earlier following the French actress Brigitte Bardot's media campaign against the killing of baby seals in Canada, which in fact had nothing to do with the Greenland hunting of seals. The re-launch was an immediate market success for Great Greenland. It turned out however, that the dominating customer group was women with an unfulfilled dream from their youth to own and to wear a seal fur. The seal fur loyalists did not possess the attributes as innovators, and they were not a point of reference for any early adopter on the prestige fashion fur market. Great Greenland had to more or less withdraw from the prestige fur market and reinvent the seal fur through redesign and a changed distribution strategy.

4.3.2 Taking a Closer Look at Loyalty Segments

Committed buyers – hard-core loyalists have low transaction costs (except in some situations high control costs) due to:

- **A monopoly-like situation** – such as oilrig fire fighting, specialised military equipment or pharmaceuticals.

- **Extensive customisation of assets** – the customer's and/or the supplier's. A golf club renting the golf course land will very much act as a committed buyer.
- **Unique brand equity.** Supporters of high profile sports clubs, certain life style products, purchase of mission specific industrial components and management of financial assets will tend to act as extreme loyalists.

For customers in the *product to be a good friend* category, entry and exit barriers to relationships still are high, but not unmanageable. Some of the motives for customers to become soft-core loyalists are:

- Confidence, trust and positive experiences, e.g. suppliers of security solutions.
- High integration in the sense that the supplier's product or service has been designed into the customer's value chain.
- Perceived high quality, which certain automobile brands magazines or service providers can offer.

The *satisfied customers with switching costs* have no reason to switch brands or supplier, although they are neither by motivation nor by instrumentality tied to the supplier or the product. Despite this apparent indifference they are loyal, repeat buyers. If the buyer perceives all competing products in the category to be almost identical, there is no reason to switch. If the buying process is reversible, low risk, low involvement, and present repeat buying routines saves the customer transaction costs.

The repeat buyer without switching costs and the *price sensitive non-loyal buyer* show rational behaviour, if the price is the only relevant choice criteria, because products are perceived to be homogenous and the pure market contract is the usual contractual arrangement. In certain niches within the capital market and in the trading of agricultural products or electricity, where exchanges are organised and handled by intermediaries, customer loyalty is not an issue.

In some bizarre situations we find relationship economic disadvantages; reward mechanisms are structured with the purpose of indirectly punishing the loyal customer. Frequent flyer programmes are structured in a way so that mileage or bonus points are granted to the cardholder, usually the business traveller personally. But it is the employer who gets the invoice from the airline. So, companies are being charged a price above the true market price. The firms are involuntarily and without much influence forced to grant their staff an indirect salary increase or a fringe benefit! In this case the customer, i.e. the company, would be better off as absolute anti-loyalist.

Loyalty segmentation in the pyramidal sense can be a pretty difficult exercise. Certain approximating techniques like measuring share of mind (attention value); share of vote (attitudinal value), customer satisfaction surveys and perceptual maps can give an indication with regard to loyalty but it is otherwise very difficult to gauge.

4.3.3 Ties as Segmentation Criteria

A somewhat different loyalty segmentation technique is to look at the kinds and levels of ties or bonds between seller and buyer.

Monetary ties imply that the customer becomes financially tied to the supplier. Monetary ties can come out of transaction costs advantages – discounts, bonuses, provisions etc – or from the price of core products. As an element in tactical marketing programmes it is quite common to create exit barriers for customers. Insight into the consumption patterns and ordering routines can be incorporated into procedures and makes the repurchase easy for the customer. Such ties represent a certain level of relational economic protection.

The question is to what extent e-trade affects the opportunity of developing and maintaining monetary ties. Last-minute auctions over flight tickets to phantom prices will inevitably threaten the monetary ties business travellers have entered with airlines. What counts the most? Exchange economic efficiency or relationship discount packages?

The effectiveness of monetary ties is a balance. If the supplier shares the relationship economic profits with the customer, monetary ties can be a viable marketing tool. If the supplier exposes the loyalty segment to too much opportunism, the strategy becomes risky. Companies paying above normal prices for travel, just because national airlines have "bought" the loyalty of the employees, will surely break these hostage-like relationships at the first possible occasion.

Social ties: Research has shown that the relationship between two parties tends to continue more or less unchanged despite managerial decisions regarding new policy directions. The informal human networks between the buying and the sales centre have created social organisational ties. This is illustrated in figure 4-4.[11]

---

11. See also different combinations of relationships in figure 7-6 in chapter 7.

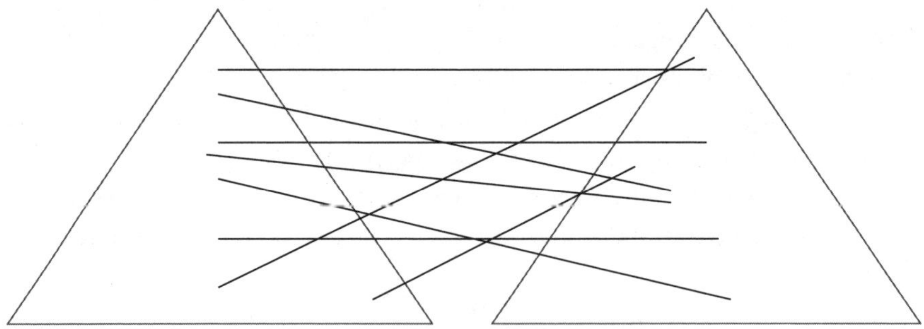

Figure 4-4: The social network. Source: Inspired by Hedaa (1991)

Such networks and informal social relationships are not intentional, as they can lead to dependency. Social networks most often facilitate exchanges and contribute to the generation of positive relationship economic effects, e.g. conflict-solving mechanisms, trust building, risk monitoring and control.

Social ties are not necessarily only two-way. The strategy in financial institutions is to develop social bonds, i.e. a customer's tie to the bank or insurance company. Annual financial reviews, advisor concepts, personal account management, making people feel they are a well-known face all lead to a feeling of goodwill. In many respects these loyalty features are favourable for the customer. Research done in a great many countries[12] document that the social tie loyalty between private households and their bank is correlated with high charges and margins. Most private households could save considerable amounts of money by switching banks. But only a very small fraction of customers actually consider switching.

Segmentation in the financial sector often has social ties as a key ingredient. The distinction between the autonomous, the transactional and the social segment represent one such model. Another almost identical typology is the service benefit segmentation dividing private banking customers into front-runners, loan seekers, value seekers and one-stop bankers.

Infomediators in private banking and insurance have experienced some success. The business idea of the (financial) infomediator is to act as a shell and filter between the "weak and loyal" individual against the "strong and non-loyal" suppliers of financial services. The infomediator:

12. Forbrugerstyrelsen in DK (2001).

1. Finds the best prices and terms on the market.
2. Minimises the transaction costs
3. Hides the identity of the individual customer in bid rounds and negotiations.
4. Protects the customer against the disadvantages of loyalty in the shape of unilateral dependency.

Institutional ties means that two business systems or hierarchies engage in a marriage-like relationship. Institutional ties cause very strong loyalty. Facility management, where a company outsources completely functional areas in their supply chain or franchising, where franchisee and franchiser agree on a symbiotic kind of relationship demonstrates the strengths of institutional ties.

The institutional bonds are in some cases not just the means, but also the purpose of the relationship, as it is the precondition for creating relationship economic advantages. As a business system, the franchising idea is explicitly built on the concept that the value chain is split up into two independent roles with separate hierarchies, linked together by a comprehensive relationship contract, stipulating concept, roles and responsibilities, key success factors, decision making process and financial guidelines.

When owners of concepts and business ideas prefer franchising instead of forward vertical integration, i.e. multiples or chain stores, it appears as if such a firm sacrifices profits and control in order to get less financial exposure. The popularity of franchising as a business system demonstrates, however, that the mutual instrumental loyalty created by institutional ties, can in fact be a very powerful unification model. Not only because franchise system allows a healthy, strong motivation towards opportunism combined with effective control but also due to the irreversibilility of the arrangement.

4.4 The Loyalty Matrix as an Approach to Segmentation

The loyalty matrix categorises the market into segments based on a buyer behavioural dimension and a buyer relationship dimension. Please refer to figure 4-5.

The loyalty matrix reflects the classical attractiveness position trade-off, where the customer – non-customer distinction reveals the position dimension, whereas the different behavioural patterns reflect true attractiveness. Buyers tend to feel that loyalists are the most attractive customers, ceteris paribus, as opposed to the switchers who are always chasing marginal advantages.

The marketer will choose the strategic priorities among the different segments in the loyalty matrix depending on the situation. However, there is no perfect solution. In figure 4-5 there is a set of hypothetical market strategic priorities for a given company. The protection of one's own loyal customers in this case has been given the highest priority, as opposed to targeting competitors' most loyal customer base.

The marketing logic behind any set of priorities can be challenged. Some companies do not in fact pay much attention to their own loyal customers, as this business is not under attack from outside. Marketing resources are instead invested in retention programs, often vis-à-vis fence sitters in order to increase the level of loyalty or in the acquisition of fence sitting customers from competitors.

	Switchers	**Fence sitters**	**Loyal**
Customers	Medium	High	Highest
Noncustomers	Low/medium	High	Low

Figure 4-5: The loyalty matrix – and it's priorities.
Source: Inspired by Pompa, Berry, Reid and Webber (1995).

4.5 A Typology for Industrial Markets

In industrial markets loyalty is assumed to stem from rational considerations and motives, the subjective and calculated balance between transaction costs on the one side and dependencies on the other. In general, low transaction costs go hand in hand with high dependence. In other words, neutralising the impact of market mechanisms may increase the risk of counterpart opportunism. In that respect loyalty can be viewed as a function of the level of dependence a customer is willing to accept in order to obtain transaction cost reductions.

By combining the two dimensions in terms of the *interaction level dependence* and the *product dependence* four archetypes of industrial markets can be established, refer to figure 4-6.

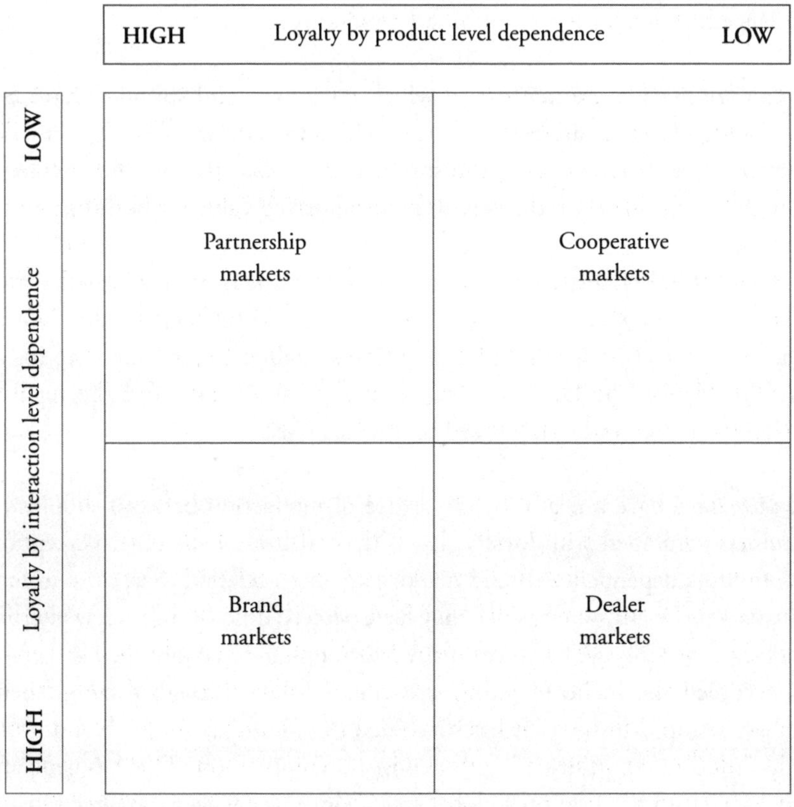

Figure 4-6: A typology of business markets. Source: Hedaa (1991; 1993; and 1996)

The four market cells should be treated as dynamic phenomena regarding customer loyalty. Therefore, a company's portfolio of customers can include relationships of all four kinds at the same time. Consider a commercial bank's relationship with business customers. Some customers tend to act extremely market-like considering the banking services to be like a commodity, always chasing the best prices. Other customers take the more holistic view treating their bank in a cooperative manner.

Customer behaviour might change over the life cycle. In the beginning, customers prefer a more arms-length relationship that in some cases can lead to deep life long partnerships.

A supplier will try to build customer loyalty by nudging their customers in the direction of dependence. Marketing programs will either seek to increase the level of interaction in a cooperative direction or stimulate to unilateral dependence through a product or brand preference.

Partnership markets are markets in which customers and suppliers have established a high level of interaction, and in which the customer experiences a high product dependence vis-à-vis the supplier. Typically, partnership markets are for highly customised products with high-perceived value for both supplier and customer.

Relationship characteristics in partnership markets are associated with the need for close cooperation between the parties and bilateral loyalty. Not only regarding interaction issues, but also in terms of allocating resources to the relationship. Hence, the level of irreversibility is rather high and the regulating mechanisms tend to develop based on mutual trust.

Brand markets have a relatively low degree of interaction between suppliers and customers combined with loyalty that is derived from a customer perception of high product dependence. Brand markets are often referred to as close to monopoly markets by customers, since they have perceived no or only a few alternative suppliers. The Chicago based company Morningstar was established in 1984 and has occupied the niche of rating investment funds through a comprehensive database set-up. Morningstar has succeeded in building a unique brand position in the "fund rating industry" with almost no competition. This has generated a truly loyal customer base on a global scale. Morningstar data have been incorporated into third party sites, as an investment services tool. Therefore, many tangible as well as intangible features are embedded in products in the brand markets, such as quality assurance, service, availability, image and reputation.

In *dealer markets* loyalty levels are notoriously low. Dealer markets can be described by a very low level of interaction between the parties coupled with low product dependence from the customer's point of view. Products or services, which are highly standardised, brought to market by equally good suppliers. No complex contact is needed, and market contracts are the prevailing regulating mechanism between the parties. The relationships between customer and supplier are purely on an on/off basis.

Co-operative markets are characterised by a high level of interaction between suppliers and customers and based on a minimum of perceived product differences. Nevertheless, close cooperation between the parties is needed. Contrary to partnership markets, customers do have the possibility of finding alternative suppliers, as these are present in the market. Still, switching costs and sunken investments in the relationship give the parties incentive to solve possible problems before considering dissolution of the relationship. Social ties as well as a multitude of human ties within the two organisations protect the relationship.

4.6 Measuring Customer Loyalty

As described earlier (1) retention, (2) efficiency and (3) value are the three core business economic terms to pay attention to when analysing the impact of loyalty on long-term profits.

4.6.1 The Business Loyalty Cube

The specific marketing objectives and programmes to be discussed and prioritised could therefore be the increased duration of customer relationships, increased share of wallet and accession of new customers as illustrated in the loyalty cube in figure 4-7.

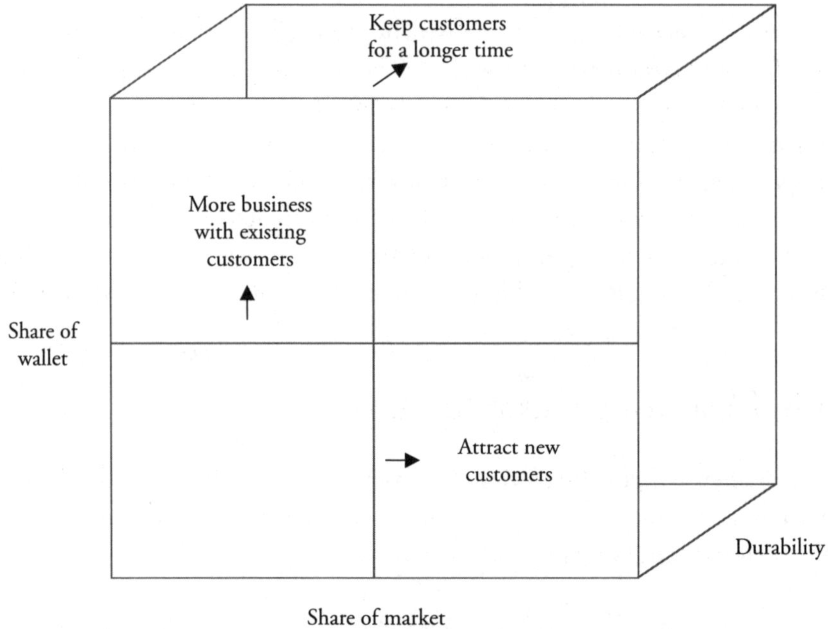

Figure 4-7: The customer loyalty cube.

The three different growth directions do of course not mutually exclude each other. Very often marketing programmes and sales force efforts are focussed on attracting new customers and existing customers tend to be overlooked as the key to growth.

The 555[13] technique is a simple "quick and dirty" marketing tool to determine which loyalty groups to target and with what expected outcome from customer bases. The technique is described in the following sections.

Direct marketing surveys show that customers who have just bought a product or service from a company will be more inclined to purchase again compared with customers where the time since the last purchase is longer.

The customer base can eventually be divided into the following loyalty cells based on their buying habits expressed by time since last purchase, buying frequency and purchasing volume.

On each of the three dimensions the customer base is divided into 20% increments according to the level. This can be shown in a grid as in figure 4-8.

13. Cumberland (1999).

	Increments 20%				
	highest				lowest
	5	4	3	2	1
Time since last purchase					
Purchasing frequency					
Purchasing volume					

Figure 4-8: Purchasing habit cells. Source: Cumberland (1999).

Results were split up into 125 target groups – from 111 to 555. The profitable loyalty segments for a given direct mail promotional campaign can be identified by a simple (static) break-even response calculation like this:

> R = cost per mail/contribution per. Sales × 100
> If a mail costs 0.5 USD and the net contribution is 7 USD pr. sales the break-even response rate R = 0.5/7 × 100 = 7%.
> All groups with an expected rate of response below 7% should be excluded as targets. The expected response levels can be validated through statistics or a test mail exercise.

This exchange-oriented methodology neglects the dynamic life cycle aspect and should be combined with net present value estimates.

Dell Computers is a company that has made measurement of customer behaviour a cornerstone of its relationship-marketing mode of doing business. The company set up a customer experience council, reporting to a corporate vice chairman, to oversee its measurement efforts and its loyalty-building programs. Senior executives from each of the company's major business lines and functions participate in the council. After studying data on customer retention, the council found three key drivers of loyalty: order fulfilment, product performance and post-sale service and support. It then identified the best summary statistics for each driver. For order fulfilment it chose "ship to target", which measures the percentage of orders delivered to customers on time with complete accuracy. For product performance, it picked "initial field incident rate", which measures the frequency of product problems encountered by customers. For service and support, it chose "on-time, first-time fix", which measures the percentage of problems That are rectified on the first visit by a service rep that arrives at the time promised.

Such ongoing or ad hoc audits of customer behaviour and loyalty drivers can help the marketer determine what drives their profit and suggest actions that can lead to long-term profitability.[14]

4.6.2 The Profit/Potential Grid

Not all customers contribute equally to a company's protitability, actually as well as potentially. The most loyal customers are not necessarily the most attractive target group for a relationship economic loyalty strategy. Acquisition may give a higher payoff than retention. Lifetime economics and retention economics must also take into consideration profits and potential.

The profit/potential grid is a practical technique to segment a firm's customer base with the purpose of formulating different strategies for the different loyalty segments, see figure 4-9.

Knowing your customer will create new opportunities in the formulation of loyalty programs. This may be old wisdom, but it is just as relevant today as ever.

14. For details of such a framework please refer to the appendix of chapter 4.

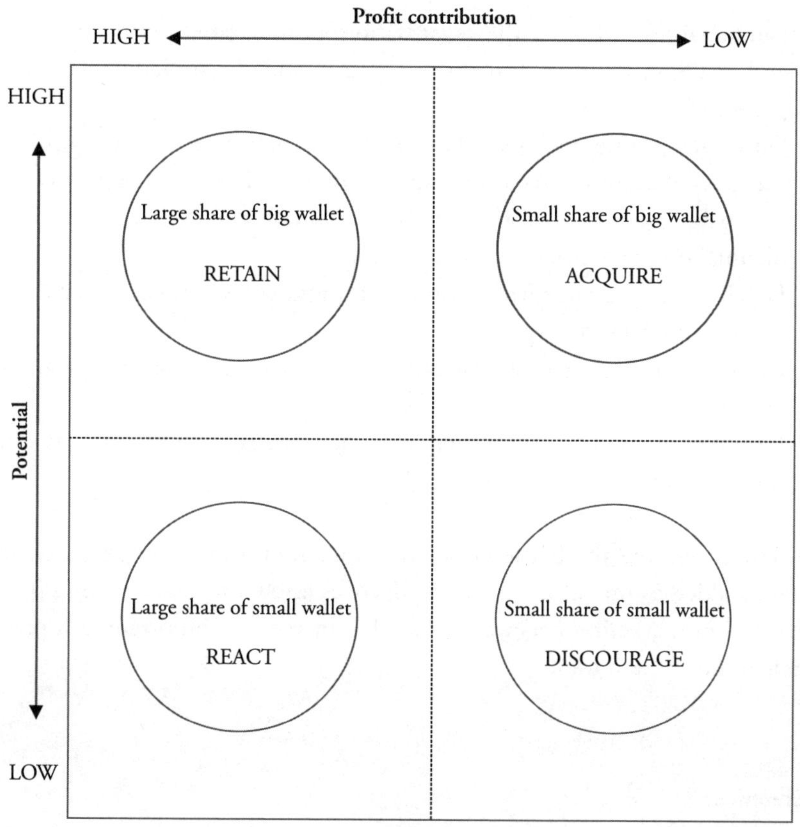

Figure 4-9: The profit/potential grid. Source: Pompa et. al. (2000).

4.6.3 A Brief Note on Customer Relationship Management (CRM)

Many of the ideas, models and rationales in this chapter constitute the analytical foundations of customer relationship management (CRM). CRM is a not just a bundle of data, tools and IT-technologies aimed at increasing the customer understanding. CRM represents a turning point in the business system of many companies now turning from an episodic business approach to a relationship-based one. According to Kelly[15] analytical CRM applications include:

15. Kelly (2000).

- Sales analysis: Offering the organisation an integrated perspective on sales and enabling the sales function to understand the underlying trends and patterns in sales data.
- Customer profile analysis: Allowing the organisation to distinguish from the mass of customer data, the individuals as well as micro segments.
- Campaign analysis: Providing the ability to measure the effectiveness of individual campaigns and different media.
- Loyalty analysis: Measuring customer loyalty with reference to the duration of customer relationships.
- Customer contact analysis: Measuring customer contact history of any individual.
- Profitability analysis: Measuring and analysing the many different dimensions of profitability.

CRM has become the battle cry of the millennium marketing society. It has been heralded as one of the greatest advances known to man. From a strategic relationship marketing perspective CRM is incredibly important as a practical mode of implementation.

References

Aaker, D. (1991) *Managing Brand Equity: Capitalizing on the Value of a Brand Name,* The Free Press.

Ahrnell, B-M. and Nicou, M. (1989) *Kunskapsföretagets marknadsföring – att utveckla förtroende, relationer och kompetens,* Liber.

Alonzo, V. (1994) *Till death do us part,* Incentive Marketing.

Barnard, N. and Ehrenberg, A. S. C. (1997) *Advertising: Strogly pervasive or nudging?,* Journal of Advertising Research.

Berry, L.L.(1983) *Relationship Marketing: Perspectives on Services Marketing,* American Marketing Association.

Cram, T. (1994) *The power of relationship marketing: How to keep the customer for life,* Financial Times.

Crosby, L.A. and Stephens, N. (1987) *Effects of Relationship Marketing on Satisfaction, Retention and Prices in the Life Insurance Industry,* Journal of Market Research.

Cumberland, F. (1999) *Markedsføring – materialesamling,* Samfundslitteratur.

Dick, A.S. and Kunal, B. (1994) *Customer Loyalty: Toward an integrated Conceptual Framework,* Journal of Academy of Marketing Science.

Egan, J. (2001): *Relationship Marketing – exploring relational strategies in Marketing,* Pearson Education.

Forbrugerstyrelsen, Denmark 2001.10.15

Fornell, C. (1992) *A National Customer Satisfaction Barometer. The Swedish Experience*, Journal of Marketing.

Gordon, I. (1998) *Relationship Marketing.* John Willey & Sons.

Guiltinan, J. and Paul, G. (1991) *Marketing Management: Strategies and programmes,* McGraw-Hill.

Gummesson, E. (1996) *Relationsmarkedsføring. Fra 4P til 30R.* KOLLE Forlag.

Gummesson, E. (1987) *The new marketing – developing long-term interactive relationships.* Long Range Planning.

Gummesson, E. (1990) *The part-time markeeer,* University of Karlstad.

Halinen, A. (1997) *Relationship Marketing in Professional Services – a study of agency-client dynamics in the advertising sector,* Routledge.

Hallén, L. (1984) *Stability and Change in Supplier Relationships.*

Hansen, F. (1972) *Consumer Choice Behaviour. A Cognitive Theor,.* Free Press.

Hedaa, L. (1996) *Customer Acquisition in Sticky Business Markets.* Copenhagen Business School.

Hedaa, L. (1993) *Distrust, Uncertainties and Disconfirmed Expectations in Supplier-Customer Relationships,* International Business Review.

Hedaa, L. (1991) *On Interorganizational Relationships in Industrial Marketing,* Samfundslitteratur.

Heskett, J. L., Jones, T. O., Loveman, G. W., Sasser W., E. Jr., and Schlesinger, L. A. (1994) *Putting the Service profit Chain to Work,* Harvard Business Review, vol. March-April, pp. 164-175.

Hougaard, S. (1995) *Relationstankegang som virksomhedsfilosofi i fremtidens pengeinstitut.* Handelshøjskolen i København.

Kelly S. (2000) *Analytical CRM: The fusion of data ad intelligence,* Interactive Marketing.

Kotler, P. (1992) *It's time for Total Marketing,* Business Week Advance Executive Brief, vol. 2.

Kunøe, G. (1994) *Metalojalitet,* Working Paper. Handelshøjskolen i København.

Nielsen, O. (1995) *Organisationers købsadfærd i grundtræk,* Samfundslitteratur.

Pompa N., Berry J. Reid J. and Webber R. (1995) *Relationship Marketing for competitive Advatage: Winning and keeping customers,* Butterworth-Heinemann.

Reichheld, F. and Schefter, P. (2000) *Your secret Weapon,* Harvard Business Review.

Reichheld, F. and Sasser, W..E. jr. (1995) *Zero defections: quality comes to services,* Harvard Business Review.

Reichheld, F. (1993) *Loyalty-Based Management,* Harvard Business Review.

Reichheld, F. (1996) *The Quest for Loyalty – Creating Value through Partnership,* Harvard.

Reilly, M. and Parkinson, T. (1985) *Individual and Product Correlates of Evoked Set Size,* Advances in Consumer Research.

Schijns, J.M.C. (1996) *Measuring relationship strenghts for segmentation purposes,* Center for Relationship Marketing.

Stenvinkel Nilsson, O. and Olsen, J. K. (1996) *En adfærdsteoretisk model til beregning af kunders levetid og værdi,* Handelshøjskolen i København.

Svanholmer, B. (1996) *Kundeloyalitet,* Børsens Forlag.

Sviokla, John J. and Shapiro, B. (1993) *Seeking Customers,* Harvard Business School Press.

Uncles, M (1994) *Do Your Customers need a loyalty scheme?,* Journal of Targeting, Measurement and Analysis.

Appendix: A framework for Customer Loyalty Review – the Service-Profit Chain Audit[16]

Scope of analysis	Abstract	Measure
Profit And Growth:		
1. How do we define loyal customers?	Customers often become more profitable over time. Loyal customers account for an unusually high proportion of the sales and profit growth.	
2. Do measures of customer profitability include profits from referrals?	Companies sometimes overlook the most important aspect of loyalty: referrals. Hence they also overlook the rewards that loyal customers should receive.	
3. What proportion of business development expenditures and incentives are directed at the retention of existing customers?	Too many companies concentrate nearly all their efforts on attracting new customers. But in a great many industries it takes four, five, six or even more years before the profit-break even point for new customers is reached	
4. Why do customers defect?	It is important to find out not only where defectors go, but also why they defect. Was it because of poor service, price or value? Exit interviews can give answers and have a real sales impact.	
Customer Satisfaction:		
5. Is customer satisfaction data gathered in an objective, consistent and periodic fashion?	Very often the weakest measurement concerns customer satisfaction. Sometimes reported customer satisfaction is contradicted by continuing declines in sales and profits. Sometimes observation reveals that data collecting methods are more or less manipulative. Third party interviews, mystery shopping etc. should be used.	
6. Where are the listening posts for obtaining customer feedback in your organisation?	Listening posts are tools for collecting data from customers and systematically translating those data into information in order to improve service and products. Reports from field sales people, letters of complaints are examples.	
7. How is information concerning customer satisfaction used to solve customer problems?	In order to handle customer problems a company must have the latitude to resolve any situation promptly. Customers and employees should be encouraged to report concerns and failures.	

16. Heskett, Jones, Loveman, Sasser, and Schlesinger (1994).

External Service Value		
8. How do you measure service value?	Value is a function not only of costs to the customer but also the results achieved for the customer. Value is always relative because it is based both on perceptions and expectations. The reasons expressed by customers for high or low value is a typical company measure.	
9. How is information concerning customers' perception of value shared with those responsible for designing a product or service?	Information on customer perception will often require the formation of teams of people responsible for sales, operations, service or design as well as the frequent assignment of service designers to tasks requiring field contact with customers	
10. To what extent are measures taken of differences between customers' perceptions of quality delivered and their expectations before delivery?	Ultimately, service quality is a function of the gap between perceptions of the actual service experienced and what the customer expected before the purchase. Measures such as reliability, empathy, functionality and authority is often used as performance indicators	
11. Do our efforts to improve external quality emphasise effective recovery from service errors in addition to providing a product or service right the first time?	A popular concept of quality in manufacturing is the importance of doing things right the first time. Often customers allow one mistake. Some companies are very good at delivering service as long as nothing goes wrong. Others organise for and thrive on service emergencies. Outstanding companies do both and allow frontline employees to do whatever they feel right in order to satisfy customers.	
Employee Productivity		
12. How do you measure employee productivity?	Employee productivity is integrated with customer satisfaction. Very rarely employees are unproductive with customers being completely satisfied	
13. To what extent do measures of productivity identify changes in the quality as well as the quantity of service produced per unit of input?	In many industries, the ultimate measure of quality may be customer satisfaction. That measure should be combined with measures of quantity to determine the total output of the organisation. Outstanding service organisations are replacing the typical either/or trade-off between quality and quantity with an and/also imperative.	
Employee Loyalty		
14. How do you create employee loyalty	Employee loyalty goes hand in hand with productivity, contradicting the conventional wisdom that successful service providers should be promoted to larger supervisory responsibilities or moved to a similar job in a larger business unit.	

15. Have we made an effort to determine the right level of employee retention?	Rarely is the right level of retention 100%. Dynamic organisations require a certain level of turnover. However in calibrating desired turnover levels, it is important to take into account the full costs of loss of key people in terms of lost sales and lack of productivity.	
Employee Satisfaction		
16. Is employee satisfaction measured in ways that can be linked to similar measures of customer satisfaction with sufficient frequency and consistency to establish trends for management use?	Customer interviews carried out on a regular basis usually include questions about employee's friendliness, professionalism and hustle. It is extremely important that employee satisfaction measures are analysed and interpreted as an integrative element in customer surveys to give management a reliable diagnosis.	
17. Are employee selection criteria and methods geared to what customers as well as managers believe are important?	Sometimes companies invite key customers to participate in selecting personnel or to define the decisive criteria in the recruitment process.	
18. To what extent are measures of customer satisfaction, customer loyalty or the quality of service output used in recognising and rewarding employees?	Employee recognition may often involve little more than informing individual employees or employees as a group about service improvements and individual successes.	
Internal Service Quality		
19. Do employees know who their customers are?	It can be particularly difficult for employees to identify their customers when those customers are internal to the company. These employees often do not know what impact their work has on other departments. Identifying internal customers requires mapping and communication characteristics of workflow, organising periodic cross-departmental meetings between "customers" and "servers" and recognising good internal service performance.	
20. Are employees satisfied with the technological and personal support they receive on the job?	The cornerstone of successful companies is the provision of the latest information technology, work scheduling and team training. This practise often leads to the establishment of self-managing teams improving the quality of work-life.	

Leadership		
21. To what extent is the company's leadership energetic, creative vs. stately conservative? Is leadership participatory, caring or removed, elitist? Listening, coaching or supervising, controlling	The corporate culture has a major impact on customer satisfaction. Values and image are inevitably linked together, and leadership is the key factor driving norms, values and beliefs in certain directions.	
22. How much time is spent by the organisation's leadership – in person – developing and maintaining a corporate culture centred on service to customers and fellow employees?	Leaders naturally have different traits and styles. But the CEO" of companies that are successfully using the value chain audit possess all or most of a set of traits that separate them from their merely good competitors. Of course different styles of leadership are appropriate for various stages in an organisation's development.	
Measuring The Relationship		
23. What are the most important relationships in your company's service-profit chain	It could be one out of six referral markets[17] or a single dimension among the 32 kinds of relationships that can be identified. Most often the customer relationship is the value star of a company.	
24. To what extent does each measure correlate with profit and growth at the frontline level?	Consistent motives, back-up function that work as well as access to information are the prerequisite for success among frontline personnel. Often these links are overlooked creating unnecessary customer distortion.	
25. Is the importance of these relationships reflected in rewards and incentives offered to employees?	Measures drive action when they are related in ways that provide managers with direction. Only if the individual measures are tied together into a comprehensive picture will the service-profit chain provide a foundation for unprecedented profit and growth.	

Source: Inspired by publications from SAP, Mercuri International, Huthwaite International and others aiming at collecting elements of the audit.

The service-profit chain audit as presented through the above 25 questions is not intended to demonstrate a universal approach to the measurement of behaviour and drivers. It is one way. Our basic message is: "What gets measured gets done!"

17. Christophe Payne and Ballantyne (1999).

PART II

Preconditions for Building Successful Relationships

CHAPTER 5

Understanding the Driving Forces of Customer Relationships

Information technology has opened up a whole new world of customer relationship marketing tools and business models. Concurrently, research on the relationship aspects of marketing has also gone up dramatically. New and somewhat controversial marketing concepts and typologies have been developed. Surveys have demonstrated that successful positioning strategies do in fact require a deep relationship understanding. And yet, mainstream marketing is still at the foot of the mountain only incorporating the relationship approach into existing theories and models.

In this chapter, the driving forces of customer relationships will be discussed and analysed. Within traditional strategic marketing theories, a deep understanding of the industry, the market, the segments and the competition is required. Likewise, a relationship centric marketing view must explicitly evaluate the driving forces behind the climate of the customer relationship.

Which actors and stakeholders affect customer relationships? Why, how and when? What situational elements link a supplier and its customers together? And which forces are attempting to replace well-established relationships and value chains?

5.1 The Reorientation of Strategic Market Analysis

Customer relationships do not exist in a vacuum. They are exposed to various influences from within the relationship as well as from outside the relationship. This forms a complicated and dynamic influence system that stems from internal and external actors who are the driving forces of the relationship and who determine its structure, stability and economic strength. Figure 5-1 identifies the following categories of driving forces behind all customer relationships.

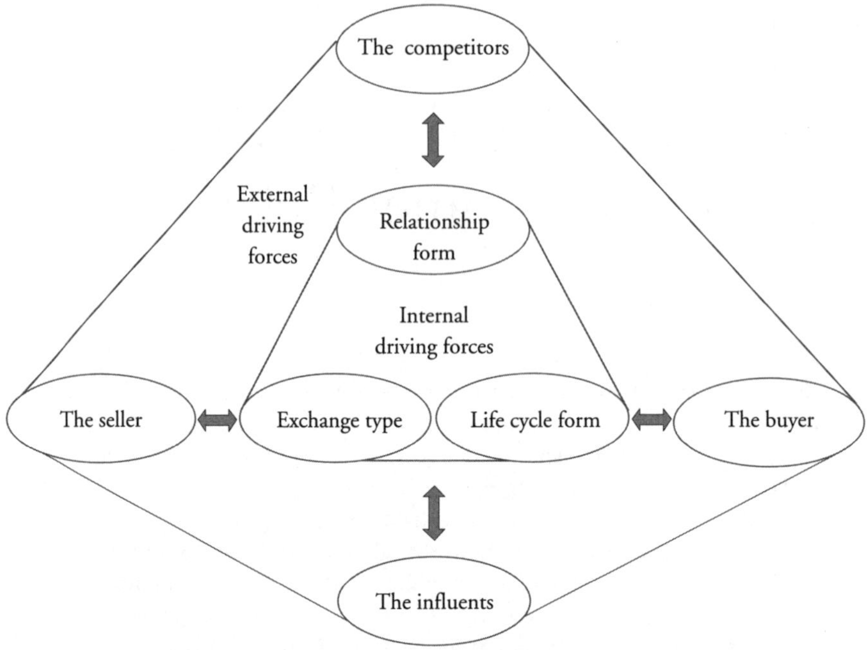

Figure 5-1: Actors and other driving forces behind customer relationships.

The *external driving forces* are the influences on the relationship that emanate from actors who either participate in the relationship or have a direct interest in affecting it. Whereas, the *internal driving forces* are the factors that influence the basic characteristics of the relationship by either strengthening or weakening it.

Hence, the driving forces comprise four distinct participant categories: (1) the direct participants, i.e. seller and buyer, (2) third parties in the form of competitors and influents, (3) the structure of exchange and (4) the exchange variables in terms of the relationship form and the customer life cycle.[1]

Almost any relationship in competitive environments has opposite forces built into it. The *self-protecting forces* seek to validate, reinforce and enrich the relationship, while the *undermining forces* constantly challenge, limit and attack its competitiveness. This organic perception of the relationship, where pressure

1. Bagozzi (1975) identified four variables influencing the transaction: (1) transaction variables (=exchange variables), (2) characteristics of the actors, (3) third parties and (4) the transactions themselves.

for growth and protection act simultaneously and in opposition to constraining and destructive mechanisms is what requires further explanation and interpretation. Meaningful marketing initiatives rest on the understanding of such alternate interaction behaviour.

Relationships possess different natures, cyclical patterns and levels of importance for the participants. The driving force model is a framework for analysis and diagnosis that is applicable across boundaries of different relationship markets. The concept behind this model is that environmental factors and changes are transmitted to the relationship via the external driving forces through the arrangements made between the participants. An exclusive distributor is, for example, exposed to the threat that the principal company will decide to internalise sales and distribution thereby establishing an affiliate company in the territory. Such action is perhaps initiated as a reaction to manoeuvring by competitors or as an offensive strike. On the other hand, strong distributors will sometimes be tempted to put a threatening pressure on their suppliers by backwards-vertical integration, that is establishing their own plants or launching private brands.

Influents are the heterogeneous bundle of stakeholders, in addition to competitors, who have the explicit purpose of breaking down, replacing or changing an ongoing customer-supplier relationship. Influent actors will typically exist in the form of *invaders* or *innovators* attempting to redefine or shorten value chains, which are described in detail later.

The internal driving forces cover the overall characteristics of the relationship, and they represent an independently working organism that must be understood. The exchange form, the relationship form and the life cycle have been identified as the three key internal driving forces. The exchange form refers to the buying-selling process, the interaction with the product; the delivery structures as well as the generic need situation. Exchanges imply different levels of involvement and impacts, functionally and financially, on the buyer. Buying nails and screws has very little in common with purchasing of tools and machines with regard to risk, reversibility, dependencies, brand loyalty, trust etc.

Regarding the attributes of the relationship form to be investigated are factors such as: Who are the parties? Are they potential competitors? What is the potential lifespan of the relationship? How is the fit and position of the deliveries in both parties' value chains? What is the contact form? etc. In total, the relationship form can have a determining influence on buying and selling strategies and the resulting match in regulating mechanisms: (1) command, (2) competition or (3) cooperation.

Driving forces in customer relationships are by nature difficult to identify, measure and diagnose. They change over time and interrelate. Isolating the impact of a single element in the driving force model therefore requires careful and patient analysis.

5.2 The Influence Position of the Seller – the Relationship Marketer

Traditional marketing is a monopoly game in the sense that high market share and *dominance efficiency* is considered to be the requirement for high profitability. Introducing mutuality and reciprocal considerations in terms of *interactive efficiency* and value driven economic principles illuminates the position of the seller. The dyadic motive and the balancing act between the establishing of barriers to entry to protect customer relationship on the one hand, and the idiosyncrasy of asset customisation on the other, play a very important role in establishing a marketing approach.

The power and influence of the seller is one of the main external driving forces in many relationships. A multitude of aspects must be dealt with in order to gain insight into the actual and the potential influential factors. Dominance has a high price as well.

5.2.1 The Value of the Relationship and the Distribution of Power

The economic value and hence the relative importance of the relationship is often a determinant for the distribution of power between the seller and the buyer. If a specific customer relationship has a high value for the supplier, but is only of minor importance to the buyer, the influence of the seller tends to be limited. The mere existence of asymmetric distribution of power in favour of the customer will as such impede the supplier. This is known as the "don't step on the lion's tail" effect.

Small companies with a special competence sometimes get substantial or strategically important orders from big companies, typically in the role as niche subcontractor or development partner. If the order requires genuine customisation of systems, design, staff, equipment etc. that is greater than the company's overall capacity, the supplier is put in a difficult marketing situation. On the one hand, the opportunity of obtaining a strategic contract resulting in rise in competence, expansion and perhaps high profitability meaning a *higher degree of future strategic freedom.* On the other hand, the risk of engaging in an uneven relationship thus gradually *weakens the range of future strategic freedom*, because customer specific assets represent a low alternative market value and because the exit barriers for the customer are relatively low.

The reverse situation, where the relationship gradually becomes more important for the buyer, is also a possibility. A producer of industrial niche plastic products once developed a polyethylene based packing material customised to suit a leading manufacturer of branded consumer products. The customer built its product branding (shape, colour, design) as well as manufacturing processes on this specific packaging concept. The supplier relationship became of vital strategic importance to the customer, but was in no way a dominant player in the customer portfolio of the, relatively small, supplying company. What happened? In fact nothing. The supplier had the opportunity of increasing prices and capitalising on the influential position, but did not. When the case was analysed at a later stage it turned out that the supplier never drew the expected conclusion about the economic value of the relationship for the customer because the supplier paid more attention to own investment in specialised tools and other equipment.

5.2.2 Interdependence of Ties and Trust between Buyer and Seller

The ties between supplier and customer reflect the strength of the relationship between them. When a relationship agreement replaces market contracts, transaction costs go down and the relationship moves into a positive reinforcing circle.

Ties will either be a result of conscious and explicit investment strategies reducing the opportunistic motives of the parties or they arise gradually over the life cycle as a consequence of implicit adjustments. Hence, we can distinguish between dyadic advantages caused by *contractual factors* as opposed to *incremental processes.*

In the *command situation,* the buyer is dependent on or is a prisoner of the supplier. Such was the case in the early days of photocopying, when Xerox was in a monopoly situation and gave customers service agreement offers they couldn't refuse.

In the *reverse command situation*, the supplier has no other choice than to accept the opportunistic moves made by the buyer. In subcontractor industries such as defence, aircraft building, metal works and certain niches in the building industry etc. this is very often the case. Not only must the supplier cope with fluctuations in demand, price pressure, delays or extensive services, the buyer is also forced to take over the commercial risk of the seller, e.g. R&D expenses or investment in capacity of expectation for later sales.

But what if bonds are interdependent? Interdependence does not necessarily lead to a corresponding fit between buyer and seller's strategies. But the parties will nevertheless tend to develop patterns of reaction enabling effective adjustment and a balanced distribution of the dyadic value creation.

As a paradox the deep and balanced interdependent relationship might suffer from the weakness that it can be difficult to organise effective decision making processes if external changes disturb the commercial logic behind the relationship. In situations with unilateral ties or a more formalistic climate of control, coordination is not primarily consensus based. Therefore, the independent party will initiate necessary adjustments.

Here is a case where interdependent ties had some bizarre negative consequences:

> Some time ago, the leisure and sportswear company Hummel experienced a significant increase in sales primarily due to the exposure of the Hummel "Chevron indefinite" logo on television. Hummel was a fast mover in the emerging sponsorship market and succeeded in acquiring sponsor contracts with top teams in soccer etc.
>
> During this period, Hummel decided to consolidate its distributor network among the varied group of independent sportswear retailers. Some shops were selected to become A-distributors. They obtained a series of advantages concerning new collections but did not get any exclusivity in their territory. Gradually Hummel put pressure the on A-distributors to place larger and larger orders on new collections and certain seasonal items. Hummel did not support the distribution network in forecasting sales with promotions or national communication. The end result was huge retail inventories of un-saleable Hummel products. Hummel's own sales curve did, however, not show any sign of weakness at that point in time.
>
> Soon after, the distributors had to sell off the stock of excess Hummel products through massive price reductions. The consequence was that the brand image eroded as it was now being promoted and

hence perceived by the consumers as cheap, old fashioned, low prestige, something everybody could afford. Furthermore, the distributors reacted negatively, creating an atmosphere of reluctance against the Hummel concept, which was at that time the market leader in sports wear. No surprise, Hummel's sales fell dramatically and the company got into deep problems.

Hummel both increased and exploited the distributor network's dependence and loyalty at the same time. This gave room for opportunism, but the end result of sub-optimising was self-destruction of Hummel's own business.

5.2.3 The Threat of Vertical Integration in Dyadic Relationships

In any relationship the influence position of the seller will vary depending on the risk or opportunity of vertical integration. The threat of vertical integration, replacing relationships with a hierarchy, is an extremely widespread opportunistic weapon in a great many business-to-business markets.

Forward vertical integration means that a company, typically a manufacturer or a brand owner, establishes its own businesses in finished goods production, wholesale, retail or service i.e. nearer to the end-user. Vertical forward integration represents an opportunity for the supplier and a threat against some distributors. Backward vertical integration has the reverse effect.

Producers of engines will often be inclined to establish business units in industries where engines is an essential component, i.e. in the industries of their customers (Honda, General Electric etc.). In contrast, auto manufacturers have a strategic motivation to control the development and production of car engines and other critical parts.

The threat and opportunity balance of vertical integration, viewed as a latent opportunistic possibility, plays a major role in understanding the influence of the supplier. Companies in the fashion industry, hi-fi and luxury products invest in creating their own brand stores. The retail retaliates by designing proprietary brands and shop-in-shop solutions asking the brand owners to share the commercial risks.

The strategic perspective behind vertical integration has to do with either efficiency economics or dominance aspects. The *efficiency economic consideration* assumes that saved transaction costs via insourcing exceed the eventual larger production plus exit costs. In opposition to this, the market dominance argument concentrates on defensive motives such as the opportunism of the other party. Some of the most apparent driving forces that stimulate vertical integration are:

- *Reduction of entry barriers.* Lower entry barriers to the customer or the supplier industry have influence on the risk-return calculations.
- *No asset customisation.* If the interdependent relationship relies on non-specific assets the costs of extrication will be lower.
- *Expected competitor moves.* If a company expects competitors to integrate vertically, and if the first mover advantages are considerable some firms tend to take the more offensive step over the doorstep backwards or forwards.
- *The quality of existing relationships.* Vertical integration can sometimes be a reaction to the opportunism of the trading partner or a lack of motivation to cooperate with regard to specifying assets to genuine needs.

5.3 Competitors as Driving Force – Direction and Level of Pressure

The triangle scenario is possible in every competitive environment.

The duel may serve as an example for reflection:

> In ancient times, suitors of beautiful women's favour settled their conflict by duelling with pistols. Once upon a time a lieutenant and an artist fell in love with the same beautiful woman and a duel with pistols was agreed. The lieutenant was an excellent shot with a 100% hit rate. The artist was somewhat narrow sighted, and although he exercised daily before the duel to improve, he never passed a 10% hit rate and faced assured death. However it turned out that there was a third suitor – namely a businessman. As was the tradition, he also challenged his two love competitors to a triangle duel with pistols. The businessman also began training and he reached a hit rate of 25%. At daybreak they all met on the duel place and each of the three was handed a pistol. How could it be that the artist actually had the greatest chance of survival despite his 10% hit rate?

Competition is about challenging, gaining and defending relationships. Although the art of relationship marketing is to resist competitive pressure, the trilateral forces are what keep patterns of trade vital. The directions of competition as influential factors can be classified into four main categories as illustrated in figure 5-2.

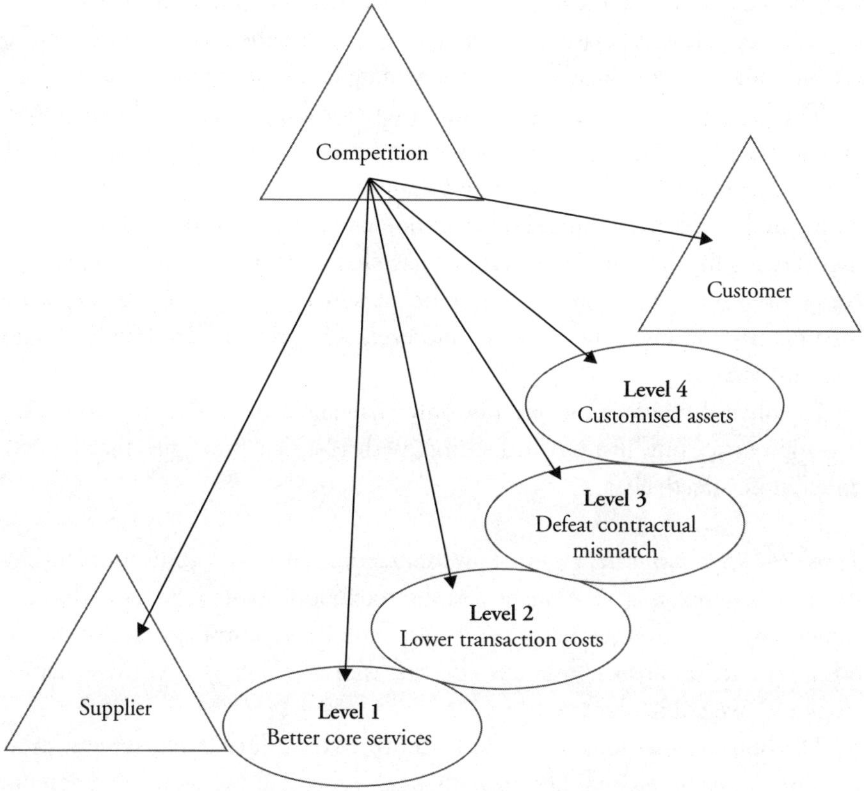

Figure 5-2: Influence of competition on established relationships.

Level 1: The core service. Not surprisingly, existing relationships get threatened if competitors offer better or less expensive core products or services. In certain industries, a successful strategy can be either relationship-oriented or exchange-centric depending on various competitive pressures. Strategies based on core services are centred on the exchange; companies following this path deliberately try to position themselves as anti relationship-oriented. They maintain that some segments perceive the relationship attributes as tricks aiming at pacifying the customer's search for the most competitive solution. We could call it trust building through clean pricing.

In the airline industry, low price companies like Southwest Airlines, Go Airlines, Ryanair or Virgin have succeeded with this non-relationship marketing strategy. The German retail chain Aldi has a tightly managed programme for product exposure in the outlets. In order to create and confirm the perception of Aldi as being absolute discount, Aldi considers it to be important that the store layout gives a clear association to a warehouse i.e. that the items are been kept in cartons indicating low handling costs, low margins and low end-user prices.

The contrast is strategies based upon relationships. Such marketing strategies seek to remove the customer's attention from core services and their generic values, considering it to be trivial and a routine, whereas other benefits are incorporated and expected to be determining choice criteria. In the airline business services like booking, check-in, luggage handling and in flight comfort are being promoted. In retail, it could be personal service, product exposure, in-store promotions, entertainment and events, interior design, dividend, club concepts etc.

Established relationships are not only challenged by differentiated marketing approaches but also by competitors with identical strategies that are executed more effectively.

Level 2: Lower transaction costs: Low transaction costs is a protection mechanism in any customer relationship, as the transaction costs is part of what customers pay for a product or service. Hence, an offensive strategy aiming at lowering transaction costs can be an effective tool to challenge existing relationships and overcome obstacles.

Distribution methods, logistics, better or faster information, service, product line extension etc. are key areas that can potentially generate a transaction cost advantage and reform the overall competitive picture.

The increasing sales of non food items in supermarkets, i.e. clothing, footwear, books, medicine, hardware etc. is in fact an effective exploitation of the opportunity of lowering customers' transaction costs, namely time and convenience. Supermarkets have gained substantial market shares with this strategy. While speciality stores have defended their position by increasing the service level.

In rare cases, an existing customer relationship can be put under pressure if a competitor in fact increases the transaction costs. This is called the *paradox of reverse pricing effect.* Competing with a nearby club for new members, the management of a golf club began asking a lot of relatively unimportant questions through questionnaires to membership applicants thereby making it more difficult to get into the club. This move, by which the transaction costs did actually go up for potential members, was very well received by candidates and prospects and was perceived as a sign of quality, esteem, selectivity and snob effect and the number of applicants went up. As Groucho Marx once stated: "I would never dream of joining a club that would accept me as a member."

Level 3: Defeating contractual misfit:
In chapter 1, relationships were classified according to the strategies of buyers and sellers in competitive, command or cooperative behaviour. Based on that the relationship contract will result in interdependence, mismatch or dependence. From this we can also draw a map of opportunities for competitors to overcome potential mismatching of existing relationships.

		Marketing strategies				
		Competitive		**Cooperative**		**Command**
Purchasing strategies	**Competitive**	Independent	←	Mismatch	→	Independent
	Cooperative	Mismatch	→	Independent	←	Dependent
	Command	Independent	→	Dependent	←	Mismatch

Figure 5-3: The direction of competitor influence in established customer relations
Source: Based on Sørensen (1997)

Figure 5-3 illustrates how competitors can put pressure on customer relationships that are not functioning very well. The arrows illustrate the competitors' opportunities for breaking a relationship, given specific marketing and purchasing strategies. See also chapter 8, specifically the sub-section on buying strategies.

Level 4: Customised assets. Customers often appreciate individualised solutions. In some cost driven industries standardisation is the name of the game in order to stay price competitive. In the 1960's and 1970's this was the case in the Scandinavian holiday travel industry. The very popular charter holidays to Mediterranean destinations became affordable for almost every citizen in the

Nordic countries. This marketing concept of standardisation relied on economies of scale to bring costs down.

New entrants in the travel market and niche tour operators saw that the demands of innovators and early adopters changed as the market matured. These segments wanted exotic destinations, adventure holidays or just individual go-as-you-please trips. This mass customisation turned out to be a major threat to the industry and gradually all players turned their products in a more flexible direction at the expense of the very low prices.

5.3.1 The Competitor Threat in Different Industry Environments

Fragmented Industries

Fragmented industries[2] means that barriers to entry and exit are low, and that economies of scale and scope are limited. Industries with fragmentation tend to have excess capacity with harsh price pressure and high buyer influence. Switching costs are typically low, with certain exceptions such as personal service sectors, based on trust in combination with social bonds between the parties. In fragmented industries, suppliers are rarely interested in investing in customised assets.

Companies in fragmented industries can in some situations protect their customer relationships through transportation or inventory costs, the lack of economies of scale, local presence and image or perceived customer dependence. So even if the competitive threat is constant, relationships are to some extent defendable.

The competitive threat is most apparent when a competitor creates uniqueness by adjusting to the cause of fragmentation or when they standardise or specialise. Law firms have begun to merge into larger entities. The local image and the close client relationships are maintained while at the same time specialising the staff of lawyers. These law firms adjust to the cause of fragmentation (i.e. the local element) as well as exploit the opportunity of building core competencies and therefore economies of scale. When pizza restaurants begin to deliver pizzas at your doorstep, they overcome the traditional barrier of proximity. Global fast food- and restaurant chains have succeeded in standardising and branding a product category that was traditionally a local mom and pop type of enterprise.

---

2. See also chapter 7 for details on industry analysis in different industry environments.

Concentrated Industries

Industry concentration does not protect customer relationships against competition, unless the structure of the customer relationships is directly linked to the driving forces that underlie industry concentration.

Traditionally, the retail sector in most countries is quite concentrated. In these markets, logistics, buyer bargaining power and organisational size, as well as marketing costs have become very critical success factors. In this industry, scale and size has almost removed the relationship and the end-user loyalty dimension from the marketing agenda.

Suppliers in concentrated industries do not tend to customise assets as a competitive marketing tool, unless the customer side is equally as concentrated.

The competitive threat against supplier/customer relationships will materialise when a competitor invests more strategically in meeting the choice criteria of vast customer segments in combination with precise timing. The Japanese automobile industry conquered the US market during the oil crisis in the 1970's. When consumers needed compact economic solutions, the Japanese companies met this need by offering more compact fuel-efficient cars. Chrysler's come back in the mid 1980's with the Voyager coincided with car owners' preference for functional comfort, social life and luxury.

Competitive pressures in new industries and product-markets in the introductory stages

New industries tend to be product and customer-centric rather than competition-oriented. In new industries, suppliers concentrate on new category users, whereas switchers are not considered the key to market leadership until in later stages of the life cycle.

In relatively immature industries such as cable networks, mobile phones, IT services and travel, a customer will typically need only one supplier. Competition is centred on what has been deemed *subscription economics.* At the outset, a mobile phone customer had to change his or her telephone number when they wanted to switch carriers. This was a very effective barrier against competitive pressure, until a company launched a service that neutralised this advantage through a forwarding protocol.

Mature and declining industries – the playground of fierce relationship competition

Mature and declining industries are characterised by a mixture of stability and turbulence. Take the newspaper business, an industry that has been in decline for decades and has extremely high barriers to entry and exit. Competition is fierce and marketing aggressive. As newspaper production has very large capacity costs and low variable costs, competitors fight for customers and subscribers with all manner of discounts and offers.

The customer relationship angle has become a serious topic as a marketing tool in the interactive sense. Reader groups are formed locally. Thereby newspapers create communities of readers. Polls are taken and results are generated immediately. Readers are able to print their views in the paper without interference or censorship. New print-shop technologies will offer a broad range of options creating the personally edited newspaper. Print and digital media will converge. Content will be published via all media channels. Newspapers will put up a kitchen staffed with top chefs in the editorial department. While cooking, the journalists write the article and TV and radio programmes are broadcast live. People can get ideas on web TV etc, where the programme is on live. Interactivity therefore becomes new source of pressure on your competitors, which they must live up to in order to remain competitive.

5.4 Buyers and Their Influence on Relationships

E-tailers, e-marketplaces, blind e-auctions etc. have not really succeeded yet[3] as profitable business models. It is not because buyers are against low prices, transparency and convenience, but relationships seem to be more competitive than the exchange centric e-speculators. In business-to-business markets, flexibility, timing, low inventory costs and effective networking create more value than low prices and anonymity.

A buyer has two opposing interests. On the one hand, autonomy orientation could be avoiding the idiosyncrasy of dependence. This phenomenon is called the *monadic-competitive driving force.* On the other hand, buyers seek stability, interactivity and smooth exchanges with low transaction costs. This is called the *dyadic-co-operative driving force.* When the level of exchange complexity increases, so does the dyadic-co-operative motivation. Buyers demand solutions not exchanges. How these contrasting concerns manifest themselves in purchasing processes and regulating mechanisms depends on a variety of situational, cultural and buyer specific elements.

At one extreme are the market environments with a high buyer concentration. In airline catering each airport hosts less than a handful of airlines each with a substantial catering need. In such situations there tends to be only a few

3. Spring 2002.

suppliers. The business atmosphere tends to develop into a cooperative direction with a considerable buyer influence. The reverse will occur in situations where many customers are in combat for a few value-adding suppliers only.

The influence of the buyer in terms of what, when, how much, does of course depend on the basic exchange situation and the importance this specific relationship has for the parties.

5.4.1 How can Buyers Increase the Importance of Relationships with Suppliers?

Customers can sometimes gain further influence over their suppliers by increasing the perception of the relative importance of the account. *Intensifying* then becomes a crucial issue in the industrial buyer's backward relationship strategy as illustrated below in figure 5-4.

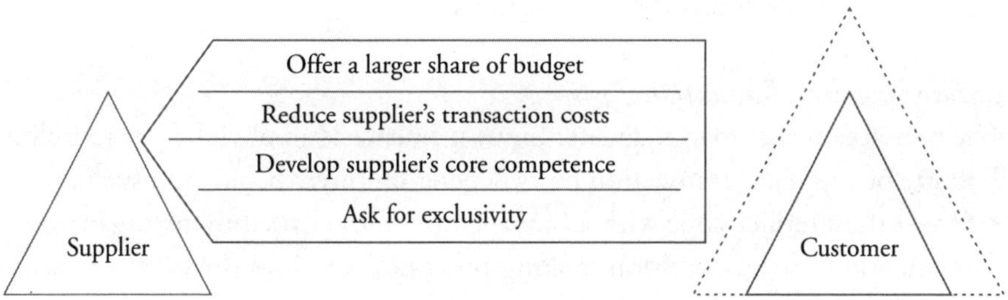

Figure 5-4: Customers Intensifying the Supplier Relationship.

Climbing the supplier's value ladder can help generate mutual benefits. This is however, not a universal truth. Careful attention should also be paid to the supplier's *response profile* in terms of assumptions, current strategy, goals and cultural inclination to strengthen customer ties.

Offer a Larger Share of the Budget

In industries with extensive use of subcontractors, companies will often invite their suppliers into closer more cooperative programmes involving R&D and hence higher risk exposure. In return, the customer offers a larger share of the budget, possibly a sole supplier-ship. That is if the supplier is willing to accept the risk of exclusivity. The strategic intention of the customer is often to increase their own cost competitiveness by moving relatively quickly down their experience curve by driving the suppliers down their learning curve. When Boeing reduced their number of subcontractors by 75% in the intense rivalry with Airbus and McDonnell Douglas unit cost calculations was the main argument for the supplier concentration. Manufacturers of defence and aircraft components in NATO countries were offered very attractive development contracts if they would team up in the design of the F16 successor fighter. This put pressure on the nation states as well. The customer offered a larger share of wallet to the supplier and asked for payment in terms of risk transfer and dependence.

Often companies designate a maximum limit for the proportion of a supplier's revenue it will purchase. Such ceilings can disqualify small companies as suppliers. The customer deliberately attempts not to become too influential and not to create a situation of dependence, image persuasion and lack of control. Therefore, when a hierarchy-like command relationship mechanism is about to evolve, customers prefer to loosen the ties in order to avoid facing costs *of dependence* imposed on the supplier.

Reduce Supplier's Transaction Costs

The transaction cost road to greater buyer influence is an obvious one to follow. The size of suppliers' transaction costs depend on buyer behaviour, such as:

- Must the supplier cope with a bureaucratic, formalistic buying organisation centre and unclear decision making processes? Or does the customer strive to minimise waste of supplier's time and money?
- How comprehensive are the customer's contractual routines, i.e.: certifications, documentation, legal framework, reps and warranties as well as risk aversion in operational details?
- What are the buying routines at the tactical level? Which and how many competing suppliers ask for bids and how?
- Does the customer have smooth informational procedures in cases of reordering, giving notice, planning for just in time etc.
- Is the quality control level sufficient to reduce supplier costs?

With good reason, public companies must live up to legislation to avoid being accused of nepotism. Very often professional purchasing units pay too little attention to the transaction costs that arise in the supplying organisation. Cost demanding hurdles in the guise of competition and documentation are used as monadic mechanisms of pressure. Is that a wise philosophy?

Develop Supplier's Core Competence
Most companies need demanding customers who can actively contribute to the development and refinement of their core skills. Some customers might take advantage of this fact and will put pressure on the supplier's price or loyalty or both.

In many companies, such as Ikea for example, creating superior and effective suppliers has become a strategic goal rather than a marginal side effect. In relationships, where a customer needs a cooperative and value chain oriented network of suppliers, and where the customer's own profitability to a large extent depends on supplier professionalism, the influence of the customer is high.

In industries with short product life cycles, frequent technological shifts and unpredictability, companies delivering end user products such as handy phones, computers and PDA's, are forced to work strategically with suppliers in the R&D phase, as solution providers and sole component suppliers. If not, development, design and procurement would be far too slow and costly, as the windows of opportunity are not open for long. Successful companies in these kinds of competitive environments will end up with a sharp profile as *aggregators*.

Ask for "Exclusivity"
In certain creative or advisory industries such as consulting, communication, PR or product development, a customer might demand exclusivity. Exclusivity places the customer in a very influential position, which depends on the economic mobility of supplier assets and skills. The customer considers it to be of vital importance that information, talents, solutions etc. remain proprietary.

In most distributor-principal discussions, the struggle for exclusivity and non-exclusivity is a recurring issue and an area of conflict. The distributor is expected to invest in sales and marketing and will seek the return through exclusivity.

5.4.2 The Supplier's Motivation to Invest in Customised Assets?

Customisation of assets to one single customer strengthens the influence of the buyer. Both because such incremental or explicit investments reflect a cooperative seller strategy and because the outcomes in terms of assets with low alternative market value make the supplier vulnerable. In some situations, customisation is the core product. Think of a bridge, an airport parking structure, a hotel or a sports arena on perpetual leasehold. The supplier of such fixed asset services can not very easily re-deploy such assets in a neighbouring county.

The more irreversible and financially immobile a customisation of assets is and hence also the opportunistic temptation, the more comprehensive contractual assurances and arrangements the supplier will request. Trust will rarely be enough of a safety precaution.

Not only is the supplier heavily influenced by asset customisation the customer is as well. The local community will hardly threaten the bridge owner that they will switch over to another bridge. Competition does not exist in this relationship.

Shipyards are forced to invest in specific assets, when they get an order for a vessel, or more frequently, a series of similar ships. The shipyard must establish a project organisation from design, construction to project management to material handling. The dock capacity may have to be changed, staff trained in special welding etc.

The ship owner orders a certain number of crafts and gets an option to contract further units. In this situation interdependence will be the result. The shipyard will have a clear preference to sacrifice other orders with the purpose of getting the maximum return on the market investment in customised assets. But the ship owner will become dependent as well in the option exercise situation because other yards will have both learning and asset efficiency economic disadvantages.

5.5 Influents as a Driving force in Customer Relationships

The triad is at the heart of the analysis of driving forces behind relationships and networks. The triad shapes the dynamic interaction between customer, supplier and competitor. The simultaneous threat of escalating market mechanisms and the necessary contractual modifications is what constitutes the fascinating framework of competing value chains.

Influents represent an independent, multifaceted driving force. From a theoretical perspective, influents are the sum of exogenous disturbances or "noise". From the point of view of the marketer, influents that are present in the close environment may provide opportunities or threats to the relationship – see also introduction of the political economy paradigm in chapter 2.

Influential forces are classified into two broad categories: Invaders versus innovators. *Invaders* are new or established players from the outside whose intention is gaining a share of the market by reformulating the relationship parameters. *Innovators* are the total number of external influents affecting the competitiveness of existing relationships and underlying strategies without having these relationships as their purpose. Whereas invaders are a threatening element, innovators are composed of both threat and opportunity elements depending on utilisation. Or as Chairman Mao said, "When the wind blows up you could either creep into a shelter or build windmills". The role of influents is visualised in figure 5-5.

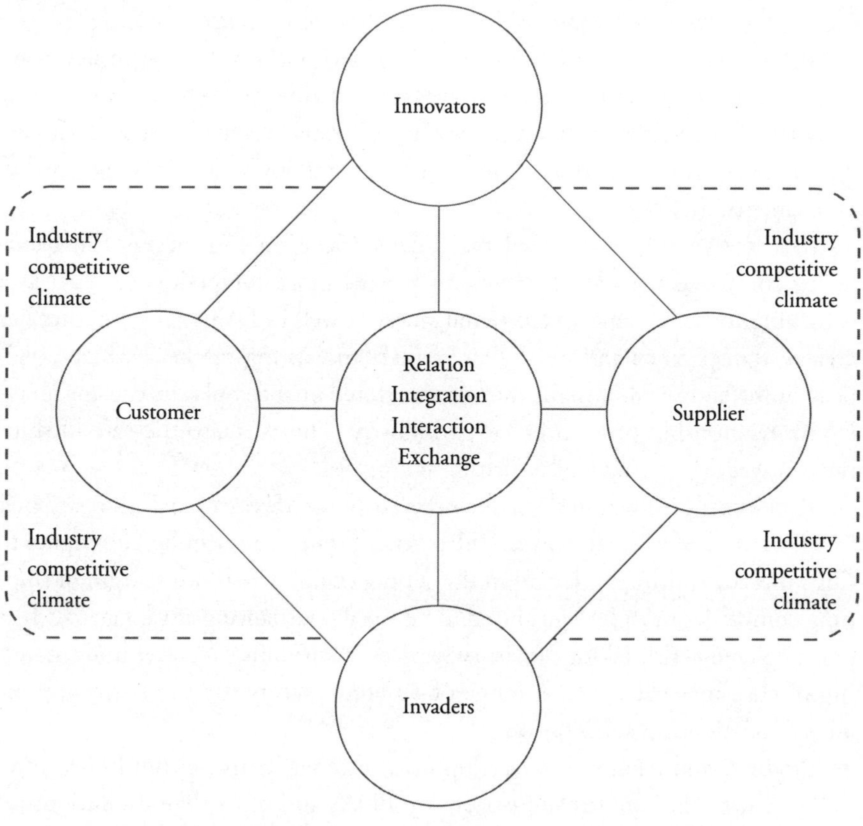

Figure 5-5: Influents in the overall customer relationship picture.

Different industries vary with respect to turbulence pressure on relationships from outside innovation and invasion. Not only does the level of pressure differ, the level of volatility and the unpredictability of changes do as well.

5.5.1 Invaders – New Players with Alternative Strategies

New entrants into an industry often as a spin off of an established firm are usually seen as the most likely type of invasion. New entrants increase the intensity of competition; they add capacity, and they potentially can also stimulate demand.

Invaders relying on a differentiated set of skills do, however, introduce completely new business models and relationship features.

Substitutes – New and Different Relationship Economic Values
Substitution means that new players satisfy generic customer needs in new ways and consequently offer customers different relationship economic values or variations. They either define the industry differently, apply existing resources differently, or they substitute existing business systems by introducing new basic elements.

In a few years it is expected that digital television and increases in bandwidth combined with micro payments will be more competitive and act as a substitute for video tape, video rental stores as well as DVD. The Internet has created transparency and nearby alternatives to existing markets, where previously information and insight were concentrated on a few players causing an effective relationship protection for an industry. This was also the case in shipping, travelling, leasing and securities trading.

Relationship substitutes are not necessarily life threatening if they are met by effective defensive strategies. Video retail groups can acquire copyrights to films thereby shifting backward in the supply chain. The profit margin of shipping companies must be legitimised in new ways, visualising advantages such as granting credit, risk taking, advisory services, positioning, a better understanding of customer needs etc. A range of different factors stimulates the appearance of relationship substitution:

- Product- and relationship development in other industries until now unrelated with the supplier industries, e.g. PDA's and other digital solutions replacing the classic paper calendar.
- New technology or new ways of distribution, dramatically reducing transaction costs while respectively increasing the relationship value, as is the case with the video band compared with a fully integrated digital solution.
- Changed focus among customers – e.g. out- or insourcing.
- New roles and applications – insurance brokers, portals, e-markets.

Invasion by Reconfiguration
A successful *reconfiguration* can develop a unique selling proposition by rearranging, reinventing or shortcutting supply chains and offering more cost-benefit attractive patterns of relationships.

Factory outlets shorten the supply chain from designer-manufacturer to customer. Suppliers of imbedded systems reconfigure the traditional value chain in the computer industry by integrating software into hardware or bundling products. One-stop shops with electronic components and IT have broken traditional borderlines between industries. Reconfiguration is also an opportunity if first mover advantages are obvious.

5.5.2 Innovators – Their Sources, Their Influence and Effects

Fundamentally, innovation is not the only driving force when using actor-based values. However, analysing the outside influential factors on customer relationships and neglecting the importance of innovation enabling forces would be like studying the cheese and leaving the holes out of the equation. We view the innovative element as structural external changes that can be exploited by the relationship participants. New legislation, technology and media are such changes enabling innovative renewal.

The development of EDI (Electronic Data Interchange) is based on new information- and network technology. EDI has changed the relationship between manufacturers, wholesalers and retailers. Reordering, order planning as well as billing become automatic routines not involving any human activity. This reduces transaction and quality costs within established relationships. EDI is an innovation implemented by customer and supplier working together.

Not all suppliers in an industry adapt to external changes and turn them into relationship innovations. In the early stages of interactive TV only a few networks and media communication companies decided to invest in set-top boxes that linked digital and analogue spheres. Interactive TV represents a radical change in the perception and the functionality of the television as media. Set-top boxes and the platform technologies underneath became the enabling factor behind a substantial relationship innovation in the TV and networks industry.

How can a marketer identify and calculate relationship innovative opportunities in the external environment? Fundamentally, there are two different working methodologies. Using the *detective, backward approach* the analyst is systematically searching for ways to improve well defined relationship benefits considered to be important for competitiveness, e.g.: "How can we reduce our customers information costs substantially?" The *screening forward approach* is where the analyst identifies major external changes, categorises and evaluates them eventually into scenarios, e.g.: "How could we possibly exploit blue tooth technology to increase the value of the relationship as perceived by our customers". In most search-learning processes, there will be several instances where both approaches will be utilised.

5.6 Internal Driving Forces of Customer Relationships

The somewhat trivial statement that the value of relationships > the value of exchanges implies that buyer rationality rests upon a relationship logic that coexists with or even defeats the pure market mechanisms. The behaviour of a buyer in any given purchasing situation, to a certain extent, is also determined by some structural elements attached to the relationship. We call such elements the internal driving forces. In figure 5-6 below we have as an example customer relationships as divided into four categories looking at two dimensions only: frequency of interaction and frequency of exchange.

The relationship between a customer and its IT supplier is usually characterised by low frequency in purchasing combined with a high frequency interaction pattern in terms of services, customer service hotline, hosting etc. This type of cooperation is usually regulated in a legal contract of some kind.

The atmosphere and the structure of the relationship is influenced by a variety of independent basic forces:

- *The exchange form* in terms of the core product. Companies do not replace their hardware and software very often, therefore the exchange frequency is low. During the rare purchasing process, when a company invests in new IT, the transaction cost level is considerable. It is not unusual that IT systems procurements run over 1-3 years. It is a very complicated and individualised purchase that involves many users who demand compatibility, integration in workflow and vice versa, technicals support security and many other factors. Furthermore, the buying company will need ongoing interaction with the supplier throughout the lifetime of the system.
- *The relationship form.* The relationship form between a customer and the IT supplier tends to develop in a cooperative rather than a competitive or command direction. The relationship is by nature long lasting and considered important by both parties. The nature of the relationship will often tie the

two organisations closer together than the formal contractual arrangement indicates.

- *The life cycle form.* In the beginning of a project, a delivery or an ongoing relationship, the parties might be unaware of the intentions, style and capabilities of the opposite party, which can lead to somewhat complicated transaction, that place weakening competitive pressure on the relationship. In the later stages, the relationship may move into long-term stability.

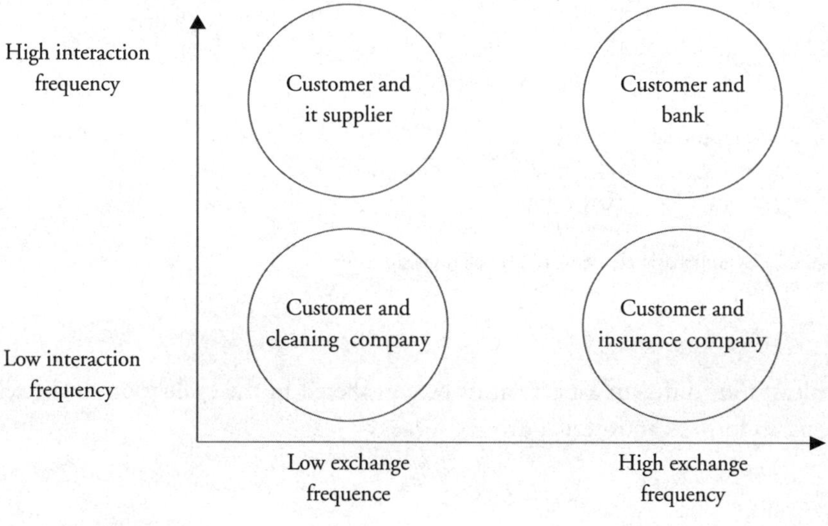

Figure 5-6: Four types of customer-supplier relationships.

5.6.1 What Impact does the Relationship Form have on the Relationship?

The relationship form is determined by the nature of the product, distribution patterns, as well as technology and industry standards. The relationship form is in no way static; it will change due to innovations and competitive pressures.

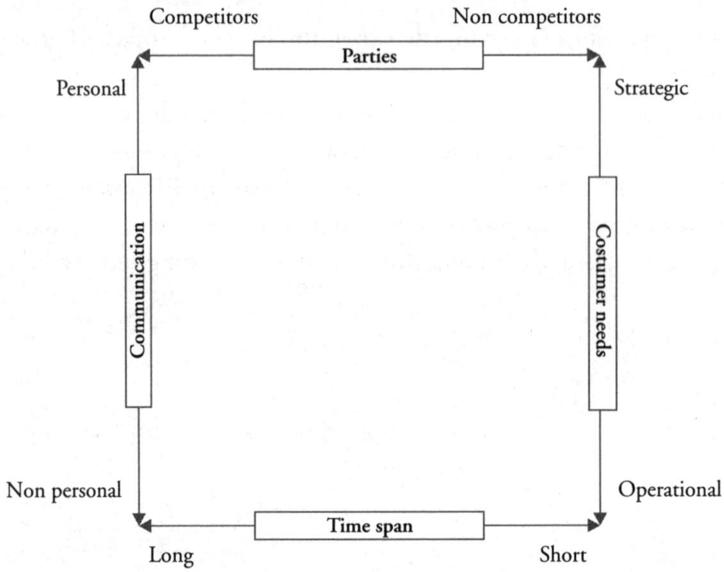

Figure 5-7: Some basic elements of the relationship form.

At least four different aspects must be considered in the evaluation of the relationship form as an internal driving force.

The Parties

In situations where the likelihood of vertical integration is minimal, the potential rivalry between buyer and seller tends to be relatively low. In the opposite case where competition lurks, the relationship form will develop in a more instrumental control-oriented direction.

The Customer Needs

Strategic customer needs in industrial markets means that the relationship form is of decisive importance to either both parties or just to one of the parties involved. JIT (just in time) cooperation between car manufacturers and their subcontractors is a relationship form of strategic importance for the whole industry. The exchanges, components, modules, parts, services, etc., do not differ from the pre-JIT deliveries from outside or from internal departments, but the functional interaction is different.

The car manufacturers have gained significant productivity improvements and cost savings, shortened the production time, as well as reached higher capacity utilisation etc. through the JIT relationship form; the same goes for the subcontractor as well.

Time Horizon

The longer time horizon determined by the relationship form the higher the impact on expectations, interaction, specificity of assets and regulating mechanisms. This is definitely the case with JIT arrangements. More and more companies have realised that a supplier relationship strategy with a promise of long-term commitment is actually advantageous in terms of total relationship economics and quality.

The Communication Pattern

Some relationships anticipate intense personal communication, whereas other relationships are characterised by no or very limited personal contact. The supplier and the customer may only have met through the product or service exchanged. In general, interactivity increases the perceived proximity and lowers the transaction costs. In most industries the increasing level of competitive pressure has forced firms to work in a relationship oriented manner.

Thus the basis of relationships is changing. No longer is it true that a series of episodic exchanges of information, products etc. are considered to be the building blocks that support the developing relationship. Increasingly we find that a different pattern exists. Periodic exchanges are not prerequisites for a relationship to exist. Rather, it is an analysis of the information flows that either is possible or else is required that determines the form that the relationship will take. Such information flows, however, do not just determine the nature of the relationship between the buyer and the supplier. They are far more important than that, they can determine the very structure of how markets operate, acting as the backbone of distribution.

5.6.2 The Exchange Form – the Critical Influential Factor

We have defined the new marketing concept as company behaviour that attracts, maintains and develops relationships that are mutually beneficial for both supplier and customer.[4] In this respect it is an imperative to include the core product characteristic as a driver of relationship elements.

The characteristics of the core product set the scene. Whereas commodities

4. See chapter 1.

like crude oil, corn or transportation services will be exchanged under pure market contracts, personal or advisory services and other types of highly differentiated products will be transacted in a distinct relationship context.

The core product can in most cases be augmented by enriching the customer-product interface developing new relationship features like self-service, do-it-yourself solutions, launching of communities, loyalty clubs etc.

The critical influence of the exchange form can be depicted in a simple model, figure 5.8, which shows the dimensions, or parameters, of the core product as a driving force.

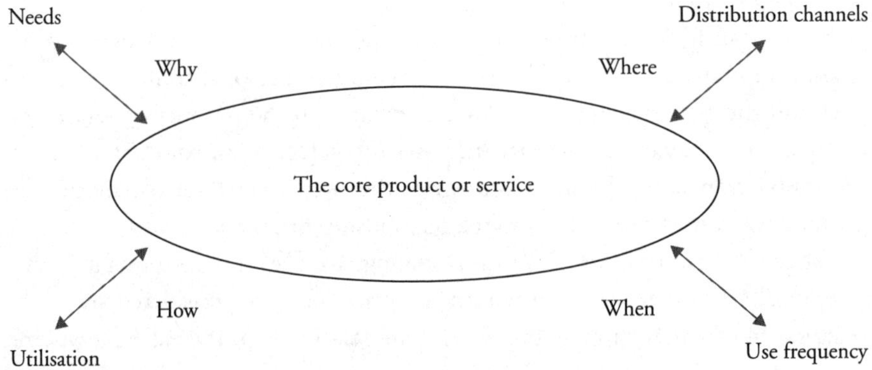

Figure 5-8: The core product as internal driving force.

The same core product covers rather *different needs*; the substance and the diversity of needs covered determines the direction and strength of the core service as driving force. Take air travel. On the same flight you find both business people, alone or in groups or tourists that are either travelling alone or in groups as part of package holidays, where the flight is but one element in the total service package.

The satisfaction of the business traveller is influenced by regularity, in-flight service, ground service level, working facilities, space between seats etc. The tourist pays attention to the movies and the quality of food.

In many cases the *channels of distribution* are crucial for the customer relationship. Those are expectations, transaction costs, risk and opportunism, ties and dependencies. Compare physical stores with Internet shopping. A consumer expects the Internet shop to have lower prices, be open 24 hours and be user friendly. On the other hand, customers do not expect to get professional personal service, and you cannot touch and feel the products on the Net. It is easy to click away and you don't have to feel embarrassed leaving the Internet shop without making a purchase.

Use frequency: Light versus heavy use of a given product or service determines what a supplier can and will do on the relationship front. Frequent buyers tend to be more inclined to engage in cooperative framework agreements. Use frequency will often be a discriminating segmentation criteria.

The *product or service utilisation* differs. Utilisation can sometimes mirror customer involvement and hence also the importance of the relationship. If utilisation of the product is integrated into the core of the customer organisation or at consumer markets and is combined with high loyalty, the impact can be substantial.

5.6.3 Customer Lifecycle – Reinforcing and Dissolution Forces of Relationships

Among the internal driving forces of the relationship customer life cycle is the most apparent. The *diffusion of relationship* is the underlying force and works in parallel to the *dissolution of relationship*. Idiosyncratic reactions tend to pull in the direction of dissolution due to conflict of interest and distrust. As opposed to that the mutual advantages of further exploration or extension of the relationship seem obvious as well.

Some products and services possess the paradoxical attribute that quality and strength erodes in the stable long time stage of the relationship. When companies break their relationship with advertising agencies after some years of intense cooperation the reason most often is that communication solutions become less creative and effective because the parties know each other too well. Adaptation to the attitudes and ideas of the other party might eventually kill creativity and will inevitably lead to conformity and value erosion.

References

Bagozzi, R. P. (1975) *Marketing as Exchange*, Journal of Marketing, vol. 39, pp. 32-39.

Berry, L.L. and Parasuramen, A. (1991) *Marketing of Services: Competing through Quality*, Free Press.

Collins, J. C. and Porras, J. I. (1995) *Skabt til succes – visionære virksomheders succeskriterier*, Børsens Forlag.

Dwyer, F.R., Schurr, P.H. and Oh, S. (1987) *Developing buyer-seller relationships*, Journal of Marketing.

Egan, J. (2001) *Relationship Marketing – exploring relational strategies in marketing*, Peason Education..

Ford, D. (1980) *The Development of Buyer-Seller Relations in Industrial Markets*, European Journal of Marketing.

Ford, D. (1990) *Understanding Business Markets: Interaction, Relationships and Networks*, Academic Press.

Ford, D., Håkansson, H. and Johanson, J. (1986) *How do companies interact?*, Industrial Marketing and Purchasing.

Freeman, R. E. (1984) *Strategic Management – a Stakeholder Approach*, Pitman.

Freytag, P. V. (1991) *Leverandørsamarbejde –Koncipering af en referencemodel Bind I og II*, Samfundslitteratur.

Halinen, A. (1997) *Relationship Marketing in Professional Services – a study of agency-client dynamcis in the advertising sector*, Routledge.

Hallén, L. (1994) *Stability and Change in Supplier Relationships.*

Halliburton, C. W. (1994) *Reconciling Global Marketing and 1-to-1 Marketing. A Global Individualisme Response*, EMAC Conference.

Hedaa, L. (1991) On *Interorganizational Relationships in Industrial Marketing*, Samfundslitteratur.

Heskett, J. L., Jones, T. O., Loveman, G. W., Sasser W., E. Jr., and Schlesinger, L. A. (1994) *Putting the Service profit Chain to Work*, Harvard Business Review, vol. March-April, pp. 164 – 175.

Håkansson, L. (1982) *International Marketing and Purchasing of Industrial Goods: An Interactive Approach*, Wiley.

Koehn, N. (2001) *Brand New: How entrepreneurs earned Consumer Trust from Wedgeod to Dell*, Harvard Business Scholl Press.

Levitt, T. (1983) *After the sale is over.* Harvard Business Review.

Monthoux de Guillet, P. B.L. (1975) *Organizational Mating and Industrial Marketing Conservatism – some Reasons why Industrial Marketing Managers resist Marketing Global Theory*, Industrial Marketing Management.

Nielsen, O. (1995) *Organisationers købsadfærd i grundtræk*, Samfundslitteratur.

Parvatiyar, A. and Sheth, J. (1995) *Contemporary Knowledge of Relationship Marketing.* Emory University.

Parvatiyar, A. and Sheth, J. (1995) *Relationship Marketing in Consumer Markets: Antecedents and Consequences.* Emory University.

Parvatiyar, A. and Sheth, J. (1995) *Toward a Theory of Relational Partnering Governance,* Presentation Materials Emory University for Meeting in Oslo.

Parvatiyar, A. (995) *Evolution of Relational Marketing,* Presentation Paper Emory University for Handelshøjskolen i København.

Penrose, E. (1959) *The Theory of The Growth of the Firm,* Basil Blackwell.

Porter, M. E. (1985) *Competitive Advantage: Creating and Sustaining Superior Performance,* Free Press.

Porter, M. E. (1982) *Competitive Strategy: Techniques for Analyzing Industries and Competitors,* Free Press.

Porter, M. E. (1990) *The Competitive Advantage of Nations,* Macmillan Press.

Prahalad, C.K. and Hamel, G. (1994) *Competing for the Future,* Harvard Business School Press.

Prahalad, C.K. and Hamel, G. (1990) *The Core Competence of the Corporation,* Harvard Business Review.

Robinson, P.J, Faris, C.W. and Wind, Y. (1967) *Industrial Buying and Creative Marketing,* Allyn & Bacon.

Sørensen, C. (1997) *Transaktionsomkostningsteori versus Relationship marketing som paradigme på business-to-business markedet,* IAØ, Handelshøjskolen i København.

Turnbull, P.W and Valla, J. P. (1986): *Strategies for International Industrial Marketing: the Management of Customer Relationships in European Industrial Markets,* Crom Helm.

Turnbull, P.W. and Valla, J. P. (1992) *Strategies for International Industrial Marketing,* Croom Helm.

Williamson, O. E. (1985) *The Economic Institutions of Capitalism – Firms, Markets, Relational Contracting.* Free Press.

Williamson, O.E. (1975) *Market and Hierarchies, Analysis and Antitrust Implications,* Free Press.

CHAPTER 6

Supplier Relationship Levels – Consequences and Contents

When considering relationships it is necessary to define the development stage of the relationship in order to understand the content and potential of the relationship and to appreciate how relationships can differ. Therefore, this chapter is dedicated to understanding the stages that relationships pass through and the types of key account management that a supplier may apply to these steps.

We also introduce the notion that it is not an automatic process where the relationship develops from one step to another on its own but that it may stop at a given step or even return to an earlier step.

Relationships and the way internal processes are organised will differ depending on which stage the relationship is in at any given time. It is this need for flexibility that dictates how the relationship is handled by the supplier as well as the resource allocation with regard to the relationship. But how many variations can be handled within one management system?

The framework introduced here is founded primarily in resource-based theory and transaction cost theory. Its practical application has been tested in a number of industries such as professional services, fast moving consumer goods, high-tech, industrial production, as well as public organisations.

6.1 The Relationship Ladder

Using a ladder to symbolise how relationships develop is not a random choice as the most important benefit of a ladder is the ability to climb up and down, safely and with minimal risk. We will use the relationship ladder to illustrate two important concepts in relationship marketing. The first is that it takes time to climb the relationship ladder. Close relationships don't develop quickly. The second is that the relationship will develop based on mutual exchanges i.e. a proven track record.

Relationship stages, or steps on the ladder, are used to describe the gradual development and different stages of the relationship. It is worth noting that dissolution of the relationship is included in one of the models, i.e. relationships are not expected to continue indefinitely when formed, but may break. Furthermore, the original descriptions of the models all stress that it is important to identify what steps of the relationship ladder are relevant for which customer. Especially important is the total portfolio of relationships, as it may indicate the strength of the supplier, i.e. a majority of high level relationships will indicate a strong strategic position.

One of the questionable preconceptions about relationship stages is that the higher the stage the more profitable the relationship is expected to be. As we discussed in chapter 3 on relationship economics, this may not always be the case. Actually in some industries, the profitability decreases due to increased investments and costs in relationships that are acknowledged to be of crucial importance.

Presented here are four different descriptions of the steps or stages describing the relationship development process. A note of caution should be highlighted here, namely that none of the models deal with how a relationship develops from one step/stage to the next. They simply identify the different and distinctive steps/stages.

Furthermore, it is important to note that relationships only exist when both parties acknowledge the possible benefits. Despite the fact that there are frequent and valuable exchanges between a supplier and a customer, it is not necessarily a close relationship, but could be regarded as a series of discrete transactions.

The four contributions[1] are quite different, and yet the similarities become quite apparent when compared and illustrated alongside each other.

1. Kurzrock (1996), Dwyer et al (1987), Payne et al. (1995), and Kotler (1997). The structure of the figure is based on Egan (2001).

	Kurzrock	Dwyer et al.	Payne et al.	Kotler
		(Dissolution)		
	Partner	Commitment	Partners	Partners
			Members	Members
	Business Consultant		Advocates	Advocates
	Preferred Provider		Clients	Clients
Relationship Marketing		Expansion		Repeat Customers
---	---	---	---	---
Traditional Marketing	Vendor		Customers	
				First time Customers
		Exploration		
	Spectator			
		Awareness	Prospects	Prospects
				Suspects

Figure 6-1: Various relationship ladders.[2]
Source: Kurzrock (1996), Dwyer et al. (1987), Christopher et al. (1991) and Kotler (1997)

An important distinction is made between the steps that relate to *traditional marketing* versus *relationship marketing*. The first group of steps includes potential customers and customers that have completed one transaction, the focus in these steps is to acquire the customer and to establish, if possible, a relationship. This group is characterised by traditional sales efforts and the initial interest in mutual exchange and if possible, making the first exchange. The second group of steps includes repeat customers where the focus is on developing and expanding the relationship. This group is characterised by ongoing exchange and the gradual development of experiences.

2. Is also worth noting the similarities to the loyalty framework introduced in chapter 3.

6.2 The Five Steps of Supplier-Customer Relationships

Treating customers as assets could indicate that suppliers regard customers as something that belongs to a supplier, but that is not the case. The fact is that it may be exactly the opposite. The implications of this are that the supplier cannot control the customer and that the customer cannot and should not be managed; however the relationship itself can and should.

Therefore, the supplier should be able to manage the supplier-customer alignment and the relationship with customers. This may prove to be quite problematic however, as customers pursue different strategies, including some of non-integration with suppliers.[3] This does not exclude the possibility of the supplier managing the relationship and the alignment between the supplier and the customer but it assigns limits to the possible depth of the relationship.

Organisational relationships between a supplier and a customer is described in 5 levels of alignment, ranging from "spectator" to "partner".[4] The five levels are presented below. The inclination of the supplier to develop a specialised transaction structure is commented on in correlation with each alignment level.[5]

Spectator

There is no sales relationship with the customer. The customer deals with the competitors but does not see a need for the supplier's products and services, or the supplier chooses not to work with the customer. This level of alignment does not motivate the supplier to develop a specialised transaction structure.

Describing potential customers as prospects or even suspects indicates that the supplier would like to establish an exchange. At this stage however, neither the supplier nor the customer knows whether or not an exchange will be mutually beneficial. Actually many sales organisations make calculations using a certain level of non-interested and non-relevant potential customers.

Vendor

The supplier is on relatively equal terms as competitors are, supplying products and services to the customer. This level of alignment may incline the supplier to develop a specialised transaction structure.

3. See sub-section 8.1 on "Strategic Behaviour".
4. Kurzrock (1996, p. 121).
5. See also the discussion regarding Aaker (1996) and the loyalty pyramid in sub-section 4.3.

Mutual exchange has taken place in this stage. The supplier focuses on how to fulfil the customer's needs and desires either better or more efficiently. Furthermore, the benefits of continued exchanges will be explored as the basis for changing the relationship from a "one among many suppliers" to "one among few suppliers" or even to be a "preferred supplier". The relationship as such will be "under development" but it is important to acknowledge that it is primarily the supplier that is the active participant.

Preferred Provider

One supplier has been chosen by the customer and has the largest total share of the customers business. The supplier advises the customer with regard to products and services. This level of alignment inclines the supplier to develop a specialised transaction structure.

This step is characterised by several or a series of transactions that have taken place and are taking place. Both parties express mutual interest and acknowledge interest in developing the relationship. Investments are made specifically to support and develop the relationship, i.e. adjustments or developments of interfaces between the two organisations in areas, such as allocation of activities and processes etc.

Business Consultant

The supplier helps the customer manage part of the business. The customer consults the supplier to meet the customer's long-term business goals. This level of alignment inclines the supplier to develop a specialised transaction structure.

The relationship is now based on the supplier's engagement in to customer's processes and activities geared towards improving the customer's benefit from the continued exchange. We see examples of this in industries where the supplier is responsible for the customer's buying and production planning processes. An example could be electricity production plants and their advice regarding when and from where high-volume customers should source electrical energy.

Partner (Ally)

The supplier manages the customer's business in the supplier's area of expertise providing bottom line value that cannot be provided without the supplier. The supplier is considered an integrated part of the customer's organisation. The supplier provides completely integrated systems to run the operation, and the product mix is often composed of the supplier's products and services as well as the competitor's. This level of alignment does incline the supplier to develop a highly specialised transaction structure.

The specialised transaction structure is at this stage idiosyncratic. Both parties acknowledge the mutual dependency and will at this stage have made internal adjustments in order to accommodate this mutual collaboration.

It is important to note that only four of the five steps actually identify a relationship between the supplier and customer, as the first step is merely a question of relationship initiation.

Hence, just four levels are of interest to relationship marketing as they are the ones that describe the interaction and exchange. Identifying the level of a relationship depends on three indicators related to the five steps of alignment, namely the nature of the relationship itself, the access to different levels in the customer's organisation, and the resources invested by the supplier. This is presented in figure 6-2.

	Key indicators		
Alignment level	**Tasks handled for the customer**	**Access to customer**	**Ressources provided**
Spectator	Providing neither products nor services	Limited, usually to gatekeepers	Few or none
Vendor	Providing products and/or services	Limited, usually to lower levels, and to gatekeepers	Product is most important resource – value-added services often provided
Preferred provider	Providing products and/or services	To low and middle levels	Products and value-added services
Business consultant	Providing consulting to help customer meet business goals	To all or most levels	Products, value-added services, and consulting beyond products
Partner/Ally	Managing a function of customer's business: often contractual	To all levels	Sharing and managing resources from both organisations

Figure 6-2: Characteristics of the five levels of alignment. Source: Kurzrock (1996, p. 122).

Figure 6-2 illustrates how tasks handled for the customer by the supplier differs depending on the various levels of alignment. The further down in the figure the more tasks are handled by the supplier. This is also reflected by the supplier's access to the customer's organisation, the further down the wider the access. The resources provided column describes how the exchanges vary in accordance with the alignment level as well.

6.3 The Origin of Key Account Management

The concept *Key Account Management* has yet to be clearly defined by the various theorists in this field. However, it is quite apparent that key account management deals with the supplier's handling of customer relationships. The structure of key account management will be introduced later on in this chapter. Quite often key account management is compared to an iceberg where only a limited part is visible, making it necessary to look beyond the visible part in order to fully understand what it is.

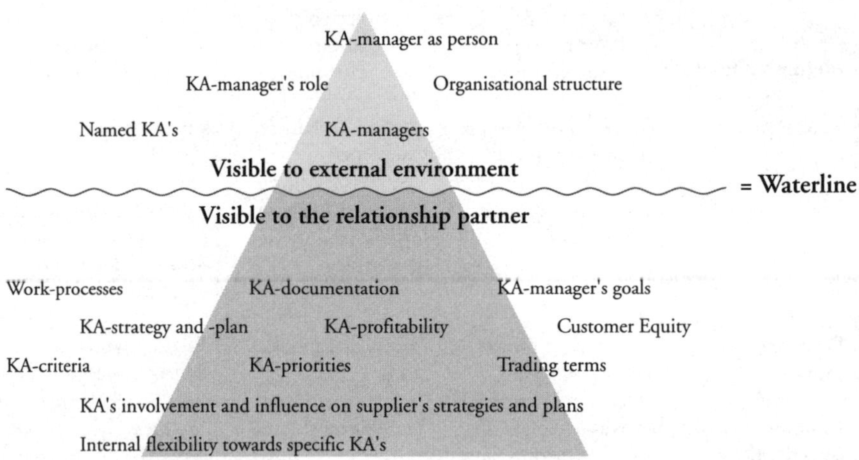

Figure 6-3: The KAM-iceberg. Source: Bjerre (1999b)

The concept *key account management* originated in the IT-sector as the need for treating "key" customers, this typically refers to volume, in a differentiated manner. The movement developed as a consequence of increased need for individualisation of the process, designing the offer to the customer, ensuring correct deliveries, implementing on schedule and ensuring a satisfactory execution.

The first positions as key account manager were filled at the end of the 1960's in the US often as the visible result of increased customer orientation within the selling organisations. Consequently, staff handling customer contacts was regarded as more important than ever and it became popular to illustrate the organisation with the management at the bottom of the illustration and sales staff at the top, see figure 6-4.

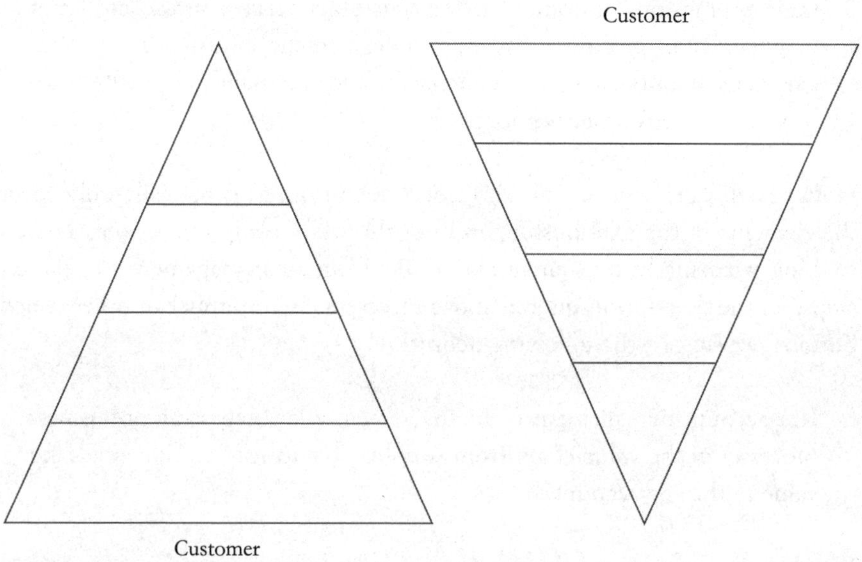

Figure 6-4: The pyramids has been turned upside down. Source: Bjerre (1999b)

Turning the pyramids upside down was introduced by the CEO of the Scandinavian Airline SAS as an attempt to ensure that the whole organisation regarded the customer as the most important person, by placing the customer at the top and the SAS organisation as a support to the customer.

The concept of key account management gradually spread to Europe during the 1970's primarily through the subsidiaries of international IT firms. The first industrial sectors to copy the concept were those characterised by long and complex relationships, i.e. exactly where you would expect to find investments in relationship marketing. By the end of the 1970's, the concept had also spread to fast moving consumer goods and later it has spread to different service industries and even to the public sector.

Defining *key account management* ranges from the very simple to the very complex. One of the more complex descriptions focuses on the elements of the relationship was presented by Moore:[6]

> ... the managerial role in relation to objectives, strategies, standards, monitoring, the coordinating role in relation to distribution department, financial department, sales, consumer marketing, trade research, trade promotion, customer buying, customer stock control, customer merchandising, customer distribution department, customer finance department, the informative role internally and externally and finally as responsible for customer negotiations.

However, this description falls short of a definition, as it basically only covers the elements of the relationship, and not the relationship as a whole. There is nothing particularly innovative about this form of management of relationships. As the description quoted above represents of a number of other contributions[7] we suggest the following definition:

> Key account management is the investment and integration of business processes in the value chain from supplier to end-user aiming at adding value to the key account.

Based on the suggestions above we will use the following definition in the rest of the book:

> Key Account Management is used to describe the supplier's appointment of senior staff that on behalf of the supplying firm is responsible for foreseeing and ensuring the best possible customer relationship. This will preserve the firm's customer portfolio criteria and protect the relationship by developing strong, competitive advantages, efficiently and profitably.

As stated previously, no relationship exists in isolation. Therefore, it is important to recognise that the supplier's investments and activities concerning each

---

6. Moore (1994).
7. Randall (1994), McDonald and Rogers (1998), Pardo. Salle and Spencer (1994).

relationship must be seen within a portfolio of relationships. Furthermore, this also reflects the need for comparing relationships in terms of value creation to the parties involved in the short and the long term.[8]

6.4 Four Types of Key Account Management

There are three distinct types of key account management, of which one can be subdivided into two. Therefore, there are four different types to discuss:

- Contact – one point relationship
- Coordinator
  - Passive Coordinator – customer reflected relationship
  - Pro-active Coordinator – supplier reflected relationship
- Integrator – joint development

The four types can be illustrated in the following manner – see figure 6-5.

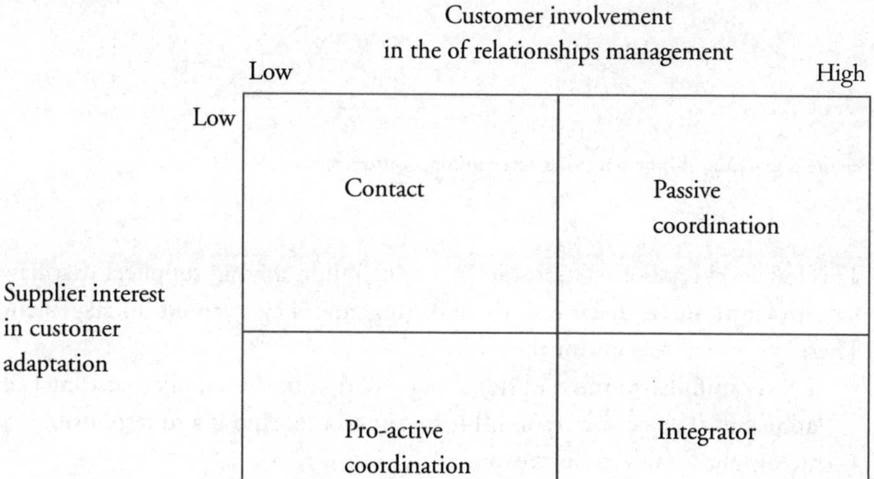

Figure 6-5: The four types as a result of customer involvement and supplier interest. Source: Hougaard and Bjerre

8. See chapter 3 on "Relationship Economics".

The four types have been tested in a number of different industries and may also be regarded as distinct and often sequential steps when a supplier has decided to invest in an organisation that has the ability to handle large and individual customer relationships.

6.4.1 Contact – the One Point Relationship

This type is characterised by the task of handling the interface role between the supplier and the customer and is often referred to as "one face to the customer" (see figure 6-6).

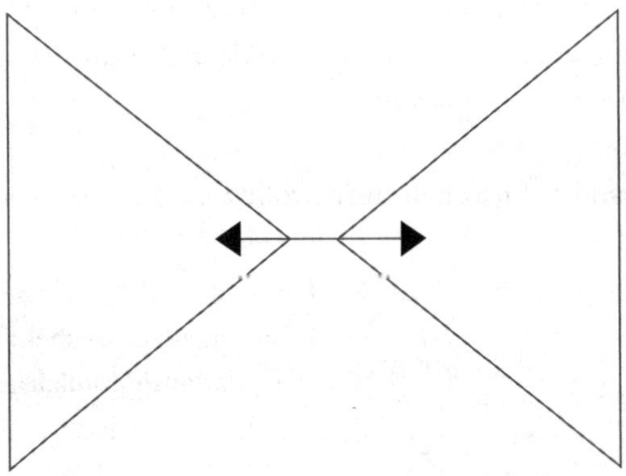

Figure 6-6: Contact – the one point relationship. Source: Bjerre (1999b)

This low level type of relationship is very common among suppliers that have recently introduced relationship marketing and key account management. There are several reasons for this:

- It is very similar to the traditional organisation of the supplier-customer relationship. The person responsible for the relationship is also responsible for the supplier's sales to the customer
- The supplier's own need for managing the relationship and related information is an important factor
- This type may co-exist with a traditional sales organisations (as the need for change is small in terms of changes in responsibility and power)
- The relationship will often be highly dependent upon personal relationships between the people involved
- The need for *new* qualifications is limited

- Recruitment may be internal or external
- Focus of the relationship will be the supplier's sales to the customer

This type is found in industries where exchanges are price focused. Price focus is often the result for one of two reasons: either there is an oversupply of more or less identical products/services, or the industry does not have any past history of developing relationships. The second reason is characteristic of value systems in which all parties independently handle their own tasks without any interference from others.

All dialogue between the supplier and the customer is channelled through the key account manager, i.e. there is no attempt to involve other parts of the supplier's organisation in the relationship.

Customer insights is the responsibility of the key account manager, meaning that information regarding the relationship lies with one individual or if the supplier uses some kind of customer database system the information will be accessible to others. Typically customer relationships are handled in the sales department.

Internal processes will typically not change significantly when the *contact* type is introduced. Actually, changes are seen as desirable at this stage, due to the need for continued handling of other customers whose relationships are not yet developed.

Evaluation of the supplier's outcome of the relationship is based on sales or volume of, in most cases, existing standard assortment of products and services. This is reflected in the choice of key customer, they tend to be large or at least have great potential.

As no idiosyncratic investments have been made, typically there are no entry or exit-barriers of any significance. Competitors can therefore establish competing relationships with the customer and may do so without large investments.

6.4.2 Passive Coordination – Customer Reflected Relationship

Passive coordination is typical of suppliers that have introduced relationship marketing and are experiencing that the customers gradually change from being passive to pro-active. If the supplier does not react to the customers taking over the initiative, it is *passive coordination.* The supplier is basically not interested in adapting either its products or services to suit individual customers, but it must do so due to demands from customers.

Initially, this means that the employee who is responsible for the customers has less time per customer and therefore the situation develops into a bottleneck effect. This situation often leads to contacts emerging between the customer and other parts of the supplier's organisation than the key account manager. What's happening is that the customer gradually makes arrangements directly with the relevant individuals in the supplier's organisation, often without the key account manager knowing about it. Gradually key account management becomes a question of finding out what happened and what has been agreed upon, rather than managing what is actually going on.

The consequence is that the customer becomes the initiating party, as illustrated in figure 6-7.

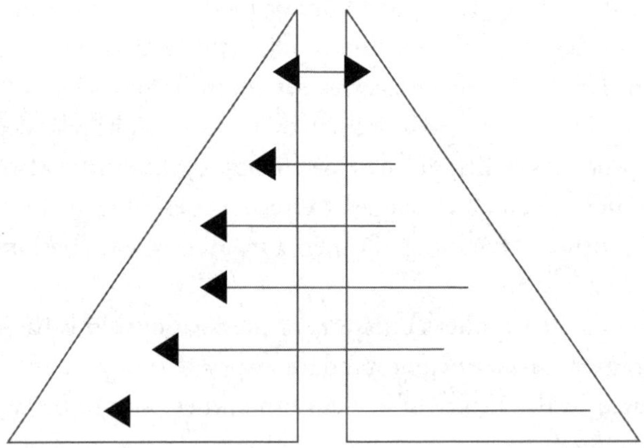

Figure 6-7: Passive Coordination – customer reflected relationship. Source: Bjerre (1999b)

This form can be found among firms with some experience in relationship marketing. Often firms with experience in dealing with powerful customers or customers that have more insight into the value system adopt this passive coordination tactic. Passive coordination can be characterised by the following:

- Passive coordination is similar to the traditional supplier-customer relationship, but differs from this as it is the customer that is the pro-active party and the supplier that is the passive, or adaptive party
- The supplier's own need for insight may to some extent be limited by the activities of the customer and in some case, the customer may know more than the supplier about the value system
- Customer orientation is a result of the relationship, but is actually not de-

sired by the management of the supplier but must be accepted due to competitor initiatives and customer initiative

- Passive coordination can work alongside a traditional sales organisation strategy but will gradually challenge existing systems and routines as demands from customers result in adaptations
- The relationship will often be supported by strong personal relationships between the key account manager and the individuals in the customer's organisation, however, this may happen between several individuals in both organisations
- Recruitment for the customer responsible positions i.e. account managers etc, may be internal or external
- Focus is on sales to the customer and gradually also on customer profitability as a result of the customer's initiatives and negotiations within various parts of the supplier's organisation

The responsibility of the key account manager may gradually increase as a result of the customer's initiatives. This may lead to significant differences between the relationships and with customers, leading to decreased standardisation and increased costs of doing business.

Typically, the key account manager will be located in the sales or marketing department as the focus is looking after the supplier's interests and avoiding any customer adaptations that are not absolutely necessary.

Evaluation of success will be based on well-known indicators such as turnover, volume and perhaps even an early attempt to measure customer profitability. Economies of scale will still prevail as the overall goal, as will the standardisation of processes, planning formats etc. This is a delicate balance, as few suppliers actually have a financial infrastructure that allows them to assign all costs to the individual customer. Actually these suppliers are basically facing the strategic choice: customer orientation vs. standardisation.

As the customer is the initiating party, suppliers often face situations where the customer suggests new modes of collaboration. Sometimes these suggestions may be based on positive experiences from the customer's collaborations with other suppliers, i.e. a supplier may benefit from the investments made by other suppliers having developed new relationship formats or methods.

Considerable entry and exit barriers may exist as the suppliers often will have made customer specific investments. In other words, if a competitor is to enter the relationship with the customer these investments must be matched.

6.4.3 Proactive Coordination – Supplier Reflected Relationship

This model is based on decisions made within the management of the supplier to use customer orientation to pursue its own goals and to recognise the possibilities for developing strong competitive advantages by developing relationships with customers. Quite often these advantages are based on competitor comparisons, i.e. the advantages are not necessarily advantages in themselves, but become so as a result of comparisons with the supplier's competitors. The increased number of contact points is illustrated in figure 6-8.

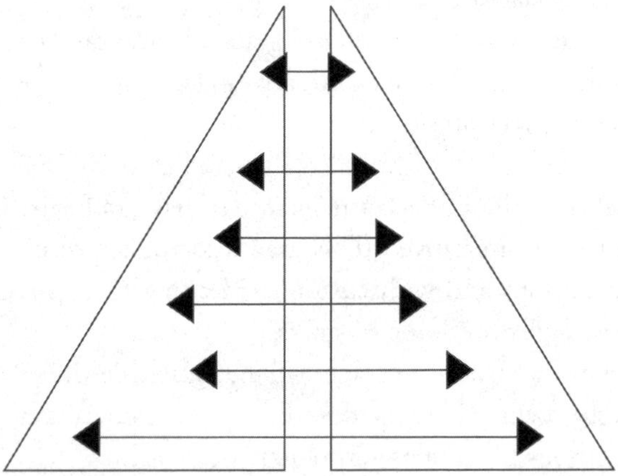

Figure 6-8: Pro-active coordination – supplier reflected relationship. Source: Bjerre (1999b)

This form of supplier-customer relationship is found in firms with considerable experience in relationship marketing and a few firms have actually used this form as their first encounter with strategic relationship marketing. Pro-active coordination can be characterised by several points:

- Pro-active coordination breaks radically with the traditional supplier-customer relationship, as it is built around the customer and relevant customer processes
- The supplier acknowledges that the necessary overview of the individual customer requires a close dialogue with the customer
- Customer orientation is seen as an opportunity to enhance relationships with selected customers while also outperforming competitors
- This form can, to some extent, co-exist with a traditional sales and marketing organisation but the challenges relating to tasks and processes will gradually increase

- The relationship between the two organisations is supported by the personal relationships between various individuals in the two organisations. Furthermore, one could call the exchange taking place a structured dialogue
- Need for new qualification is quite high as many new areas of exchange are included in the relationship
- Recruitment of customer responsible individuals, i.e. account managers, will primarily be internal, as external recruitment will demand substantial resources for training with regard to the supplier's organisation, processes, culture and attitudes
- The role as customer responsible is regarded as being significant in the tactical and strategic development of the supplier
- Focus will be on developing and strengthening the supplier-customer relationship, customer profitability and the customer's profit from doing business with the supplier. Furthermore the aim will be to strengthen the customer's competitive advantages at the operational, tactical and strategic level vis-à-vis competitors
- There will be management recognition and interest in investing in the specific supplier-customer relationship and also idiosyncratic investments.

Furthermore, pro-active coordination requires highly flexible internal management systems and processes. It is not sufficient to have the interest in strategic relationship marketing, the ability or competency is also necessary.

The customer responsible individual will often be part of the sales and marketing department. In some instances, suppliers have chosen to establish separate key account departments, often to highlight focus on these customers. In practice, this will reflect the combination of external customer focus and internal competence/department division. More often this is not a "one man band" but a team with members from all relevant departments in the supplier's organisation. The staffing of the team may change over time, especially when the collaboration is characterised by projects.

This form of the supplier-customer relationship may also lead to situations where either the supplier or the customer will act on behalf of the other, i.e. suppliers ordering on behalf of the customer or involving supplier competencies in the customer's dialogue with the customer's customers.

Such mutual collaboration also leads to considerable mutual impact on each other's business models and processes and possibly a mutually developed management and monitoring system.

Evaluation of the success of the relationship will be based on the supplier's and the customer's benefits from the continued exchange, and the impact of the relationship on the customer's strategic goals. The precise common success criteria should be defined and monitored.

The relationship will be based on considerable, mutual investments specifically geared towards enhancing and developing the exchanges taking place within the relationship. Mutual does not mean shared, but it should be noted that as both parties invest, they both take a risk if the collaboration breaks.

Coordination will also develop informal networks within the two organisations but it is the responsibility of the customer responsible individual that all these networks are known and to some extent coordinated.

6.4.4 Integrator – Joint Development

The integrator model describes a relationship that is very close.

Actually it is so close that it may be difficult to distinguish between the supplier and the customer in terms of organisation, activities, processes and individuals. The term integrator is an attempt to describe the collaboration that has evolved into integration at least in relation to some exchanges. Please refer to figure 6-9 for illustration.

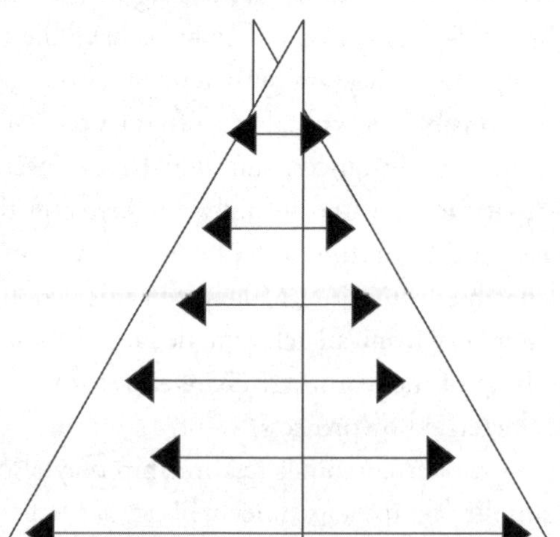

Figure 6-9: Integrator – joint development. Source: Bjerre (1999b)

It is a model that is most commonly known in industries dominated by large, complex and longitudinal projects. The integrator type is only identified in relation to suppliers that have gained experience by applying relationship-marketing principles. It is characterised by the following statements:

- The integrator model breaks radically with traditional supplier-customer relationships as the customer and customer related processes are the basis for all activities and processes within the supplier's organisation
- The individual customer is regarded as an individual market (and may be compared to a geographical market in terms of size and priority)
- The supplier will base its own strategic development on close and strong relationships to chosen customers and will furthermore regard these relationships as the precondition for outperforming competitors
- The integrator model cannot co-exist with traditional sales and marketing organisation, as the challenges to competencies and processes are far too great. The sales process also changes considerably, as the relationship comes into focus, the exchanges taking place within the relationship literally take a backseat
- The relationship between the two organisations is supported by the personal relationships between various individuals in the two organisations. Furthermore, one could call the exchange that is taking place a structured dialogue. This will involve every level of the two organisations from clerks to board members
- Recruitment of customer responsible individuals is only based on internal candidates, as the role often is equivalent to that of a managing director. However, in this situation the individual is not responsible for the whole firm, but for a significant part of it
- As indicated, the role will have significant strategic impact for both the supplier and the customer
- Focus will be on developing and strengthening the supplier-customer relationship, customer profitability and the customer's profits generated by doing business with the supplier. Furthermore, the aim will be to strengthen the customer's competitive advantages at the operational, tactical and strategic level vis-à-vis competitors
- There will be management recognition and interest in investing in the specific supplier-customer relationship as well as idiosyncratic investments. Investments will be planned and evaluated as any other internal investment.

As indicated, the consequences of the integrator model are considerable both internally and in the way the supplier-customer relationship is maintained. Therefore, it is important to decide which criteria to apply when choosing customers as potential candidates for integrator relationships. With this in mind, three basic criteria must be met:

- They have strategic importance
- They are large or have high potential
- They share the relationship marketing mindset

The integrator form is found in industries where a close collaboration will provide opportunities for product and/or service development. It is important to remember that these relationships often will be exclusive, i.e. it is not possible to have similar or identical relationships with competitors of the customer or vice versa. The supplier and the customer must choose.

Describing an *integrator* manager or customer responsible can be compared to the responsibility of a managing director of a subsidiary.

In terms of the organisational solution, this model often requires a separate department or even a separate location. Compared with the three other models, the integrator model represents managerial challenges, primarily related to internal learning from the individual relationships, which are often confidential.

The integrator model is characterised by mutual investments supporting and developing the collaboration that is quite often shared by the supplier and the customer and based on common specifications. Both face the possibility of losing these investments, no matter the reason for the termination.

Evaluation of the relationship is based on audits carried out by both parties in full view, as the supplier will know the criteria used by the customer, and vice versa. As indicated earlier the entry and exit barriers are high and there are serious consequences for both parties if the relationship if it is broken.

The four forms of key account management cover very different types of relationships. Seen from a management point of view it is important to decide which of the relationship models to focus on. This choice should be based on the supplier's own strategic goals and on an evaluation of the potential customer's strategic[9] goals.

We do not regard any one of the four models to be superior, but market conditions and the specific customer's strategy will be decisive factors when choosing the most effective model. Furthermore, it is not a necessity that the supplier changes from the contact to the integrator model, but it is a possibility. Actually we have seen examples of suppliers that have left the coordination

9. See chapter 8 on "The Individualised Approach to Customer Behaviour".

model in favour of the contact model, as a result of changes in the customer's buying strategy and behaviour.

6.5 Is there a Limit to the Number of Customers per Key Account Manager?

A central question in relationship marketing is the number of customers one customer responsible individual can handle, especially if the answer is more than one, then how many?

There is no simple answer to this, but based on the different supplier-customer relationship levels presented above, a number of suggestions emerge. Generally speaking, the number will depend on the level of the supplier-customer relationship and the form of key account management applied. If the contact model is used the number will be higher than if the coordination model is utilised and yet again higher if the integrator model is chosen.

Another consideration is as to the future development of the relationship. If changes and developments are expected to be small and far apart, then there is basically no need for reserving resources or time to invest. But if the potential for change and development is high, the need for reserving resources and time is also high, i.e. handling fewer supplier-customer relationships.

Actually, one individual may not be sufficient based on the resources and competencies needed or simply due to the sheer size of the tasks. Therefore, it is necessary to assign a number of individuals to support the customer responsible individual, partly to ensure sufficient resources and partly to ensure relevant resources.

No matter how many resources the supplier-customer relationship needs, there are a number of different principles that can be used for inspiration when deciding how to combine the handling of more than one customer per account manager or team:

- Customers are allocated based on their buying strategy
- Groups of customers are defined in a way in which they reflect the mix of the total customer portfolio
- Competing customers are handled by different individuals or teams
- Customers are allocated in accordance with the competency requirements within the supplier's organisation

If several customers with the same buying strategy are to be handled by one individual or team, the primary purpose is often to optimise the internal processes of the supplier. The purpose is to learn from one relationship and to transfer learning from one relationship to other relationships. That way, fewer resources are necessary to develop and enhance future relationships. A precondition is that the transfer of learning does not reveal customer sensitive information to other customers.

The portfolio principle may serve several purposes. First of all, the same individual or team will not handle directly competing customers. Secondly, the individual or team will acquire experience by dealing with different types of customers and relationships, and thirdly this diversity may support the development of a holistic understanding of the competencies and capabilities of the supplier's organisation.

Separation of directly competing customers often stems from the customers themselves. In some situations the customer may force the supplier to choose what customer(s) to serve based on the perception that "the relationship to my supplier is a strategic precondition for as well as a part of the continued development of competitive advantages within my company".

Customer demands for supplier competencies may also be used as guiding criteria when deciding which individuals or teams are going to handle which customers. The supplier may actually benefit considerably from this, as the individual or team in question may sharpen the required competencies.

6.5.1 Multinational Relationships – Increased Complexity

Multi-national relationships are characterised by the customer's presence in several geographical markets. Matching such supplier-customer relationships in all markets may prove difficult as the situation often is either:

- *Supplier over-coverage*, meaning that the supplier is represented in more markets than the customer, or
- *Customer over-coverage*, meaning that the customer is represented in more markets than the supplier

Supplier over-coverage is typically easy to handle for the supplier, as the customer can be informed of the markets in which the supplier will be able to establish and operate local relationships. Problems may arise if the supplier's market position varies considerably from market to market or if the customer's market position varies considerably from market to market. The problems are linked to the mutual expectations of performance within the local relationships, especially where there are situations of "mismatch" between the supplier and customer, i.e. a market where there are considerable differences in the supplier's and the customer's market position. These situations may be illustrated in figure 6-10 below.

Customer market position \ Supplier market position	Weak	Strong
Strong	Customer drive to force supplier to expand Mismatch	Perfect match – worthwhile
Weak	"Perfect Match", but is it worthwhile?	Supplier drive to force customer to expand Mismatch

Figure 6-10: Supplier versus customer market position grid.

As can be seen in figure 6-10, the relationships may face difficulties is the "mismatch" situations as the risk for opposing or at least conflicting strategic, tactical and operational goals is eminent.

References

Aaker, D. (1996) *Building strong brands*, The Free Press.

Bjerre, M. (1999) *Key Account Management of Complex Strategic Relationships*, Ph.D. dissertation Copenhagen Business Scholl.

Bjerre, M. (1999b) *Key Account Management – et strategisk værktøj*, Børsens Forlag.

Christopher, M., Payne, A. and Baalatyne, D. (1991) *Relationship Marketing*, Butterworth-Heinemann.

Dwyer, R. F., Schurr, P. H. and Oh, S. (1987) *Developing Buyer-Seller Relationships*, Journal of Marketing, vol. 51, pp. 11-27.

Egan, J. (2001): *Relationship Marketing – exploring relational strategies in Marketing*, Pearson.

Håkansson, H. (1982) *International Marketing and Purchasing of Industrial Goods – An Interaction Approach*, Wiley.

Håkansson, H. and Snehota, I. (1995) *Developing Relationships in Business Networks*, Routledge.

Kotler, P. (1997) *Method for the millenium*, Marketing Business, vol. February.

Kurzrock, W. (1996), The Sales Strategist, Irwin

MacDonald, M. and Rogers, B. (1998) *Key Account Management*, Butterworth-Heinemann

Miller, R. B. and Heiman S. E. (1991) *Successful large account management*, Warner Books.

Millman, T. (1995) *Key Account Management in Business-to-Business Markets*, in A. Payne (ed.) Advances in Relationship Marketing, Kogan Page

Moriarty, R. T. and Sharpiro, B. P. (1980) *National Account Management*, MSI Report, pp. 80-104.

Moriarty, R. T. and Sharpiro, B. P. (1981) *National Account Management – Emerging Insights*, MSI Report, pp. 82-100.

Moriarty, R. T. and Sharpiro, B. P. (1984) *Organizing the National Account Force*, MSI Report, pp. 84-101.

Pardo, C., Salle, R. and Spencer, R. (1994) *The Key Accountization of the Firm*, Industrial Marketing Management, vol. 22, pp. 123-134.

Randall, G. (1994) *Trade Marketing Strategies: The partnership between manufacturers, brands and retailers*, Butterworth-Heinemann.

Rottenberger-Murtha, K. (1992) *A NAM by Any Other Name*, Sales and Marketing Management, vol. 144, no. 15, pp. 40-46.

CHAPTER 7

Relationships in Different Environments

Why is it that relationships seem to develop differently across industries? And why is it that relationships seem to change over time within different industries? Is it due to changes in the environment? Or is it because the conditions in the industry change as they develop?

In this chapter, some of the factors considered to be decisive to the emergence and development of relationships will be discussed. There is no such thing as the "perfect" relationship, but rather relationships are formed and developed under various forms of external and internal constraints.[1]

The classical 5-forces framework is utilised in order to identify and analyse three different relationship spheres; I – the customer's competitive situation as foundation for strategic behaviour, II – the relationship value system, and III – the potential competitors to the relationship value system.

This chapter is divided into three parts; the first part introduces industry characteristics and relationships and discusses digitalisation of value chains as part of the potential competitive analysis. The second part presents reasons for entering relationships, and finally the third part examines the exchanges taking place within a relationship.

7.1 Industry Characteristics and How They Affect Relationships

Relationships do not exist *per se*, and they are not necessarily beneficial to any of the parties involved! The environment influences whether relationships may develop as well as their characteristics. This implies that the relationship partly

1. Internal and external refers to the concept of the political economy paradigm, i.e. internal and external is related to the dyadic relationship between the organisations in focus.

will reflect the external conditions within the industry in which the partners of the relationship operate.[2]

Defining the origin and environment of the relationship, the industry, is complicated due to the changing concept of an industry, from categorising firms according to their output to categorising them according to the benefit they provide to their customers or the problem they provide solutions for.[3] This means that we don't necessarily define an industry by its product or service any longer, but by its placement. This could for example be an industry like marine paints that are defined as part of the marine asset protective industry, or the wallpaper industry that is defined as part of the home decoration industry.

Despite these developments, the original approach[4] to the concept of an industry still holds as it includes a number of relevant analytical tools and frameworks. Dependency on industry characteristics must therefore be described in terms of a number of different analyses and frameworks.

The guidelines on how to analyse an industry are included in several textbooks on marketing. This section is based on the "Noble Art of Industry Analysis",[5] which outlines a three-step approach as described below. However before this analysis, the question of defining industry boundaries must be addressed.

Industry analysis or the definition of an industry, basically builds on the customer needs that are satisfied by the company's product or service. Another way to define the boundaries of an industry could be geography, i.e. the North American car industry, products i.e. dairy products or operational mode i.e. the franchise industry. The boundaries are important, as they reflect the unit of analysis. Furthermore the industry defined by customer needs may allow for identification of potential competitors that do not provide the same product but who fill the same need. For example, when decorating a home the manufacturers of lamps are competing with wallpaper manufacturers, paint manufactures, etc.

In principle, an industry analysis will provide a static and up to date description of the situation, which may not be sufficient to evaluate market potential. Therefore, the analysis should be supplemented by considerations about future developments and trends in the industry. If one were to look at in-

---

2. See also chapter 5 on the "Driving forces of Customer Relationships".
3. Eriksen (1992) and Foss (1993).
4. Porter (1980).
5. Hayes, Jenster and Aaby (1996).This section has been taken much further in "Industry Analysis" in Jenster and Hussey (2001).

ternet-based sales of fast moving consumer goods at this point in time the numbers are not impressive, however expectations for future revenue are extremely high.

Assessing the effects of changes in the industry is difficult, partly because changes are hard to foresee and partly because effects of changes are not always apparent. One way to handle this would be to try to answer the following question: "What could change the way we do business today to the extent that we could no longer sell our existing products/services?" To answer this question the three steps approach may be utilised:

I Customer's competitive situation which is closely linked to the traditional analysis of industry attractiveness

II Relationship value system – may be compared to the business systems analysis, and

III Potential competitor analysis as illustrated in figure 7-1 below.

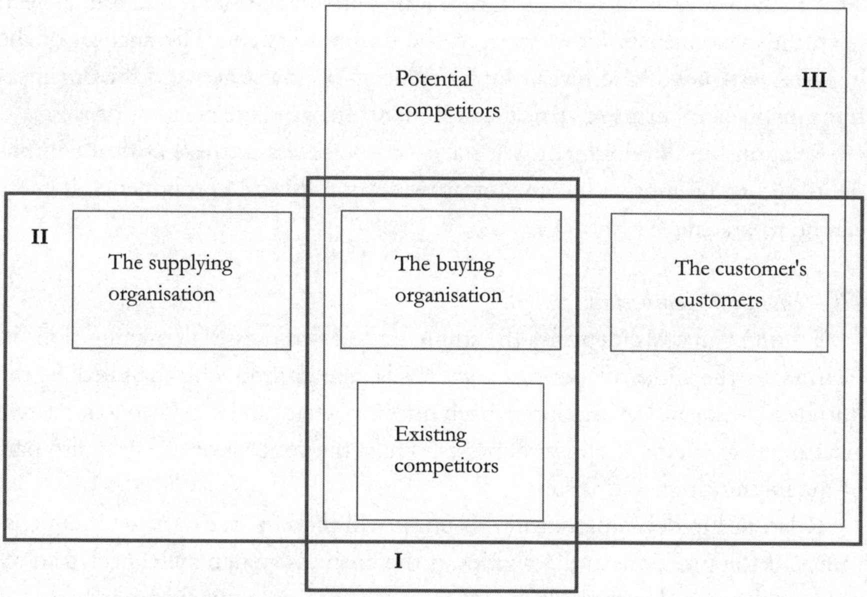

Figure 7-1: Industry analysis – the three step relationship approach.
Source: Inspired by Hayes, Jenster and Aaby (1996, pp. 123-148)

I – Customer's Competitive Situation (Industry Attractiveness)

This first step will ascertain the level of profitability and this level may give an indication as to whether or not it would be interesting to invest in a relationship with a customer in this industry. If profitability levels are high, the inclination to invest in relationships is high, as it is of strategic importance in order to ensure access to the business system of which the customer is a part. Furthermore, if profitability levels are high in one part of the business system, that part may look for opportunities to expand its role in the business system by adding more functions and /or activities.

If profitability levels are low, it may not be attractive to invest in relationships, as it would be difficult to identify the benefits for the selling organisation. However, in this situation it is expected that organisations in the industry may look to suppliers to assist in increasing industry attractiveness, either by relationship development or by enhancing competition among suppliers.[6]

II – Relationship Value System (Business System Analysis)

This analysis reveals the critical and unique parts of the value creation, as seen from the customer's point of view, in the business system. The analysis of the business system will also reveal the distribution of power between the organisations involved in terms of critical components in the value creation process.

Relationship development will focus on the access to these critical components and to be more reluctant towards the non-critical components, if these can be separated.

III – Potential Competitor Analysis

This form of analysis identifies the strengths and weaknesses of organisations in relation to the industry performance levels, the components handled in the business system and in relation to each other or what can be termed as a relative assessment of strengths and weaknesses. Thus, the concept of power is also part of the implications of this step.

Relationship development in this phase will then focus on the winning customers if the functions and activities in the business system are expected to remain unchanged. However, if the business system is in a transitional phase or is undergoing radical change, relationship development may focus on the organisations where changes in the business system are expected and welcome.

One might pause to ask, have you performed an industry analysis on cus-

6. See subsection on risks related to relationships in chapter 3.

tomers, suppliers or even your own company? Few companies do this, primarily because the workload is considerable and because it may be difficult to invest in the resources necessary.

These three steps are examined in more detail in the following three sub-sections.

7.1.1 The Customer's Competitive Position

Analysing the competitors of a customer often provides relevant information related to the strategy, policies and behaviour of that specific company, especially in terms of manoeuvrability and potential. Key elements of competitor analysis are the assessment of the following characteristics:

- Strategies pursued by competitors – basically identifying cost focus and or differentiation focus, serving many or few segments, acting as the innovator or follower, etc.
- Market performance – which implies a description of the players in the industry, their size, their market share, product and service range(s), price, customer relationships and a description of their use of distribution channels.
- Operational performance – in terms of use of resources, use of production capacity and factors such as human resource management, organisational structures and recruitment.
- Financial performance – searching for key drivers of economies of scale, economies of scope etc.

The central point of competitor analysis in the context of strategic relationship marketing is to evaluate the relative strength of the partner in the partner's industry.

The status of the competitive situation may be supplemented by a future scenario by generating strategic options for the competitors and thereby be able to assess the SWOT of the company in focus. If the relationship develops you have to realise that your partner's strengths are an important part of the relationship's potential, and your partner's weaknesses are also an important part of the relationship's challenges.

In order to accurately evaluate a customer's potential for future development, it is also important to analyse the attractiveness of the industry of which the customer is a part. As seen from a supplier's point of view, it is also a question of choosing where supplier resources are expected to produce the highest profitability.

The key issues to assess when evaluating industry attractiveness in a relationship are as follows:

- Profitability – the financial return on capital compared with competitors to the industry, i.e. is it worthwhile to invest at the moment?
- Growth – the opportunity to grow businesses organically by keeping up with basic demand, or is growth acquired by merger and acquisitions?
- Size – must be large enough to be "significant" to "serious players", i.e. economy of relationships must be attainable.
- Customer/risk – the more customers the less risk, see the following section on industry concentration.
- Is it possible to identify potential for changes in these first four elements due to closer relationships to specific customers in the industry?
- Barriers to entry – specifically the analysis of the potential for investing in customised assets and thereby creating difficulties for new players looking to enter the industry, due to capital requirements, special competencies, existing relationships between players in the industry, capacity, etc.
- Characterising the relationship climate in the industry – is there risk of opportunism in the industry?
- Capital intensity – the relative amount of capital required to support revenue stream(s), the more intense the less attraction.

Industry attractiveness may turn out to vary depending on the industry of the observer. It is worthwhile to note that attractiveness may vary at different levels of the business system. For example, an industry may have many suppliers of raw materials, but few production plants, or few manufacturers of computer chips, but many potential customers who produce computers and other electronic devises using computer chips.

The industry attractiveness analysis may prove to be of great importance when assessing the supplier's interest in future relationship developments as illustrated in figure 7-2, presented later.

7.1.2 Relationship Value System

Traditionally, analysis of a business system was based on deconstructing the system into separate activities and identifying the sequence in which they are performed. Taking it a step further, it is then possible to link the sequence critical competencies and critical resources necessary to perform these activities. This we label the "Outside-in Perspective" in the relationship value system.[7]

The business system is defined by the organisation in question, its existing competitors, its suppliers and its customers.

An example of a relationship value system is the media surveillance industry serving its customers by providing news clippings and news summaries. Acquiring news channel access, identifying articles and other points of interest to customers, clipping, organising themes/clusters of news, writing summaries, editing summaries as well as packaging and bundling themes/news.

When analysing the business system, the primary component is the individual activity performed. Initially it is not a question of who does what but what they do. Having identified the components, they are then placed in the sequence in which they are performed. It is important to note that it is common that business systems display more than one linear sequence of components, i.e. may be loops, parallels, doubles (identical sequence copied) or even pauses. Some of these sequences may be performed by different organisations in the business system or within the boundaries of a single organisation.

It is important to stress that the value system analysis is dynamic. Therefore it is not sufficient to analyse the existing business system, but it is as important to identify changes and trends in the business system as well. The dynamic part of the analysis can also provide value to the potential relationship partner as the selling organisation may play an important part in realising changes and new sequences of functions and activities in a modified business system, as is done in detail in the potential competitor analysis.

Knowing and understanding the business systems within which a buying organisation plays a part is important when considering what aspect to focus on in relationship development.

However, another approach to industry analysis is identifying value creation in the business system focusing on scarce resources[8] in the system, such as competencies,[9] tangible and intangible assets or customisation of assets.[10] This analysis is based on the combination of these resources and assets and the output of these. This will often illustrate a whole range of output in which the industry in

7. See also chapter 2 introducing the Political Economy Paradigm.
8. Nelson and Winter (1982).
9. Penrose (1959).
10. Williamson (1975), and the asset specificity.

focus may have a large share. This is called the "Inside-out Perspective" of the business system.

Implications of the inside-out perspective are primarily that existing relationships may develop into others based on valuable competencies and resources applied outside the industry's boundaries. With regard to the earlier example of the media surveillance industry the inside–out perspective would ask: can competencies and resources be used in relation to other partners or other products or services? Or more specifically can resources and competencies such as having offices open at night, staff working at night, knowledge of the individual customer preferences and interest areas, packaging, journalism, writing skills, etc. be used elsewhere?

The important point is to ensure the reader's knowledge of more than just one way of defining competition for competencies and resources. Furthermore the "Inside-out" has the advantage over the "Outside-in" as it originates from the company in question, and not from an analytical point of departure open to all competitors.

Furthermore, it is important not to stop at dyadic relationships but also to focus increasingly on value systems that combine a number of firms. This development runs parallel with Supply Chain Management and some new approaches might be outsourcing or third-party partners or maybe even fourth-party partners.

7.1.3 Potential Competitor Analysis

Analysing the potential competitors of a customer, who will also indirectly be in competition with the relationship value system, will provide insights related to how the customer's customers may be served by different value systems. It is important to note that this analysis goes beyond the existing competitors, as they are part of the first step.

- Potential competitors are identified by using the findings in Step II – Relationship Value System to basically identify the value delivered by the business system no matter whether it is serving many or few segments, acting as the innovator or follower, etc.
- Once the value is identified the search begins for alternative ways of delivering this value. In principle this is a classical analysis of customer benefits that is supplemented by analysis of the alternative value system's strengths and weaknesses.
- Once the alternative value systems have been identified, the search for com-

petitive advantage vis-à-vis these value systems, begins by dissecting in all processes and activities of the relationship value system. These may be found in:

- Market performance – the key success drivers size, market share, product and/or service range(s), price level and/or range, investments in developing and retaining customer relationships, or in use of distribution channels.
- Operational performance – in terms of the use of resources, use of production capacity and factors such as human resource management, organisational structures, recruitment.
- Financial performance – the key drivers of economies of scale, economies of scope etc.

The central point of the potential competitor analysis in a strategic relationship marketing context is to evaluate the relative strength of the customer in the customer's industry as well as the relative strength of the relationship value system compared to value systems outside the customer's industry.[11]

The status of the competitive situation may be supplemented by future scenarios in order to generate strategic options for the potential competitors and thereby be able to assess the SWOT of the customer in focus. If the relationship develops you have to realise that your customer's strengts are an important part of the relationship value system's potential, and your customer's weaknesses are also important parts of the relationship value system's challenges.

Combining findings from the customer's competitive situation with findings in the relationship value system analysis and the potential competitor analysis will provide a matrix illustrating where to focus on relationship development and where not to do so. These considerations are summarised in figure 7-2.

11. See sub-section 7.3 on relationships in digital value chains.

		Relationship value system strength		
		High	**Medium**	**Low**
Customer's position vis-à-vis competitors	**Strong**	Invest in relationship for growth	Protect and improve relation and profit	Exploit relationship and improve profits
	Medium	Improve relationship and profitability	Ensure relation	Invest only to harvest and reduce costs
	Weak	Focus on profit, not on the relationship	Avoid investments or development of relationship	Prepare to exit or slow wind down

Figure 7-2: Prioritising where to develop relationships and with what purpose.

This matrix suggests where to invest in relationship development and where not to. It also suggests the purpose of relationship development. The combination of high relationship value system strength and the strong competitive situation of the potential customer, suggests investment in relationship development with the focus on growth, i.e. go with industry leaders and assist them in maintaining their position. However a combination of low relationship value system strength and the weak competitive situation of the potential customer suggests that investments should be withdrawn from the relationship as neither the industry nor the potential customer appears to be attractive.

As illustrated above, the spotlight is not on industry analysis per se, but on the strategic decisions related to relationship marketing, with special focus on the impact of the customer's strategic situation.

7.2 Industry Concentration

Industries often share "paradigms" for relationships in terms of type and content. In some industries, such as telecommunications, joint ventures are sometimes formed between competitors. But only if the joint venture is active in a geographic market where the parties do not compete. In this way, relationships among competitors can exist and develop across organisational boundaries.

In other industries, such as the ice cream industry, competition is fierce in the local as well as international markets. Situations have occurred where ice cream manufacturers have physically removed the freezer and its contents of its competitor from several retail outlets and replaced the freezer and its contents with its own brand. Therefore, relationships between competitors are not possible in this industry.

Besides industry characteristics[12] supporting these paradigms, the concentration of the industry also plays an important role in how relationships develop in a specific industry. As initially mentioned in chapter 2, all relationships possess both inner and outer environmental influences. The industry concentration is located in the outer environment. Industries can also be described in terms of market share distribution or concentration as well as the number of companies that exist within the industry as a whole as illustrated in figure 7-3.

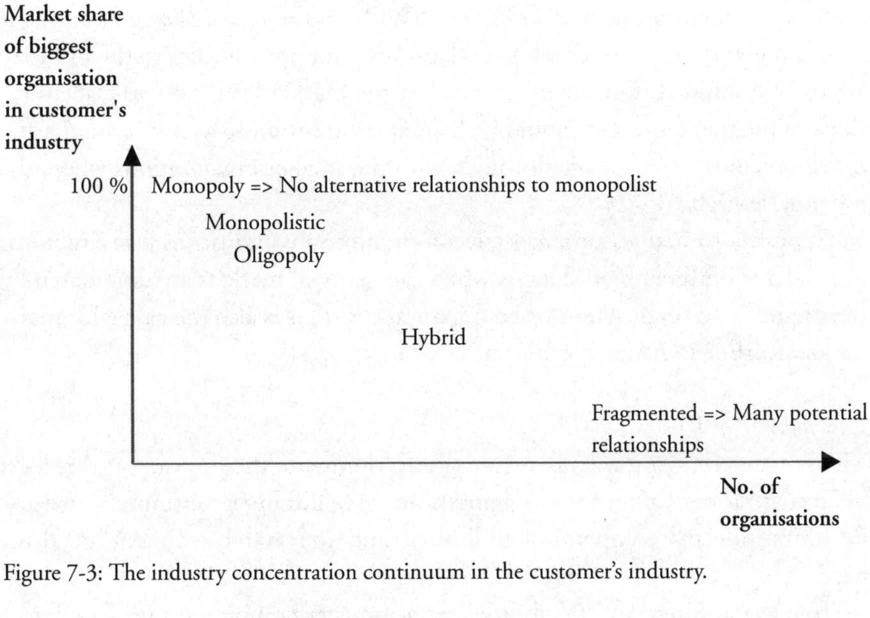

Figure 7-3: The industry concentration continuum in the customer's industry.

Figure 7-3 indicates whether or not a supplier has the choice between many different alternative relationships, or if the supplier is more or less forced to establish a relationship to the only customer in the industry. This is merely to ensure that we discuss the supplier's interest in developing relationships with a

12. See also chapter 5 on driving forces of relationship development.

customer in the industry concentration context, as will also be discussed under the "Monopoly" heading.

Monopoly

This type of industry is characterised by just one organisation dominating the market or, as is often the case, the industry may be labelled monopolistic when there is one very big organisation and several small ones.

Smaller companies will constantly challenge the market leader, either by lower prices or by specialisation in serving niches or segments also labelled *segment nippers.*

The expected relationship[13] strategy in this case would be to develop relationships with the market leader. However, market dynamics may suggest relationship development with one or more of the challengers as well, depending on the assessment of the market leader's SWOT. If the market leader is strong it is absolutely necessary to develop a relationship if opportunities in the industry are to be examined. On the other hand, if the market leader is weak, relationships to the market leader should be kept at a minimum so as not to hinder the development of strategic relationships with the smaller organisations where the potential is high.

Suppliers to many European telecommunications industries face situations like the one outlined here. That is when the national markets are dominated by the original and often state-owned organisation. This is also the case with many national airline industries in Europe.

Oligopoly

This is when only a few large organisations dominate the industry at this level of concentration. Often these organisations serve different consumer segments, i.e. intra-industry competition is limited and they rarely compete head-to-head.

In relationship terms, the limited intra-industry competition implies that it may be possible to develop relationships with all these organisations at the same time. However, the contents and the structures of the relationships may vary considerably depending on the potential partner's strategy. Relationships beyond the operational level may be mutually exclusive, as strategic relationships may be used as a basis for future competition.

The international airline industry is an example of an oligopoly where

---

13. See also the contribution by Reichheld in figure 9-1.

many organisations serve several airlines, for example airline catering at a specific airport. But when it comes to developing new menu's or new dishes, or even more radical elements such as developing new food processing techniques, the relationship often becomes strategically oriented and therefore results are not shared outside the dyad.

Hybrid

Hybrid industries are characterised by some medium-sized, some small and some developing organisations. Market dynamics are often high and changes are frequent.

At this level industry concentration competition is intense, and it may be quite difficult to develop simultaneous relationships to organisations within the industry, as they can be difficult to handle. Competing organisations may demand either exclusivity or guaranties of confidentiality. This situation will force the selling organisation to be careful when choosing which organisation to approach first, second, third, etc. as relationships to these "first choices" may prevent the development of relationships to other organisations.

As is often the case, many examples of "real-life" can be found in the middle of the relationship development continuum. This is also the case for the hybrid level of industry concentration. Examples of such industries are advertising and communications, FMCG retail, home furnishing, among others.

Fragmented industries – in principle close to "perfect competition"

In this case, basically no industry concentration is observed. All organisations in the industry are small in terms of market share. The competition is typically fierce, margins are generally low and the search for lowered production costs is intense. Very few organisations will attempt to pursue a differentiation strategy in order to fulfil niche demands.

Relationship development at this level of industry concentration will typically be based on a low investment approach and a desire to re-use solutions and processes in as many relationships as possible.

One example of a fragmented industry is the metal shops that serve the windmill industry. Although the metal shops may desire to develop tighter relationships with a specific producer, the producer does not see the need for this, as the risks of not having a relationship are considered minor.

The different levels of industry concentration summarised above all describe a static situation. However, most industries are in a constant state of flux either at a slow or fast pace. The consequences are that the level of industry concentration may change, or that the conclusions regarding the individual organisation may change, i.e. that an organisation previously considered to have a strong position has weakened or vice versa.

Industries in transformation pose a more intriguing problem, as this raises several questions seen from a seller's point of view. Actually the points stressed below are equally relevant to buying and supplying organisations. These issues specifically concern the business system, i.e. the division of activities in the industry. Basically, an organisation may change the business system in four different ways:

Active approach to industry transformation
- Take-over – Acquire the partner
- Change – Choose another partner
- Do-it-Ourselves – Develop the process, the resource etc. ourselves

Passive approach to industry transformation
- Wait – Let the battle be fought – waiting to see a winner

These options address key elements of the company's own strategy and how the organisation perceives itself. But they also emerge from your partner's point of view, i.e. in times of transformation the uncertainty increases choosing which relationships to enter and which to break can be very difficult.

Take-over
This step requires that a take-over be considered a strategic advantage to include the activities and processes of the partner. Reasons for this may include exclusivity of the output and competencies of the partner, or it may focus on potential benefits stemming from improved coordination, improved exchange etc.

Change
Choosing another partner is dependent on the existence of other potential customers, and that these potential customers are also interested and willing to do business with you. This is where the identification of future winners among potential partners is necessary.

Do-it-Ourselves
This means building and developing the necessary competencies and capabilities within the organisation. To evaluate this will often be a "make or buy" decision, applying economic tools and principles.

Wait
This is the patient method. Keep cool and let the process of "natural selection" go undisturbed. In terms of relationship marketing, there is not much strategy related to this approach.

One of the ways of coping with change is to try to lock-on to the development among the company's customers, i.e. to develop and nurture relationships with the winners among your customers. This is how LEGO has decided to cope with changes among their retail customers around the world. Lego's statement with regard to the realisation of its goals is: "We will achieve our goals by growing with the leading customers".

The LEGO example raises another important question having to do with relationships, namely the geographical reach of the relationship. This may be a decisive factor as costs of match and content of match must be investigated. Some of the levels of the geographic reach are:

- Local – typically a one to one firm relationship
- National – often a one to one firm relationship
- Regional – often a several to several firms relationship
- International – typically a several to several firms relationship
- Global – always a several to several firms relationship

Global relationships are present among a number of multinational corporations (IBM, ABB, DHL, Siemens, Procter & Gamble, etc.) that are organised into a lobby called a Global Forum. They meet to discuss how global relationships may be improved simultaneously from both a supplier and customer viewpoint.

An interesting point in these discussions is the focus on one relationship at a time, i.e. although they spoke of "programmes, systems and the like", nothing is standardised to the point where the specific characteristics of the individual partner is set aside.

7.3 Relationships in Digital Value Chains

Relationships in the physical world have been the basis for most contributions so far. But going digital opens up new relationship possibilities in terms of communication and collaboration. In a strategic relationship-marketing context these possibilities are interesting and exciting. Therefore digital value chains deserve closer examination.

Information technology plus the Internet has pushed modern economies in a network and virtually oriented direction. There is no doubt that this mainstream development creates a different kind of environment for a marketer. Not only are relationships at all levels influenced by this new interactive one-to-one mode of communication, so are products and services. The big question is whether this *digitalisation push* has any impact on our understanding of what relationship marketing strategy is all about. And whether or not the basic definition of marketing must be revised.

We believe that virtualisation actually will inspire and improve relationship marketing possibilities, not the reverse, even though customers' switching costs decrease:[14]

> Customers in bricks-and-mortar stores leave no record of their behaviour unless they buy something and even then the data is incomplete. But in virtual stores, their shopping purchase patterns are transparent. Every move they make can be documented electronically, click-by-click. If a customer exits a website when the price screen appears, it's a fair bet that he is price sensitive. If he jumps from page to page without ever initiating a transaction, he's probably frustrated at being unable to find what he wants.

Basically, the Internet has caused a reduction in transaction costs. Some observers have seen this trend as a return to a situation of market perfection, where relationships are considered to be disturbances and are irrational. Minimal transaction costs will more or less eliminate idiosyncrasy, as it is easy to escape and return to pure market mechanisms.

A recent Michael Porter[15] article seems to represent a return to fundamentals:

> It is hard to come to any firm understanding of the impact of the Internet on business by looking at the results to date. But two broad conclusions can be drawn. First, many businesses active on the Internet are (were!, ed.) artificial businesses competing by artificial means and

---

14. Reichheld and Schefter (2000).
15. Porter (2001).

> propped up by readily available capital. Second, in *periods of transition* such as the one we have been going through, it often appears as if there are new rules of competition. But as market forces play out, as they are now, the old rules regain their currency. The creation of true economic value once again becomes the final arbiter of business success.

According to Michael Porter, in the early days Internet market signals were unreliable. This *distortion of market signals* have inspired a lot of well established companies and all the dot.coms to change their view of relationships in the direction of pure exchange. Furthermore, it is now assumed that traditional supply chains could be easily outperformed by new, short cost effective value chains.

The virtual environment of business has definitely lowered switching costs. A relationship market strategy based on transaction cost leadership[16] therefore has two opponents to defeat: The first is the mere transaction cost decrease which all suppliers can benefit from due to the common breakthrough of technology. The second is the perception of low friction, which influences other areas over and above transaction costs.

The Internet has made it easier to customise packages and obtain *network effects.* Both forces act in favour of a differentiation based relationship marketing strategy.[17] A network effect means that a product or service becomes more valuable as more customers use it. A number of important Internet applications displays network effects, including e-mail, instant messaging, auctions or communities. Where such effects are significant, they can create demand-side economies of scale and raise barriers to entry. Relationship thinking will often imply network effects.

Internet technologies have made it easier for companies to coordinate with their suppliers leading to more partnering based on outsourcing. *The virtual enterprise* is a business largely created out of purchased products, components and services. A virtual enterprise is a conductor that leaves the majority of the value chain profits with their partners:

> Networks can flourish only if their orchestrators protect the welfare of all companies on which they depend – partner or customer.

16. See chapter 9 on "Generic Relationship Strategies".
17. See chapter 9 on "Generic Relationship Strategies".

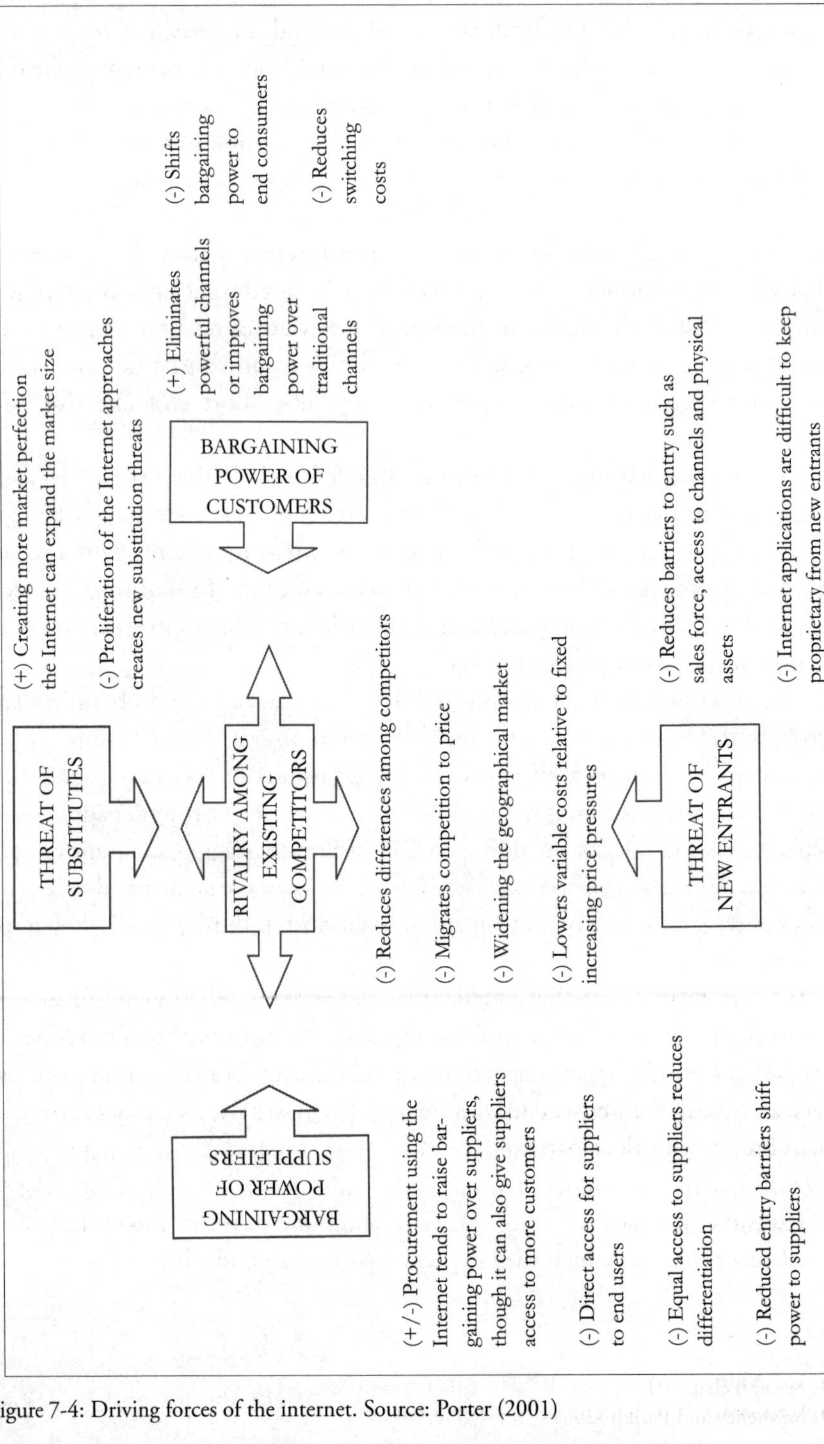

Figure 7-4: Driving forces of the internet. Source: Porter (2001)

This idea supports the cooperative regulating mechanism of relationships leading to interdependence as opposed to a win-lose command or a competitive marketing rationale.

How the Internet influences industry structure and hence also the relationship environment is illustrated as in figure 7-4.

Virtual value chains change the whole marketing environment. The value of a network is its functionality. That is the ability to distribute, store, assemble, utilise and modify information. Networks combine richness and reach of information[18] and create an atmosphere of power in relationships based on information distribution. Therefore, a network where partners do not share intelligence in the dyad is not likely to gain competitive strength.

Both the marketer and the customer will try to capitalise on what is called *intelligence migration strategies.*[19]

Arbitrage

Because intelligence can be located anywhere in a network, there are often opportunities for moving particular types of intelligence to new areas where the costs of maintaining the intelligence is lower. These are typically labour-intensive operations.

Aggregation

As intelligence de-couples, companies have the opportunity of combining formerly isolated pools of dedicated infrastructure that can be provided over a network. Consulting firms do so through curriculum vitae databases and personal competence profiles. Portals such as Netdoctor.com (health) and Smartforce.com (e-learning) have the aggregation of knowledge as their value proposition.

Rewiring

In essence, this strategy involves creating an information network that all participants connect to and establishing an information exchange standard that allows participants to communicate. Virtual office solutions that enable people to work together on the same project, sharing documents and background information is an example.

18. See also chapter 1.
19. Sawheney and Parikh (2001).

Reassembly

Another new kind of intermediary creates value by aggregating, reorganising and configuring disparate pieces of intelligence into coherent, personalised packages for customers. This is the case with a company called Morningstar.[20] Morningstar collects a comprehensive amount of data from and about investment funds. Morningstar measures funds using 80 different benchmarks. The data collected are sold to the investment funds as in-frames, advisor tools, ratings, co-publishing etc. Morningstar adds reassembly value and the funds are both suppliers and customers – the dog eating his own tail!

Digitalisation is a puzzle for companies across industry boundaries. No one can avoid the disturbances, which can be both opportunities as well as threats, in the transition to virtual value chains.

If relationships are like diamonds, one could ask: Are diamonds forever or will virtual value chains gradually erode the concept of loyalty?

7.4 Relationships Across the Industry Life Cycle

Having discussed the industry attractiveness and concentration, the business system and possible changes due to digitalisation as well as competitor analysis techniques, it is now time to turn to the development stage of the industry.

The actual stage of the industry life cycle tends to influence the inclination to develop relationships, especially strategic relationships. Therefore there are links between the stages of the industry life cycle and possible relationships.

But first the concept of power must be considered, as power is one factor discussed jointly with relationships. The presence of power centres may be the reason for developing a relationship even when there are not necessarily shared interests per se. Power centres can be quite diverse and can be discussed in terms of size, resources, expertise, information, future potential, etc.

A one-sided relationship[21] is when one party forces the other to enter and maintain the relationship, despite the opposite party's intention. At best, the one-sided relationship is beneficial to one party and without negative consequences for the other.

Power as a concept has been defined earlier, but the way power may support a one-sided relationship is as follows:

---

20. See page 126.
21. Reichheld and Schefter (2000).

- Size – the customer has a large share of our business, and we cannot afford to lose this business. Often very important in companies basing their performance on economies of scale
- Resources – the supplier has a monopoly on certain resources, or plays a significant role for our value creation
- Expertise – we cannot do without the specific element/item/component – an example could be Intel microprocessors
- Information – we need to know what is going on in our customer's business – or at the next level of the business system
- Future potential – we cannot develop our business without the relationship, as the partner is regarded as a first mover
- Future winner – we stick to the winners of the future, if they survive and we have a relationship with them then we survive also.

It may be assumed that relationships develop as the industry develops. Industry development stages are defined in the following text.

Embryonic

Embryonic industries are characterised by low or no price competition as there is a customer or demand surplus in the industry, i.e. customers and demand is plentiful. This is of course related to the identification of undiscovered needs or the fulfilment of known needs superior to present offerings.

As most players in the industry are new, and thus unknown and without a reputation, there is low brand loyalty as few preferences have developed among customers. References do basically not exist and the level of information uncertainty is rather high.

Limited competition between the organisations in the industry is reflected by the low level of rivalry that exists, i.e. resources and production have not yet reached the level of full capacity and the demand exceeds supply.

At this stage in the industry life cycle, a central question is: "Why bother with developing relationships?" Furthermore, at this stage everybody will have a chance to survive the following stages of development, and it is far too early to identify winners, their strategic behaviour and the competencies and assets they posses. This may be a cynical approach but what can be done about it?

Although relationships at this stage of industry development are rarely close, experience shows that they may have considerable impact at later stages. This is an extremely important point, namely that relationship development also should be seen in terms of path dependency. This path dependency reflects once again that a relationship rarely exists without any external influence either current or historic. This form of dependency will therefore reflect all past exchanges and the way in which the involved organisations and individuals behaved along the way. Actually, there is a parallel that can be drawn from our own lives. This concept works the same with personal relationships as some develop positively and continue to do so, while other relationships deteriorate either gradually or abruptly.

Growth

As the industry expands its supply, more and more customers see that their needs and desires are fulfilled. However, demand still exceeds supply and price competition is low.

The industry is still young and the brand awareness is low, as is the loyalty towards these brands. The primary reason is lack of experience with the individual brand and insight into comparisons between the brands and the organisations behind them. Rivalry between members of the industry is low, primarily because the winning strategies in the industry haven't as yet revealed themselves clearly.

The industry will gradually approach equilibrium between demand and supply. This means that the overall rivalry in the industry will be low except in specific areas such as special competencies, use of patents etc. this may be different.

Developing relationships becomes more visible as they gradually emerge between companies who share a collaborative strategy and who also share a willingness to devote resources to relationships. Another type of relationship may develop namely the one-sided relationship as attempts to develop relationships are carried out. Relationships are thus characterised by strong belief in and expectation of future benefits.

Shakeout

As competition increases and the supply gradually exceeds demand, rules of the game will change. Price fluctuation will often be the first reaction to increased competition, and the secondary set of reactions is that the players will begin to look outside their organisational boundaries to identify opportunities for cost reductions.

The third set of reactions is often to focus on differential opportunities, i.e. where it is possible to differentiate our offering to the customers. This will lead to an increased or at least emerging interest in customers' preferences and investigations into where and how relationships may be established. Differentiated market offerings may gradually lead to brand awareness and brand loyalty.

Competition will, beyond price, also be dependent on who gets which business with which customers as the level of rivalry increases. Therefore, some of the players in the industry will begin to look beyond their borders to identify opportunities for differentiation and value creation.

It may become strategically relevant to develop relationships when battle really begins in the industry. Gradually the companies setting the pace in the industry emerge and separate from the followers. During this process the company must aim at the potential partners with an optimal fit.[22]

As the winners will take it all, it is crucial to identify the winners and to identify generic winning strategies and the related key success factors. The focal point of analysis should be where could we, together with our customer, strengthen the *relevant key success factors.* At the same time it is important to identify areas where a relationship basically would make no difference and thus to stay away.

Mature

Mature industries typically display either low or medium price competition, depending on the size of the exit barriers, as the remaining firms have often settled in terms of maintaining customer demands. This reflects the situation where there is low or medium rivalry between the organisations as they focus on optimising their supply to the customers rather than acquiring new customers.

Reputation and experience exist between suppliers and customers, i.e. high brand loyalty is quite common.

Mature industries tend to possess common understandings or paradigms regarding the nature of relationships exist and the content. Mature industries are often characterised by strong strategic interest in developing and maintaining relationships. This is also important, as changes in the industry are slow and when changes take place, for example when one supplier is replaced with another, it often has considerable impact on the supplier that looses the relationship. Relationships are at this stage of the industry life cycle very important, and often to be regarded as strategic assets.

Decline

Declining industries may display both low or high price competition and ri-

22. See chapter 10 on relationship balance system.

valry. It depends on the capacity and the exit barriers within the industry. In some situations organisations leave the industry due to lack of future potential and such industries may continue to be profitable for the surviving organisations. Such industries will display high brand loyalty at least among the remaining customers.

Industries in decline must be regarded as strategic cash cows, and existing relationships should be protected. However, investing in new relationships or expanding existing ones does not seem to have strategic impact or make sense.

Summarising these arguments, figure 7-5 emerges.

	Price competition	**Brand loyalty**	**Overall rivalry**	**Relationship**
Embryonic	Low	Low	Low	Why bother
Growth	Low	Low	Low	Developing
Shakeout	High	High	High	Strategic relevant
Mature	Low/medium	High	Medium/high	Strategic interest
Decline	Low/high	High	Low/high	Strategic cash cow

Figure 7-5: Relationships related to the industry life cycle. Source: Modified from Hill and Jones (1992)

7.5 Relationship Contents

When analysing relationships, it is rarely specified what is exchanged within the relationship. Therefore, a central question is what is actually exchanged in the relationship, i.e. the relationship is primarily a vehicle for exchange and ongoing development of the mutual relationship and business.

With regard to different types of relationships, the level of interaction may differ, and this is also true when focusing on what is exchanged.

Before discussing what is exchanged, a model to describe exchanges taking place within the dyad will be introduced. That is Ford's definition of "episodes" or specific exchanges or transactions and the relationship atmosphere, which is regarded as the result of a series of episodes. Therefore, a relationship must be regarded at more than one level – as we have earlier referred to as the internal and external level:[23]

- Internal – the exchange between the partners
  - Episodes – product or service
  - Information exchange
  - Social exchange – leading to relationship atmosphere
  - Financial exchanges
  - Balance – power and dependency
  - History and experiences
  - Expectations

- External – factors influencing the internal exchange
  - Alternative partners – i.e. industry concentration
  - Industry dynamics – i.e. trends
  - Role in the business system – power and dependency
  - Opportunities to change activity sequence in business system

As highlighted in the industry analysis sub-section, it is important to distinguish between the short-term episodes and the long-term relationships. This is important as the line between what is internal and external may change over time, as the relationship develops and the companies involved adapt and institutionalise the exchange.

However, exchange may also involve external parties or third parties, either supplying one of the organisations in the dyad or both.[24] As described previously, other relationships may influence the specific dyad.[25]

The organisations supporting the exchanges taking place are gradually changing from one-way flows to two-way flows to disperse flows (see figure 7-6 below) and from nipple to multiplex relationships.

But what is actually exchanged? Which functions/departments are involved when exchanges take place and what are some of the obvious benefits that these functions/departments may develop from these exchanges?

Sales representation and the buying function within the buying organisation are the traditional focus of a relationship and will typically coincide with the conditions for the exchange between the organisations, such as:

---

23. See section on Political Economy Paradigm in chapter 2.
24. See chapter 2.
25. Gummesson (1996).

- Information regarding product/service
- Information regarding trading conditions and payment terms

Sales representative and marketing department of the buying organisation may share insights on:

- Possible improvements of customer's product/service
- Promotional material
- Product development

Sales representative and logistics department of the buying organisation may design and discuss how to:

- Improve inbound logistics
- Lot sizes
- Forecasting
- Frequency

Sales representative and HRM department of the buying organisation may exchange information and details concerning:

- Training
- Recruitment
- Career development

Sales representative and finance department of the buying organisation may exchange information and details concerning:

- Payments and payments made
- Planning investments
- Evaluating financial performance

Remember that exchange may involve more than the traditional two members of a dyad. In order to distinguish between different types of exchanges, this book has separated them into four distinct types (see figure 7-6). The four types cover the traditional one-to-one handling of exchanges to the "spiders web" gradually developing from just one line of contact to several lines and into a network.

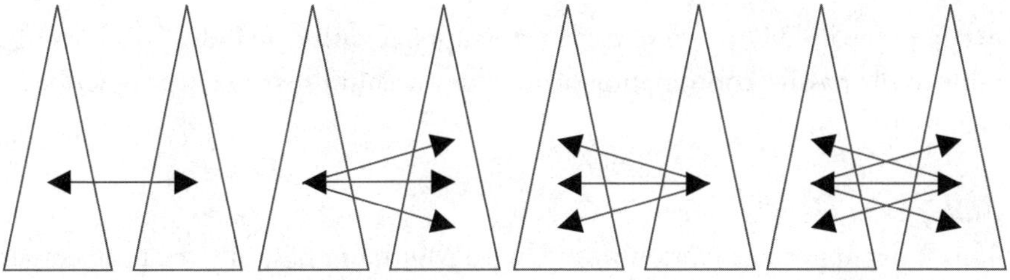

Figure 7-6: The different combinations of uniplex and multiplex relationships.

In principle, the process is simple and quite easy to describe as the organisations move from single contacts to contact-webs.

Uniplex

Uniplex is the traditional relationship and the traditional way of organising the exchange with one representative from each. This is comparable to the contact form of key account management described in chapter 6.

The greatest weakness of uniplex is its dependency on individuals in the two organisations. Therefore efforts to avoid potential loss of information and data will be supported by reporting structures, databases, minutes of meetings etc. Historically almost all this data would be stored individually.

The flexibility and the individuality is an important strength, meaning that the individual will often regard the relationship as having personal relevance and will defend it accordingly.

Uniplex to Multiplex – One to Team

This consists of selling relationships to several functions/persons in the customer's organisation. This is not necessarily a permanent arrangement, but can be related to projects where desired competencies and insights are part of the organisation handling the exchange.

The coordination of the elements of the relationship and the exchanges that relate to other parts of the supplying organisation other than the sales department are a considerable challenge. The individual handling the relationship will be faced not only with a number of questions and issues, but also choices with regard to if these issues should be handled alone or with others.

One risk is that the balance between the supplier and customer will become uneven and one-sided, i.e. that the customer takes over the initiative or simply occupies the individual representing the supplier with demands. This is comparable to the passive coordination form of key account management described in chapter 6.

Multiplex to Uniplex – Team to One

This is the opposite situation from Uni to Multi, but basically the problems are identical. The buyer handles relationships with several functions/persons in the supplier's organisation and is faced with the same challenges and choices as the seller in the Uniplex-Multi relationship.

Coordination of the internal elements of the relationship and the exchanges therein are only handled by one of the organisations involved: the buying organisation. This is comparable to the pro-active coordination form of key account management described in chapter 6.

Multiplex – Team to Team

Multiplex relationships means several representatives representing each company involved.

Tacit knowledge may develop within the group and both organisations will often attempt to share experiences internally and aim at best practice.[26] The drawback of this is that it may be difficult to share experiences with individuals outside the relationship. This is comparable to the integrator form of key account management described in chapter 6.

The team-to-team approach may be institutionalised further, for example by devoting parts of the company solely to handling the relationship with one partner. Tacit knowledge develops within the group and across the organisational boundaries, often working within it's own set of boundaries and practices.

Supporting the relationship by developing a unique organisational structure by perhaps developing that structure into an independent company. Thereby moving into limited merger situations where the firms decide to share some of their competencies and resources.

Finally, when looking for external factors of considerable importance to a relationship, you must never assess your own value to your customer or to your supplier. Basically, the following tough questions must be answered: Could the three areas in which we provide our customers/suppliers with value/benefit be obtained anywhere else? Or put another way: what is a result from our relationship that cannot be copied?

---

26. Nonaka and Takeuchi (1995).

References

Eriksen, B. (1992) *The Resource-Based Theory of the Firm: A New Paradigm for Strategy Research?*, Management Research Institute, CBS.

Ford, D. (ed.) (1995) *Understanding Business Marketing*, Dryden Press.

Foss, N. J. (1993) *Theories of the Firm, Contractual and Competence Perspectives*, Journal of Evolutionary Economics.

Gummesson, E. (1996) *Towards a Theoretical Framework of Relationship Marketing*, Proceedings of the International Conference on Relationship Marketing, Berlin, pp. 5-18.

Hayes, H. M., Jenster, P. V. and Aaby, N.-E. (1996) *Business Marketing – A Global Perspective*, Irwin.

Hamel, G. and Prahalad, C. K. (1989) *Strategic Intent*, Harvard Business Review, vol. May-June, pp. 63-76.

Hill, C. W. L., and Jones, G. R. (1992) *Strategic Management Theory: An Integrated Approach*, Houghton Mifflin Company.

Jenster, P. V. and Hussey, D. (2001), *Company Analysis – Determining Strategic Capability*, Wiley.

Sawhney, M. and Parikh, D. (2001) *Where Value lives in a networked world?*, Harvard Business Review, vol. January.

Nelson, R. R. and Winter, S. (1982) *An Evolutionary Theory of Economic Change*, Harvard University Press.

Nonaka, I. and Takeuchi, H. (1995) *The Knowledge-Creating Company*, Oxford.

Penrose, E. T. (1959) *The Theory of the Growth of the Firm*, Oxford University Press.

Porter, M. E. (1980) *Competitive Advantage*, Free Press.

Porter, M. E. (2001) *Strategy and the Internet*, Harvard Business Review, vol. March.

Reichheld, F. and Schefter, P. (2000) *E-loyalty – your secret weapon on the web*, Harvard Business Review, vol. July-August.

Williamson, O. E. (1975) *Markets and Hierarchies – Analysis and Antitrust Implications*, The Free Press.

PART III

Relationship Marketing Strategies

CHAPTER 8

The Individualised Approach to Relationships

Taking an individualised approach to relationships implies that each relationship is analysed in it's own right, and entered into as such. Basically this is an outside-in approach based on the individual customer, not the market or other variables that can be applied to groups of customers etc. The outcome of the individualised approach is an understanding of the potential customer's situation and theoretical or expected perception of the potential relationship.

The individualised approach identifies reasons for either entering relationships or abstaining, linked to the strategic behaviour of the potential customer. It also provides suggestions for designing strategic relationship marketing practices with regard to which departments the supplier should use in order to enhance relationships.

The following typology and analytical framework identifies and characterises different types of strategic behaviour in order to describe how the potential customer behaves. The answer to this will then lead to the potential customer's reasons for developing relationships or not depending on the strategy pursued.

Supplementing these principal types of behaviour is the perception of the potential risks involved in going further with the relationship, as seen from the potential customer's perspective. Presented here is a modern buying framework that assesses risk from both an internal or operational perspective as well an external or strategic one.

Taking an individualised approach to relationships implies that the result is that the seller will engage in different types of relationships as well as relationships that contain different elements or dynamics.

8.1 Typology of Strategic Behaviour

Within the strategic planning literature a number of typologies have been presented that focus on how firms react to the outer environment.[1] There have traditionally been two different foundations for these typologies: one has been based on theoretical arguments leading to for example the model of Competitive Advantages,[2] and the other has been based on empirical studies aiming at describing what has been observed. Belonging to the first are the Three Modes of Strategy Making,[3] which are the Entrepreneurial Mode, the Adaptive Mode and the Planning Mode. Within the second mode are the Four Interpretation Modes[4] and a second model[5] had been introduced earlier that includes four different strategic patterns based on empirical studies of several and diverse industries. The description of customer behaviour presented in this book is based on the three modes of strategy processes that have been observed among various firms. Most strategic processes actually carry examples from each of the three modes, reflecting that strategy decisions are complex and dependent upon various contributions. Furthermore, the three modes contain different priorities as to what is relevant when deciding on a strategy similar to the strategy processes many firms encounter.

Using typologies for analysis should always be carried out with caution, as a typology cannot describe all the characteristics of an organisation. But the central point of a typology is that it helps bring order in an incredibly cluttered conceptual landscape. This advantage may be fully utilised when deciding where to aim at relationship development resources and what results to expect.

Although the typology presented and used here is not new,[6] it has been chosen for a number of reasons:

- It is empirically based
- It has recently been used by researchers to describe strategic behaviour and the implications of this[7]
- It does not imply transformation from one type to another will take place, but that it can take place

---

1. See chapter 2 on the political economy paradigm for reference.
2. Porter (1980).
3. Mintzberg and Waters (1985).
4. Daft and Weick's (1984).
5. Miles and Snow (1978).
6. Miles and Snow (1978).
7. McDaniel and Kolari (1987);Zahra, and Pearce (1990); Floyd and Wooldridge (1992); James and Hatten (1995); Slater and Olson (2000).

- And finally, that it is well suited to describe and analyse a customer's behaviour and decision making logic

Originally, the typology of strategies pursued by firms was based on three empirical studies. These studies covered different types of organisations, and the goal was to develop a general typology that would be applicable in different areas of economic life. The typology was narrowed down to four different archetypes of relationship behaviour. A second aim was to present a typology describing various adaptation patterns for organisations. Both purposes have been fulfilled[8] in a clear-cut and forthright way by discussing several cases and examples.

The result of the original empirical studies was a typology with four archetypes, namely *Defenders, Prospectors, Analysers,* and *Reactors.*

8.1.1. The Concept of Fit

"Fit" is used to describe a situation in which there is alignment between the strategy pursued by an organisation, the organisational structure and its management processes. Successful firms are well aligned and therefore the strategy, structure and management processes "fit" together in an optimal way. These elements within less successful firms however, do not work as well together and therefore do not "fit" as well. The degree of fit will also reflect the organisation's ability to pursue consistent strategies meaning that low fit implies that some parts of an organisation aims for objectives and goals that are not necessarily shared by other parts of the organisation. Seen in a relationship context, this means that it is difficult to develop close relationships to all parts of an organisation having low fit, whereas this is possible with an organisation with high fit. The concept of fit is partly a description of process and partly of situation:[9]

> ... a dynamic search that seeks to align the organisation with its environment and to arrange resources internally in support of that alignment. In practical terms, the basic alignment mechanism is strategy, and the internal arrangements are organisation structure and management processes. Because in a changing environment it is very difficult to keep these major organisational components tightly integrated, perfect fit is most often a condition to be striven for rather than accomplished.

---

8. Tollin (1990).
9. Miles and Snow (1978, p. 11).

Within each archetype an adaptive cycle exists. An adaptive cycle is the organisation's ability to change in terms of product, market domain and technology. The reason for looking at the adaptive cycle is the dynamics it represents, i.e. the strategic archetype does not merely characterise the organisation, but also the way the organisations react to changes in the environment. Furthermore, the adaptive cycle describes the transition between the strategic type and the tactical and operational levels and thereby also the responsiveness towards strategies pursued by potential buyers or sellers.

The basic principle of the typology is that it is possible to identify a pattern by the way organisations move through the adaptive circle and at the same time solving the problems and making the necessary decisions.[10] How this takes place differs depending on the strategic archetype. The adaptive cycle is illustrated below in figure 8-1.

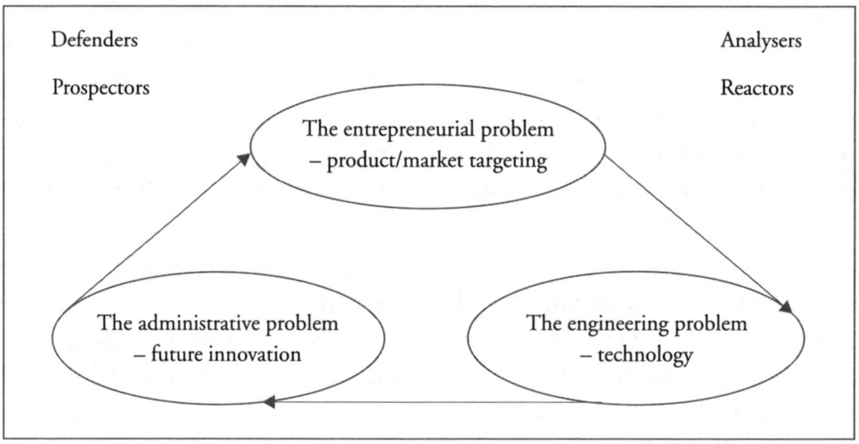

Figure 8-1: The Adaptive Cycle. Source: Based on Miles & Snow, 1978, p. 24.

8.1.2 The Entrepreneurial Problem

The entrepreneurial problem deals with the choice of product(s), market(s) and domain(s) i.e. the choice of specific product(s) or service(s), and target market(s) or market segment(s). This is not a one-time problem, but one that continues to play an important role in the organisation's continuous passing through the adaptation cycle process. The adaptation cycle process is defined as

10. The three step approach introduced in chapter 7 will be beneficial here.

an organisational capability that influences the degree and type of change the organisation can handle at any given time as related to choices of products, markets, and technology. In a relationship context this will influence the areas of focus for the relationship as well as where the customer looks for support from it's suppliers in order to serve the chosen market(s) with the chosen product(s). This deals with relationship content and the question of what is exchanged.

Thus, the tactical and operational areas of decision involve:

- Product(s)
- Assortment, width and breadth
- Customer(s)
- Segments
- Quality and price level and range
- Service(s) and level of service
- Branding
- Promotion
- Positioning
- Etc.

8.1.3 The Administrative Problem

The administrative problem here deals with reduction of internal insecurity and the creation of stabilising elements that will support future development of the firm. Thus, internal processes are key areas. In the relationship context this is where the exchange between supplier and customer could focus on enhancing the customer's internal processes, improving forecasts, utilising competencies and assets etc. In terms of required information, the administrative problem calls for intimate knowledge and insight into the customer's processes, activities and decision-making structures.

Thus, the tactical and operational areas of decision involve:

- Organisational structure and principles
- Support and monitoring relationships (contracts, dialogue)
- Decision making policies
- Processes, design and monitoring
- Flexibility versus standardisation
- Automation of processes

8.1.4 The Engineering Problem

The engineering problem deals with the creation of a system that supports the choice of product and market. Thus this area is related to the choice of technology for production and distribution. Development of suitable control and information systems is a key part of the engineering problem. In a relationship context this is where the supplier may be able to influence the infrastructure of the customer's operation.

Thus, the tactical and operational areas of decision involve:

- Production technology
- In- or outsourcing
- Competency developments
- Product development processes
- Differentiation between core competencies and others
- Distribution
- Use of support systems by partners

The adaptive cycle displays several important features and observations, all based on the empirical application of the principles:

- The adaptive cycle despicts the a general physiology of organisational behaviour.
- The three adaptive problems – entrepreneurial, engineering, administrative are intricately interwoven.
- Adaptation frequently occurs by moving sequentially through the entrepreneurial, engineering and administrative phases.
- Adaptive decisions made today tend to become permanent aspects of tomorrow's structure.
- Understanding how a customer goes through the three adaptive problems will reveal valuable insight regarding what a relationship must provide as seen from the customer's point of view.

8.2 The Four Archetypes

As indicated earlier, the different strategic archetypes may pass through the adaptive cycle in different ways, resulting in different strategies. In the original typology[11] two clear-cut opposing strategic types were identified they are defenders and prospectors. Defenders are characterised by their consistency and by isolating themselves from the outer environment, as opposed to prospectors, who are characterised by a continuous change of procedures and structures.

However, a combination of the two opposing types was also identified they are the analysers. Analysers are described as a compromise between defenders and prospectors. Consistency and renewal thus characterise analysers. A fourth type was, somewhat reluctantly also identified:[12]

> ... the Reactor, exhibits a pattern of adjustment to its environment that is both inconsistent and unstable; this type lacks a set response mechanism, which it can consistently put into effect when faced with a changing environment. Consequently Reactors exist in a state of almost perpetual instability.... Thus, the Reactor is a residual strategy, arising when one of the other three strategies is improperly pursued.

The unit of analysis is the concept of customer as a whole. A note of caution may be highlighted here; namely that traditions for handling the adaptive cycle may differ between various parts of an organisation or at least the attention the various parts of the cycle receives. It is therefore important to go beyond the superficial level of analysis if the strategic type is to be identified, and not merely analyse one or two parts of the organisation in question.

8.2.1 Defenders – It is All about Costs

Typical for organisations of this type is a relatively narrow product and/or market domain. Furthermore, the decision-makers in these organisations consider the environment to be simple and stable. This leads to a managerial focus on only a few indicators in the environment and no focus on indicators that do not directly impact the internal operations or the domain in which the organisation as active. The managers in defender organisations may be characterised as follows:[13]

---

11. Miles and Snow (1978).
12. Miles et al. (1988, p. 529).
13. Miles and Snow (1978, pp. 37-38) and Thompson (1973).

> Managers in Defenders usually restrict their perceptions to a narrow range of external stimuli, which are expected to influence the organisation (mostly related to technological developments). Typically they allocate a small amount of administration and staff to monitoring other organisations, events, and trends. In addition, environmental scanning is performed only by a few top executives and their staffs.

As defenders view their environment as relatively stable and simple, they focus on "doing things right", once they have identified what the right things are. Another consequence is that managerial focus is primarily internal and with emphasis on the engineering and administrative portion of the adaptive cycle.

In other words, they will stick to their strategy and their positioning as long as possible and will only change when they acknowledge that the environment is markedly different from their internal dominant perception. This also means that there is no intention of involving others in the decisions related to the entrepreneurial part of the adaptive cycle. The main focus is on cost efficiency of internal distribution and production systems. For defenders, low price is a central issue in their marketing strategy and their positioning.

The long-term strategic goal is to maintain the position of cost leader as compared to competitors, and it should be noted that all initiatives that potentially may help sustain this goal could be of interest to a defender.

Relationships to suppliers are, generally speaking, not regarded as beneficial but as boundaries that limit the defender's management options to choose among potential suppliers and customers, depending on where the best deals can be made. Relationships therefore concern the administrative and/or the engineering part of the adaptive cycle but are not considered to be of strategic importance. However, it should be noted that relationships are generally regarded as limiting the management's ability to control the organisation.

Defenders are well known, for example in FMCG-retailing a perfect example is the German retailer Aldi. Aldi relies heavily on advanced systems for scanning, control and follow-up. The defined key measurement factors are for example: SKU coding, turnover per hour, turnover per employee, etc. Other key factors are: DPP and Space Management which are used and managed internally, systems that create the basis for simple operations and the ability to use low qualified staff. Information is only shared with suppliers and only if it suits Aldi. Collaboration is used to minimise Aldi's net costs in terms of handling, transportation, storage, shelving, interest, etc. Suppliers have to adapt to the retailer's systems and processes. Positioning is based on low cost, secondary location, standard inventory, efficient in terms of refilling shelves, palettes can be driven directly into parts of the sales area, stores are almost 100 % identical and if possible the retailer prefers to design the location as opposed to accepting an existing one.

Other examples are firms in the construction industry, Korean shipyards and the position of car manufacturers in the former Eastern Europe.

8.2.2 Prospectors – It's Got to Develop

Prospectors are opposed to defenders as they constantly seek new opportunities and attack the existing and dominant perspective in a business sector. Thus, prospectors look for new positioning opportunities, focusing on the outer environment. The prospector can be described as:[14]

> In order to constantly develop new areas of opportunity, the Prospector must develop and maintain the capacity to monitor a wide range of environmental conditions, trends, and events.
>
> The Prospector, therefore, invests heavily in individuals and groups who can scan the environment for potential opportunities. One means of spotting and exploiting opportunities is to develop and elaborate surveillance capacity by decentralising and scanning activities to appropriate sub-units within the organisation.

The prospector strategy reflects a high level of initiative with regard to the environment. The environment is seen as changing and thus constantly providing the organisation with new opportunities. The organisation develops new products and undertakes new initiatives and is therefore highly focused on the entrepreneurial part of the adaptive cycle.

The environment is considered to be complex and characterised by constant change, and therefore new initiatives must constantly be tested. These new initiatives will typically relate to the positioning, regarding the administrative and engineering parts of the adaptive cycle as instruments supporting the initiatives. Internal flexibility and dynamics are key capabilities.

A prospector's long-term goal is to be *the* innovator of the industry they are part of, or to redefine the industry and the way the supply chain functions. Several of the well-known prospector organisations have done exactly this.

Relationships are regarded as beneficial as long as they can keep up with the

14. Miles and Snow (1978, p. 56).

development pace of the prospector, and as long as the relationship does not limit the possibilities of developing other relationships. Relationships are considered of strategic importance to a prospector when related to the entrepreneurial part of the adaptive cycle. This does not imply that prospectors do not have other relationships, just that these are not strategic.

One prominent example of a prospector is SONY whose CEO has been quoted as saying: "My most important task is to ensure that we through our own product development are able to make our old products obsolete before our competitors do so". Other examples of prospectors would be Apple Computers in the IT-sector, Amazon.com redefining bookstores and other "first movers" in an industry. Apple's launch of the iMac is a brilliant example of changing the way a product looks, the colours it can have and of course whole idea of making the product partly transparent. Apple has also been involved in setting up their own retail operation and the unsuccessful result of this stresses that prospectors take risks, often great ones.

8.2.3 Analysers – Rather be Safe than First

Analysers play it safe, and they can be characterised as a combination of cost- and risk-minimisers (defenders), and opportunity seekers (prospectors). Therefore, analysers are often the organisations that are one step behind in terms of innovation, but are nevertheless often organisations that their partners can rely on and that have clear positioning within their market.

This is possible due to the division of the organisation in two, the base part providing the majority of income and the development part that is used for trial and error activities. External stimuli are transferred to the base part, after proof of the significance in the development part of the organisation. To do this successfully, analysers rely on other organisations to lead the way; they thus follow in the footsteps of prospectors, if these developments are applicable within the base part of the analyser's organisation.

In an analysers outer environment there will be a number of prospectors from whom analysers can detect new business opportunities. It is important to note that the analysers often have a global perspective on prospectors in their markets, i.e. an analyser may be the first to introduce a new product or service in a market, having noted the success of a prospector in another, typically geographic, market.

The analyser's norm for cost efficiency is that of the defender. This will apply due to the innovative delay of the analyser as compared to the prospector, which gives the analyser the opportunity to analyse how the strategy should be pursued as related to all three problems of the adaptive cycle. Analysers thus typically copy and follow the prospectors, but ensure that a positive result is not jeopardised by new initiatives.

The analyser focuses on all three parts of the adaptive cycle and it is important to note that the analyser is the type where the frequency and the speed of the adaptation is by far the highest of the four types. Furthermore, going through the parts of the adaptive cycle is often regarded as a process in itself. An analyser is quite conscious about continuously monitoring changes internally and externally, in particular focusing on the successes and failures of competitors and colleagues internationally.

The use of all parts of the adaptive cycle also implies that it is possible to develop strategic relationships that concern each part of the adaptive cycle.

An analyser's long-term goal is often very clear in terms of positioning and vision of how to get there. They know what they want. The consequence of this is that analysers often engage in relationships especially if these relationships support the overall strategic developments of the analyser.

Examples of analysers would be organisations such as IBM, Maersk Sealand, and General Motors. These firms share the motto: "We would rather be safe then first" and encourage thorough analysis and caution.

8.2.4 Reactors – Let's Move

Reactors are "followers" in the sense that they react to new trends from competitors by attempting to duplicate the success of the competitor, but do not have the managerial systems or capabilities to analyse or investigate why and how competitors do what they do.

Reactors survive in stable industries or in industries where competition leaves room for organisations that do not exhibit superior performance or focus.

The result is that they do not pursue any consistent strategy or development path and will apply any possible technique or tool, if they have the impression that others are doing so successfully. This type of behaviour is very open to input from others and can change existing routines.

Reactors are organisations that stick to earlier successful business models and they will typically end up in a situation where they are not able to choose a positioning strategy with regard to price, quality or innovation. Thus, they do not focus on specific products or markets.

All parts of the adaptive cycle may be considered equally important, and changes are often decided upon as result of desired changes in other parts of the adaptive cycle, i.e. changes in the IT processes are a result of needs in the entrepreneurial area. Therefore, strategic relationships may be developed in areas concerning all parts of the adaptive cycle.

Basically a reactor does not operate within any decisive timeframe and therefore a relationship to a reactor may serve as a basis for new developments, testing new products or services, testing new ways of cooperation etc. The possibilities are almost limitless. Generally, relationship development with other partners is regarded as a way of ensuring vital inputs such as information, competencies or as a catalyst for change.

Examples of reactors are typically found among the COOP's in the dairy industry, farmers and retailers. This is due to internal structural problems in the administrative part of the adaptive cycle as well as the lack of internal clear priority of goals and means. Reactors are caught between the interests of the organisation, i.e. the need for funds to invest in product/service developments, production facilities etc., and the need to financially satisfy their members in terms of the highest possible prices for production inputs, dividends etc.

The implications of the four types as illustrated in figure 8-2 focus on what part of the adaptive cycle is most relevant to the development of strategic relationships.

Cost focus \ **Differentiation focus**	Low	High
Low	Defender Short-term focus Administrative ands engineering part of adaptive cycle	Analyser Long and short-term focus Entrepreneurial, administrative and adaptive cycle
High	Reactor No time focus Entrepreneurial administrative and engineering part of adaptive cycle	Prospector Long-term focus Entrepreneurial part of adaptive cycle

Figure 8-2: Areas in which strategic relationships can be developed.

The consequences of these four types can also be expressed in terms of what kind of benefit a supplier may get from developing a relationship to these customers, i.e. are the customers interested in developing relationships, and if so, what would be their primary focus? This is outlined in figure 8-3.

Cost focus ↓ / **Differentiation focus** →	Low	High
Low	Defender Will pursue flexibility avoid investing in specific assets Rationalisation Focus of lowest possible specific transaction costs The seller's Transaction Cost Leader Strategy will be applicable	Analyser Investing in specific assets Coping with customer "cherry-picking" Partnering projects Focus on lowest possible specific transaction costs and specific developments The seller's Transaction Cost Niche Strategy and/or the Quality Segment Specialist Strategy will be applicable
High	Reactor Testing new ways of working and processes developing new forms Educating new staff Focus on lowest possible generic transaction costs The seller's Relationship Differentiator and/or Transaction Cost Leader Strategy may be applicable	Prospector Product development Process development Investing in specific assets Partnering projects Focus on creativity and innovative skills The seller's Quality Segment Specialist Strategy and/or Relationship Differentiator Strategy may be applicable

Figure 8-3: Consequences of the four types in terms of their focus and the seller strategies that may apply.

The intent of introducing the typology of strategic behaviour was to classify different types of behaviour and different strategic needs and opportunities related to the individual organisation. But in order to take the individualised approach to strategic relationship marketing a step further, a framework for assessing the importance of a potential partner as seen from the potential partner's point of view must be introduced.[15] Others have attempted to describe the consequences of the four types in terms of sales management focus. The buying organisation's perspective will therefore be adopted when discussing whether or not to engage in strategic relationships.

8.3 Strategies related to buying

Buyers or buying organisations segment their suppliers just as suppliers segment their customers and ultimately these segments contain one organisation. This statement seems to surprise many sales and marketing organisations despite the fact that this situation comes up quite often. The introduction to supplier segmentation has been developed within the Supply Chain Management (SCM) framework, which in principle is geared towards:

> ...the integration of business processes from end user through original suppliers that provides products, services and information that add value for customers.[16]

And in practice this means:

> The management of upstream and downstream relationships with suppliers and customers to deliver superior customer value at less cost to the supply chain as a whole.[17]

Of course not all relationships are equally important or have equal impact on business processes within the supply chain. Therefore, most buying organisations focus on getting the most out of their, often limited, resources. One increasingly popular approach[18] is to prioritise resources and choice of focus based on the risks associated with cooperation with a supplier, as perceived by the buying organisation. The risks are evaluated both internally and externally.

15. Cron and Levy (1987).
16. As defined by The International Center for Competitive Excellence (1994).
17. Christopher (1998).
18. Krajlik (1983).

Internal risks are those that:

- May cause potential loss of profit, due to:
  - Lack of delivery
  - Quality deficiencies.
- Have high importance of delivery, as they are crucial for the ongoing production.
- Incur set-up costs in case of re-starting the production – could involve costs for cleaning, waste due to production stop, ... etc.
- Have high complexity in terms of delivery and degree of mutual integration between the supplier and the customer.

Internal risks are all related to the internal consequences of the supplier's failure or inability to fulfil contracts and/or other obligations.

External risks are related to:

- The number of suppliers.
  - Potential, in terms of ability to fulfil need.
  - Those, that can and want to deliver, in terms of ability to meet the needs and demands of the customer.
- The barriers to entry for new suppliers, the higher entry barrier the higher risk.
- Negotiation strength of the supplier(s), the relative importance of the customer to the supplier.
- Degree of commodity in the delivery, the more standardised the lower the risk.

External risks are all related to difficulties and risks of exchanging an existing relationship between the customer and a supplier.

If the internal and the external risks are divided into low and high risks, and combined in a matrix, the result is as illustrated in figure 8-4. This table illustrates the rationale, as seen from a buyer's perspective, concerning where to focus and where to engage in strategic relationships with external partners.

External risks ↓ / Internal risks →	Low	High
Low	Bottleneck materials and services **Ensure supply** (E-procurement)	Strategic materials and services **Partnering** (Co-operation and integration)
High	Non-critical materials and services **Hands off** (Auctions)	Synergy materials and services **Encourage competition** (Marketplace portal)

Figure 8-4: Supplier segmentation. Source: Based on Krajlik (1983)

When risks are high, internally and externally, strategic relationships may be developed due to the importance and consequences in case of failure. The aim of the relationship is to ensure the supplier's attention and interest in continued cooperation.

When either the internal risks or the external risks are considered high, it may also be possible to develop strategic relationships. However, in a strategic relationship marketing perspective, it is important to remember what the purpose of the relationship is as seen from the buyer's point of view. High internal risks combined with low external risks will encourage relationships that are focused on the administrative and especially the engineering parts of the adaptive cycle. In opposition to this, low internal risks combined with high external risks will encourage relationships focusing on the entrepreneurial part of the adaptive cycle.

In both groups, risks are considered to be low as it is difficult to claim that strategic relationships are a necessity. The modern[19] buying approach is based on the buying function's role in realising the strategic goals of the organisation. The cooperational principles of this modern buying approach are:

19. Kjeldsen (1997).

- Potential is more interesting than actual performance
- Performance over time – relational content
- Supplier's interest in development
- Joint interests in a strategic perspective

The term "supplier management" has also emerged within SCM literature[20] as a way to enhance product development, smooth out order and buying processes with regard to invoicing and payments. The main task of supplier management is supplier development, i.e. developing a profitable and strategic relationship to the chosen suppliers, as these relationships are regarded as the basis for increased productivity, quality, flexibility, innovation and process alignment. As an interesting parallel to the suppliers focus on key customers through key account management, a number of buying organisations have developed key supplier managers to ensure focus on key suppliers. As indicated earlier, the SCM concept does not apply equally well to all four strategic types of behaviour, especially not to the defender strategy.

This development has been phrased "Buyer Initiative" as it is seen in a classical marketing context[21] where it is quite often the customer that chooses the supplier and not the other way around as is typically taught in traditional marketing courses.

This section has focused on the buyer as an independent function or buying as an activity in the organisation. Individuals located in other parts of an organisation may have some difficulty relating to the relevance to them and in their own functions. However, these buying principles will gradually be applied in all parts of the organisation, especially now that modern buying departments increasingly regard themselves as internal advisory functions, assisting other functions choosing and prioritising resources and partners.

In the preceding sections, different types of strategic behaviour of potential partners have been presented. This discussion was then extended to include the identification of possible areas of strategic relationship development. The next step was introducing the importance of a selling organisation to a buying organisation and thereby be able to identify the buying organisation's interest in developing strategic relationships, and the area of focus. This implies that it is now possible to describe the basic elements of an individualised approach:

---

20. Shapiro (1985), Krajlik (1983) and Tanskanen (1994).
21. Kjeldsen (1997).

- The strategic behaviour in terms of archetype
  - Strategic goal
  - Time horizon
  - Basic approach to relationship development
  - Area of the adaptive cycle in which relationships may de developed
- The type(s) of seller strategy applicable
- The importance in terms of risk
  - Potential impact of failure
  - Purpose of relationship, if developed
  - Area of the adaptive cycle in which relationships may be developed

Based on the information and the analysis method presented above, it is possible to develop a suitable approach to strategic relationship marketing for an individual organisation.

References

Bjerre, M. (1999) *Key Account Management of Complex Strategic Relationships*, Ph.D. dissertation, Copenhagen Business School.

Christopher, M. (1998) *Logistics and Supply Chain Management*, Pitman Publishing.

Cron, W. L. and Levy, M. (1987) *Sales Management Performance Evaluation: A Residual Income Perspective*, Journal of Personal Selling and Sales Management, vol. August.

Daft, R. L. and Weick, K. E. (1984) *Toward a Model of Organisations as Interpretation Systems*, Academy of Management Review, vol. 9, No. 2, pp. 284-295.

Floyd, S. and Wooldridge, R. (1992) *Middle Management involvement in strategy and its association with strategic type*, Strategic Management Journal, Summer Special Issue, vol. 13, pp. 153-167.

James, W. and Hatten, K. (1995) *Further evidence on the validity of the self typing paragraph approach; Miles and Snow strategic archetypes in banking*, Strategic Management Journal, vol. 16(2), pp. 161-168.

Kjeldsen, J. (1997) *Køberinitiativ, indkøbsmarketing og leverandørsamarbejde*, Ledelse & Erhvervsøkonomi, vol. 2, pp. 145-157.

Krajlik, P. (1983) *Purchasing must become supply management*, Harvard Business Review, SEP-OCT, vol. 61, 5

McDaniel, S. W. and Kolari, J. (1987) *Marketing strategy implications of the Miles and Snow strategic typology*, Journal of Marketing, vol. 51(4), pp. 19-30.

Miles, R. E. et al (1988) *Organisational Strategy, Structure, and Process*, in The Strategy Process: Concepts, Context and Cases, Ed. By Quinn, Brian, et al. Prentice Hall, pp. 524-530.

Miles, R. E. and Snow, C. C. (1978) *Organisational Strategy, Structure, and Process*, McGraw-Hill.

Mintzberg, H. and Waters, J. A. (1985) *Of Strategies, Deliberate and Emergent*, Strategic Management Journal, pp. 257-272.

Porter, M. (1980) *Competitive Strategy*, The Free Press.

Shapiro, R. D. (1985) *Toward Effective Supplier Management: International Comparisons*, Harvard Business School Working Paper.

Slater, S. F. and Olson, E. M. (2000) *Strategy type and performance: the influence of sales force management*, Strategic Management Journal, vol. 21, pp. 813-829.

Tanskanen, K. (1994) *Supplier Management in Just-in-time Manufacturing*, Acta Polytechnica Scandinavia, The Finnish Academy of Technology.

Thompson, J. D. (1973) *Hur organisationer fungerar*, Bokförlaget Prisma.

Tollin, K. (1990) *Konsumentbilder i Marknadsföringen av Livsmedel*, Stockholms Universitet, Akademitryck.

Zahra, S. and Pearce, J. (1990) *Research evidence on the Miles-Snow Typology*, Journal of Management, vol. 16(4), pp. 751-768.

CHAPTER 9

Generic Relationship Marketing Strategies

In this chapter, the concept of relationship oriented marketing strategy as a very convincing and effective method of developing sustainable competitive advantage will be presented. The term generic relationship marketing strategy will be used in this context. The term generic in this context means that in order to achieve long-term outstanding performance, the company must be very clear about the main relationship benefit sources behind the strategy and their sustainability within a framework of competitive understanding.

Unique customer relationships will inevitably be reflected by strong customer loyalty. Strong loyalty assumes *extraordinary* customer satisfaction, which then becomes a clear vision for any successful relationship marketing strategy.

In the process of developing a strategy, a company will either aim at gaining relationship economic advantages in terms of a leading position in transaction cost efficiency or aim at perceived unique relationship quality advantages. Both of these strategic directions can be successful, whether geared towards the total market or focuses on specific market segments or niches.

Relationship marketing strategies have to be defendable as do the various generic strategies with regard to what competitor initiatives they are potentially vulnerable to.

9.1 The Narrow, Decisive Track to Outstanding Performance

These examples will illustrate how much a company's profitability depends on loyalty:

It costs \$51 to win a new account; profits earned grow annually from \$30 in year 1 through \$42, \$44, \$49 to \$55 in subsequent years.

> Clearly, a customer relationship must last into the second year before break-even is reached.[1]
>
> Increasing customer retention by 5% adds more than 3 years to the average customer lifetime. Defection declines markedly across customer tenure with a financial institution and account usage per relationship increasing over time... In the same publication an analysis from Cumberland Bank reveals the following about the top 5% of their customer base: These top customers generate 40% of the bank's total deposits. A 5% increase in retention among top customers yields a 24% increase in overall profitability...

Why is it that some companies succeed in creating a high and outstanding level of customer loyalty while others do not? According to the idea of so-called *meta loyalty*,[2] *internal loyalty* from employees is a prerequisite for the development of *external loyalty* in terms of customer attitudes, propensity for repurchase etc. But is that all?

In economic terms, the idea of customer *relationship profitability* is a reflection of different marginal revenues generated at the transactional level of the relationship. This generates higher prices, larger volume, lower costs of servicing the customer, lower defection rates, reduced sales- and marketing expenses, increased buying frequency etc. What the company must sometimes do, in order to maximise transaction economy, i.e. the relationship generated plus-revenue streams, is to investment in customer specific assets. These assets will typically be idiosyncratic due to eventual asset redeployment losses and hence dependence and vulnerability in terms of loss of bargaining power.

When customers tend to rebuy and behave as loyalists over a longer period of time and when this behaviour contributes to the financial success of the supplier, it can to some extent be explained by a similar relationship economic logic. Depending on the category of product or service and the fit within the regulating mechanisms, a customer gets more value for "loyalty money" in the sense that the perceived marginal transaction costs going through an extended purchasing process exceed the expected benefit that such a process could possibly generate.

Therefore, the main thesis is that it may pay off for the customer to demonstrate loyalty from an economic, technical or psychological standpoint. This how-

---

1. Buttle (1996, p. 106).
2. Kunøe (1994) and Buttle (1996).

ever may sometimes be modified by the overall strategic approach pursued by the organisation in question. Relationship oriented buying adds more net value than control and autonomy in combination with somewhat higher transaction costs.

But which kinds of competencies are then required from a supplier in order to develop sustainable, relationship advantages? What does it take to build such competencies, and which kinds of strategies must support them? Why do some companies succeed in creating extraordinary customer loyalty, while others miss such a great opportunity? And how can a company reduce or eliminate the risks and the idiosyncratic reactions arising from the execution of relationship based marketing strategies? The coherence profitability, loyalty and satisfaction are illustrated in figure 9-1.

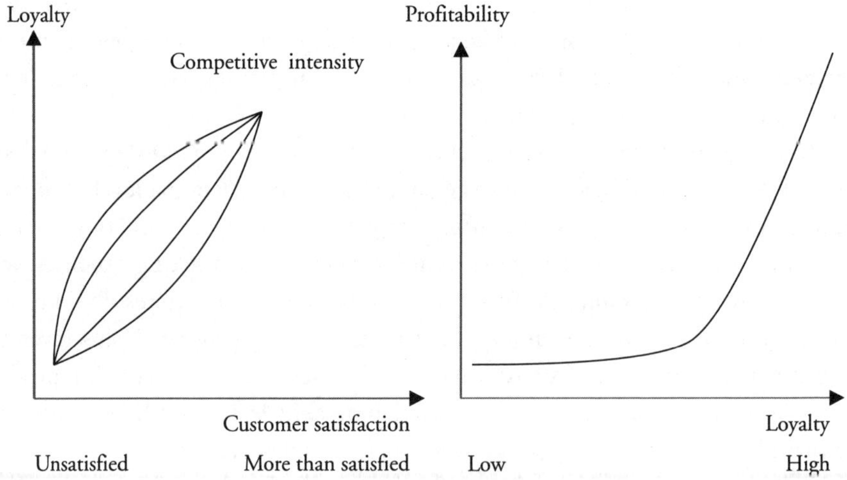

Figure 9-1: Coherence of profitability, loyalty and customer satisfaction.
Source: Based on Reichheld (1996).

Most companies on a regular basis carry out customer satisfaction studies. The traditional customer satisfaction survey typically leads to a conclusion like this: "The vast majority of our customers are satisfied with our products and services. Our total customer satisfaction average score is 4 on a 1-5 index scale." Despite such positive feedback from the customer base, many companies still suffer from high customer loss rates, complaints, brand switching, price pressure and painful attacks from competitors indicating that customer behaviour is far from loyal. But why is it so, when survey indicators usually show overall satisfaction? We call this discrepancy the *loyalty-satisfaction paradox*.

The idea is that only customers who are extremely satisfied are true loyalists as shown on the left side of figure 9-1 above. This correlation is particularly significant in buying situations with high involvement and intense competitive pressure. In these cases customers go through an extended purchasing process and evaluate several alternatives.

In more regulated or monopoly-like markets with low or no competition, customers will for obvious reasons behave as loyalists even when they are rather unsatisfied with the supplier as alternatives are more or less out of reach. This was the case with old monopoly sectors like telecommunication, electricity, airlines, television, healthcare, electricity etc. And it is also the case in IT industries. When a company has decided to acquire a certain technology or a new system it is obliged to use the service staff and the concepts of the supplier.

Even in cases where competition is effective, customers who indicate an attitude level less than extremely satisfied still have high repurchasing rates of certain products and services. In other words, their behaviour is loyal despite a clear satisfaction gap. This apparent discrepancy can be explained by the product category deemed as low involvement, high reversibility or low risk. The question is; can satisfied customers with a certain but not extremely high re-buying propensity lead to competitive advantage and outstanding performance?

If above average profitability assumes high loyalty (figure 9-1), and if such strong loyalty requires extraordinary customer satisfaction, then the crucial strategic question in conjunction with customer relationships is not "how do we obtain and retain satisfied customers?" but instead "how do we develop *extremely* satisfied customers?" Successful strategic development founded on customer relationship development and maintenance means creating extraordinary characteristics not just sufficient ones. Why? Because outstanding performance that separates the company from the crowd depends on the "last step on the ladder" breaching the gap between satisfied and extremely satisfied customers, as illustrated in figure 9-2.

It should be noted that "satisfaction" must be dealt with in a relative sense i.e. relative to expectations and competitors. In addition, some companies may find that marginal investments in customer services and loyalty programs are less attractive than investments in the core product.

For companies in highly competitive environments the whole idea of extreme customer satisfaction seems like nonsense. In such environments, focusing on relationships is not a critical success factor at all. This could well be the case on commodity markets and other markets with many substitutes or low switching costs. The correlation between customer satisfaction and customer loyalty is illustrated in figure 9-2.

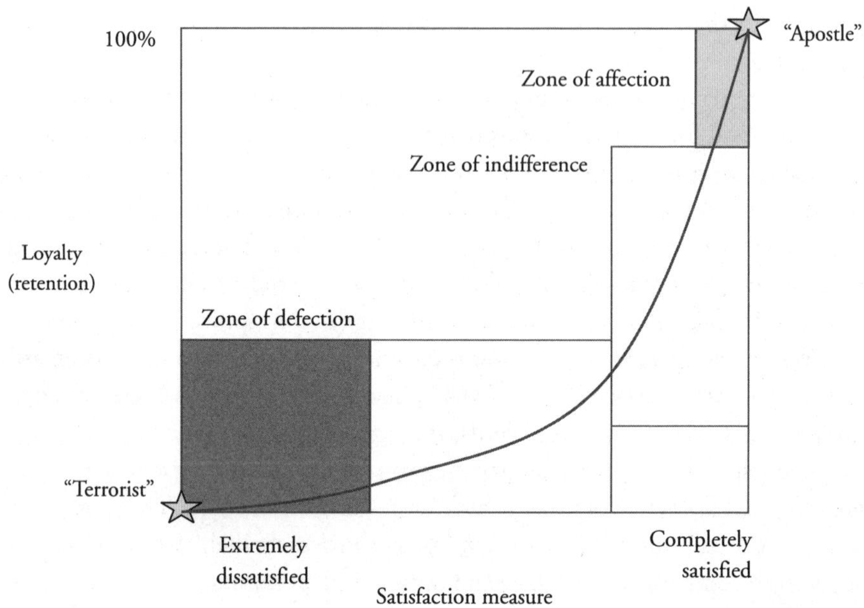

Figure 9-2: A satisfied customer is loyal. Source: Heskett, Jones, Loveman, Sasser and Schlesinger (1994)

There are important modifications to the above rationale that customer satisfaction sustains loyalty[3]:

> Customer loyalty is not always based on a positive attitude, and long-term relationships do not necessarily require positive commitment from the customers. The distinction is important because it challenges the idea that customer satisfaction (attitudinal dimension) leads to long-lasting relationships (behavioural dimension).

So, the simple model that customer satisfaction leads to customer retention, which in turn leads to profitability, might be too simplistic and possibly mis-

3. Storbacka (1994).

leading for many businesses. While intuitively the goal of increased customer satisfaction might prove productive, it might well increase expectations and almost by definition lead to increased dissatisfaction rates. When you decrease your expectation, you increase your chance of happiness.

Also the *service paradox* found in some studies indicates that less profitable customers are frequently the most satisfied, and vice versa. This was what the airline SAS observed and hence led to the creation of the businessman's airline in the early 1980s.

Therefore, even the most profitable and the most satisfied customer might be a brand switcher in absolute terms. The idea of creating extraordinary customer satisfaction as the prime loyalty source should therefore always calculated along with the marginal contribution it can provide and the costs of an increased expectation level. Our rationale must therefore be perceived relative to competitors and relative to alternatives.

9.2 Why base the Marketing Strategy on a Relationship Philosophy?

The term *relationship marketing strategy* implies that a company defines its strategic direction by mere relationship benefit judgment. The core offer to customers and hence the key determinant of competitive advantage consists of a relationship based understanding between supplier and customer. The rule of thumb is that all companies and business units must include the relationship aspect in their operations due to the strong correlation between loyalty and profitability. This is more or less a correct observation.

But the interesting phenomenon to work with here is not necessarily the tactical considerations that any marketing management team must handle in order to maximise the relationship economy of their business. Instead it is important to understand why some companies take a big step further and concentrate their *overall strategic positioning* around a relationship based business concepts.

Acknowledged innovative companies such as Charles Schwab, Amazon.com and Dell Computers all belong to this category. Charles Schwab offers round the clock securities trading as their core concept. Amazon.com introduced e-tailing in books, entertainment etc., which means a new relationship based on convenience that has a revolutionary impact on the life cycle. Dell Computers offers perceived customisation, enabling the customer to configure his or her own computer, combined with direct contact to end users cutting off traditional distributors.

In some countries, households can lease appliances such as washing machines instead of buying them. Suppliers offer services and regular maintenance. They guarantee that the old model can be replaced regularly with an updated model. Private insurance portals on the Net are a completely new kind of supplier. The private customer provides the portal with an overview of his or her present insurance portfolio. The portal company screens the market and comes up with better or more cost effective insurance solutions. A company like Last-Minute.com specialised in bringing supply and demand together focusing on situations with last-minute transactions as the value driver. Even a company like Ikea has relationships as the foundation of its strategy. The idea is that the customer assembles the furniture and adds a completely new dimension to the product-user interface in terms of the joy of creating your own home.

It is interesting to observe that companies nurturing the relationship element as their Unique Selling Proposition (USP) can be found at all the stages of the industry life cycle. Household appliances and furniture are mature industries whereas e-business is in the emerging phase.

Parallel with the relationship based marketing strategies aimed at gaining market leadership for some firms in an industry, there are also traditional and successful strategies rooted in more conventional marketing thinking in the same sectors and with the same objective. Barnes & Noble, the strong market leader in brick and mortar book retailing is a good example. Furthermore the perceived benefits of choosing relationship-focused strategies can be found across all stages of the *buyer-experience life cycle*: Amazon.com (purchasing stage), Ikea (delivery stage) and appliance leasing (use and disposal stage) among others.

How can a company identify and assess the opportunity of a relationship based marketing strategy as opposed to a traditional marketing approach? Which internal and external factors should be considered? The questions to be asked are presented below:

- Does there appear to be a potential for relevant, feasible and profitable improvements in the interface with the customer during the buyer experience life cycle: Purchase, delivery, use, supplements, maintenance or disposal?
- Can we identify attractive market segments where the relationship element seems to be the determining choice criteria?
- If we review and calculate transaction costs – contact, contract and control costs – what is the cost level, and where could a renewed or reengineered relationship with customers lead to substantial cost reductions?

- Can we spot any innovations in channel structures or communication technologies enabling new relationship forms to break through?
- The customer life cycle perspective transitions over the life cycle might a different relationship attitude lead to significantly higher customer retention rates, e.g. from introduction to growth, from growth to maturity etc.
- Is there anything in our market position indicating an unrealised relationship potential?
- Do competitors use the relationship philosophy as their main strategic marketing tool? If yes who, how and with what impact. If no, does the industry history contain cases or events where a relationship strategy was the cause of successful outcome?

In BtB trade, most suppliers would definitely be better off using a relationship oriented marketing approach, as business customers tend to respond positively to cooperative formats. Roadblocks like mistrust, breach of trust, opportunism and other monadic motives can be hard to overcome.

9.3 Generic Relationship Marketing Strategies

Sustainable competitive advantage via a relationship strategy assumes that a company is able to create and maintain extraordinary customer satisfaction that is superior to its competitors. Customer satisfaction determines loyalty, which is the main profitability driver through the loyalty economic effects (see chapter 3).

In the following section, the concept of generic relationship marketing strategies and the underlying rationales behind their functionality and competitiveness will be discussed. The starting point of this discussion consists of two basic and rather concrete positioning issues:

- Where in the market does the company seek to create a unique relationship positioning? In the total market or only in specific segments or niches?
- Which sources in terms of core competencies or other performance variables determine the keys to extraordinary customer satisfaction?

These two questions, the where and how to compete with a relationship oriented marketing approach, both require insight into industry and market factors as well as a flair for timing and careful analysis of the company's strength profile.

9.3.1 Looking for a Unique Relationship Position?

Customer needs and wants vary. Some consumers prefer low touch-high tech shopping with extended self-service and discount prices. Others look for high touch outlets with professional staff to guide and give service and accept the somewhat higher prices. Industrial services do not differ substantially from this pattern. Some companies reject bundled solutions assuming they are too high priced; instead they will chase offers on single components on a transactional basis. Other firms appreciate good, confident long withstanding cooperation with their suppliers, not just for the sake of convenience but because it saves time and leads to higher quality or lower costs. Therefore, a specific mix of relationship features can have different appeal to different segments.

In some cases companies reach the conclusion that the total market is the only relevant target for a successful relationship marketing strategy. This could be deduced based on the following market characteristics:

- The market is highly fragmented; no single segment has substantial size or growth rates to motivate a focus.
- Economies of scale are more apparent than economies of scope for which reason share of the total market becomes the main objective and not the conquering of a certain niche.
- Customer needs are rather similar. No segment appears to have differentiated relationship preferences.
- The market dynamic is volatile and unpredictable. It would therefore be too risky to specialise in one or a few segments; they could suddenly vanish or change dramatically.
- The company does not possess resources to explore, develop and defend a leading position in any segment and would be more vulnerable by making such an attempt.

The strategic options concerning where to compete and whether or not to found a generic strategy on the relationship continuum as opposed to a more traditional attitude can be summarised as illustrated in figure 9-3.

	Total market focus	Segment focus	Individual customer focus
Non relationship based marketing strategy	1	2	3
Relationship based marketing strategy	4	5	6

Figure 9-3: Strategic options – where are they and what should the marketing foundation be?

A relationship based strategy individualised for every single customer is the ultimate relationship segment focus. In heavy contracting industries such as ship building or facility management such an approach is the term of trade.

A relationship-based strategy is derived from a business opportunity analysis. Whether or not the relationship marketing foundation is a feasible way for a company to succeed depends.

Which of the six strategic options would be the best for a business unit to concentrate on can to some extent be derived from a strategic diagnosis. The relationship aspects can, however, in particular be rather difficult to identify and evaluate. Most quantitative as well as qualitative data in companies, regarding markets, customers, competitors etc. and the most traditional managerial methods do not really encompass the relationship aspect of the business. Relationships are viewed as add-on's, as augmentations to core product benefits, as intangibles "nice but not necessary" to the overall marketing strategy. That's why strong *innovative skills* are needed in order to sew the seeds of strategic relationship marketing principles.

9.3.2 Detecting Relationship-based Sustainable Competitive Advantages

Innovations in most real life situations are the outcome of creativity, intuition and careful analysis blended together in a balanced cocktail. That is, the art of detecting potential sustainable competitive advantages requires innovative skills. A functional methodology could be to draw the *customer relationship benefit grid* as an idea – generating and screening tool, see figure 9-4.

In the benefit grid model we distinguish between the *when-in-the-relationship-benefit* aspect as symbolised by the six stages in the customer life cycle and the *which-relationship-benefit* attribute illustrated by the six relationship benefit levers. Furthermore, we have separated the benefit levers into two main categories, i.e. the relationship economic versus the relationship quality dimension.

The customer relationship benefit grid can be a useful framework in the strategic process as:

- It enables the marketer to analyse attractiveness and significance: Which benefit elements are potentially important for which market segments and in which stages of the life cycle?
- Describe the relationship benefit profile of the company's target segments
- Identify gaps and opportunities
- Describe our relative relationship benefit position as perceived by our target customers compared with their perception of competing offers and relationships – strengths and weaknesses
- Find discrepancies between what our customers think we do and what we actually do. That is a gap between perceived and physical position. If yes, where in the grid, why is it so and which corrective action can be taken?

As a problem-opportunity generation tool the customer relationship benefit grid can also produce an overview of business portfolios and competitive positions within an industry. In figure 9-5 below we present a few business examples, where companies' USP's are rated using a relationship benefit perspective.

The conscious consumers pay increasing attention to the quality of food including meat. Not only do they consider ethics, animal welfare and ecology as important product characteristics, they take it one step further. They want to see the livestock live, before they buy the beef in the supermarket.

The company Net Beef (fictitious name) has television cameras in the stables of cattle farms. The consumers can watch the cow or the calf, enjoy their behaviour, and track all their data before ordering the net beef delivered to their home within 24 hours.

The unique relationship benefit that Net Beef provides is concentrated in the pre-relationship and initial stages of the customer relationship. The relationship quality factors are what Net Beef concentrates on, giving the consumer a feeling of convenience, conceptualisation and individualisation. Additionally, the perceived risk, i.e. contract costs, is reduced compared with the more conventional alternatives in the supermarket.

More and more companies have chosen to outsource their logistics such as inventory, transportation, inbound material handling and even purchasing functions. This leads to a transaction cost reduction and hence relationship

Relationship benefit levers		Stages of customer life cycle					
		Pre-relationship stage	Initial stage	Growth stage	Maturity stage	Decline stage	Exit stage
Relationship economic levers	Contact cost						
	Contract cost						
	Control cost						
Relationship quality levers	Customisation						
	Convenience						
	Comfort						

Figure 9-4: Customer relationship benefit grid.

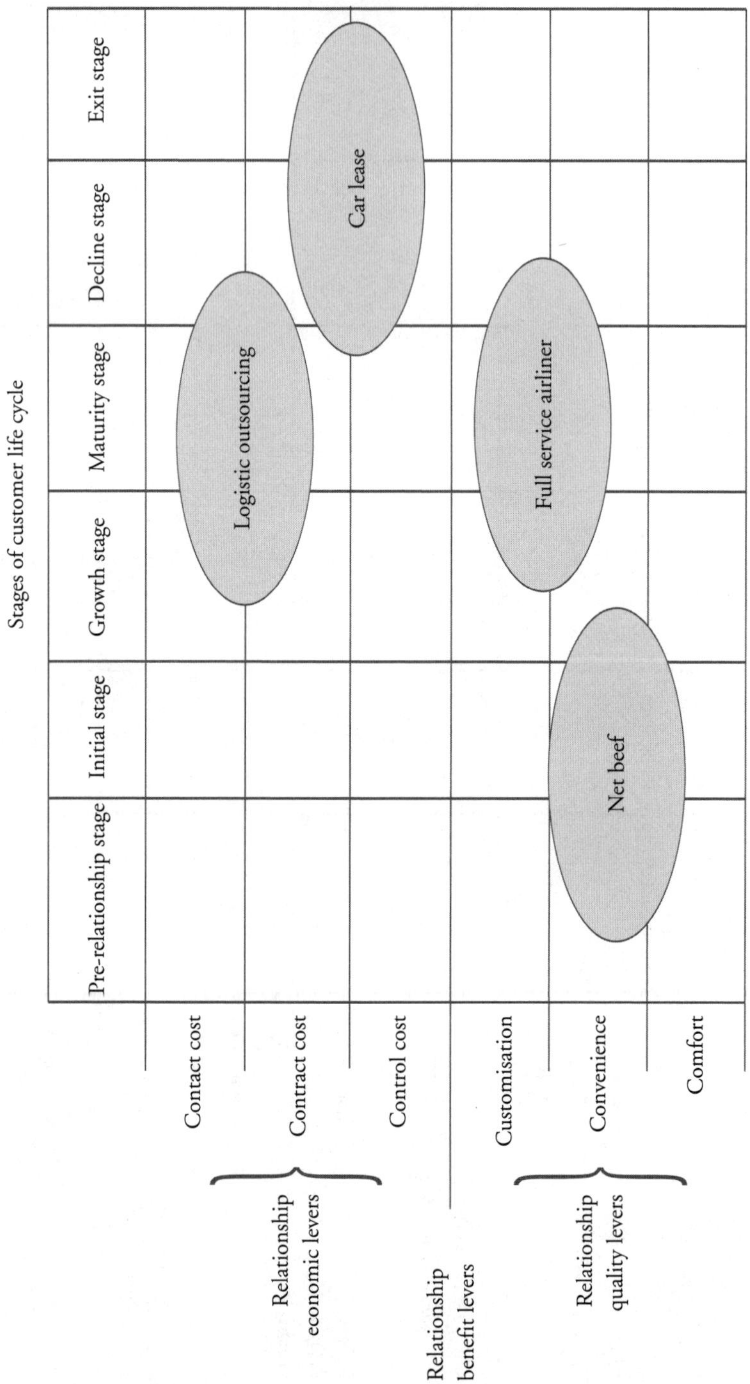

Figure 9-5: Customer relationship benefit grid – Examples.

economic advantages in the use phase of the customer life cycle, as the partner will take care of operations backwards in the supply chain.

Discount airline companies like Ryanair or Go have made it very easy to make reservations and get tickets. By fax the customer receives a one page combined confirmation voucher and ticket and that is the end of the transaction, simple. The full-service airlines concentrate their marketing efforts on the delivery stages. They offer packaged solutions including baggage handling, hotel reservations, lounge services, leisure activities, mileage programs etc. Features with the purpose of creating quality relationship benefits to certain customer segments.

Car leasing as opposed to car buying gives the customer a package of flexibility, variability and other transaction cost savings in terms of insurance, regular garage service etc. One extra, often-overlooked benefit of a leasing arrangement concerns the disposal stage. Trade-in of a second hand car when buying a new one can be problematic for many car owners due to the extreme depreciation of new cars. The leasing arrangement removes this relationship problem between the car owner and the car itself and gives a stronger sense of freedom regarding what kind of car to buy and when to trade in the old car for a new one.

The customer relationship benefit grid does not indicate that a company could only operate with one peak benefit cell. Neither does the grid recommend picking one specific *relationship economic lever* and excluding a combination with one or more *relationship quality levers.*

Strong customer loyalty generates long-term above average profitability. Developing and maintaining extraordinary customer satisfaction is the fuel in the loyalty creating process. Instead of establishing a scattered pattern of relationship benefit peaks in the grid, it makes more sense to compete by selecting a cluster of benefits, which support and reinforce each other. Because they will draw on the same kinds of core competencies like R&D, production, distribution or branding. And because a unique competitive positioning is easier to establish and defend by concentrating on a few keys to competitiveness instead of a basket of diversity.

9.4 Modelling Generic Relationship Marketing Strategies

Combining the “where” discussion, niche versus total market, with the “how” discussion in terms of relationship utility levers as unique selling propositions throughout the customer life cycle now enables us to orchestrate a new typology for understanding relationship marketing strategies. We have named this typology generic relationship marketing strategies (see figure 9-6). The label – *generic* – underlines the fact that the strategies are genuine and bound together in a system of mutual business economic logic and that sustainable competitive advantage depends on different and distinct sources.

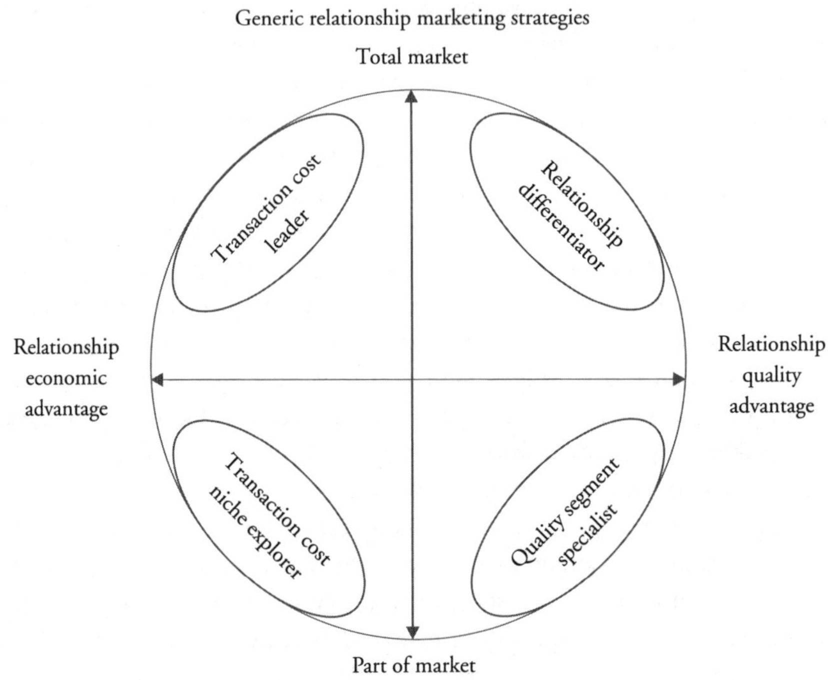

Figure 9-6: Four generic relationship marketing strategies. Source: Inspired by Porterian thinking

Product markets appear to be in an attractive strategic position as they don't possess clear differentiation opportunities and they do possess high frequency in the purchasing pattern as well as obvious economies of scale and transaction cost leadership.

Transaction cost leadership means that a company acquires sustainable and decisive relationship economic advantages within the total market. Such transaction cost advantages over competitors lead to higher profitability. A very loyal and extremely satisfied customer portfolio will among other advantages result in considerably lower sales and marketing costs.

Although it is the relative transaction cost position of the company that generates the above average financial performance and hence the sustainable advantage, the other side of the transaction cost leadership coin is about the advantages that the customers receive. The low perceived transaction cost level in terms of extraordinary security, standardisation, re-utilisation, optimised regulating mechanisms and so forth, becomes the heart of the relationship incentive for the customer, whereas the loyalty from the customer is the reward that the transaction cost leader receives.

Differential based relationship advantages can be a successful strategy for companies aiming at market leadership. A *relationship differentiator* addresses the market as a whole, either with a highly *standardised* concept, through attributes like convenience, simplicity, productivity, comfort etc., or with *mass customisation* such as e.g. the eyeglass industry. Relationship differentiators harvest extra profits on a quality-generated loyalty that can be translated into higher prices, lower marketing and service expenses or extension and prolongation of the customer life cycles.

Differentiation advantages in the relationship sense can either stem from structural strategic moves at critical points in the industry life cycle, such as discount stores in the mature retail market, or by early adaptation to emerging market needs, such as interactive television.

In addition to the generic relationship strategies targeting the total market, substantial competitive advantages can instead be obtained by focusing on specific relationship segments which possess a preference for certain relationship attributes. By *quality segment specialisation* a company decides to specify its assets and competencies to well-defined segments or individual customers leaving the rest of the market out of consideration. The more distinct, the more attractive and accessible special relationship segments are, the higher likelihood for success within a quality segment. Specialisation does imply that a company specifies its products to suit certain target groups or even individual customers with the purpose of fulfilling relationship needs better than competitors or substitutes. The suppliers attract customers who are not completely satisfied with the relationship offerings from cost leaders or differentiators and increase their switching costs through a relationship quality offering.

A Scandinavian Internet weather forecast company has specialised in "micro-weather", forecasting weather conditions with extreme time accuracy, 24 hours service, with predictions for every square mile of land, constantly updating the forecasts. This net-met service firm forwards messages to computers and as SMS messages to PDA's. The climate of the country in question changes frequently and suddenly. The target market segments for this service are farmers and the construction industry. There are tremendous cost savings for companies in these sectors if they can tailor the workflow to suit the weather conditions, not only in terms of waste of labour costs but also optimisation of processes vulnerable to temperature, humidity etc. The general weather forecast institutions do not give exact information at the building site or individual farm level. Hence, there is room for a relationship-based strategy in terms of quality segment specialisation.

A *transaction cost niche* is focused on selected customer segments that demand very specific relationship economic advantages. It could be access, self-service, transparency, reversibility, special kinds of deliveries etc. Lastminute.com, offering last minute services such as travel, tickets etc, gives the customer the transaction cost advantage by postponing the decision until last moment. The transaction cost niche seeker will explore the opportunity of being more competitive than the overall transaction cost leader by investing in features, services or transaction cost elements that a well defined customer segment considers extremely important.

Each of the four generic relationship strategies highlights distinct pathways to increased loyalty and hence outstanding performance. Relationship economy and relationship quality represent two such distinctly different directions where clear positioning and unique competencies support each other.

9.5 Transaction Cost Leadership: The Gate to Market Leadership

Transaction cost leadership means that a company acquires competitive advantages, i.e. stronger *true and sustainable loyalty* than its competitors through the development of a unique transaction cost position as perceived by the market:

- Without disqualifying the company in terms of a higher price or a lower quality of the core product.
- Creating a position that competitors are not able to imitate, neutralise or defeat.
- Retaining customers without customisation of assets or other types of dependence.

Long term success based on transaction cost leadership assumes that a company combines bundles of resources into a unique competence that enables it to adapt to or manage the driving forces in the industry that are determinants for the level of transaction costs. These kinds of skills lead to the lowest transaction costs in the buyer-seller relationship in the industry and stimulate customer loyalty, the key to outstanding performance. Loyalty is the supplier's cost leadership reward and transaction cost minimisation is the benefit for customers.

9.5.1 Elements Stimulating Transaction Cost Leadership

In industries where the transactional system, i.e. the terms of trade, is characterised by a high transaction cost levels or if core products are homogeneous, suppliers will sometimes strive for market leadership through transaction cost reductions.

The starting point for the systematic strategic development of relationship economic advantages is a deep understanding of the transaction cost *drivers* within the industry in question. Transaction costs differ through the customer relationship life cycle and through the industry life cycle as well. The anticipation of counterpart's monadic motives, the existence of triad relationships and mismatches in relationship contracts influence them. They can be counterbalanced by dyadic behaviour as well as by reducing the customers' perceived risks through *optimisation.* Some of the main parameters that a supplier can manipulate while reaching out for a transaction cost leadership position are described in the following as factors.

Factors Influencing the Frequency of Purchasing

The purchasing frequency represents a main cost driver in many buyer-seller relationships. Influencing the frequency of customers' buying processes is a key determining factor for a transaction cost leader. The modification of market mechanisms through relationship contracts leading to straight rebuy scenarios will dampen the overall friction between the two parties and hence reduce the transaction costs. The positive dyadic circle can work in all levels in the *purchasing process hierarchy:*[4]

- At the *transactional level* – how often a purchasing transaction is actually undertaken by customers.

---

4. Nielsen and Wilke (1999).

- At the *commercial level* – how often a customer considers alternative suppliers going through an extended repurchasing process.
- At the *technological level* – how often an industrial buyer evaluates and decides on different technologies fulfilling the same needs.
- At the *strategic level* – how often a purchasing process is initiated by an investment in new products or new strategic business areas.

Not surprisingly, the impact of transaction costs by establishing a straight rebuy routine, i.e. reducing customers' purchasing frequency, depends on the level and the importance of frequency in the specific buyer-seller relationship. High buying frequency, in particular at the higher levels in the customer's purchasing process hierarchy, where the risks, importance and irreversibility are significant, transaction cost leadership strategy is even more attractive.

Factors Reducing or Increasing the Uncertainty

The perception of high uncertainty inevitably makes a purchasing process more resource demanding for a buyer. The buying centre will have to take steps to minimise the risks by initiating contact with more suppliers, going into greater detail in negotiations and setting up protective mechanisms to best control the deliveries. They will have to be more careful and study possible future scenarios. This means cost increases both for suppliers and the customers.

Risk must be dealt with as a cost, and activities aiming at managing risks give rise to transaction costs. The consequence of risk is that purchasing processes are extended and formalised. Increased transaction costs caused by risk factors are, however, not necessarily always negative. The trade-off between living with risks and living with transaction costs that dampen the risks is very often in favour of the acceptance of high costs.

The point is that a marketer has the opportunity of driving down transaction costs to the benefit of both parties. Doing so faster, more determined or at a lower investment than competitors can create market leadership. What can a supplier do to develop competitive advantages by reducing the costs of contact, contract and control? There are several means:

- *Financial means* by which the supplier shares or keeps the financial risk such as is the case with trade-in guarantees for second hand equipment, operational leasing, cure-pay arrangements or insurance solutions.
- *Transparency means*, where the supplier is the customer's agent screening the market for the best offer. This is has been a successful business model for several Internet portals.

- *Social and psychological means.* Informal networks of relationships at the personal level across organisational boundaries create confidence and a sense of mutual bonding and commitment. Experience with a supplier is probably the most effective reducing factor for any buyer either business-to-business or business-to-consumer.
- *Institutional means.* Even in contexts where the buying centre is supposed to act rationally, institutional factors such as corporate image, technology or previous experience with the supplier can play a major role in the reducing perception.

Integration and Quasi Integration as the Key to Transaction Cost Leadership
As discussed earlier, long lasting customer relationships tend to develop in an integrative direction. Integration means that cooperative behavioural elements of both parties suppress command or competition oriented buying and selling strategies[5] or intention. Suppliers concentrating on dyadic motives and *communication convergence* will in some cases be able to drive down the customers' transaction costs and reinforce positive loyalty circles.

In some countries the interaction between supermarket chains and suppliers has developed into what we could call *quasi integration.*[6] The supplier takes responsibility for the ordering of products in every store. The sales force, in some cases merchandisers, visits each supermarket store on a regular basis. Equipped with hand terminals they are entitled to order goods from the chain's central terminal or directly from the supplier. The staff of the supplier is also in charge of rearranging their own shelf space in order to present the products in the most attractive way.

The leading supplier within a given product category in some cases is given the role of category manager. This supplier role means deciding how to organise the total shelf space area for the whole product category in the stores including competing products. The space manager uses market data and category expertise in areas like direct product profitability, shelf mirroring and shelf "temperature" to optimise the customer's business.

This type of quasi integration can actually be very effective despite the customer's somewhat higher control costs. The supermarket chain simplifies and reduces the internal workflow; as a customer the chain benefits from the fact that the sales reps inspecting and maintaining the stock are co-responsible for

5. See also chapter 3.
6. See also chapter 6 on the five steps of supplier-customer relationships.

the reordering, so that stock out situations are avoided. This arrangement is attractive to both parties.

Timing in the Product Life Cycle as a Transaction Cost Driving Force
Timing can be crucial for a company's future transaction cost level. Companies with a *first mover strategy* look for the opportunity of establishing a dominant market position at the early stages of the product life cycle. Early leadership positioning can place a company in a favourable transaction cost position in the later phases. The first mover obtains brand awareness, brand recognition and distribution access in a market with lower communication as well as distribution costs, as there is no competition.

Number one gets attention, number two does not. Who was the first man on the moon? Neil Armstrong, correct. Who was the second?

This cost advantage can be turned into lower transaction costs throughout the life cycle. In industries with very short product life cycles even small delays in product introductions can mean that "the train has left the station".

9.5.2 Developing Transaction Cost Leadership through Routinisation

Routinisation means developing, defending and reinforcing buying patterns, where customers rebuy your product or service without investigating alternatives and without much negotiation.

The advantages that an industrial buyer gets from such a transaction cost minimising purchasing behaviour can be summarised under headlines such as: Economies of scale, the saved transaction costs obtained by less frequent purchasing processes, better supplier service, easier adaptation of products in the internal supply chain etc.

For the buyer the outcome of routinisation will be loyalty through transaction cost advantages as well as unilateral dependence. The motivation for a company to accept the power of a supplier through open routinisation is that transaction cost effectiveness advantage exceeds marginal costs of the expected opportunism of the seller.

Companies like IBM, Microsoft and the global oil companies have succeeded in developing transaction cost leadership through routinisation. IBM has established and successfully defended a dominant position on the mainframe computer market. It is the experience of many IBM customers that it requires much less effort in the purchasing process to choose technology and machines under the IBM brand than it would require to switch to a competing brand. This is not only a question of experience, integration and compatibility, but also because of the sense of quality and certainty associated with the IBM brand. Additionally, IBM is able to control the timing of the launching of new generations of hardware. This strategy could be called *routinisation by branding.* In the early stages of the personal computer, Microsoft decided to almost give away the DOS operating system to end-users. This *first mover routinisation* positioning created Microsoft's large, loyal customer base enjoying low perceived transaction costs in all future upgradings just by rebuying a Microsoft package, from DOS to windows etc.

The global oil companies produce and sell completely identical core products at the same prices in the same markets through outlets with the same location and service profiles. On the consumer gasoline market, company credit cards have been a key to customer loyalty. Although gasoline stations in most countries accept bank credit cards as well, consumers driving in their private car or company car feel that it is easier to pay with the proprietary card issued by the oil company. Therefore the customers have reasonably strong preferences for that specific brand. This is a very subtle and effective transaction cost leadership strategy based on *routinisation by a contractual advantage.*

9.5.3 How can Transaction Cost Leadership be Attacked and Defended?

Market leaders are always under attack from competitors and substitutes. Companies with a strong portfolio of extremely loyal customers due to relatively low transaction costs are no exception to this rule. Competitors will try to either replicate the successful strategy of the transaction cost leader or attempt to develop other types of relationship advantage considered to be attractive by buyers or segments of buyers.

Imitation

In some situations competitors can imitate the successful transaction cost leader by offering the same cost saving schemes such as subscription advantages, services, guarantees integration attributes, accessibility, transparency etc. This is the case when oil companies, mortgage institutions, credit card companies, hotel chains and airlines immediately copy successful initiatives based on relationship advantages. Imitation is feasible only when transaction cost leadership is not rooted in unique capabilities and competencies.

In industries where high market share obtained by the experience curve effect is a prerequisite for transaction cost leadership, a challenger strategy founded on imitation will presumably fail. Here, the learning curve represents an effective barrier to entry for challengers with a copycat relationship oriented strategy.

Concentrate Marketing Efforts on Most Important Decision Criteria

Competitors may attempt to strike back at the transaction cost leader by concentrating on other important choice criteria than transaction costs. This can be in terms of low price on the core products or by developing new, differentiated relationship advantage within a quality-focused framework.

Whether or not such types of competitive moves lead to sustainable advantages depends on the specific circumstances within the market. Generally, customers tend to prefer the low transaction cost scenario to the low price on the core product scenario.

Reconfiguration

A commercial bank with a widespread net of branches or a provider of electronic components operating huge warehouses in multiple locations are perceived as easy accessible suppliers offering full service, immediate delivery and perceived confidence. Substitutes or newcomers can, however, threaten the position of the transaction cost leader, if their value proposal is based on completely different value dimensions.

Suppliers of IT services will face another ball game if customers decide to outsource IT services. E-businesses and e-marketplaces destroy existing value chains and bring a revolutionary reduction in both the transaction costs and the core product price to the market.

Reconfiguration capabilities rely on product or technology innovations. In some cases, new distribution strategies can alter the perceptions of relationship economics. In the 1970's Timex created a dramatic and promising shift in the watch market. Timex simply introduced inexpensive bulk watches in supermarkets and convenience stores as buy-use-throw-away products. Until then consumers considered watches to be jewellery, status symbols, partners for life. Watches were expensive and transaction costs were high. Specialty stores staffed with professionals originally distributed watches. Suddenly not only the price of the core product went down but also transaction costs dropped to almost nothing through accessibility, affordability, and scrapability.

9.6 The Relationship Differentiator: Overall Relationship Quality

Perceived quality is one out of the determining elements of a brand's equity value together with awareness, associations and loyalty.

Relationship differentiation is a market leader strategy founded on the idea of creating unique *relationship quality advantages* as opposed to *relationship economic advantages*. Such perceived and sustainable relationship quality advantages in some cases can generate customer satisfaction, loyalty and outstanding performance.

Relationship differentiators address their marketing efforts towards the total market and not just certain market segments which demand special relationship quality levers like customisation, special convenience or individualised comfort. The rationale behind relationship differentiation as a generic relationship marketing strategy can either be derived from a positioning perspective, *the open window of opportunity*, or be rooted in a unique set of competencies, *company skills applied in one among several product-markets*. Or maybe both.

The rapid penetration of the Internet in mid 1990s opened the window of opportunity for relationship differentiators like Internet banks, auction houses and all kinds of e-tailers. Microwave ovens in private homes did the same to the popcorn industry and created the microwave popcorn as a product category.

The health care portal Netdoctor.com gives individuals easy, instant access to a huge database that contains specific, scientifically based information about any disease, access to top medical specialists and hospital doctors, the opportunity to participate in information sharing and support communities etc. Netdoctor.com establishes an environment of direct relationships among individuals suffering from the same diseases and also between doctors and patients. The networks of medical research centres, medical authors and medical editors established through Netdoctor constitute a unique bundle of resources and competencies, which are prerequisites for relationship differentiation.

The Scandinavian company Home-Ice has built a fantastic company on the business idea of selling ice cream, the same products and brands as in supermarkets, directly to private households in residential neighbourhoods. At the core this idea is a relationship differentiation marketing strategy. The Home-Ice Van drives up the road and rings the big brass bell, a sound all children and adults immediately recognise as the "Home-Ice sound". Home-Ice comes to your door and offers a purchasing experience between family members and neighbours. And the freezing of the ice cream is much more effective than bringing ice cream in bags from the supermarket to the deep-freezers at home.

The window of opportunity for Home-Ice was the rapid rate of penetration of deep-freezers in the 1970's. The business innovation Home-Ice created was a relationship marketing innovation that established a direct relationship with the end-user characterised by quality elements like convenience and conceptualisation. Home-Ice involves the consumer much more in the buying process. People spend time buying ice cream and for the children the Home-Ice van is fun and exciting. The brass bell sound activates emotional response mechanisms, and the customer prepares for the Home-Ice experience even when the van is two blocks away.

A successful relationship differentiator strategy must be defendable against competitors. In the case of Home-Ice, direct imitation is not likely as there is no room in the market for a number 2. Hence, the first mover advantages in terms of the marketing innovation can represent effective barriers to entry for competitors.

9.6.1 Elements Promoting Relationship Differentiator Leadership Strategy

In a great many industries, relationship economic advantages are not the primary concern for the customers. In these situations companies must work with other strategic elements than transaction costs to develop extraordinary customer satisfaction and overall market leadership. This could be the case if:

- Customers give the routinisation effect relatively low priority as decision criteria compared with relationship quality. This type of buying behaviour is often found in knowledge based service industries like management consulting, IT-development etc.
- All major suppliers are structurally bound by identical supply chains and product lines. That is the case for many wholesale distributors.

The utility levers of a successful relationship differentiation might be divided into two broad categories: convenience vs. comfort.

How can the benefits of a relationship differentiator strategy possibly provide customers with convenience or comfort, e.g. cost reductions in the internal supply chain? A marketing strategist will try to identify the most important cost drivers in the value chain of the customers that can be eliminated by adding value to utility levers, thereby changing the nature of the buyer-seller relationship. He or she will also analyse how much extra customer satisfaction and loyalty could possibly be created through relational developments and ask if a position as differentiator can be built, consolidated and defended.

Just in time delivery is a typical differentiation relationship marketing strategy requiring special competencies that reduce inventory-holding costs within the customer organisation. The benefit: cost reduction through convenience.

The Danish company called Arte offered corporate customers a whole cultural service package comprised of theatre ticket services, event services, administration of customer clubs and sponsoring of cultural events. Culture is a part of corporate policies in most Scandinavian companies and an area where the internal planning, decision and implementation costs legitimise a package solution.

Relationship differentiation based on value adding to the customer's value chain is another way of obtaining competitive advantage. This could be generated by comfort attributes such as, flexibility, support, opening hours, training and education or logistical services. But how is it possible to identify and measure the opportunity of a strategic move in a direction that is perceived by the industry as generic relationship differentiation?

Outside Industry Differentiation Openers

Internet penetration paved the way for Internet banking, webvans and e-dating. The increasing proportion of active women in the labour market caused families to invest in deep-freezer capacity in private homes and opened up the market for Home-Ice. Changes outside an industry act as differentiation openers because such changes:

- Give room for completely new – differentiated kinds of relationships, which existing suppliers have difficulties grasping due to factors such as cannibalisation or decreasing capacity utilisation.
- Are absolute conditions for new customer behaviour and hence prerequisites for profitable innovative investments in relationship differentiation.
- Influence the overall competitive climate of the industry.

Changing Buyer Behaviour

Changes in customer behaviour sometimes can have a substantial impact on relationship strategies in supplier industries. The 7-eleven convenience chain offers a different relationship quality in terms of long opening hours combined with high quality food. New life styles among consumer i.e. flexible working hours, home offices, hard working IT and internet youngsters as well as more relaxed shopping habits, has made the 7-eleven business model viable.

The overwhelming outsourcing trend in almost all industries leads to much more dependence of suppliers and requires new marketing as well as new relational skills.

Intensified Rivalry in the Industry
In mature stage industries, rivalry tends to become fierce as a result of low market growth. Furthermore, it is difficult and expensive to gain substantial new market shares from competitors; at least it requires huge investments in R&D, communication, price cuts, better distribution coverage to win new customers. Not to mention the reduction of retaliation.

Relationship differentiation is often facilitated by intensified industry rivalry, e.g. struggle for economies of scale. Before the changes of SEC regulations in the US, the global accounting firms tended to offer their customers a broad spectrum client team with experts in auditing, tax planning, environment reporting, corporate finance, IT services etc.[7] This relationship differentiation, which some customers considered to be attractive, contributed to end the second tier accounting firms because size was the precondition for the type and level of non-audit service expertise.

For decades, newspapers in Europe and the US have suffered from declining sales. At the same time, digital TV and the Internet have conquered substantial market share from the newspapers, both in the news market as well as advertising revenues, e.g. jobportals like Stepstone. As a consequence of the intense rivalry between media houses, relationship differentiation has become a defensive strategic tool for the newspaper publishers. These defensive measures can be seen in terms of on-line editions of the newspapers, development of interactive services, vertical portals, communities, mass customisation, personalisation of the newspaper, *i.e. decide which content you want and we print a daily personalised edition of the newspaper for you.*

9.6.2 Developing a Strong Position as Relationship Differentiator

What does it require to develop a strong market position based on a relationship marketing strategy, targeting the total market and differentiating the company distinctly from its competitors? The relationship differentiation building can be viewed as a process in which all three elements are interdependent as illustrated in figure 9-7.

---

7. Financial Times, 2002/01/12 refers to a Standford study reporting that non-accounting services amount to 2.7 times the auditing fees among the big five account firms.

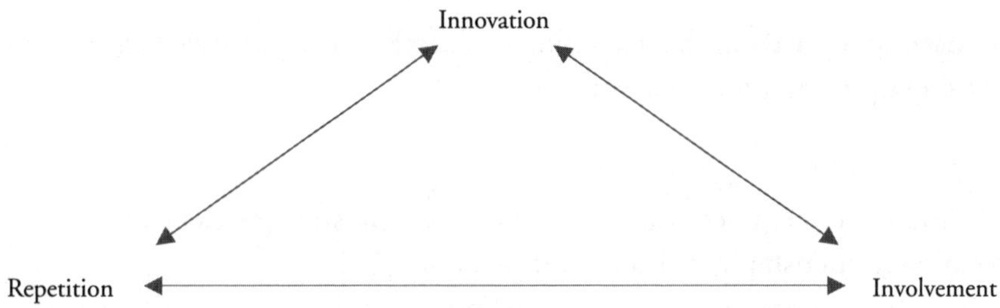

Figure 9-7: Innovation, involvement, and repetition.

In the *innovative* stages, a company detects opportunities to relate to customers in new ways: patterns of demand change. The driving competitive forces in the customer's industry shift. New technologies or infrastructures are breaking new ground in purchasing, usage, maintenance or disposal. Or perhaps the innovation comes from the discovery of new relationship utility potentials of a company's competency structures.

ISS is the global market leader in the cleaning industry. The core competence of ISS, developing and producing reliable, cost effective professional services, has enabled the firm to also innovate in the direction of relationship differentiation in terms of new tasks such as catering services or security. Strategically, ISS has moved its position from being perceived as a cost effective subcontractor in cleaning services only into a total solution provider of business services.

A shift in the level or in the type of *involvement* of the customer is usually an integrated element of a relationship differentiating marketing strategy. Do-it-yourself products seek to increase the involvement of the consumer. Just as process management consulting does as opposed to the expert-client or even the doctor-patient kind of interaction between the consultant and the customer.

Packaged solutions of all different kinds, ranging from packaged tours to the outsourcing of major business functions, imply a lower involvement level and leave more functions to the supplier and fewer transactions to the customer.

New involvement concepts are what turn a satisfied customer into an extraordinarily satisfied and loyal customer. Involvement can be the key to increased benefit and competitive advantage.

Repetition means that the relationship becomes an integrated part of the dyadic structure. Appreciation of the differentiator's offer is what leads to repeat buying and modification of the market mechanisms to the advantage of the seller in terms of premium price or lower sales costs.

Each of the 4 P's in the marketing mix can be an effective element in a relationship differentiation strategy:

P for Product

Product development can be a rather powerful strategic element in creating relationship based competitive advantages.

40 years ago, postal book clubs became very popular in Northern Europe. Signing up as a member of a book club you would automatically receive series of books of various types at very low prices compared with bookstore prices. The book club as a product innovation established a different generic relationship between the customer and the book as product category and the club as postal outlet.

P for Promotion

The World Wide Web has already presented overwhelming evidence that new patterns of communication can in fact be the drivers of radical new strategies.

On-line games usually involve a certain number of players interacting in game universes created by one single supplier. On-line gaming can, however, be even more amusing when different types of games and more players are involved under the umbrella of an organiser arranging tournaments.

This bundle of services creates a completely new relationship between the end user and the game community on the Internet.

P for Place

Buyer-seller relationships are determined by the distribution context or the interaction environment, in which they take place. By crossing traditional boundaries in its distribution strategy, a company can in effect create differentiated relationship moments. Commercial banks with staffed outlets in department stores, virtual fairs running parallel with and supplemented physical fairs, post offices selling theatre tickets have demonstrated the benefit of establishing new arenas for the customer contact.

Bang & Olufsen, famous in the luxury hi-fi market, refuses to distribute their products through discount store chains. They claim that a B&O distributor must reserve a special corner in the store in order to create an atmosphere of high quality relationships with end users.

P for Price
Price can be an influential mechanism in customer relationships. In the financial sector, fees on services can have a major impact on customer behaviour. Transaction fees on money and check exchanges have increased the popularity of electronic payment systems. The level and structure of fees is a litmus test for the customer relationship. Some financial institutions have decided to continue to give their customers transactional and advisory services free of charge leading to closer contacts with customers.

9.6.3 How Can Relationship Differentiation Leadership be Defended?

Whether or not a relationship differentiator will be able to obtain long-term return on loyalty depends not only on the short-term internal and the external driving forces. Sustainable advantage means that the sources of differentiation are renewable and adaptable to environmental changes. Examples of these are:

Changing Value Perceptions
What is an important relationship value generator today may have less impact on the market tomorrow. Customers get new ideas. Fulfilment of certain relationship preferences becomes a matter of course – once they are an integral element in the dyad such benefits loose their decisive influence. Both perceptions and importance of utility levers are dynamic and volatile.

Imitation Risk
If differentiation advantages rely on one sole visible and determining variable only there is a tendency towards imitation. When a strong loyalty position is instead composed of a variety of dimensions and competencies, imitation is less likely to occur.

External Driving Forces that can Lead to Erosion of Differentiation Advantages
In some cases external driving forces lead to the shortening the customer life cycle. The result is that investments in relationship differentiation never reach a stage of profitability. Special appliance stores in the mobile telephone market with the business segment as the main target group and that are staffed with professional sales people have been replaced by consumer electronic and TV stores with broader distribution and OTC selling.

Substitutes and Counterattacks

Instead of attacking the market leader by imitation, competitors will sometimes attempt to neutralise or substitute relationship advantages by changing the game of competition via price cuts or transaction cost leadership.

When railroads argue that they offer the business traveller unique relational qualities such as convenience, comfort, spaciousness, working facilities and conference rooms, the airlines strike back by focussing on the number of departures and the travelling time. Both utility levers are about price in terms of time value of money.

Does it Pay Off to defend Relationship Differentiation Advantages?

Relationship quality and service concepts have always been treated as strong marketing instruments. But it is by far a law of nature that the loyalty generated revenues stemming from such programmes exceeds the cost of acquiring such revenues through differentiation. In other words: Does it pay off to defend relationship differentiation advantages?

In the late 1970's, the Danish bank Privatbanken introduced their bank advisor concept, which was at that time a revolutionary relationship innovation for all household customers who now got their own personal bank advisor. The bank advisor should, would and could handle all kinds of financial services from portfolio management strategy to mortgage loans, overdrafts and pension planning. Before the introduction of the bank advisor, a private customer had to run the gauntlet between the different functional sections in the branch. The bank advisor was a revolution as bank branches at that time were organised along functionary lines. The target customer of the bank advisor was the more high net worth individuals, the segment where the return on loyalty investment was the highest. The bank advisor concept never paid off for Privatbanken. Why not? It turned out that it was financially the weakest, the most time consuming, and the least profitable customer who demanded the majority of the bank advisors time and who used up the banks precious resources. Whereas, the high net worth target group received and accepted the standard service level.

9.7 The Relationship Quality Segment Specialist

Transaction cost leadership and relationship differentiation are generic relationship strategies geared towards overall market leadership and industry wide leadership recognition.

In many industries, niche market segments, however, can be identified based on relationship preferences as segmentation criteria. Segments with different relationship requirements in terms of convenience, comfort or customisation will tend to buy what they prefer, if they can get it.

A relationship marketing strategy focusing on segments demanding special relationship features can therefore be a successful way to a genuine loyalty position: Either as a reactive, adaptation-like strategic move; *follow your customer*, or proactive initiatives; *your customers follow you.*

In the photo development industry, customers are offered a whole range of alternative service levels regarding delivery time. From instant (1 hour) development of the film to 72 hours delivery, very different convenience levels at very different prices. Consumers can decide themselves which relationship quality segment they belong to.

In asset management of institutional security portfolios, the asset management agreement determines the service quality on a set of different relationship type characteristics: responsibilities of the asset manager in terms of the mandate, reporting, transfer of data, transfer of knowledge etc. Some investment banking houses focus on specific client segments who prefer not to be involved in any operational decisions and who only require quarterly statements.

Working out an opportunity matrix with the purpose of spotting interesting relationship quality segments can be a helpful tool (see figure 9-8).

		Importance of relationship quality		
		Strong	**Middle**	**Weak**
Market segment attractiveness	**High**	1	2	3
			Area of opportunity	
	Middle	4	5	6
	Low	7	8	9

Figure 9-8: Opportunity matrix in relationship quality segmentation.

The size, growth and accessibility of such segments not only determine the attractiveness of relationship quality segments but also the importance and significance of the relationship quality attributes. For a market segment to be highly attractive, the specific relationship benefits demanded must also play a decisive role.

Evaluation of the company's overall position requires an insight into core competencies as well as knowledge about competitors. Despite a rather mediocre position in attractive segments, a relationship quality strategy can turn out to be worth consideration if the dominant players pay greatest attention to industry wide positioning.

Bang & Olufsen has built a unique and strong position in a narrow upscale hi-fi segment, where relationship benefits, design and lifestyle, encompass virtually their whole marketing strategy. In IT services, a customer segment like process industries, will choose an IT service supplier offering premium support services on a round the clock basis. This relationship quality factor may be superior to all others.

9.7.1 Elements in Favour of Relationship Specialist Marketing Strategy

Not all industries and markets contain relationship quality niches that are worthwhile cultivating. Either because competitive advantages are easy to neutralise or off balance, or because customers do not care enough about the quality features.

Some examples of the criteria that indicates the existence and accessibility of relationship quality niches of substantial value are:

How different are customers' needs and wants?
As mentioned earlier, specialisation assumes the existence of niches or market segments that have significantly different relationship preferences than the rest of the market. This is not the case in all markets. An *expectation based* relationship marketing strategy can still be interesting for some companies if they anticipate the relationship segments to expand in the future, even if they are non-existent today. Furthermore, relationship specialisation may turn out to be the only feasible outsider strategy, if overall market leadership is out of reach.

Variations in relationship demands do not necessarily stem from absolute buyer characteristics such as demographics, geography, magnitude, industry type, type of company in business-to-business markets etc. Discovering varieties in patterns of customer needs in many cases are dynamic and determined by situational factors. Consider restaurant consumption. Depending on situational factors like time, occasion, personal taste etc., our relationship demand differs considerably – do we want slow food, fast food etc.

When analysing a market for the purpose of discovering possible and robust relationship quality segments, the marketer should go through the following steps:

Step 1: Outline the broad list of relationship utility levels at play on the market.
Step 2: Describe typical customer life cycles and the transitions between the different phases.
Step 3: Rank the relationship utility levers and the customer life cycle phases. Answer questions like: Which relationship quality elements are important? How important are they? For all or only for some customers? Why?
Step 4: Ask if the customer or relationship need segments identified in step 1-3 are substantial in numbers, potential revenues over time and regarding differentiation relationship differences?

In the management consulting industry there are very different relationship quality strategies to handle the same set of client problems, e.g. corporate strategy. Some customers prefer a process oriented, enduring relationship to the consulting supplier. Some companies seek a more ad hoc quantitative expert solution with clean-cut diagnosis and recommendations. To go even one step further, some consulting firms de facto take over the management of the client firm during the period of restructuring. This is called deep pocket consulting.

Here is an anecdote reflecting these different relationship quality strategies in the field of management consulting:

> The Board of a major manufacturing company called in three different consulting companies for a briefing. At the end of the briefing, the president of the company asked the representatives from each consulting firm this simple question: "What time is it?" The first consulting firm representative looked at his watch: "It is ten to two". The senior partner in the second consulting firm: "Thanks for asking the question. We'll make a study on that". And the third said: "Well, Mr. President – what time would you like it to be?"

The Perceived Value of Customised Relationship Assets

The customer considers customisation of the product or service in some cases an important relationship value driver. Mass customisation means that the assets of the supplier within certain intervals create individualised solutions as the key to extreme customer satisfaction. Eyeglasses manufacturing, dental design, automobile, and architecture of private homes and print-on-demand are examples of this. Genuine customisation goes some steps further, by specifying groups of supplier assets to one and only one single customer with extensive consequences for the regulating mechanisms between the parties.

Mass customisation will often be the core element in a relationship differentiation strategy targeting the total market. But in some contexts customisation as a relationship value driver is only relevant for some segments of buyers. For luxury consumer goods segments in clothing or jewellery individualisation is an absolute must for a supplier to live up to if he wants to do business with that segment. Subcontractors of modules and components to device industries like hearing aids or mobile telephones with rapid growth and rapid technological renewals have to customise all their resources to the needs of the customer. The ability of such strategic subcontractors to cope with and create value during interaction with customers is a crucial strategic factor.

Core Competencies Behind Segment Focused Relationship Quality

The design capabilities of hâut couture houses like Ungaro, Kenzo or Gucci are the long-term key to maintaining the loyalty of the small segment of repeat customers at the very peak of the image hierarchy. The role of this segment is to certify and increase the equity of the brand vis-a-vis the much larger prêt-á porter market. The design competence is very much attached to the relationship between the fashion house, their designers and the individual customer. The ideas and models created in interactive iterations between the couture and the customer contributes significantly to the relationship value.

Changes in the Driving Forces of the Industry

Changes in the driving forces of an industry can stimulate a firm to move in the direction of a marketing strategy composed of relationship specialisation. Such driving forces could be:

- Structural changes developing new relationship preferences in specific market segments. Intensified competition forcing the customer segment to develop a new balance between market mechanisms/transactional focuses on the one hand and relationship contracting on the other hand can cause such changes. This creates opportunities for relationship specialists.
- Consolidation of industries forges new competitive positions. When the big five global airline alliances were formed in the mid 1990's following privatisation and liberalisation in Europe, discount airlines targeting the low quality segments and suddenly gained foothold on the market.

9.7.3 Competitive Advantages in Relationship Quality Segments

The above discussion of the factors that stimulate a company to invest in quality segment leadership assumes that such a business strategy originates from an ex ante explicit marketing strategic process. But marketing strategies are often emerging instead of being consciously planned. They develop out of evolutionary behaviour, interactive experiences with customers and an ex post rationalisation. So by asking the question "how do we actually think and work in our company?" it is possible for marketing management to paraphrase a generic strategy.

Sustainable and successful relationship marketing strategies in any case require that a company is concentrating all its efforts on this specific strategy element. A relationship strategy is by no means a clinical phenomenon that can be monitored and adjusted by a few skilled strategists. All employees, functions and business units are integral parts of the formulation and participate in providing the concrete offer and execution of the relationship marketing strategy. The company's interface with customers is multifunctional and not imbedded in a core product separated from the human dimension.

Therefore, the organisation viewed as a holistic organism is the marketer. Competitive advantages assume that this organism is able to leverage and orchestrate its resources relative to competitors in a relationship framework focusing on the quality levers of the segment through concerted behaviour. But why can the building, enhancing and defending of decisive relationship advantages in a specific relationship, quality sensitive niche, most of all be considered a matter of resource leverage?

First, because the strategy as relationship quality specialist is the typical no. 2 or no. 3 position in an industry, for which reason strategic focus becomes even more crucial. Focus means full consensus of strategic goals and high learning skills within the organisation itself. Second, the relationship quality dimensions that the focus segment cares about and which legitimise the specialist position must be continually secured, emphasised, developed further and internalised in every nerve and cell of the company. Finally, the overall benefits of customisation in terms of asset specificity depend on the excellence of resource leverage. As discussed earlier, customer orientation of any asset is a kind of double-edged sword. On the one hand, weakening the bargaining power of the supplier in the relationship contract, as the asset has less economic value in other uses if any at all. On the other hand, customisation of assets towards single customers or segments is clearly a dyadic strength and a key to competitive advantage. In any case, resource leveraging is an essential element in developing effective relationship quality specialisation. The categories of resource leveraging, the building blocks of unique quality competencies can be expressed as in figure 9-8.

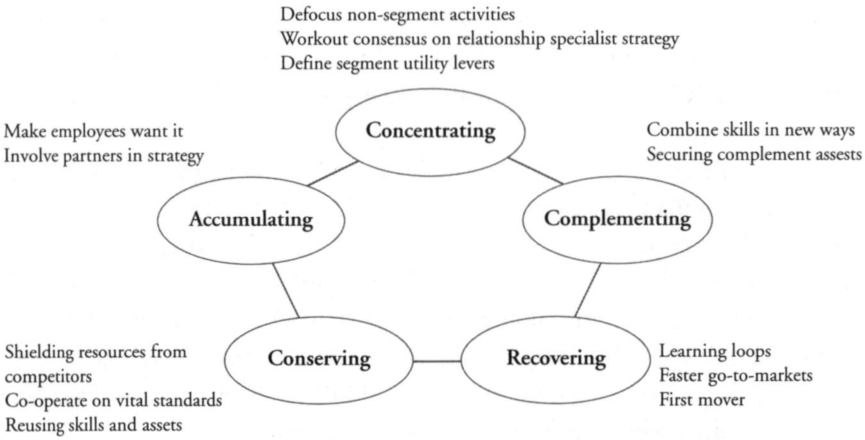

Figure 9-9: The resource leverage pentagon for the relationship quality specialist.

Sufficient concentration means that activities and processes are addressed to the quality segment and non-core activities are spun out or reoriented. The *concentration* leverage factor creates focus. *Accumulating* is the aspect of resource leverage by which experience and organisational learning creates effectiveness synergies, because they are centred on the relationship niche.

Complementation stretches the capabilities of the organisation in new ways by meeting the customers' requirements and securing access to new assets. Reusing, co-operating and protecting is the resource *conserving* leverage mechanisms. Whereas, *recovering* strengthens the skills of speed through effective learning loops and involvement of customers in the value creation.

One conclusion that can be drawn is that developing competitive advantages through the firm's ability to create unique relationship quality experiences for a specific segment and leaving the rest of the market to competitors, requires an innovative marketing strategy. More important are the invisible and immaterial organic skills in terms of resource leverage.

9.7.3 When is a Relationship Quality Niche Threatened?

The relationship quality niche is a mono segment marketing strategy. As is the case with the positioning strategy of the monotype, it is threatened if:

- The demand and decision criteria of the segment changes. Repositioning becomes the more difficult and painful the stronger perceptions of a company's products are within the segment
- The segment decreases in size or value
- The competitors move. Competitors discovering new decision criteria in the segment will develop new attributes or utilise their cost efficient position to reduce the price level. It is difficult for the relationship segment specialist to fight back, as all its resources are dedicated to specific relationship needs in specific segments
- New technologies or other external driving forces threaten the dyad
- The company itself reformulates its strategy in a multi-segment direction. In this case there is a reduction as the organisation looses its focus and thus weakens the loyalty of customers in the niche. This was the experience of a travel agency specialised in exotic, adventure small group travel packages They decided to broaden their scope and offer the more standard type of charter travel oriented towards the mass market. The broader focus gave room for their competitors in the basic adventurer segment to gain market share.

In summary, a relationship quality niche strategy can be very profitable and is for some companies the only feasible way to gain competitive advantage. But following the customers can be difficult, if they do not follow you. Put in another way: *customers don't care how much we know, before they know how much we care.*

9.8 Engineering The Transaction Cost Niche Explorer Strategy

A transaction cost niche is a segment of customers who demand other relationship economic elements than the rest of the market in all or some stages of the customer relationship life cycle. The key to strong loyalty and niche dominance is to reduce the perceived transaction costs for customers in the segment in an above-normal profitable way. Often a company seeking transaction cost leadership must accept the role as niche explorer, as it is difficult to predict the existence and size of the niche beforehand.

A hotel chain once made the public announcement that any guest who was not fully satisfied with his or her stay at the hotel would be granted 100% refund of the invoice at the cashier's desk when checking out without discussion or documentation of any kind. This relationship's offer, free stay if you so wish, had strong appeal to a certain audience. As a supplier would never make such an offer, if he expected customers to make use of it. Maybe customers who tended to be unsatisfied with hotels anyway, maybe just security seekers, maybe pure opportunists or maybe customers who interpreted this guarantee given by the hotel as a quality assurance. Some customers saw the offer as a substantial transaction cost reduction, no other group of hotels could offer. Why not choose that one when all other elements of the product were fully competitive. The investment turned out to be very profitable.

An innovation in the insurance industry is a service where an insurance broker investigates areas where a company can possibly reduce its insurance costs. They do so on behalf of the customer. In essence they target their service towards customer segments that are willing to externalise their purchasing process. The brokers not only offer possibly lower rates; they also offer minimisation of the transaction costs in a field, which is difficult for an outsider to understand.

Success with a relationship marketing strategy as transaction cost niche explorer both assumes the discovery and cultivation of an attractive, profitable niche, but also that local leadership is attainable. The competitive advantage of the hotel chain above could easily vanish, if their competitors just copied the idea offering the same service quality guarantee. It is therefore of great importance that the transaction cost niche allows the niche to build and defend entry barriers.

9.8.1 Elements Promoting Transaction Cost Niche Strategies

A position whereby a company has successfully lowered the sum of its own and its customers' transaction costs, i.e. the costs of running the total economic system in a particular segment is not easily obtained. Many of the elements applicable for relationship segmentation specialists also hold true for cost niche dominance. When are the structural and the situational elements in favour of establishing a transaction cost niche? When are they not?

A manufacturer in the food industry decided to focus entirely on a business model comprising the design and production of no name brands and private labels to store chains that have the strategy of selling their own proprietary brands.

Either exclusively or as counter positioning to the well established brands. This manufacturer experienced minimal sales and marketing expenses and obtained low production costs through high capacity utilisation. Store chains often make aggressive attempts to persuade producers of strong brands to provide them with a proprietary brand as well – using their purchasing power as a main argument. Even when the relationship between the big retail groups and brand suppliers include private label contracting, this kind of relationship is rarely amenable, which implies a lot of excess transaction costs in a non-cooperative atmosphere.

Indications of a transaction cost niche opportunity are:

- The strategies within customer industries create relationship economic niches for supplier industries. Some segments of buyers strive for competitive advantages by deliberately reducing their transaction costs based on a cooperative buying strategy. In cases, where they also request idiosyncratic investments from the supplier, the transaction cost niche is unsafe.
- The market leaders in the supplier industry work with strategic paradigms that are unable to respond to transaction cost niches, as a positive response would cannibalise heavily on the existing business structure. The widespread fear for e-business solutions reveals clearly such a situation.
- Substitution opportunities. Sometimes a completely different environment for transactions with customers can be set. Substitution relationships do in fact represent a transaction cost niche. When commercial banks in Europe begin to sell insurance, mortgages and pension schemes they tried to reduce the transaction costs dramatically, as banking customers tend to trust their bank more than they trust other service suppliers.

9.8.2 Developing a Company into a Transaction Cost Niche Explorer

A position as transaction cost niche can be very strong and difficult for competitors to attack. But it can also be hard to explore and consolidate.

On some productmarkets, relationship economics only plays an inferior role. If reversibility is high, distribution widespread, involvement low etc, there are limits to a company's ability to build very strong loyalty by adopting a relationship approach to marketing planning. Developing a position as transaction cost niches involves steps such as identifying and sizing the niche, exploring the opportunity through pilot tests, focusing the internal resources and investing in segment specific assets in order to drive down the transaction costs.

Exploring a transaction cost niche implies attention to two different relationship economic dimensions:

- The investment characteristic, i.e. whether or not the exploration process requires investment in specific assets.
- The frequency of interaction between buyer and seller.

A strategy based on non-specific assets will most often use the market mechanism as regulator. Complete customisation in terms of idiosyncratic investments will require extended bilateral coordination among the parties, e.g. the seller builds a factory to produce customer specified items only. In between we find mixed investments with elements of both non-specification and customisation. Modular products are a good example.

Frequency of interaction and purchasing can have a significant impact on the level and the structure of transaction costs. Recurrent purchases of the strategic type with extended information gathering is a niche characterised by very high transaction costs.

Combining the two axes, the interaction pattern and asset customisation, the following typology emerges (see figure 9-10).

		Asset customisation	
		Non customised	**Customised**
Frequency of interaction	**Occasional**	Niche: Bundling	Niche: Dyadic contract
	Recurrent	Niche: Easy access	Niche: Co-operation

Figure 9-10: Some transaction cost niche positions.

Niche – Easy Access

Segments of customers or clusters of needs with high frequency of purchasing compared to the rest of the market, i.e. heavy users, who demand non-customised investments. Easy access becomes the key to reducing the transaction costs in the system, e.g. mass distribution, EDI, functional outsourcing.

Niche – Bundling

Occasional purchasing of standardised goods or services with high reduction, high complexity and irreversibility gives rise to extended transaction costs. Not only in the initial stages but also in contracting. Some segments prefer to acquire a bundled solution leaving it to the supplier to provide a *plug and play* solution. Bundling as opposed to single products supply is a focus marketing strategy, which is aimed at loyalty preservation replacing transaction costs with a higher price on the core service. The concept of *all reducing insurance* is a genuine bundling solution.

Niche – Dyadic Contract

Industrial buying of key components, modules, systems and machinery is occasional and in many cases combined with all the elements of opportunism, self-interest, idiosyncrasy, mismatch in buyer-seller strategy etc. A seller strategy could be to gradually develop a position as dyadic contractor. The target segment for the dyadic contractor is customers both demanding customisation and with a behavioural fit vis-à-vis the seller strategy.

Niche: Cooperation

Recurrent purchases of customised material will typically be relatively reversible for the buying organisation and does not involve the kind of huge high reducing, hyper idiosyncratic investment for the seller. In this niche position the buyer will tend to act in a cooperative way, as the inducement to opportunism is relatively low because the seller can reemploy his assets in other relationships. Additionally, the transaction is less costly to undertake both for buyer and seller if they cooperate. The relationship between a firm and its advertising agency or accounting firm reveals such a situation.

In the first growth stage of the Internet, service firms adopted quite diverse relationship strategies. Some of the firms decided not to work for dot.com's and focused strongly on customer segments in the *old economy* that preferred relatively strong retainer contracts as the framework for cooperation. These accounts were difficult to acquire, and furthermore the relationship focus sacrificed the skyrocketing budgets of the dot.com e-tailers. After the burst of the Internet bubble in 2000-2001 the strategy as transaction cost niche turned out to be relatively successful.

9.8.3 Is the Transaction Cost Niche Defendable?

When a supplier has leveraged its resources to the relationship economic priorities of a given transaction cost segment it can be quite difficult for competitors or new entrants to threaten such a position.

Customers will of course control the supplier on a regular basis in a triadic game, in which competitors will try also to break the relationship often motivated by positive signals from customers. But they rarely succeed. The transaction cost niche and its customer base has developed into a committed relationship.

References

Abell, D. and Hammond, J. S. (1979) *Strategic Marketing Planning – Problems and Analytical Approaches*, Prentice Hall.

Andersen, U. (1997) *Strategiens økonomi – Vækstbaseanalyser som ledelsesinstrument.* Handelshøjskolens Forlag.

Berry, L.L. and Parasuramen, A. (1991) *Marketing of Services: Competing through Quality.* Free Press.

Buttle, F. (ed.) (1996) *Relationship Marketing – Theory and Practice.* Paul Chapman Publishing.

Buzzell, R. D. and Gale, B. (1985) *The PIMS principles. Linking strategy to performance.* The Free Press.

Chan, W. K. and Mauborgne, R. (2000) *Knowing a winning business idea when you see one*, Harvard Business Review, vol. September.

Cravens, D. W. (1994) *Strategic Marketing.* Irwin.

Cyert, R.M. and March, J.G. (1963) *A Behavioural Theory of the Firm*, Prentice Hall.

Ford, D. (1980) *The Development of Buyer-Seller Relations in Industrial Markets*, European Journal of Marketing.

Ford, D. (1990) *Understanding Business Markets: Interaction, Relationships and Networks.* Academic Press.

Ford, D., Håkonsson, H. and Johanson, J. (1986) *How do companies interact?*, Industrial Marketing and Purchasing.

Guiltinan, J. & Paul, G. (1994) *Marketing Management: Strategies and programmes*, McGraw-Hill.

Heskett, J., Jones, T. O., Loveman, G., Sasser, E. and Schlesiger, L. (1994) *Putting the Service Profit Chain to Work*, Harvard Business Review, vol. March.

Hovell, P. (1990) *The Marketing Concept and Corporate Strategy: A Well-o-the-Wisp Relationship*, Journal of Marketing.

Håkansson, H. & Snehota, I. (1995) *Developing Relationships in Business Networks.* Routledge.

Kunøe, G. (1993) *Metaloyalitet.*

Larreché, J.C. & Gatignon, H. (1990) *Markstrat – A Marketing Management Simulation*, The Scientific Press.

Nielsen, O. and Wilke, R. (1999) *Organisationers købsadfærd i grundtræk*, Samfundslitteratur.

Owusu, R. (1997) *Relationship Marketing and the Interactioninetwork Approach*, Svenska Handelshögskolan in Helsinki.

Penrose, E. (1959) *The Theory of The Growth of the Firm*, Basil Blackwell.

Porter, M. E. (1985) *Competitive Advantage: Creating and Sustaining Superior Performance*, Free Press.

Porter, M. E. (1982) *Competitive Strategy: Techniques for Analyzing Industries and Competitors*, Free Press.

Porter, M. E. (1990) *The Competitive Advantage of Nations*, Macmillan Press.

Prahalad, C.K. and Hamel, G. (1994) *Competing for the Future*, Harvard Business School Press.

Prahalad, C.K. and Hamel, G. (1990) *The Core Competence of the Corporation*, Harvard Business Review.

Reichheld, F. and Sasser, W.E. jr. (1995) *Zero defections: quality comes to services*, Harvard Business Review.

Reichheld, F. (1993) *Loyalty-Based Management*, Harvard Business Review.

Reichheld, F. (1996) *The Quest for Loyalty – Creating Value through Partnership*. Harvard.

Simon, H. A. (1955) *A Behavioural Model of Rational Choice*, Quarterly Journal of Economics.

Storbacka, K. (1994) *The Nature of Customer Relationship Profitability – Analysis of Relationships and Customer Bases in Retail Banking*, Ekoomi och Samhälle Svenska Handelshögskolan. Helsingfors.

CHAPTER 10

Risks and Benefits of Relationships

Relationships are not beneficial in and of themselves, but can potentially offer benefits of varying importance to the parties involved. This chapter focuses on the benefits of relationships for the involved parties, typically the selling and the buying organisation. In keeping with the previous chapters, consequences will be assessed both inside and outside the dyad.

These benefits will be analysed in relation to time. In the short-term these benefits are generally considered to be operational and tactical. Whereas in the long-term they tend to often be both strategic as well as tactical. Depending on the customer's willingness, and interest, the relationship benefits acquired in the initial part of the relationship may turn out to be all there was to gain. What happens if the benefits are not sustainable? Must a relationship show continuous improvement in order to survive?

Although it is the benefits in focus here, the limitations must be identified and assessed as well. Would you consider a relationship to be beneficial if one party received all the benefits? On the other hand, is the party who gains no benefits disadvantaged by this situation?

10.1 Supplier Benefits – as a Relationship Partner

Benefits the selling organisation may obtain will of course depend on the relationship type and the customer involved. Before going into specifics, the general benefits a supplier can expect from strategic relationship marketing will be presented. The benefits obtained from a relationship may differ considerably. Consider a supplier's relationship to a defender,[1] this type of relationship may provide opportunities for rationalisation and increased efficiency in the selling organisation, whereas

1. See chapter 8 for a detailed discussion of the four strategic types of behaviour.

a relationship to a prospector may provide increased creativity and improved processes related to product development within the selling organisation.

		Differentiation focus	
		Low	High
Cost focus	**High**	*Defender* Short term focus – risk of opportunism Flexibility – may avoid investing in specific assets Focus on value in processes Efficiency Rationalisation Focus of lowest possible specific transaction costs Will support the seller's transaction cost leader strategy[2]	*Analyser* Long and short term focus often supported by contracts Ensuring profitable investments in customised assets Coping with customer "cherry-picking" Partnering projects Focus on lowest possible specific transaction and costs and specific developments Will support the seller's transaction cost niche strategy and/or the quality segment specialist strategy
	Low	*Reactor* No time focus – low risk of opportunism Testing new ways of working and processes Developing new form of delivery systems Educating new staff Focus on lowest posible generic transaction costs Will moderately support the seller's relationship differentiatior and /or transaction cost leader strategy	*Prospector* Long term focus often supported by contracts Product development Process development Ensuring that investments in customised assets are profitable Partnering projects Focus on creativity and innovative skills Will support the seller's quality segment specialist strategy and/or relationship differentiator strategy

Figure 10-1: Supplier benefits to be expected.

2. See chapter 9 for a closer definition of these generic relationship strategies.

The benefits can be described in relation to the four different types of strategic behaviour introduced in chapter 8 as illustrated in figure 10-1. This figure shows that more than one of the generic relationship strategies may be applied to each of the four types. However, it is important to ensure that the possible benefits actually fit the strategic goals of the selling organisation in the short and long-term.

The central point is that obtaining benefits at the customer's expense is not an option within the framework of strategic relationship marketing; the relationship must benefit both parties. Furthermore, these benefits are highly dependent upon the strategy pursued by the partner, as illustrated in figure 10-1, as well as on the strategy pursued by the selling organisation itself.

Bang & Olufsen, for example, would have great difficulty supplying a discount retail chain due in part to diverging goals and understandings of why consumers buy and in part to the differences in the operational set-up. Bang & Olufsen focuses on high quality and exclusive consumer perceptions of product and service, whereas a discount retailer focuses on low prices and no service to enhance the perception of low prices.

When a manufacturer of tables and chairs looks for a supplier of bolts and screws it is typically a question of price and price alone. Therefore, it may be quite difficult to hope for any other supplier benefits than flexibility and efficiency.

Obtaining benefits will often be a result of decisions involving trade-offs and the dilemmas related to strategic relationships. If the industry is characterised by mutually exclusive relationships, the supplier will have to choose between different opportunities. In the FMCG-sector it's quite rare that a supplier has equally close relationships with competing retail chains. Actually, the supplier will often play a strategic role for the retail chain either in terms of product development, marketing or both.

But even if relationships can be developed with all potential customers, most organisations face limited resources and will therefore have to be selective and choose where to focus. Discussing benefits is a way to assess the opportunities and make educated decisions.

Organisations do not enter a relationship expecting a negative outcome. A positive outcome is expected or at least a neutral one if compared to the situation before entering the relationship. Beware of the risk of over-investment without reward. Many selling organisations have convinced themselves that a prospective relationship justifies significant investments in specific assets, only to realise that the customer didn't have the same interest.[3] What we see here is the *expectation*

3. See chapter 1, figure 1-5.

paradox; namely that the benefits expected in the long-term are much higher than the realised benefits in the short-term. However, if a small supplier is interested in doing business with a very large customer, the supplier may be faced with a "take-it-or-leave-it" relationship. Developing a relationship in this context may lead to a "one-sided relationship" and is generally not recommended.

Lowering transaction costs may be possible as the exchange between the partners is repeated. This can be due to the learning curve, customisation of assets, long-term contracts etc. Furthermore, continued exchanges will gradually internalise the routines and processes supporting the exchanges and the relationship will become part of everyday routine. This will ensure a smooth and continuous exchange without having to search for alternatives or substitutes. An important question to pose here is: Is filling the designated need of the buyer in the strategic interests of the seller?

Getting the most out of idiosyncratic assets is an example of the benefits gained from investments in production facilities, service facilities, individuals, etc. These are resources dedicated to handling exchanges between the supplier and a specific customer. For example most IT companies have dedicated individual salespeople to specific customers. This is partly based on the person's insight and knowledge of an industry and partly based on the person's psychological profile.

As described previously in chapter 8, the benefits may also depend on the strategic behaviour of the partner. This will reflect the type of behaviour, i.e. the defender will make your organisation more efficient and slim, the prospector will enhance creativity and flexibility, the analyser will do both, and the reactor may prove to be a testing ground for new products, new processes or a new exchange method.

The stage in the customer life cycle is relevant as well. In the early stages, benefits are related to operational activities, as this is where the supplier and customer are willing to share information. As the relationship develops over time, tactical and even strategic benefits may emerge as the parties gradually acknowledge themselves as part of a value chain. However, if a relationship wears out it may become very difficult to hold on to former benefits, either due to lack of interest in continued cooperation or simply because the supplier or customer return to a "I-want-to-safeguard-my own interests" mindset. This is typically a strategic mismatch or simply a question of different priorities with regard to the expected benefits of the relationship. But it is also the result of a failure. Namely, that it wasn't possible to develop mutual benefits valuable enough in order to sustain the relationship.

When benefits are expected to increase over time, is it partly due to the gradual emergence of mutual trust and the gradual acquisition of insights into each other's structures, processes, and activities. Benefits also stem from mutual understanding of the others culture and gradual development of exit barriers as adaptations are constructed.

Generally, relationships are expected to generate supplier benefits such as the types illustrated in figure 10-2.

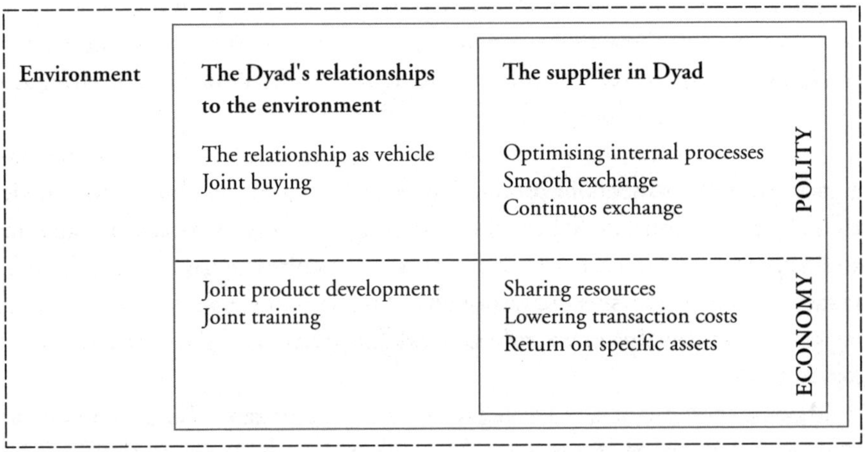

Figure 10-2: Supplier benefits related to the political economy framework.
Source: Based on figure 2-1, in chapter 2.

Supplier benefits may be classified into three categories within the supplier's organisation: Monadic benefits, within the dyad – Dyadic benefits, and taking the dyad further – Triadic benefits.

Monadic Benefits – Primarily Transaction Cost Reduction

Focusing on internal benefits within the partner's organisation was originally a core reason for developing relationships.[4] However, the original approach to relationship development was based on a "we-invest-then-we-harvest" methodology, which has since given way to a "we-both-invest-and-we-both-harvest" methodology, the basic benefits to each of the partners should not be neglected.

4. Grönroos (1995), Gummesson (1996), Christopher, Payne, and Ballantyne (1991).

- Relationships may be a catalyst for including new areas in the exchange, i.e. opening informational exchanges other than just product relevant information – but are there areas of information you cannot reveal or do not want to reveal?
- Smoothness, no friction (or transaction costs) will maintain the relationship and mutual trust will assist in resolving misunderstandings, events to be interpreted positively.
- No disruptions, i.e. a continuous flow of exchange (no start/stop costs) – is this type of benefit shared? And how?
- ROI from specific assets because the relationship ensures economies of scale for the specific investments made to support the relationships and the exchanges taking place within the relationship, but who gets the economic benefit?

Dyadic Benefits – within the Dyad

Uneven distribution of benefits may not be sufficient to maintain the relationship. However, in the short-term it will be sufficient to ensure that one party will do whatever it takes maintain the relationship. But in the long run this will be an up-hill battle. Such a situation is only sustainable if there is information asymmetry or if the party that is aware that distribution of benefits is uneven does not possess either the strength or the resources to change it.

Dyadic Benefits – Benefiting the Supplier

Many relationships have been developed with the expectation that the supplier initiating the relationship will gain from this. Basically this is a sound argument, however, relationship marketing focuses on taking this further, also ensuring benefits to the customer. Some of the most common reasons for developing relationships are:

- Cost reductions – could also affect partners outside the relationships, i.e. third party
- Process development, based on joint input and alignment
  - Data capture, based on joint alignment.
  - Forecasting, based on joint alignment.
- Product development based on unsolved needs of the customer.
- Increasing utilisation and profitability from investments in specific assets.
- Utilising the relationship as internal benchmark to educate and develop internal resources.

Dyadic Benefits – Benefiting Both

Benefits to both partners in the dyad leads to a strong long-term relationship. Basically these benefits can only be realised if the two partners exchange information and share insights. Therefore, most of the benefits identified have a *joint* or *share* as prefix.

- Joint cost reductions – could also affect partners outside the relationship, i.e. third party
  - Joint process development
  - Reusing data captured
  - Improving forecasting, stock and sales data
- Joint product development
- Sharing resources
- Sharing competencies
- Sharing information regarding future developments, needs, expectations.

Triadic Benefits – the Relationship as Vehicle for Further Benefits

Benefits to partners outside the dyad develops the relationship further and allows it expand, initiating a positive cycle

- Vehicle for exchanges beyond core product/service. This could be a joint relationship with an external partner to the dyad
- Possible access to different levels of the organisation
- Influence of sourcing and supply chain management decisions
- Trial and error acceptance related to new technology, need for joint learning and other types of experiments, etc.

As illustrated in figure 10-3, relationship benefits to the supplier may be divided into three levels – the strategic, the tactical and operational level. This table indicates that there is a need for operational benefits to maintain the relationship and strategic benefits can only be expected in the long run.

Figure 10-3 illuminates the fact that obtaining strategic benefits from relationships takes time, but it can also be used as a reminder to investigate the possibilities for reaching strategic benefits when relationships mature.

When considering relationship opportunities, the supplier should not look to relationships as a way of squeezing more out of the customer. On the contrary, you should keep a constant focus on your ability to learn from the customer and to enhance your customer's benefit from having a relationship specifically with you. That is the dyadic paradigm in a nutshell.

	Short term	Long term
Strategic benefits	Hardly any	Can be
Tactical benefits	Could be	Should be
Operational benefits	Must be	Must be

Figure 10-3: Benefit expectations in relation to time.

10.2 Customer Benefits – as a Relationship Partner

Customer benefits or benefits to the buying organisation in BtB markets will of course depend on the relationship type, the purchasing strategy pursued by the customer as well as a number of other factors. Actually, quite a few of the benefits identified in BtB markets may also apply in BtC markets.

Lowering transaction costs is often a key expectation when a customer enters a relationship. In other words, this is often the single most important reason for entering a relationship. This is particularly relevant for organisations pursuing a defender or analyser strategy because their focus is on low price and efficiency.

Getting a satisfactory return on investment on idiosyncratic assets is rarely problematic, at least not during the initial steps of the relationship, as the investment tends to be supported by contractual obligations. However, this may change considerably as the relationship develops and focus shifts to extracting the most out of the strategic behaviour of the supplier.

Smoother and repeated exchange as a result of relationship longevity is the key expectation of many relationships. Furthermore, it is also important that the customer is constantly reassured that the supplier does not gain monadic benefits from the relationship.

Avoiding negative effects on one's own power base(s) is often a central concern to customers, as a relationship may, at least for a period of time, limit the possibilities for entering other relationships.

The relevance of benefits rests on each individual's perception. Actually it is the expectation of the buying organisation, or individual to which is to be used as a benchmark to evaluate the benefits and their relevance. Although a benefit may seem relevant to the salesperson, it may not be, if the buyer does not regard it as such. What is relevant and important to a low cost operator such as ALDI may only have a marginal relevance to a prospector like Apple.

Generally customer benefits fall into the same three categories as supplier benefits: within the customer's organisation, within the dyad, and outside the dyad.

Monadic Benefits – Benefits to the Buying Organisation

Customer benefits may differ depending on the strategy pursued by the customer, not just in terms of the overall strategic type, but also in terms of the buying policy applied.[5] Some of the more common benefits are:

- Ensure buying criteria are met, i.e. that internal procedures for identifying and choosing suppliers are followed and fulfilled
- Minimises risk of partner "taking advantage of the relationship at our expense", i.e. that it is not necessary to continuously check prices and trading conditions of the supplier's competitors
- Provide access to different organisational levels of partner, i.e. that access to the supplier's organisation is not limited to one or very few individuals
- Will automatically being informed about developments and innovations within the supplier's industry.

Dyadic Benefits – Benefits to the Buying Organisation

Benefits to the customer are often based on receiving free resources via the exchanges with a specific supplier and then using them elsewhere. If this is to succeed some of the following expectations must be fulfilled:

- Communication is understood and interpreted as intended by sender
- Smoothness, no friction (or transaction costs), no hassle
- No disruptions, i.e. continuous flow of exchange, supply safety
- Joint cost reductions – this could also affect partners outside the relationships, i.e. third party
  - Access to production scheduling
  - Access to warehouse, distribution and supply chain data.

Dyadic Benefits – Benefits to Both Parties

Benefits to both parties are quite similar to those mentioned in the subsection on supplier's benefits. However, a few are different in that they come from the customer's point of view. These are:

---

5. See chapter 8.

- Joint developments
- Joint actions such as joint buying
- Sharing resources
- Sharing competencies
- Vehicle for exchanges beyond core product/service
- Possible impact of strategy formulation
- Possibly part of strategy planning process – at least concerning the specific relationship.

Triadic Benefits

Taking customer benefits beyond the dyad often happens in more mature relationships, as both the supplier and customer have acknowledged that the benefits outweigh the drawbacks.

- Utilising insights in relation to other suppliers, i.e. processes, routines and procedures.
- Together serving new customer segment(s).

Generally, relationships are expected to generate different types customer benefits as illustrated in figure 10-4.

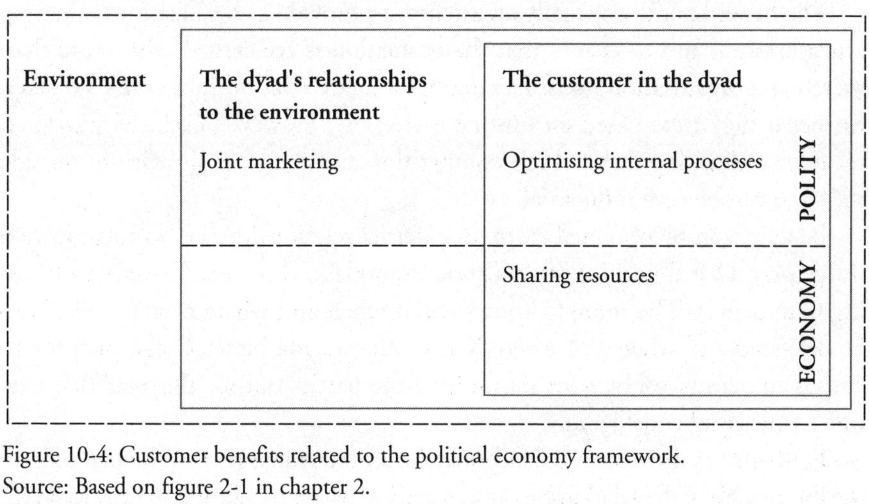

Figure 10-4: Customer benefits related to the political economy framework.
Source: Based on figure 2-1 in chapter 2.

As for the supplier, strategic benefits can be expected in the long run, whereas operational benefits must be obvious in the short-term in order to support the relationship and to make it develop.

Some customers have taken relationship-marketing strategies a step further and introduced *reverse marketing*[6] or what could be termed *key supplier management.*[7] This concept is closely related to the buyer initiative as it focuses on the need for making the "right" choices among the potential suppliers. As noted previously, strategic relationship marketing aims upstream as well as downstream in the business system.

10.3 The Relationship Audit – Evaluating the Relationship

The benefit audit is an individual assessment of the pros and cons of specific relationships. It is based on the supplier and customer being involved and their perception of the relationship rewards.

The relationship audit assesses the benefits individually. These benefits are then sorted into two groups: short and long term. Finally, each of the benefits is evaluated in terms of the future expectations – will they decrease, stay as they are, or increase?

The benefit audit is actually an attempt to provide a checklist for evaluating a relationship, and to ensure that the evaluation is concerned with more than merely the organisation itself. For example, many relationships could be taken further if they were based on mutual exclusivity. However, exclusivity is often regarded as limiting free and fair competition and therefore limitations outside the dyad can be very influential.

Benefits can be obtained from an external relationship, i.e. in relation to a third party. Distribution is often a good example in this area; A sells X to B, using C to deliver. The more C knows about when and where B would like X to be delivered and when and where X is produced, the better C can plan for it. This is an example of benefits stemming from parties outside the dyad that may impact the dyad considerably.

Furthermore the benefit balance may be an integrated part of the planning of the future state of the relationship with regard to where to take it and how to do it.

6. The customer's marketing effort aimed at suppliers.
7. Kjeldsen (1997).

	Short term	Long term
Monadic: Benefits within the organisation Limitations within the organisation		
Dyadic: Benefits within the dyad Limitations within the dyad		
Triadic: Benefits outside the dyad Limitations outside the dyad		

Figure 10-5: The benefit audit table.

10.4 Strategic Selling as opposed to Traditional Selling

Traditional selling is based on fulfilling the interests, needs, and desires of the customers and generating a profit for the supplier. Hence, the traditional sales process focuses on identifying the interests, needs and desires that are expressed by the customer, which could either be an individual or a group.

Mutual loyalty implies that you do not put your own interests first, but the well being of the relationship. Mutual loyalty is a concept developed in reaction to the prevailing concept of loyalty, which is often based on the loyal customer's behaviour towards the company. But why is it that we always speak about customer loyalty, i.e. the customer's loyalty towards the supplier, and not the other way around? What is the other way around, anyway?

It is called *reverse loyalty*, i.e. the loyalty from the initiator of the loyalty program towards the partners. The indicators of reverse loyalty are:

- A supplier's loyal behaviour towards the customer is to ensure that the customer's demands and needs are met, perhaps even setting one's own interests aside. This is merely possible in the short-term, because if it is in the long-term, the supplier should not enter into the relationship.
- Looking at one's own company (and competitors) from the customer's point of view and acknowledging strengths and weaknesses.
- Aiming at enhancing the performance and potential of the relationship in a value chain perspective, not merely one's own performance.

Mutual loyalty is thus a combination of the traditional concept of loyalty and reverse loyalty. One of the consequences of mutual loyalty is that it may create a situation where the company may disregard its own product/service. This could be due to lack of competitiveness, knowledge about new product generations coming up, lack of ability to benefit fully from product/service features, etc. Consider the situation where you know that the new version of the software product you sell will be launched in three months time. The stock level of the existing version is still high. Will you continue selling the existing version or inform your customers that a new version is coming soon?

This approach challenges traditional success criteria and compensation schemes in transactional oriented sales organisations as these are typically based on sales within a specified period, a month, a quarter, or a fiscal year. How could you defend postponing a sure sale to a customer until the new version is launched? An even more challenging question is: how about suggesting a competitor's product?

Discussions regarding sales strategies have traditionally centred on uncovering the customer's interests, needs and desires.[8] A useful framework for sales processes is the SPIN-process based on a series of questions designed to reveal the customer's:

- Situation
- Problem(s)
- Implication(s) of solution
- Need(s) and payoff(s)

Strategic sales is based on enhancing the supplier's and the customer's benefits from the relationship. In order to promote this new selling mindset, a new sales approach is needed. The major differences are listed below in figure 10-6.

8. See SPIN-process or AAB-process – attributes, advantages, benefits.

	Traditional sales	Strategic sales
Unit of analysis	The dyad	Internal and external environment of the dyad
Organisational principle	Products/geography	Customers
Timeframe	Transaction	Planning period
Success measured	Individually	Jointly
Success measured in terms of	Own benefit	Mutual benefit
Evaluation	Individually	Jointly
Information sharing	Need to know	As much as possible
Learning	No collection of learning's as many individuals are involved	Sharing experiences and building insights through workshops/meetings
Conflict resolution	Conflicts/negotiations	Win-Win

Figure 10-6: Important differences between traditional sales and strategic sales.

The discussion throughout this book has focused on the characteristics and indicators of strategic relationship marketing. This section deals with an extension of this thesis by analysing the changes within the sales organisation that are required in order support a relationship marketing strategy. Although this book builds on the original relationship characteristics identified by the relationship researchers, it is just as essential to consider the behavioural and operational implications as well. It is also important to note that one of the main prerequisites for strategic sales is that the sales organisation can and will to work according to the principles. These principles are based on:

- Mutual (business system) approach
- Focusing on partner's competitiveness and strategic potential
- Timeframe beyond ordinary planning period – actually often several planning periods
- Considering the relationship as the basis for exchange beyond products/services
- Considering the customer as a market and organising accordingly
- Opening own organisation towards partner

Knowing your customer's business is the key to understanding where the customer will look for relationship benefits. Acquiring knowledge about your customer's business is described in more detail in chapter 8.

Information and data is required, from all levels of both the customer' and the seller's organisations. This is where the IT side of many CRM systems becomes highly relevant. This becomes especially important when many parts and individuals in an organisation have relationships with other parts[9] and individuals from other organisations. Keeping control over this information and staying up to date becomes difficult in itself. Most CRM-systems are therefore a vehicle for internal information in several directions: registration, presentation, opportunities and limitations. Despite the undeniable benefits from these systems, one should be aware of the important distinction between *need to know* and *nice to know.*

The outcome of an industry analysis should centre on opportunities for increasing your customer's competitiveness vis-à-vis your customer's competitors as part of the strategic sales process. This will involve an array of operational, tactical, and strategic activities in the short as well as the long run.

Organising for strategic selling is not merely a question of logistics and infrastructure, but a managerial attitude towards relationship marketing also needs to be developed. It is not possible to employ strategic relationship marketing techniques in an organisation where the prevailing business mindset is gaining the most for yourself, regardless of the cost to others.

10.5 Relationship Traps

"Of course you can have your car in any colour you like – as long as it's black".[10]

As with most concepts, strategic relationship marketing is faced with a number of obstacles that typically come up when management changes from the strategic and tactical mode to the operational mode. Its like saying: "In principle this is fine, but in practise..."

Therefore, it is necessary to examine some of the traps experienced by companies in the past and provide suggestions for how to avoid some of these traps (please refer to relationship strategies introduced in chapters 8 and 9).

9. Multiplex relationships as described in figure 7-6.
10. Allegedly Henry Ford's comment when asked about standardisation.

Although the theoretical models favour dealing with partners individually, many organisations face limited resources and limited competencies, uneven distribution of power or often factors influencing the standardisation/customisation issues. Therefore, implementation of strategic relationship marketing concepts is often faced with constraints. What are the constraints in and around your organisation?

One of the most common traps is based on resource limitations leaving no room for individualisation of the interface or relationships between the company and it's partners. Standardisation is the operational key to such companies. The opposite trap is individualising interfaces and relationships with all partners without considering the individual relationship benefits or the resource and competency situation. The lack of standardisation, however, can be costly and inflexible.

Institutionalising the relationship undermines it; this is potentially the greatest threat to a dynamic relationship. Relationships can lose energy and drive. In some relationships institutionalisation leads to a lower level of attention and less continuous monitoring, which causes the relationship to be less effective. This lack of attention does in some cases lead to a kind *of relationship paralysis* where both partners leave the relationship unattended. Actually, hybrid governance may in some cases proves to be more dynamic, as everyone involved is constantly searching for the best possible relational fit.

10.5.1 The Standardisation Trap

Although standardisation is rarely discussed as a central part of relationship marketing, it is often the key to ensuring a satisfactory return on investment. These four generic strategies are based on varying degrees of standardisation. Which strategy possesses the highest degree of standardisation? And which the lowest?

- Transaction cost leadership
- Relationship differentiator
- Quality segment specialisation
- Transaction cost niche explorer

It is not easy to answer – right? The argument here is that standardisation and customisation can be found in many different areas and levels of concentration – i.e. you have to be specific to answer the question at the beginning of this paragraph. Therefore, the concept of standardisation must be explored in some detail in order to reveal what actually is standardised, whether or not its at the interface between the supplier and customer, whether or not its in terms of processes and activities etc.

The two strategies: *transaction cost leadership* and *transaction cost niche explorer* represent strategies where individualisation is present to a lesser degree than is the case for the two other strategies.

The concept of *mass customisation* is actually a mix of standardised processes and activities and individualised outputs. This reflects the need to examine how it is standardised, where it is standardised and when it is standardised – see illustration in figure 10-7.

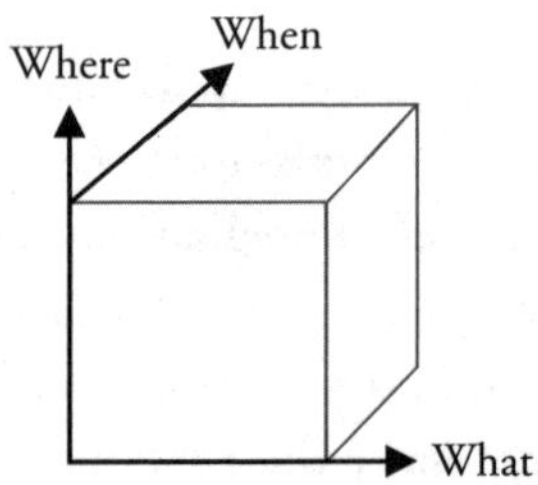

Figure 10-7: Standardisation dimensions.

What standardisation refers to is the degree of routine or the level of adaptability. The less adaptable, the more standardised the activity or asset is.[11]

- How activities and processes interplay – see components of the business system analysis
- How assets are used
- How competencies are utilised

This is the type of customer analysis that is used for classification of customer type, customer strategy etc. And could also be used to analyse distribution systems, IT-systems, packaging facilities etc.

Where refers to whether or not standardisation is within the supplier's organisation or outside the supplier's organisation:

11. The opposite is the idiosyncratic assets, i.e. assets that have only one use.

- Where inside the supplier's organisation?
- Where outside the supplier's organisation?
- Where outside the supplier's organisation, but standardised in relation to groups of customers?

Examples would be that all customers are treated identically when they approach the supplier, or when the supplier defines sales arguments and the like. Where also relates closely to the concept of the value chain, as analysis here will identify where value is created.

When refers to:
- When in the production process, interface process, etc.?
- Can it be delayed?
- Can it be stored?

Examples are based on individualisation in all areas or merely within a defined set of criteria. This is where we expect to see massive differences between BtB and BtC industries. In BtB industries we expect to see standardisation in what is not visible to the customer, internally within the supplier's organisation and primarily in the processes. This is due to the large size of the individual transaction and the high frequency of transactions. In BtC industries, standardisation is apparent to a greater extent, often due to the small size of the individual transaction and the low frequency of transactions.

However, one of the most important distinctions concerning standardisation is the distinction between how the seller sees it and how the buyer perceives it. Dell is a brilliant example of standardised components configured according to customers' specifications. Dell has refined the production process and actually delays the final configuration of their products until the customers' orders have been received. The customers regard the final products as one produced exactly according to their specification. But remember who designed the customer's design and specification options.

The most common trap is often seen in companies introducing a "relationship program" or other systems based on the notion that all relationships will develop according to a predetermined number of steps and in a predetermined sequence. The basic concept here is to treat everyone identically, i.e. a "one size fits all" approach.

Standardisation may be regarded as a conduit for internal knowledge transfer, ensuring that data and information are manageable. Management-wise this is a trade-off between several considerations; competitors' activities and policies, customers' desires and influence, assets available and their alternative use etc. In other words, there may be considerable benefits from not treating customers individually and these must be addressed when relationship marketing is considered:

- Internal flexibility is high, i.e. resources are not linked to only one use, but can be applied where they provide the highest profit
- Resources are highly mobile and can be applied where the need is
- No dependencies outside the company, internal control is kept
- Not dependent on individuals, i.e. no individual possesses information and tacit knowledge or has developed relationships to individuals in the customer's organisation.[12] This will be supplemented by a systematic approach to all external partners
- Routines can be standardised – i.e. easy to document and monitor
- Joint format for documentation of exchanges and uniform data and information processing, i.e. if data has been captured they are organised in a specific system
- Re-use of existing solutions and processes, depreciating the investment over as many situations as possible
- Low transaction costs, due to high capacity utilisation

The drawbacks of standardisation are often referred in the relationship marketing literature. Actually, these drawbacks are often identified as key reasons for developing relationships. However, some of the drawbacks are sometimes used as reasons why the company has been successful so far and therefore, standardisation is not in itself undesirable. Each of the drawbacks must therefore be considered individually:

- Lack of adaptability and flexibility, i.e. the organisation focuses at what they are good at to ensure a present and future level of ROI
- High level of transactions costs for customer and other external partners, as they have to adapt to "the supplier's" systems
- Experience and development must come from within the organisation, i.e. new knowledge is not absorbed from the environment
- Missed opportunities in relation to product development, process rationalisation etc.

---

12. Several organisations actually have a policy where individuals change position and/or responsibility every 2-3 years in order to avoid the development of tacit knowledge or personal relationships.

The drawbacks of standardisation will of course depend on the strategy pursued by the customer. In relation to the relationship partner it could also be the case that the customer actually prefers the "standardised approach" because it is easy to understand and assess. Please see elaboration in figure 10-8.

<table>
<tr><td colspan="2"></td><td colspan="2">Differentiation focus</td></tr>
<tr><td colspan="2"></td><td>Low</td><td>High</td></tr>
<tr><td rowspan="2">Cost focus</td><td>High</td><td>Defender
Standardisation makes choise(s) easy, as alternatives can be compared</td><td>Analyser
Standardisation is preferable where is assists in keeping prices down
Dislikes standardisation due to the implicit "same solution to all"</td></tr>
<tr><td>Low</td><td>Reactor
Indifferent to standardisation</td><td>Prospector
Dislikes standardisation due to the implicit "same solution to all"</td></tr>
</table>

Figure 10-8: Implications of standardisation vs. customer's strategic type – seen from the customer's point of view.

As was discussed in chapters 2, 3 and 4, standardisation may be decided either by dyadic factors or factors outside the dyad as part of the industry characteristics. Actually in some industries there may be an existing industry paradigm pertaining to relationships, including preconceptions concerning key success factors of the industry. One such example was provided by bookstores prior to Amazon.com. Before that point in time, customer data were considered interesting, but far too expensive to register, store, analyse and use for marketing purposes. The customers didn't ask for individualisation and were satisfied with the standardised approach, as it turns out very much so, and they couldn't even imagine the service provided by Amazon.com.

10.5.2 The Individualisation Trap

Individualisation is not necessarily a part of the generic relationship strategy, although most relationship marketing texts imply that a standardised approach is not *comme il faut.* Which of the four generic strategies would have the highest level of individualisation? The second highest? Etc.

- Transaction cost leadership?
- Relationship differentiator?
- Quality segment specialisation?
- Transaction cost niche explorer?

The two strategies of *relationship differentiator* and *quality segment specialisation* are where we expect to find individualisation to a higher degree than is the case of the two other strategies.

Individualisation is a threat to standardisation and flexibility. It is a threat to economies of scale and scope; therefore it may influence the ROI negatively.

Customer as a market[13] is a popular notion that highlights the need for individualisation. However, despite the differences around the world, many multinational companies actually group markets according to a segmentation process.

Costs will go through the roof as it becomes more difficult to reuse solutions, as investments in assets will have limited use, some merely within one relationship, and as resource limitations lead to fewer relationships. Some of the more apparent limitations are:

- Lack of economies of scale, the individual relationship will define the boundaries – could also be question of prioritising where to allocate what resources
- Lack of economies of scope – across relationships and developing competencies
- Lack of knowledge resources – as they may be tied up in one relationship
- Lack of flexibility – asset specificity too high, and tied up.
- Limited career development – as individuals are locked into specific relationships

Individualisation stresses the need for the prioritising of relationships using portfolio approach to ensure that the most attractive relationships receive access to the relevant resources.

When the customisation of assets increases too much, *one-sided* risk and dependency goes too far. *Too far* may be applied to a set of objective criteria, to

13. Customer as market was developed to describe that the seller regards individual customers to as important as geographical markets. One of the most significant consequences will be if the seller organises accordingly – i.e. that the organisation serving one customer includes all the functions, processes and activities that would have been applied to a geographical market.

other relationships or to the output of the benefit audit. Asset specificity can be divided into six groups:[14] location, physical, human, dedicated, brand, and temporal asset specificity.

Increasing asset specificity leads to customised assets and in strategic relationship marketing we are also able to name the customer and are not limited to discussing specificity in a generic sense.

Combining individualisation with the strategic types presented in chapter 8, illustrates that not all customers will find individualisation to be beneficial. Please see figure 10-9.

		Differentiation focus	
		Low	**High**
Cost focus	**High**	*Defender* Individualisation makes choice(s) difficult and as alternatives can not be compared	*Analyser* Individualisation is preferable where it assists in ensuring the desired positioning
	Low	*Reactor* Indifferent to individualisation	*Prospector* Prefers individualisation as this is the core of this strategy

Figure 10-9: Implications of individualisation vs. customer's strategic type – seen from the customer's point of view.

Individualisation or customisation seems to be the next step forward. However, based on the previous chapters of this book, two crucial preconditions must to be met:

- Pursue a strategic relationship marketing strategy that fits to your own platform in terms of resources, competencies and desired future development.
- Pursue a strategic relationship marketing strategy that makes it possible to develop sustainable competitive advantages in the relationships you develop with your chosen customers.

14. Williamson, 1981, p. 555; Williamson, 1985, p. 55; Williamson, 1989, p. 143; Williamson, 1991, p. 28.

One last quote seems to be appropriate:[15]

> A relationship, I think, is like a shark. You know, it has to constantly move forward or it dies...

References

Christopher, M., Payne, A. and Ballantyne, D (1991) *Relationship Marketing*, Butterworth-Heinemann

Grönroos, C. (1995) *The Rebirth of Modern Marketing*. Meddelande från svenka Handelshöskolan i Helsinki.

Gummesson E. (1996) *Relationsmarkedsføring. Fra 4P til 30R*. KOLLE Forlag.

Kjeldsen, J. (1997) *Køberinitiativ, indkøbsmarketing og leverandørsamarbejde*, Ledelse & Erhvervsøkonomi, vol. 2, pp. 145-157.

Peppers, D. and Rogers, M (1996) *One-to-One marketing*, Wiley

Rackham, N. (1988) *Account Strategy for Major Sales*, Gower.

Rackham, N. (1991) *The SPIN-technique*, Gower

Williamson, O. E. (1981) *The Economics of Organization: The Transaction Cost Approach*, American Journal of Sociology, vol. 87, pp. 548-577.

Williamson, O. E. (1983) *Credible Commitment: Using Hostages to Support Exchange*, American Economic Review, vol. 73, pp. 519-540.

Williamson, O. E. (1985) *The Economic Institution of Capitalism*, The Free Press.

Williamson, O. E. (1989) *Transaction Cost Economics*. In R. Scmalenese and R. Willig (eds.), Handbook of Industrial Organization, vol. 1. Elsevier Science Publishers.

Williamson, O. E. (1991) *Comparative Economic Organization: The Analysis of Discrete Structural Alternatives*, Administrative Science Quarterly, vol. 36, pp. 269-296.

www.huthwaite.co.uk

15. Woody Allen from the movie Annie Hall

CHAPTER 11

11. Cases[1]

11.1: Sanisteel: The Dyadic Power of Supply Chain Management

The Industry and Company Background

With 35 offices in Denmark, Germany and the Baltic, Sanisteel is a leading wholesaler and distributor of industrial products. The range of products supplied by Sanisteel can be divided into three main categories: (1) heating and sanitary products and appliances, (2) steel and metals and (3) technical industrial components and tools. The range of products comprises approximately 90,000 items from more than 4,000 suppliers generating annual revenues totalling approximately €500,000,000.

The customer base includes a broad spectrum of industries, usage patterns and company sizes. Original Equipment Manufacturer (OEM) manufacturers of various types represent one of Sanisteel's core customer segments, both in terms of volume and regarding the future potential for relationship building.

Competition among distributors of industrial products is fierce and very much focused on prices at the transactional level. Customers bargain for discounts within a pattern of "maverick buying" facing low switching costs among local suppliers of often homogenous products.

Customers are offered annual discounts or bonuses according to a volume-based scheme and influenced by the negotiation power of the individual customer. Hence, the wholesalers such as Sanisteel are under constant pressure to lower prices thereby sweeping away profitability.

1. Prepared by Hougaard & Bjerre.

The Traditional Purchasing Process

The typical purchasing process, i.e. the exchange, between Sanisteel and its customer's involved more than 20 activities with a total duration of 8-13 days with the exclusion of manufacturing and delivery:

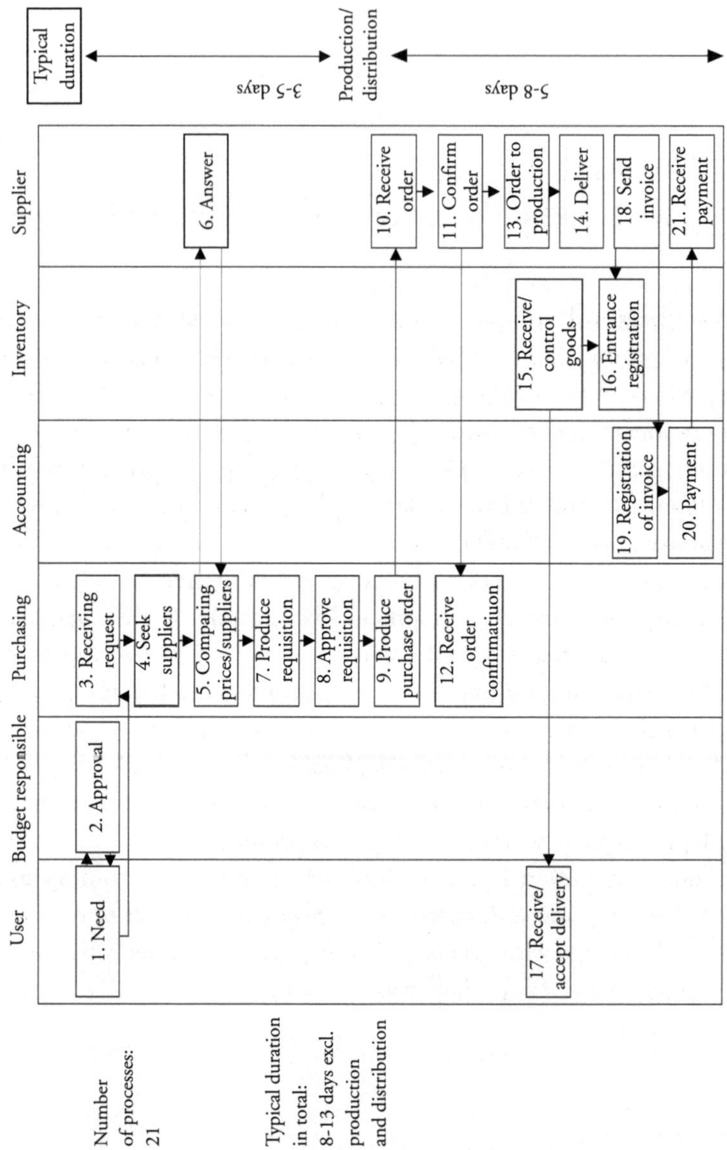

Figure 11-1: The pre SCM purchasing procedure. Source: Internal material, Sanisteel

The transaction cost of one single exchange/transaction was estimated at € 150 (year 2001 prices). As most customers made purchases on a more or less daily basis utilising an arm's length purchasing philosophy, the transaction costs were huge, which motivated the parties to sub-optimise, stimulating a climate of win-loose.

Exploring a Relationship Based Concept

In that scenario, Sanisteel decided to introduce a new dyadic relationship concept to major customers, namely Supply Chain Management (SCM). The principles behind SCM are illustrated in figure 11-2.

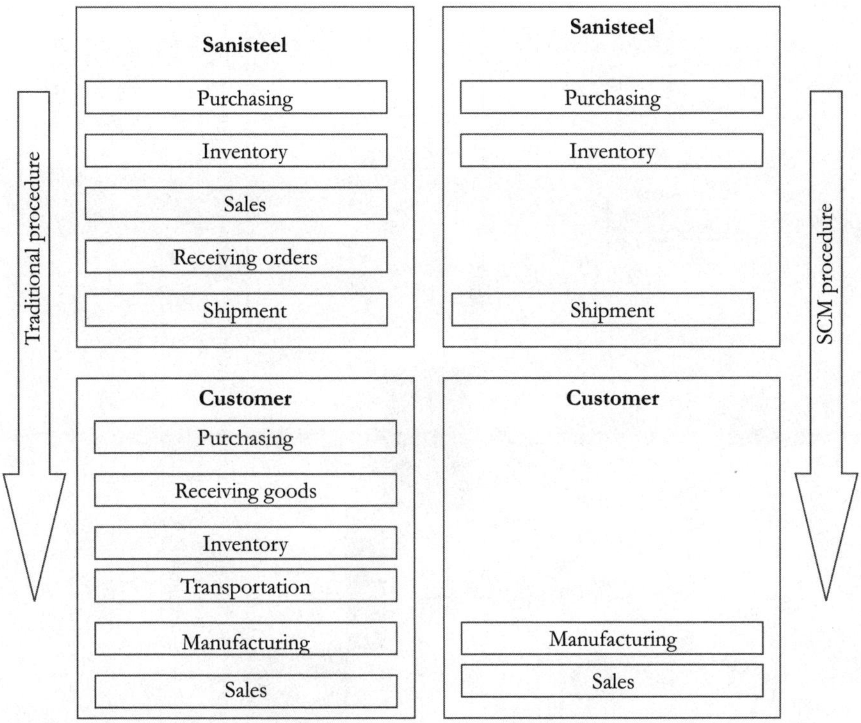

Figure 11-2: The principles behind SCM. Source: Internal material, Sanisteel

E-buying is one of the elements in the SCM system introduced by Sanisteel. The introduction of e-buying and EDI cut the number of processes in every

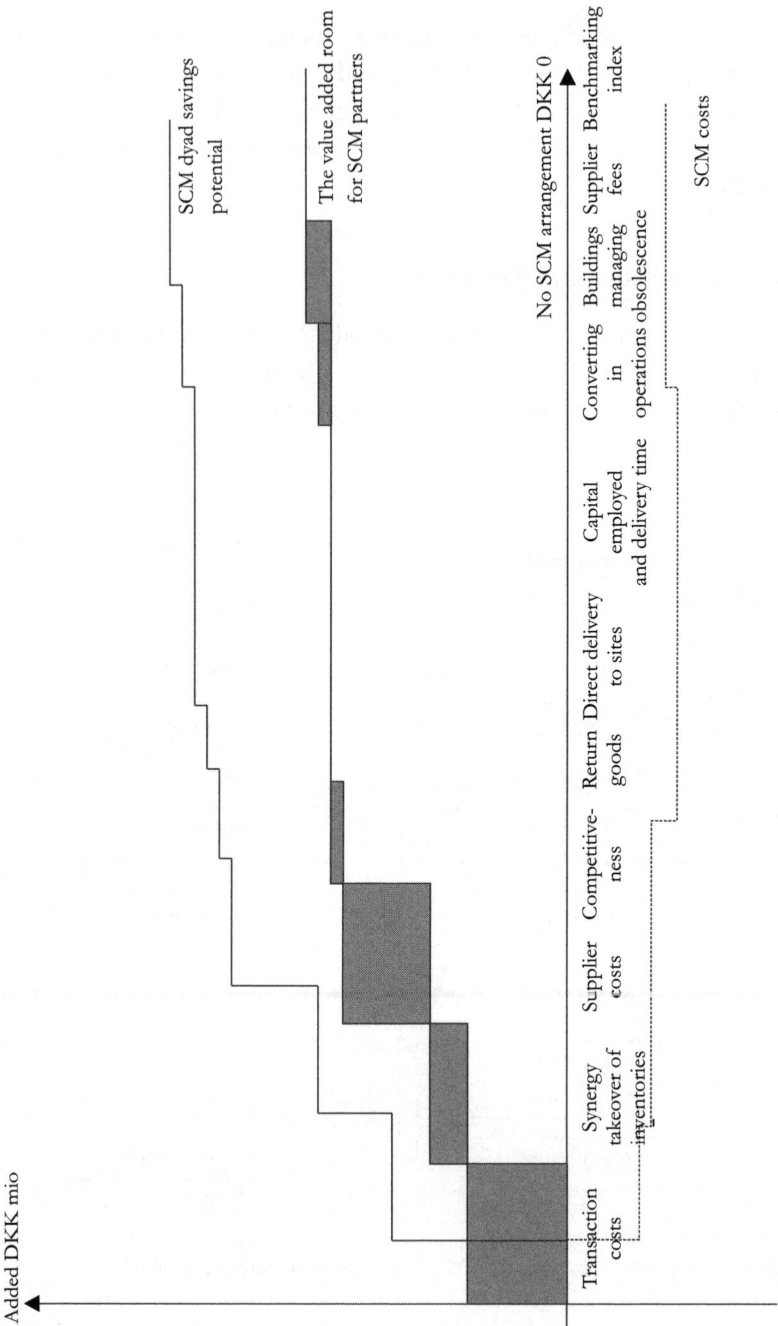

Figure 11-3: The value adding model for SCM partnerships. Source: Internal material, Sanisteel

purchasing transaction from 20 to less than 10; it shortened the transaction from 8-13 days to 7 hours thus leading to marked reduction of the transaction costs.

Under the SCM concept, a customer would fundamentally change its buying behaviour, no longer purchasing on a case-to-case basis. Not having 100-200 different suppliers allowed them to concentrate on less than a handful based on relational win-win contracts which galvinised the overall supply chain.

In order to convince reluctant customers, Sanisteel introduced what was called the Value Adding Model (VAM).

In order to quantify and validate the perspectives of SCM as relationship concept, VAM suggested that Sanisteel and the customer should cooperatively generate a joint analysis in order to estimate and verify the costs and benefits attached to SCM. Sanisteel suggested that the analysis be made for different SCM scenarios to also detect cross-organisational cost generators as well as the advantages and disadvantages of different SCM solutions.

The value-adding model illuminates the feasiblility of adding value to the drivers of costs and benefits.

From the outset customers were reluctant, believing they would become prisoners of Sanisteel. As one senior purchasing manager expressed it during a seminar hosted by Sanisteel: "Well, I recognise that economic advantages can be obtained compared to our present way of doing business with each other. But if we say yes to the Sanisteel SCM package, we loose autonomy, and it is so easy for our counterpart to milk the cow instead of staying competitive on prices and delivery quality. Fighting for every order is what keeps suppliers on their toes!"

The Dyad Snapshot Analysis

Following the seminar, the Sanisteel SCM manager and the specific customer however agreed to carry out a joint snapshot analysis of the value adding potential for the customer company. This company was a middle sized OEM manufacturer of agro-mechanical devices. The analysis took less than two weeks and revealed a substantial potential for the creation of added value within the dyad, see figure 11-4.

SCM DRIVER	SCM VARIABLE		CUSTOMER			SANISTEEL		DYAD
DKK in thousands		**No SCM**	**SCM Impact**	**Value Added**	**No SCM**	**SCM Impact**	**Value Added**	**Value Added**
	Invoicing							
	Calculation							
	Invoice control							
	Accounting							
	Supplier dialogue							
	Searching/ordering							
	Price negotiation							
	Internal transportation							
Transaction costs	Requiring external freight							
	Technical updating							
	Market information							
	Product knowledge							
	Item data registration							
	Order confirmation							
	Administration							
	Maintaining soft data							
	CIF							
	Receiving shipments							
	Value Added, transaction costs	2.668	2.028	640	0	1.144	- 1-143	- 503
	Supplier maintainaince							
Supplier costs	Fewer suppliers							
	Value Added, supplier costs	90	3	87	0	0	0	87
	Freight costs							
	Purchasing prices							
	Labelling							
	Product guarantees							
Competitiveness	QA							
	Value added –fix std.							
	Packaging							
	Certification							
	Misc. documentation							
	Value Added, competitiveness	0	- 305	305	0	- 1.155	1.155	1.460
Return goods	Return goods							
	Value Added, return goods	114	69	44	0	23	-23	22
Direct delivery	On site delivery							
	Value Added, on site delivery				0		0	0
	Hours							
	1 day							
	2 days							
	Changes in delivery time							
Capital employed	Last minute orders							
	Capital employed							
	Forecast							
	Customised goods							
	Delivery terms							
	Value Added, capital employed	130	91	39	0	2	2	37
Line values	Low value order lines							
	Value Added, line values	29	7	21	0	0	0	21

Figure 11-4: SCM value adding scheme for customer x. Source: Internal material, Sanisteel

Moving from the traditional exchange based terms of trade to a relationship based SCM system for this particular customer created an annual dyadic value of DKK 1,878,566 (approx. €270,000)

The key account manager of Sanisteel was convincing at the presentation where the results of the snap shot were communicated to the customer and he concluded: "There is no doubt that we can together build a business case with two winners creating substantial benefits for both organisations".

What should the next step be?

The customer's senior purchasing manager had the last word: "I do believe the report is valid and that the potential for value generation exists, at least on paper. We would like Sanisteel to work out a specific offer and in particular address and answer the following questions:

- Our company today has very favourable price and delivery terms with a multitude of suppliers. How will Sanisteel assure us that net price increases do not outbalance our piece of the value-adding amount identified by VAM?
- Is Sanisteel willing to unconditionally meet reference prices that we can gather from the "market"?
- Concerning key performance quality indicators such as: delays, residues, wrong quantities, damages etc. Will Sanisteel accept a set of financial mechanisms that effectively protect we, the customer, against de facto monopoly laissez –faire?

Topics to Discuss:

1. How would you describe the relationship marketing strategy of Sanisteel?
2. Which factors within customer organisations impede relationship contracts like Sanisteel?
3. How can a supplier possibly overcome impeding factors?
4. Should a customer company accept the potential risk of supplier opportunism and engage in arrangements of the relationship type? Which contractual and control mechanisms would you recommend?

11.2: The Golden Relationship Secrets of Ikea[2]

The Miracle of Ikea

Ikea has developed from a small Swedish post order company to global retail chain in the area of home furnishings and accessories. In this industry, very few companies expand outside their domestic market; Ikea has created a global network of more than 130 outlets. In 1996, more than 125 million customers visited Ikea delivering of revenues totalling $4.3 billion. Ikea is profitable and growth-oriented with a 10 -15% annual growth rate employing a staff more than 30,000.

The key factors behind Ikea's successful business development are well known: Simple, modern furniture based on Scandinavian design; global procurement policies and consistent outsourcing; furniture that the customer assembles at home; big, visible outlets in metropolis peripheries with easy access and good parking facilities. These are also supplemented services such as bistros, info kiosks, entertainment and playgrounds for the kids.

Ikea as a Relationship Concept

A proportion of Ikea's savings on procurement, inventories and self-service are passed on to the consumers in terms of very competitive pricing which has created Ikea's reputation as a low price outlet.

Focusing on Ikea's low costs and prices would be a superficial assessment at best, because the real originality of the Ikea lies in innovation. Ikea is able to keep costs and prices down because the roles, relationships and organisational philosophy within the value chain have been systematically redefined. The result is an integrated business system, considered to be very valuable by the consumers and completely different from conventional wisdom in the furniture retail business.

Consider Ikea's customer relationships. Ikea offers much more to the customers than just low prices. Ikea offers a new division of labour: If the consumer is willing to take over a part of the traditional role of the manufacturer and the retailer – assembly and delivery – Ikea promises well designed products at very competitive prices.

All parts of the business system at Ikea have been designed in order to make

2. Prepared by Hougaard and Bjerre, based on internal material and interviews.

it easier for the consumer to undertake his or her new role. Ikea prints more than 58 million catalogues in 10 different languages. Although the catalogue only covers 30-40% of Ikea's 12,000 products, it is like a script explaining the role of each actor in Ikea's business system. Recently Ikea introduced a family club with the purpose of further strengthening the interactive engagement of its customers.

The idea is to develop Ikea into a family event and not just a home furnishings department store. Covering customer needs at a reasonable price in warm and attractive surroundings is the focus of Ikea's image.

A Brief Glance at an Ikea Shop

As soon as the customer walks in, they receive catalogues, pens and notebooks enabling them to guide themselves through the store without much assistance from Ikea staff.

The products are not grouped in categories, but according to style and environment. Each item has an easy-to-read label with product name and price. Additionally you find information about the materials used, formats, colours and cleaning as well as maintenance instructions. Also, it is indicated where exactly in the storage area, you can pick up the product.

After payment, the consumer brings the product out to his or her car. If the car's luggage space is too small, Ikea will rent you a roof rack.

The Promises of Ikea and the Mutual Benefits in the Supply Chain

Ikea works hard to create the perception that the role of the customer is far from the passive; instead, the customer is treated as an active value creator. Ikea offers families much more than just tool kit furniture in a lower price range; Ikea offers improvements in the quality of people's lives. It is all about creative partnership, design and arrangement, security, information, assurance and entertainment.

Calling these services just an added convenience would be a gross underestimation of their importance as the strategic drivers behind the Ikea concept. "To understand how people can create their own value supported by a business system that enables this in better ways. Ikea's aim is not to relieve the customer from executing certain tasks, but to motivate them to do things, they never tried before easily and conveniently". In other words: Ikea creates value by enabling their customers to perform their own value generating activities. "Give a man a fish, and you make him happy for one day. Teach a man how to fish and you make him happy for the rest of his life".

In order to motivate their customers to create value, Ikea has teamed up with 2,400 suppliers in more than 50 countries.

In order to be able to live up to the promises communicated to the consumers concerning division of labour, Ikea has to find suppliers that can provide both low price and a high quality.

It is difficult to find and evaluate potential suppliers and prepare them to join the Ikea business system. They have 30 procurement offices dedicated to this task working to identify prospective suppliers. The designers, based at Ikea's headquarters in Älmhult, Sweden are always 2-3 years ahead of the introduction of new collections. They decide which suppliers should be involved in the production of their designs.

When suppliers become participants in the Ikea system they not only gain access to a global marketplace, but also to technical services and expertise, equipment and advise in quality management as well as just in time and workflow processes.

Ikea's unconditional requirement of low purchase prices has two major consequences. First of all, the component suppliers are geographically scattered. The back and the seat of a chair might be produced in Poland, the legs in France and the screws in Spain. Secondly, Ikea has to purchase in high volume. Both factors require an extremely efficient logistical system including order and inventory handling.

Innovative Ikea

Traditional supply chains do not include the complexity of roles and relationships that have been built into Ikea's business system. Ikea did not position itself deliberately with the purpose of adding value to every single point in a planned chain of activities.

Instead Ikea innovated a systematic way of developing value and built a business system through a variety of participants who both deliver and receive value.

Therefore, Ikea is not just a chain of furniture and home decoration stores but a fixture in a system of services, goods, design, management, support, logistics and entertainment. The outcome has been a fantastic global success.

Vision, Mission and Strategic Values of Ikea

Extract from Ikea Information

"The testament of a furniture dealer":

"Once and for all we have decided to stand on the side of the many people. What is good for our customers is in the long term good for us as well. This is a vision with deep obligation.

In all countries and societies a disproportionate share of the resources are allocated to satisfy the needs and wants of a small fraction of the population. In our industry almost all the new and the beautiful is reserved to a small segment of the wealthiest. This fact has shaped our goal.

After twenty years we have reached a good result. A famous Swedish industrialist and politician said that Ikea has had greater impact on the process of democratisation than the sum of political decisions! We do also believe that our style has inspired many of our colleagues to work in the same direction. Ikea's "domestic market", which is Scandinavia, has become a benchmark for the whole world. Much of the new has from the beginning been created for the many people – all whose resources are limited. We are the leaders in this development.

But we have big ambitions. We think we can be of use in markets all over the world. We think we can contribute in the process of democratisation not just in Scandinavia. We also know that larger series of production will bring new advantages to our domestic market at the same time reducing our market risks. Therefore we must expand.

The means we use in reaching our goals are all characterised by our "different line" and we strive for simplicity and directness in the way we communicate with each other and our environment. Lifestyle is a big word, but I do not hesitate to use it. In order to get a better life you must also be able to disengage from social status and conventions to become freer as human beings. Our goal is to identify ourselves with this concept in this field, for our joy and to inspire the world...

Topics to Discuss:

1. Does Ikea live up to the relationship marketing definition?
2. How would you describe the business system of Ikea?
3. Is Ikea truly dyadic in their way of thinking and doing?
4. Do you in fact consider Ikea to be a relationship-oriented company regarding customers and suppliers?
5. Discuss if any of the generic relationship strategies can explain the Ikea behaviour?

11.3: Flight Bonus: The Most Successful Loyalty Program Ever[3]

The Brink of Deregulation

Flight bonus programmes (FBP) are a result of the deregulation of the air transportation market in the US in the late 1970's, where competition between airline companies was given free reign. Free, perfect competition means that the customers get a free choice compared with a situation where the market is regulated, restricted or even non-existant in the sense that customers are given no alternatives at all.

The free choice of the customers implies that the suppliers must work extra hard in order to communicate their unique offerings to the customers and also to strive for delivering the services and performance they actually have promised to the customers. Free competition and customer choice are the top marketing priorities in this situation.

Thus, deregulation of the airlines stimulated the airline companies to invent new marketing strategies. Competition among suppliers is a key driving force behind innovation in marketing.

Of all the different experiments in the market, FBP soon turned out to be the most effective. By far, American Airlines was first with a well thoughtout program called AAadvantage. AAadvantage was introduced in 1981, and even if the programme was shortly after copied by competitors such as United, Delta

3. Based on Hedaa (1998).

and TWA, AA is still the market leader in FBP with the largest FBP membership base.

While deregulation was the driving force behind FBP, it was the breakthrough of information technology that was the enabler. AA developed a computer reservation system (CRS) named Sabre. Sabre made it possible to identify 150,000 frequent travellers, who became the first to be enrolled as members in the program and give it critical mass.

As air transportation became deregulated in other parts of the world as well, FBP followed immediately after. In Europe British Airways was the first. That was in 1991 following the European Councils second package of deregulation. Globally, more than 70 FBP's had by now had been implemented, and as Sir Colin Marshall (former BA chairman) expressed it: ".... frequent-flier miles, which has become a commodity, a price of entry into the market...". Most airlines run FBP's for defensive reasons, because experience shows that competing without a FBP will result in loss of substantial market share.

What is a Flight Bonus Program?

An FBP can be defined as a system that rewards a travellers repurchase of a certain airline company's services within passenger transportation. FBP is a behaviour modification programme that rewards certain behaviour in order to obtain repetition. FBP induces propensity to repurchase measured on actual behaviour not attitudinally but by stimulus-response, a clear case of operational conditioning.

FBP functions in a way by which the traveller is given credit in terms of bonus points depending on the length, type, timing and comfort of the travel. When a certain number of bonus points have been earned, they can be turned in for free tickets or upgrades. The addition and the value of bonus points are non-linear. Depending on the number of bonus points earned within a given period of time, the FBP members are classified into different groups with different levels of privileges; more bonus points means more privileges. This means that the last points that must be earned to move one privilege level up have a higher value for the member than the first points earned. The mini-case below illustrates the behaviour modification of FBP:

Case

"Here's how my brother Eric spent his Christmas vacation – or part of it anyway. On Dec 26. he left his home in Manhattan and drove to Newark Airport, where he boarded a Continental flight for Washington D.C just after noon. He arrived on schedule. Deplaned. Had a coke in the airline lounge. And made his return trip. By 4.30 p.m. he was back in his apartment. Is he crazy? Not necessarily. Eric made his excursion – the shortest, cheapest one possible – because he needed to rack up 750 frequent-flier miles before the end of the year to reach the Gold level of Continental's OnePass program. He will now get unlimited free first-class upgrades, free companion upgrades and a 125% bonus on miles earned".

Jean Shermn Chatzky: Manage your miles. Money, March 1999

In its most simplistic form FBP is a volume discount like "buy 10 and get number 11 for free", but because the frequent travellers are on business trips, the flight bonus programmes have been designed to create confusion about who the customer in fact is. The most influential FBP's considers the actual passenger and not the company that pays the bill as the customer. In the principal-agent terminology the airline company considers the agent to be the customer and not the principal, although the agent acts on behalf of the principal and on his account. And, as we shall see, this implies that the traveller is rewarded, if he takes care of the interest of the supplier (the airline) at the expense of the interests of his employer. The company pays the bill, but the employee receives the added value.

The loyalty towards the airline company is augmented at the expense of the loyalty against the employer. This type of phenomenon is sometimes and in other contexts called secret commission or even bribery!

The Business Traveller as Loyal Customer

A business trip can be defined as a trip made by one or more individuals on behalf of and with the purpose of undertaking duties for a company, which is paid for by that company. When an employee is a business traveller, he behaves loyal to his company, if he chooses the kind of travel that is the cheapest and the fastest assuming that certain minimum requirements such as comfort and security are fulfilled. There should not be unproductive waste of time before, during or after the trip. The comfort should not deviate significantly from the level the person is used to as part of his work or when he is on vacation. The employment and compensation package of the frequent flier has been agreed upon including the inconveniences the job might cause. Hence, a supplier is not supposed to offer any special compensation for inconvenience or sacrifices.

The business traveller is loyal to any supplier of passenger transportation, if he chooses the specific supplier, if the transportation is more expensive, slower and leads to waste of time relative to alternatives, or if he lets himself transport unnecessarily. Whether the traveller is a loyal customer or a loyal employee in cases of a decision conflict depends on which element is decisive in a choice situation.

Case

A manager, who often participated in international meetings on behalf of his employer, told about the difficulties in agreeing on meeting dates that could fit into the travel plans of all participants without someone not getting his or her bonus points.

Own interviews

There is a clear indication that the loyalty of the travelling person is directed towards the FBP and not against the airline company and their overall services. Some people are willing to tolerate relatively bad service in order to gain the bonus points. Loyalty viewed as the rebuying propensity of the traveller depends more on the personal opportunistic maximisation of benefits than on an affective preference based on a positive experience.

By nature, it is difficult to study motivations and preferences among travellers concerning the influence of FBP. Who will admit that they are strongly and consciously inclined to exploit the resources of their employers! In a recent study covering 520 travel agencies in the US, the General Accounting Office found that approx. 60% of all business travellers always or almost always travel based on FBP. Another survey among the internal travel arrangement departments in 204 companies showed that 80% of the respondents thought that FBP resulted customers booking unnecessarily expensive plane tickets. And 72% said that FBP resulted in inefficient travel plans. Finally, 62% felt that employees made unnecessary trips. In 1986, the total loss to US companies due to FBP was estimated at more than $4 billion.

Loyalty Against Distributors?

Business travel agencies facilitate approx. 70% of all business trips. Until now that is.

They are being undermined and disintermediated and this is not only due of the Internet. FBP and CRS have strengthened the direct contact between the airline company and the businessman. Hence, the travel agencies do not have the same, strong role to play in the future. In the first phase, the increasing bargaining power of the airlines led to a substantial reduction in the commissions paid to the distributors. So the travel agencies contribute actively to their own destruction. Pressure on their margins meant that the travel agencies had to impose new fees on their corporate clients for a service that the individual FBP member is not interested in, if he has already chosen his preferred FBP. Additionally the FBP member normally earns more bonus points, if he orders the travel directly at the airline or on the Internet instead of using a travel agency.

But the Changes Continue

Following deregulation, markets became less transparent. Competitive offers developed in a less comparable direction, and experiences become outdated rather fast. That makes it both complicated and expensive to secure updated well-functioning loyalty programmes, especially in business-to-business markets, where dyadic relationships are the main focus. Due to confusion with regard to the customer definition as either user or the payer, FBP can be seen as a hybrid between a consumer market and BtB.

Should the airline companies drop FBP and concentrate on good service, honest pricing, and regularity... or?

Topics to Discuss:

1. How would you describe the level and the type of loyalty in FBP programmes from a theoretical perspective?
2. What are the advantages and disadvantages of FBP in the strategic relationship marketing sense?
3. And from a business ethics standpoint?
4. Which kinds of non-FBP relationship marketing strategies could possibly compete with FBP programmes, why and how?

11.4: Danish Pharmacies – "If the Pharmacy doesn't have it – it doesn't exist"[4]

If you can get it in the pharmacy, you don't get it any better

The Happy Days of a Monopoly

Twenty years ago the political debate about deregulation of industries and sectors at that time monopolised by the Danish state began. The facing of the tearing down of old, well established monopolies, among them also the health care sector, appeared to be a tremendous threat to the existing Danish pharmacaceutical system and the total business system they were running.

The pharmacies in Denmark are privately owned, however under close government control. The pharmacies had always had a politically decided and approved exclusivity on the sales of prescriptive as well as over the counter or non-prescriptive drugs. Furthermore, pharmaceuticals as an industry had a license to produce drugs. This meant that they were able to compete directly with their own suppliers as long as they just did not violate patents and other types of proprietary rights.

As a genuine monopoly the retail prices of the pharmacies had to be approved by the Ministry of Health based on negotiations with the Association of Pharmacies. Not surprisingly, the retail prices left the pharmacies with a fair profit, and the industry model definitely did not motivate the players to increase productivity or behave innovatively.

---

4. Based on Normann and Ramirez 1983.

Decades with these rigid industry conditions, however, made the pharmacies vulnerable to competition, when and if the monopoly was ever dissolved by the parliament.

The Need to Reinvent The Business – Chasing Core Competencies

In this situation the pharmacies decided to reinvent themselves. When the political winds blew in the direction of deregulation, focusing on the true costs of the public health care systems, the time came for the pharmacies to take new directions.

The first step was to evaluate the strengths and weaknesses of this industry. The most apparent asset was the corps of local, independent chemists. They were well-educated and professional advisors who possessed broad and diverse knowledge in many areas of health care. Another distinct strength was the network of over 300 chemists with more than 1,600 outlets scattered all over the country.

This network of distribution was a very effective sales channel to the Danish population. Not only because of the geographical distribution coverage, but also because consumers respected and had confidence in the pharmacy as an institution.

Within this same period the lifestyle and habits of the population went through a major transition and went in a more health oriented direction. Furthermore, there was an increasing attitudional change going on in the sense that health and well-being was viewed as the responsibility of each individual, not an issue taken care of by society or the government. The Danes demanded more and more information and advice about how to live a healthy life.

These strengths and changes in the business environment were an excellent opportunity for the pharmaceutical sector to reposition the offering and renew their basic business concept. This gelled in the following strategic objective: To develop the pharmacy into an advanced knowledge and service centre for healthcare and well-being.

From Monopoly to Relationship Partner

For obvious reasons, the pharmacies had a strong motivation to keep their monopoly on drug distribution and also the control over wholesale. In addition, there was an increasing motivation to put a pressure on the system to create a dynamic, business orientated and cost effective environment in every single pharmacy.

The pharmacies began to change their product offerings based on this new and much broader vision. From the previous mission definition "delivering drugs and accessories to drugs" the concept had become "health and well-being in a broader sense". With this new focus in mind, pharmacies took the opportunity of maintaining a strong position in the healthcare system while at the same time gaining access to the new, fast growing market for holistic remedies and quality of life.

The range of products was extended to include health and diet products, herbal or oriental medicines, skin products and cosmetics. Pharmacies began collaborating with suppliers in areas such as quality assurance and product declaration.

The pharmacy outlets upgraded their customer information and services, created in-store information kiosks available with video healthcare programs of various kinds. Likewise, pharmacies started publishing books and pamphlets on health, exercise etc. This was a new service for citizens that combined information, recommendations and guidance. Patient information exchange networks were also among the initiatives taken to move in a customer-oriented direction.

Another example was information campaigns aimed at school children concerning contraception and an extensive non-smoking campaign that included education and group therapy. The pharmacies developed databases on drugs and their side effects and introduced an electronic prescription service for doctors and hospitals.

New Market Needs and New Relationship Strategy Despite Resistance

In later stages there was also launched a line of preventative products and treatment of sports injuries, health and recovery packages for people after hospitalisation, tools to check your own blood pressure as well as special services for allergy suffers.

These changes were far from successful in the beginning; practising doctors found that the illness treating initiatives of the pharmacies exceeded written and unwritten borders. The hospital sector found the offers to ex-patients irrelevant and intervening. Suppliers and potential competitors thought that the Association of Pharmacies attempted to capitalise on the legally defined monopoly status. This criticism was highlighted by the fact that the pharmacies at that time were also involved in the production of drugs.

In 1994 the purchasing and marketing company Apoteam was established to handle a new series of branded products in areas such as skin care, vitamins, food contribution, herbal medicine etc. In 1996 the periferal products accounted for 15% of the total revenues. The strategy worked.

Today the pharmacies have a distinctively different profile than before due to the different type of customer. Not only did they renew their promises, but they also created a business strategy based on interactivity, i.e. a relationship oriented idea.

Danish pharmacies succeeded in maintaining their monopoly within the distribution of drugs. By divesting of certain activities, i.e. wholesale functions and manufacturing, and through a reforging of their relationships with authorities, interest groups, the healthcare community and most importantly the customers, the pharmacies were able to build a new and positive atmosphere around the sector.

If extraordinary customer satisfaction is what creates true loyalty then pharmacies made it. Despite being a monopoly and hence having the customers and users as their prisoners, they were able to act in a market-oriented way and reinvent the psychological contracts with their customers.

Topics to Discuss:

1. Describe and discuss driving forces of the pharmacy-customer relationship?
2. Which kinds of relationships (30 R model) can be identified in the business system of Danish pharmacies?
3. What are the risks and benefits of a relationship based marketing formula within this system?
4. Do you think customer loyalty in this case is real?
5. How will you describe the marketing strategy of the pharmacies from a relationship point of view?

11.5: Economics of Customer Relationships in e-business[5]

Our Starting Point

Although many e-commerce businesses used to collect cost and usage data about their websites, few of them understood how to interpret such data as well as how to become more efficient over time. As long as venture capitalists were

5. Based on McKinsey Quarterly (2001).

willing to throw money at dot.coms it didn't really matter. Or did it? After the burst of the Internet bobble in spring 2000, it definitely did.

A comprehensive study carried out by McKinsey & Company consultants in 1999-2000 helped us to achieve a new level of understanding of the relationship economics in e-businesses.

At least six months before the collapse of dot.coms, the data showed that Internet companies suffered from a kind of fatal attraction. They were successful at luring visitors to their sites but not at getting these visitors to buy or at turning occasional buyers into frequent ones. Indeed, the more visitors the sites drew, the more money they lost.

A small but solid group of leaders did, however, succeed in becoming profitable by turning visitors into customers and getting them to return.

Fatal Attraction

At that time most measures of e-performance tracked variations in traffic, page views, advertising impressions served, unique users and so on. But the foundation of long-term profitability is the lifetime customer value. That is the revenue customers generate over their lives, less the cost of acquiring, converting and retaining them.

Attraction

- Visitor base
- Visitor acquisition cost
- Visitor advertising revenue

Conversion

- Customer base
- Customer acquisition cost
- Customer conversion rate
- Number of transactions per customer
- Revenue per transaction
- Revenue per customer
- Customer gross income
- Customer maintenance cost
- Customer operating income
- Customer churn rate
- Customer operating income before marketing spending

Retention

- Repeat-customer base
- Repeat customer acquisition cost
- Repeat customer conversion rate
- Number of transactions per repeat customer
- Revenue per transaction of
- Repeat-customer
- Revenue per repeat-customer
- Revenue-customer churn rate

Figure 11-5: Inside the e-performance scorecard: The indicators. Source: McKinsey Quarterly (2001).

The researchers studied consumer behaviour over two consecutive periods, the first and the second half of 1999. More than 650 million visitors to eight kinds of web sites were tracked. These visitors made 2.7 billion visits to sites, conducted 27 million transactions and paid $4 billion to 224 companies based in North America, Europe and Latin America.

The Traditional Marketing Campaign Trap

Almost none of the e-companies that lavished large sums on e-marketing campaigns achieved above-average visitor growth.

The first discovery was, no surprise today, that the intense early focus on e-businesses attracting the public to their sites went pretty well, but remained universally un-rewarded. Almost none of the companies that lavished large sums on e-marketing campaigns achieved above average visitor growth or conversion rates.

Data from the first half of 1999 suggested that fewer than 4.5% of site visitors resulted in sales and fewer than 10% of visitors who made initial purchases made later ones. By the second half of 1999, consumer choices had proliferated so much that only 2.5% of site visits resulted in sales. An increase in repeat buying to 18% seemed impressive, but the net effect was only to undo the deterioration in the conversion rate.

Companies were spending a little less to acquire customers but still losing money on each of them. During the first half of 1999 it cost on average, more than $1,100 to acquire a customer, who would typically spend a total of $400 on at least two purchases in that period. Similar customers in the second half of the year cost only $800 to acquire; though their spending still didn't exceed $400.

A number of unpleasant facts lurked behind the numbers. First, the content rather than commerce sphere was significantly overpopulated. Second, providing decent coverage and continually creating and updating content requires a large and talented staff. Third, the high off-line costs of production, marketing and distribution have been not so much eliminated as been replaced by those of on-line technology, customer acquisition and brand creation.

Naturally, companies have sought to modify their business models in response to these problems, most often by moving into e-commerce. But only 20% of all content aggregators had been able to abandon the pure advertising model by the end of second half of 1999. Those that moved into e-tailing generally leaped from the frying pan into the fire.

The fourth quarter of 1999 was an improvement to the third. Visitor bases increased by 64%, conversion rates by 65% and revenues per customer by 28%; and 12% of the businesses were profitable.

But this apparently encouraging record wasn't nearly good enough to make e-business profitable overall. The performance of the content sector was particularly dismal. Just a small number of players were gaining a disproportionate share of all revenues. The 20/80 Pareto rule was applicable to e-businesses.

Fixing the Vicious Cycle

But the success of this small number of websites indicates that the fatal attraction is not necessarily an immutable fact of e-life. The leading companies in our survey achieved visitor conversion rates of 12%, customer churn rates below 20% and repeat purchase rates of around 60%. These businesses generate nearly three times as much gross income from repeat customers as from one-time buyers.

Since the strategies of e-tailers are well known and for the most part easy to replicate, the difference between top-and bottom quartile performers must result directly from superior underlying operational skills in acquiring, converting and retaining customers. Moreover, contrary to the widespread view that e-commerce is solely about business experimentation, top performing content aggregators succeeded by marrying innovation to three tried-and-true principles from the brick-and-mortar world:

1. *Match value propositions of segments.* The business focus on core product or service propositions that fit the needs of well-defined consumer segments and has relatively sustainable revenue models. That is, such businesses can generate a positive gross margin without achieving monumental scale or unrealistic conversion levels. The resulting average revenue per customer of these businesses is four times of the entire sample.

2. *Control extensions of product lines and business models.* Under pressure to generate new revenue streams, many e-businesses have greatly expanded their product lines. This approach to fixing weak underlying operational models has generally led to highly confused offerings and to a loss of management focus. Fewer than 20% of the companies in the study sample generated significant non-core revenue streams.

   Best practise players focus on deepening their current offerings and on adding complementary products or content services geared towards the same customer segment that was targeted by their initial business model.

3. *Avoid bleeding-edge technology.* Sites that rush to acquire the latest software or to offer the coolest features tend to develop flaws in the original design before long. By contrast, the best companies, rather than spending millions on, say the latest piece of psychographic-profiling software, have concentrated on ensuring the flawless operation of basic product presentation features, customer service tools and logistics. With the aid of disciplined outsourcing, these businesses have attracted and retained their customers while spending from 50 to 75% less than the average company.

The Rules of the Game

Accompanying such general imperatives are a number of specific rules for attracting, converting and retaining buyers.

Attraction

Getting customers to a site for the first time remains expensive. You can save a lot of money by honing your targeting skills early on and making sure that partnerships you enter into deliver large numbers of new customers at a relatively low cost.

Some untargeted mass marketing may be appropriate at the launch stage in order to generate name awareness. Even then, companies should avoid extravagant campaigns like the $2 million to $3 million that some dot-coms paid for 30-second spots during January 2000 Superbowl, and eccentric flourishes such as efforts to put company-logo stickers on fruit or to persuade towns to rename themselves after companies.

As the business refines its value proposition over time, marketing should focus on the pursuit of only those customer segments that have demonstrated their attraction to the business model. Affiliate deals with narrowly targeted sites end e-mail campaigns directed at segments grouped by purchase histories and demographic traits, are 10 to 15 times more likely than banner ads on generic portals to attract prospects who click through the purchase screens.

Partnerships are the lifeblood of e-commerce companies. Best practice ones invest a good part of their resources in building a team capable of negotiating contracts that pay partners only for actual results, unlike the large number of companies that signed partnership deals with no up-front, mutually acceptable performance targets.

Conversion

The strongest sites have conversion rates as high as 12%, compared with 2.5% for average sites and 0.4% for poorly performing ones. Why is this so?

First, the simpler the purchase process, the more visitors will be converted from viewers into buyers. Too many sites ask users for all sorts of data regarding their preferences and behaviour. Some e-businesses have improved their conversion rates by 5% as a result of simplifying the purchase process.

Second, to make it easier to get to the point of purchase, good sites provide real-time assistance meaning on-line customer support and virtual customer service agents. They also make payments easy, safe and reliable. They accept several payment methods and they actively promote consumer protection charters.

Third, good sites seek to personalise their offerings, even for first-time visitors.

Retention

Perhaps the most important finding is the power of retention. A 10% increase in the rate at which visitors are converted into repeat customers drives a 10% improvement in the net present value of a company's expected cash flows.

Early on, there was much talk about customer loyalty but insufficient investment in promoting it. E-businesses typically spent three to five times less retaining customers than did equivalent brick-and-mortar- businesses. Most of the money e-businesses did spend financed simplistic loyalty programs that awarded, say $10 vouchers to customers when they had spent $2.50! Such programmes significantly affect the surfing and purchasing behaviour of fewer than 20% of on-line consumers.

The common trait of the companies that hung on to their customers was their reliability in basic operational execution. Their sites downloaded quickly; they responded to customer queries quickly; they delivered more than 95% of their orders on time; and they made it easy for customers to return or exchange purchases.

Moreover, best-practice companies maintain current profiles of customers and send promotions keyed not only to their needs but also to their value. At the most basic level, this is about retaining and leveraging past interaction histories to ensure that the customer never has to answer the same question twice. More sophisticated companies seek to re-create the notion of the personal shopper by, for example, remembering key anniversaries of their customers!

Finally, personalisation is emerging as a driver of retention as well as conversion is. Sophisticated personalisation is a nice-to-have, not a must-have feature. The must-have that helps make e-business profitable permits you to find your natural customers efficiently, to offer them what they want in an appropriately segmented way, and to deliver it reliably.

Topics to Discuss:

1. Discuss the relationship economic concepts in the case?
2. Do the figures surprise you? Why or why not?
3. How can lifetime as well as value-added relationship economy be introduced in e-business
4. Do you think that e-trade has substantial impact on loyalty?
5. How does e-business affect driving forces of customer relationships?
6. Does e-business influence the generic relationship marketing strategies differently?

11. 6: And Then Came TGI Friday's[6]

US in Origin

The first TGI Friday's was opened on New York's First Avenue in 1965. Today there are TGI Friday's restaurants in 47 states and 170 restaurants outside the US.

The restaurants boast the same red and white striped awnings, wooden flooring, and Tiffany lamp shades, bentwood chairs and striped tablecloths as retained in every restaurant in the chain. Both in the US and internationally, TGI Friday's are identical.

TGI was an instant hit with young New Yorkers, quickly becoming *the* place to meet.

TGI Friday's is an American diner operating from 3,500 square metre sites

6. Based on Dibb and Simkin (2001). Quelch et alt. (1994).

including the parking lot. They offer full cocktail bar and restaurant service. Whether it is a simple coffee, an unpronounceable cocktail, a bowl of chips or a five-course menu, TGI Friday's will provide every customer, or guest, with a truly memorable experience.

The Concept

The Friday's concept centres on a simple layout: A raised bar in the centre with dining area around the periphery of the single story building. All the artefacts/atmospherics are genuinely American shipped from the American host company to the European franchisees. Perhaps the most striking feature of the restaurants is what Friday's terms "elegant clutter". Half an eight-man rowing scull, an antique wood aeroplane propeller, a pair of old skating boots and a rocking horse are all at home at Friday's, as is the rest of the clutter items, each piece with a story to tell.

The staff is encouraged to express their personalities through wearing their own hats, braces and badges. They are trained to help guests relax and every member of staff provides the willing, professional service that is a keynote of the successful American restaurants.

At TGI's, guest satisfaction is of ultimate importance.

The menu is culturally diverse, offering more than 70 American, Tex-Mex, Cajun and Italian dishes, plus over 500 cocktails.

Training

Staff training and selection is a fundamental priority, with staff being selected for personality and dedication to looking after the guests. The company has its own full time programme, but for international restaurants, TGI imports experienced US trainers. US trainer Cheryl Domitrovic: "We have to adjust our training methods to the British personality. In the UK we have to teach Friday's staff to make people comfortable and to treat customers as real guests, as real people. We also have to encourage new staff to show their personalities at work. This does not come spontaneously to the more reticent British. But once we have showed how, employees quickly catch on, suddenly work can be tremendous fun, rewarding and enjoyable! In a way, training in the UK is more rewarding than in the US because transformation is so much greater".

Attention to Detail

The focus on all facets of staff training is echoed by the management's control and expertise in running the successful UK concept within the UK. Restaurant menus are carefully thought through to offer variety and "mix and match" dining. Despite the elegant clutter and artefacts, hygiene and cleanliness standards are high. Rigorous cleaning and maintenance programmes and tight management controls result in few problems for customers to worry about.

The attention to detail is extreme. Once recruited, before working in a TGI's restaurant, staff members learn in a classroom and from numerous manuals how to look after all parts of the business. Although the button-badged adorned striped shirts and trousers with braces may look haphazard, there *is* a uniform and dress code that is stringently enforced and specifies everything from the suitability of button badges, to length of hair and fingernails, use of plasters for cuts and grazes etc. Once selected to work in the restaurant, new recruits must pass step-by-step tests, immediately losing the job if they fail to progress satisfactorily. This level of training, financial commitment and attention to detail are all somewhat unusual for in what is often a cost-focused industry.

The Feel and the Guests

"If all the world is a stage, then Friday's must compare to a first night on Broadway", remarked DD, Friday's CEO. In the UK, research shows that 25% of customers return once a month. It is seen as an addictive experience for customers: "You will have a good time, but it won't be yours, it will be ours". The vibrant buzz in the atmosphere is deliberate and well orchestrated. The buzz and vitality are the essence of the service product offered by Friday's.

The Friday's experience and atmosphere are difficult to communicate to non-users. The typical customer is in their thirties, intellectually secure, confident enough to dress down to go out in the evening, someone who can relax, sit, watch and enjoy the experience. However, the customer profile switches throughout the day; business lunches, families in the afternoon an early evening, couples and adults in the later evening. Typical weekday guests are professional people between 25 and 49 years old. At weekends, Friday's is particularly popular among families with children. High chairs for babies, helium-filled balloons and a special kid's menu make it easier to eat out with young children.

Customer and staff loyalty is phenomenally high for the catering and restaurant industry. The whole theme concept is very much a carousel that goes faster and faster as the night goes on, with both staff and guests living on adrenaline and the TGI brand of excitement. Regular visitors to Friday's live and talk about the Friday's experience; the buzzing atmosphere, flamboyant decor and friendly staff who aim to please.

What Next?

Friday's has its critics. Not everyone wants to eat in the middle of a circus. No matter how good the management and quality control, sometimes the guests may be disappointed. Not every meal is cooked to perfection or "dub-tub" waiter right on the ball. Success and popularity also bring the occasional queue and delay. However, the management philosophy is unbending, believing that there is an equal partnership at stake between the three components or elements of business success:

> The guest, the employee and the company.

This Friday's calls the *Triangle Theory*. There must be an equal balance between guests (customers), employees and the company, and if the balance and the status quo are disturbed, the success of the concept will be put into jeopardy. No single element must become dominant, nor must one component weaken.

The company is aware of the need to move forward.

As with other good service concepts, Friday's is being copied. There are relatively low barriers to entry, except financial and employee resources, for potential copycat competitors.

In some ways, Friday's has been victim of its own success. Because of its commitment to training and authentically sourced artefacts for its restaurants as well as the desire for carefully selected sites, it has not been able to expand nationally in UK as quickly as it would like. Where branches have been opened, the impact on the local customer base has been dramatic with high foot traffic and terrific brand loyalty. However, this clear success has inspired many national and local rival restaurant operators to target this new market, which in many ways has been created by Friday's, a market which is no longer associated with the traditional steakhouse offering, pub grub or fast food snack.

Topics to Discuss:

1. Try to discuss the concept of Friday's from a relationship benefits and with a customer life cycle approach. Why is the customer relationship unique?
2. How do you think the different types of customers (i.e. business people, families and twenty somethings) view TGI Friday's in terms of level of loyalty? What are the motivations for this loyalty within each group? What motivations do these groups have in common and which ones are different?
3. How would you compete against Friday's if you were a local restaurant?
4. How would you structure the relationship and the regulating mechanism between Friday's as a company and every single restaurant? Hierarchy? Or a contractual relationship arrangement

11.7: How the Flames Died for Firestone and Ford[7]

When the relationship between companies becomes as close as a marriage, the eventual break-up is often very painful

What made Firestone do it?

That was the question that came to mind when the tire manufacturer broke off its century-old relationship with Ford. It was clear why Ford might want to move on. The car company was desperate to control the damages of its sports utility vehicle (SUV) disaster.

But it was not so clear why Firestone would take action. After all, the break-up is more likely to hurt Firestone and its parent, Bridgestone, than to hurt Ford. It is hard to imagine how Firestone, which sells about a fifth of US tires, can thrive without its big customer. The subsequent dip in Bridgestone's share price shows that markets were also concerned. What's more, Ford insisted, in public at least, that it did not want to push out its old partner. "We did not plan any draconian action", said William Ford Jr.

Many corporations would have taken Fords official position as an opportunity to grovel. Not Firestone. Instead, John Lampe, Bridgestone/Firestone's US chief executive, fired off a "Dear John letter". "Business relationships, like personal ones, are built on mutual respect", he wrote. "We have come to the conclu-

7. Financial Times (2001).

sion that we can no longer supply tires to Ford since the basic foundation of our relationship has been seriously eroded". Mr. Lampe's aggrieved tone seems disconcerting, given that he was supposedly talking about business, not marriage.

The Ending of a Marriage

"Except that he *was* talking about marriage, or a kind of marriage", says Nancy Koehn of Harvard Business School. The Ford/Firestone split might have appeared to be about responsibility for those troubled SUV accidents", says Ms. Koehn, the author of a book on loyalty and corporations. "But it was really about something more: a relationship as hot – and as idealistic – as a personal one. There are a lot of examples about loyalty between companies that is not purely transactional", she says.

Such business marriages usually begin with friendship between the founders of great companies and a firm business purpose. Ford/Firestone was born when Harvey Firestone sold four tyres to Henry Ford for his Quadricycle. Soon the arrangement goes beyond business issues. Eventually, says Ms. Koehn, these partnerships can come to have an outsized importance for both companies, so great in fact that partners will forego business opportunities elsewhere. And, inevitably, like marriages between people, business marriages do end through the death of a partner, because of the action of a powerful interloper, or in fiery scenes like the one staged by Firestone.

The marital analogy is not perfect but it does shed light on some old corporate history.

Partnerships that Last

Consider the partnership of Wedgwood & Bentley and Boulton & Fothergill in 18th-century England. Wedgwood and Bentley made the consumer earthenware that was the predecessor of the Wedgwood we know today. Matthew Boulton, England's great pioneer, established Boulton & Fothergill in the use of iron and metalwork. The companies teamed up to make buckles, buttons, vases and brooches, Wedgwood and Bentley crafting the pottery component and Boulton supplying the metal casings and frames. Both Josiah Wedgwood and Matthew Boulton, Ms. Koehn relates, passed up other opportunities in order to preserve their relationship.

"Matthew could have made vases on his own, but he did not", she says. Only the death of Wedgwood ended the link.

Then there was the relationship, perhaps more a liaison than a marriage, between Marshall Field, the mighty Chicago merchant, and Alexandra Napoleon, a smaller French company. Back in the 1860's the retailer saw the city's nouveaux riches craved European goods to confirm their social status. Kid gloves made by Alexandra Napoleon proved to be just the ticket. By 1880 Marshall Field, the department store, had become such a colossus that it could have dallied with cheaper suppliers, says Ms. Koehn. But it remained true to Alexandre Napoleon, demanding only the exclusive rights to its merchandise.

Next there was Dupont and General Motors, another car industry pair. According to Randall Kroszner of University of Chicago, Dupont supplied paint, varnish and artificial leather to the carmaker. It also held many GM shares. By the late 1940's the relationship had become so close that the US antitrust authorities demanded a divorce.

Another example of divorce, in this case a good divorce, involved Henry Clay Frick and Andrew Carnegie. Frick supplied coke for Carnegie's steel and the two men became allies. Eventually, Frick went to work at Carnegie Steel. Like the Firestone/Ford break-up, this split was apparently triggered by a catastrophe. When labour troubles arose, Carnegie stumbled off to Europe, leaving Frick and his plant manager to manage the 1892 Homestead strike. Frick hired Pinkerton Security hands, which fired on the protesters who were getting violent. Frick and Carnegie blamed each other and eventually Frick left. But he took with him a sizeable settlement in the form of equity sufficient to leave legacies such as the Frick art collection.

The marital model is useful when it comes to cases such as that with Firestone. One might propose that the break-up was overdue, since Harvey and Henry died many years ago. Or one could look at the split in the terms of an emotional dynamic. After all, with the blame that Ford unloaded on Firestone, it probably felt good to post that break-up letter. Like a divorcing spouse, the company may have decided that anything was better than the awful status quo.

Alas for Firestone, in this instance, that may not be the case.

The Cost of Exit – Who is to Blame for the Divorce?

Ford Motor Company attempted to justify its net \$ 2.1 billion charge for the controversial recall of 13 m Firestone tyres with detailed evidence alleging inferior quality and potentially dangerous failure rates in tyres supplied by the Japanese owned manufacturer.

The charge followed an intensive 10 month investigation costing more than

$30 million by Ford engineers and independent technical experts commissioned by the world's second largest carmaker. The potential liability for 174 road traffic deaths linked to accidents involving Ford vehicles and Firestone tyres was at stake.

Ford presented its findings to the National Highway Traffic Safety Administration, who was conducting its own investigations and used it in deciding to proceed with the second recall of Wilderness AT tyres.

However, its decision to discuss the issue further with analysts seemed to reflect concern that Wall Street was questioning why Ford was prepared to spend more than $2 billion of shareholders' money on a second, larger recall when there was no regulatory obligation and Firestone strongly disputed the need for this. Some analysts have been worried about the impact on the brand-image of Ford's products when competition is intensifying.

Firestone, who angrily severed its long running links with Ford, claims design issues on Ford's best selling sports utility vehicle rather than problems with tyres contributed to many of the accidents.

"We welcome all investigations to prove the Explorer is safe", a spokesman for Ford said. "But Firestone does not agree with our data and does not agree with our conclusions. We believe this incident has revealed the need to upgrade the industry standards and prevent less than adequate tyres getting on the market".

Topics to Discuss:

1. Why do you think Firestone decided to "divorce"?
2. Why couldn't the conflict between Ford and Firestone be solved within dyadic regulating mechanisms?
3. Do you think that the relationship economic benefits in the Ford-Firestone marriage, which they now sacrifice, exceed the damages? Or will one or both have to monadically absorb the damages?
4. What could have been done to prevent termination?
5. Discuss the advantages and disadvantages of life long marriages between two companies.

11.8: Scandinavian Airlines System – Turning around a Supertanker by Relationship Marketing[8]

The Back Against the Wall

The oil crises of the 1970s and a worldwide recession at the end of the decade had cut deeply into the airline industry. Most airlines had experienced a deficit, and many carriers had had to resort to dramatic survival tactics to stay in business. At the same time the first wave of US airline deregulation started being felt in Europe in the shape of keen price competition on transatlantic routes from upstart new carriers. At the same time, new lower-cost Asian competitors also appeared in the skies.

Scandinavian Airline System (SAS), the national carrier of Denmark, Norway and Sweden, had not been spared during the crises years. By 1981 SAS was struggling with a severe downturn in business and an accumulated two-year deficit of £39 million. At this time, a young and energetic Jan Carlzon was brought in as the new SAS CEO.

Carlzon: "We Fly People – Not Planes"

Carlzon believed that SAS had become an introverted operation focused organisation that had lost its awareness of the customers' needs. "Management had focused on machines instead of people", he stated. "But SAS", Carlzon pointed out, "is not the airline, or head office, or an overhaul station:

> It is nothing tangible. It is the contact and the "contract" between one customer and one SAS employee in the front line". He referred to this concept as "the moment of truth", that is any episode where a customer would come into contact with some aspect of the company, however remote, and thereby have an opportunity to form an impression. "SAS", he said, "had 50,000 moments of truth out in the market every day". That meant 50,000 opportunities to satisfy or dissatisfy customers. "We have only one real asset and that is the relationship with satisfied customers prepared to come back to SAS and pay for our costs once more.

8. Based on Dibb and Simkin (2001) and Quelch et alt. (1994).

In June 1981 Carlzon was ready to take the big jump. Carlzon: "In the beginning we had to decide what part of the market SAS should do business with, so that all our services and transactions could be designed to meet those specific market needs and no other. This included reducing the total costs this market was not prepared to pay and eventually eliminating them, so that every resource of expense was profitable. In the past, we had hurt ourselves a little more every year by cutting away at services that customers were prepared to pay for. And we got stuck with administration overheads that they were unprepared to support.

The Businessman's Strategy: Managing the Focus

While competitors were cutting back on new product development and promotions, SAS invested heavily in the Businessman's Airline Programme. By positioning SAS as the "businessman's airline", Carlzon hoped to steal passengers from such other carriers such as Air France and British Airways, which were upgrading their service but also charging high prices for it.

Research was conducted to establish what aspects of the travel experience factors businessmen regarded as important before, during and after flying. Safety and punctuality came out on the top. Carlzon asked management to find ideas to deliver new improved services for business travellers. They came back with recommendations for more than 150 projects. These proposals were followed, in rapid succession, by the development and introduction of a series of new services. The projects chosen were to accomplish one of two objectives: to improve the experience of the frequent traveller or to save his time.

Since the business traveller's most important consideration was *arriving* rather than leaving on time, Carlzon instituted a leave-on-time punctuality drive, which he was said to have supervised personally.

Carlzon was also trying to influence aircraft manufacturers to construct and produce the "passenger-pleasing plane". Its design would be unorthodox, with 75-80% of the fuselage allocated to passenger comfort and in-cabin baggage storage, instead of the usual 35%. He said, "For the 1990's our starting point is that we need an aircraft which the business passengers want. Then we can add engine and the cockpit, not the other way round. He tried to persuade the manufacturers to look beyond what was being built now or was on the drawing board for the business traveller, and to generate their interest in building a passenger-pleasing plane. But he had little success.

A marginal strategy was designed to sell to the leisure travel market whatever capacity the business traveller couldn't use. The major thrust of this effort was geared to price differentiation, low fair tickets on scheduled flights departing at times not favourable for the businessman.

The business traveller and the leisure traveller could often be the same person in different guises and, depending on his or her role at the time, demands and expectations could vary. Also the pattern for leisure travel was different. Business travels usually followed general economic trends. For the business traveller, travel was frequently part of the job. Such travel was the best way to create and maintain contacts, survey new markets, pick up new business ideas and carry out deals. Trips were an investment in present and future business and required special airline services.

For the leisure traveller, travel was nearly always associated with recreation and escape from everyday life – a chance to see new places and make new acquaintances. The trip itself was part of the pleasure. In contrast to business trips, vacations were planned far in advance and were seldom changed. For the tourist, price was a very important factor. The pattern of leisure travel was somewhat different, too. Demand could often rise during a recession, possibly because households would reduce investments in capital goods and, instead, spend their money on leisure pursuits. Business and tourist travel patterns showed wide seasonal variations as well.

Inverting the Organisational Pyramid of SAS

Carlzon's "little red book" was the first step towards involving all SAS employees in the new way of thinking. In the beginning, people were somewhat surprised by this unusual form of communication, but they got used to it in time and even came to expect it. Resistance came mainly from the technical side of the operation, especially from the older pilots.

The idea of differentiating service for different customers was partly foreign to the Scandinavian norms and values of egalitarism. But internal marketing lifted anxieties, and morale steadily improved. In fact, employees became excited by the new strategy.

In the organisation structure erased in mid 1981, Carlzon erased the pyramid and redrew his concept of the new organisation as a kind of wheel with the CEO at the hub and operation departments around him. Whereas frontline workers with the most customer contact had formerly been at the bottom of the chart, Carlzon put them on the top. It became every one else's responsibility including his, to "serve" those who directly served the customer. In his own words he wanted to put workers in charge and have management serve as consultants to the organisation!

Telling people what to do only succeeds in putting limitations on them. Information, on the other hand, permits them to know their opportunities and possibilities, to free someone from rigorous control of instructions, policies and orders and to give that person freedom to take responsibility for his ideas, decisions and actions. It releases hidden resources that would otherwise remain inaccessible to both the individual and the company. A person who has information and a sense of direction cannot avoid taking responsibility.

So, What Happened?

By the end of 1982, SAS had achieved a total image transformation. It had become the most punctual airline in Europe as well as the number one choice for Scandinavian businessmen. The financial picture had also changed unrecognisably. Corporate overheads had been reduced by 25% and the company came back from a $10 million loss to achieving a significant increase in profitability.

After the turnaround, SAS entered a period of consolidation followed by several years of steady growth. Near the end of the 1980's, US deregulation posed a further threat to SAS. To stay in business, SAS needed a strategy that would work successfully in the 1990′s, a period that was likely to be volatile for all. Carlzon wanted to securely position the airline in what was going to be a highly competitive and much altered airline market.

One of SAS' moves was to acquire Intercontinental Hotels thereby forming the basis of a solid worldwide total travel package service concept. For example, following the SAS philosophy to save customer time, special kiosks at hotels would arrange for boarding the baggage and provide other services to business travellers. To ensure the strategy's success, it was crucial that all activities moved smoothly, linking one part of the chain to the next. One such example was to provide hotel check-ins at the airport and airport check-ins at the hotels.

The 1990's, however, turned out to question the former relationship marketing strategy of SAS.

Topics to Discuss:

1. How would you describe the relationship marketing strategy of SAS?
2. What do you think SAS should focus on during implementation?

3. Does the concept of "business man's" airline have any impact on transaction costs?
4. What could eventually threaten the strategy of SAS?

11.9: The Promise of Mass Customisation – True or False?[9]

Is Mass Customisation Feasible and Attractive for all Industries?

For more than two decades, mass customisation has been the future of manufacturing. On the face of it, mass customisation is a remarkably attractive proposition for consumers, manufacturers and their suppliers alike. Consumers get a reasonably priced, tailor-made product reflecting their personal selection of colours, features, functions and style. Producers, for their part, get to reduce their inventories and manufacturing overhead costs, to eliminate waste in their supply chains and to obtain more accurate information about demand. In short a win-win proposition.

But is mass customisation equally feasible for all goods? Assembling cars, for example, is more complex and difficult than building computers. Still, auto companies have high hopes for the build-to-order (BTO) approach, a variant of mass customisation. The benefits to customers are numerous, and the many difficult challenges they face in implementing BTO can be overcome. Or can they?

The Transition from Push to Pull Production System

The challenges of implementing BTO in the auto industry are daunting and it isn't clear that economics alone will work. Moving from a mass manufacturing or push system to a BTO or pull system will require significant operational and organisational changes throughout the auto industry value as shown in the figure below:

9. Based on McKinsey Quarterly (2001).

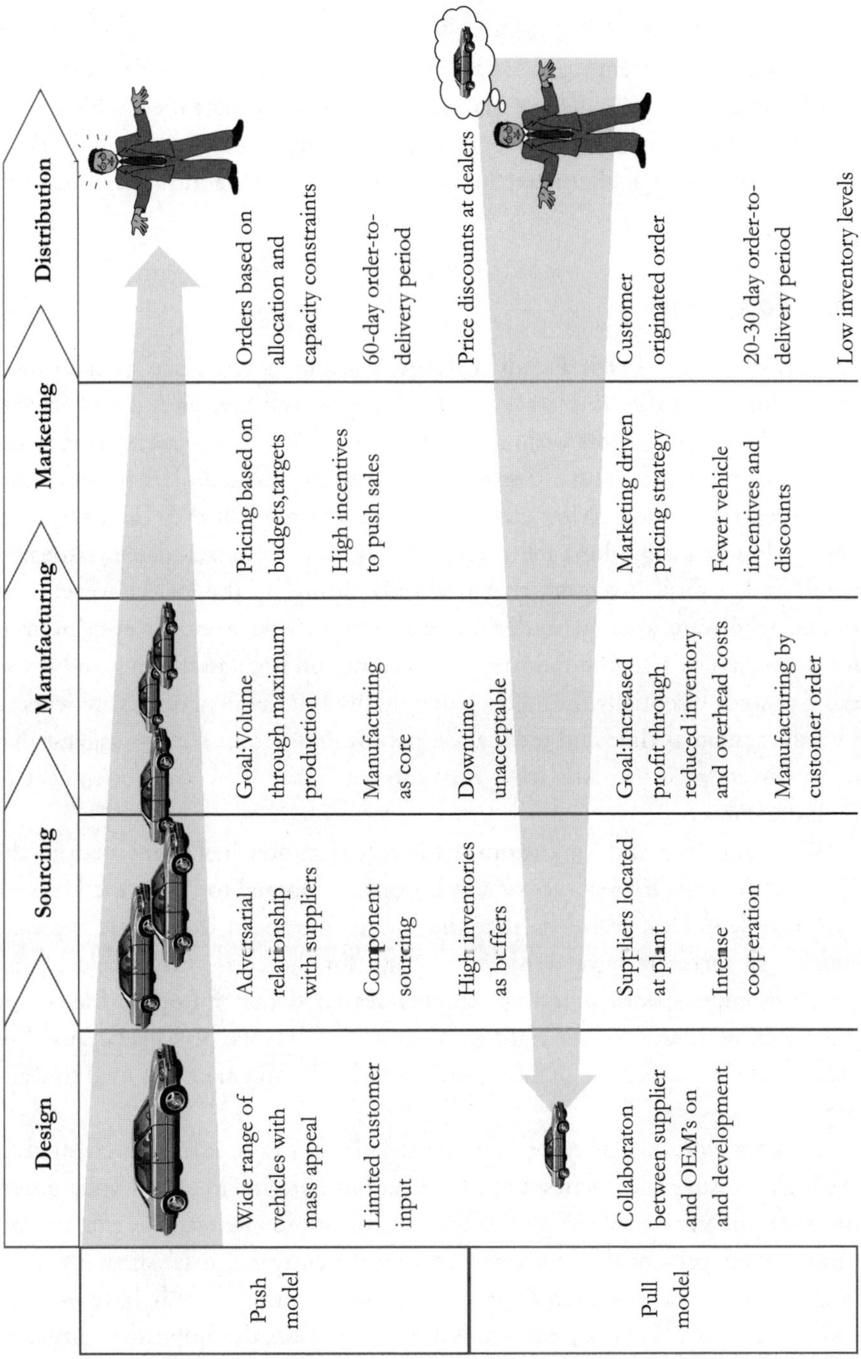

Figure 11-6: The push versus the pull system. Source: McKinsey Quarterly (2001)

Luxury car buyers seem eager to specify their preferences in great detail. But it is still too early to tell whether mainstream customers want their vehicle built to order, let alone how much they would be willing to pay for this. Will BTO develop into a virtual alternative for customers? Will BTO turn out to be profitable?

The Promise of BTO

Broadly defined, BTO is already a reality. Customers can place special orders for cars today. At the simplest level, customers as well as dealers can check the inventories of various lots within a given geographical area to see whether a car being sought already exists. Customer can also ask their dealers to order cars from the manufacturer. Most customers are not aware that they can order cars, and dealers generally don't tell them. This is quite understandable, as dealers would rather push inventory that is already sitting on the lot. However, customers who want a special-order car may have to wait weeks or even months for delivery. The US auto industry is geared to building, assembling and delivering of stock essentially through a batch method. Individual orders are worked into the system as time and inclination permit. Numerous surveys suggest that many buyers prefer to take what they can get rather than wait for the car of their dreams.

Consumer demand for custom-made cars is greater in Europe than in the US. In 2000 app. 19% of cars sold in Europe as opposed to 7% in the US were special orders. One reason is that the lots of European dealers are typically smaller, so there are fewer vehicles on-hand for the consumer to select from which prompts special ordering. Another reason is that European buyers are more willing to wait for the right car than are US buyers, perhaps because Europeans are less impulsive in their purchasing habits and are more used to waiting.

Another cultural difference between the US and European sales channels is the high-pressure sales tactics that all US car buyers come to expect upon entering a car lot. Salespeople in the US are as a rule more interested in effective inventory management than making sure that the customer is satisfied. They are taught to motivate potential buyers to buy the cars they already have in stock and to drive it off the lot the same day, preying on the impulsive nature of American consumers.

Automakers in general are nevertheless united in their conviction that they could raise prices somewhat and reduce costs substantially, if the majority of their customers bought special-order cars. Prices could be raised because customers would have difficulty comparison shopping, and they would be getting exactly what they wanted. At the same time, dealers and original equipment manufacturers probably could cut back on the enormous discounts often required to "move the metal" from the back of the dealer's lot.

But the greater lure of BTO for auto manufacturers lies in the hope of lower supply chain costs. A true pull system would mean a massive reduction in finished goods and in component inventories. Industry analysts estimate that if customers bought the majority of cars built to order, the industry could capture as much as 70% of the capital that is lost when inventory becomes obsolete following a change in models, production processes, and assembly structures, or that is locked up in metal and components kept on the shelf to meet unanticipated demand. Nissan Motors, for one, has estimated that this could amount to savings of up to $ 3,600 a vehicle.

Daunting Challenges Ahead

Making mass customisation in the auto industry a reality would require carmakers to deal with enormous changes in design, sourcing, manufacturing, marketing and distribution.

Mass customisation will require manufacturers to rethink the way they absorb fluctuations in production as well as managing people when unionised labour must be sent home still getting paid.

Customers may like to choose the colour of their cars, for instance, but paint shops at car plants run in batch mode to cut costs and to minimise the emissions and waste that are generated every time paint guns receiving new colours are flushed.

Carmakers could achieve BTO by modularising – that is, by fabricating individual cars not from thousands of distinct parts but from mere dozens of larger mix-and-match modules. But because carmakers might have to carry a range of modules, this could create greater inventory redundancy and waste within the supply chain than to the non-modular components, which can be configured according to demand.

BTO introduces even bigger challenges upstream of the assembly plant in the supply chain. Currently the chain is designed to deliver, on time and to the right location, mass quantities of standard components without the capability of adjusting the output mix according to individual orders. The ladder approach would tend to require shorter supply links, yet the low-wage areas where many current suppliers are located happen to be at a great distance from the carmakers' assembly plants.

In some countries dealers are still likely to view BTO as a threat. They feel that BTO could be the first step for the manufacturers to sell directly to the consumers. Furthermore the dealers actually *value* large stocks up to a point. As one dealer stated: "A large number of cars on my lot shows I am healthy, open for business and offering wide choice. Why should I trade that in for two demo cars in a dinky showroom?"

Will Consumers Buy It?

Assuming BTO can be implemented, will it appeal to consumers? Automakers point to the growing evidence that their customers would welcome a BTO option. In 2000 a survey by J.D. Power & Associates revealed that 17% of North American car buyers would buy a BTO vehicle next time if they didn't have to pay more and got what they have ordered in six weeks or less.

The true depth and extent of consumer demand for BTO cars are still largely unknown. Carmakers cannot gauge the receptiveness of buyers of mass-market cars in either Europe or North America. Specifically, carmakers haven't identified the incremental factors, such as time to delivery, that prompt customer to switch from option to another or prevent them from doing so. Is it two weeks? Five days? Will customers accept delivery times that could vary? In addition, some customers have said in surveys that they place greater value on the dealer's ability to help them understand whether one option or another would either enhance or undercut a vehicle's resale value than they do on expanded choice.

BTO won't become a reality until the industry has a better understanding of what it is about BTO that customer' value. Is it getting their specifications met? If so, how much delay will customers tolerate to accept that? Also, are some segments of the market willing to pay extra for BTO and, if so, how much? Would they pay an extra $100 for red paint so that they did not have to settle for white, say?

A Virtual Alternative

In view of these mysteries and obstacles, it is fortunate that an alternative path for OEM's exists. Indeed some are already pursuing it, admittedly, in a quiet way, given the supposed political correctness of the pure BTO model. They are finding that the alternative offers many of the benefits of a true BTO system while lacking its operational and organisational drawbacks. The alternative does so by connecting customers, either over the Internet or in a dealer's showroom, to the vast, albeit far-flung, array of cars already in existence, including vehicles on dealers' lots, in transit, on the assembly line, and scheduled for production. In this way, customers are likely to find a vehicle with the colour and the options they must want. Automakers would not have to *build* to order; rather, they would enhance the customers' ability to *locate* to order.

Customers shouldn't care whether the car they purchased was built expressly for them or found for them somewhere in the supply chain, as long as it had the features they wanted and they got it in a reasonable amount of time. For carmakers this is a low cost solution that is easier to implement than BTO yet likely to provide high customer satisfaction. Just as important, this approach offers automakers access to customer data and insight into customer preferences for features, options, colours and so on equal to what real BTO promises.

Will BTO come true? Making the complete attainment of true BTO the goal when the changes required are mammoth and the returns so uncertain is another matter entirely. The auto industry has a history of disappointing returns from massive changes. OEM suppliers might not have the skills to live up to the requirements. Dealer networks tend to be an obstacle and do the consumers really care?

Topics to Discuss:

1. Will customers be willing to pay a higher price for BTO?
2. Will supply chain costs go down, and will the automaker be more dependent on subcontractors, who can then act opportunistic?
3. Will dealers and distributors be threatened, if BTO breaks through?
4. Do you think that the virtual alternative is competitive?
5. Which relationship marketing strategy could possibly be a successful BTO direction for an automaker

11.10: The Bank as Life Companion[10]

Be My Life Companion!

When a Dane becomes a bank customer, he or she has in effect chosen an economic life companion.

Eight out of ten Danes have been customers in their bank for more than five years. On average the banking relationships last much longer than marriages! Banks are like diamonds: "They last forever". And when Danes on rare occasions switch from one bank to another, the main reason is bad service or because people move from one part of the country to another.

The very low bank customer mobility stands in sharp contrast to consumer behaviour in general. The average Danish family shops in at least three different supermarket chains every month without any sense of breaking loyalty ties to supermarket employees or the concept of the specific chain. We are chasing special offers, discounts and other kinds of advantages as never before. This is even the case in private damage insurance, an area that almost all consumers consider being a complicated and low involvement area. Consumers are willing to switch insurance supplier, if a competitor offers marginally better or cheaper products.

Not surprisingly, the deep customer bank loyalty walks hand in hand with very high profit margins in the private customer business of the banking sector. The theory holds that when the market mechanisms are eliminated, then the supplier tends to increase prices.

But why is it that the financial consumers behave as they do? Why have they become voluntary prisoners? Are they stupid and irrational? Or can we find logical and rational explanations?

Unilateral or Bilateral Loyalty at Play?

When discussing loyalty as a construct one can raise the question; does true loyalty require mutuality, meaning loyalty both ways? In our case, a loyal bank customer can count on the bank as an equally loyal partner as well. In practice, the loyalty codex of banks does not assume mutuality. The bank does not guarantee the lowest prices or the highest quality. And on a rainy day the bank will hardly grant you a loan although you have been a loyal customer for decades. So when it comes down to it, the bank considers risk exposure and hence prof-

10. Based on Hougaard (1995).

itability to be more important than the customer relationship. "Yes, of course", one would say, "a bank is a business like other businesses"!

What is interesting here is that bank customers are happy to accept the one-way relationship treaty without asking for anything at all in return. Apparently the loyalty does not pay off. Or does it?

No Holes in the Customer Palisade

The banks in Denmark have delivered overwhelming evidence that a relationship oriented business model is far superior over strategies focusing on products or transactional benefits. The banking sector has been excellent in cultivating and strengthening the relationship aspect and they have succeeded in developing and refining the super loyal banking customer.

In fact, it has required more than one generation of strategic marketing efforts to reach the present loyalty position. From the invention of wage and household budget accounts almost two generations ago, the creation of dominance over financial infrastructures and cash flow of society through pension schemes, personal banking advisor arrangements to life stage products. Every gap in the customer need spectrum has been immediately and effectively covered. In recent years, the banks have introduced bond and mortgage loans and private insurance's very successfully leading to further consolidation of the impregnable customer relationships.

And what about the customers? For the vast majority the one-stop money shopping is perceived to be convenient. The super loyal customer has transaction costs close to zero. When you have one supplier and you fully trust him as you would a life companion, then exchanges run at a very smooth level. The loyalty award that the banking customer gets is first and foremost in the shape of saved transaction costs.

Who Should Pay for the Net-bank?

No surprise, the banks have also succeeded in transferring their customers to their net-banks, which have conquered a substantial market share very rapidly. Apparently the loyalty was not so much oriented towards a certain channel, the branch office, in a situation where the virtual branch can offer convenience and sufficient service.

The banks are charging their customers for access to the net-bank, the main argument being that the costs of operating the net-bank should be paid by the people using it and not by all customers. In general, customers find this explanation fair. However, this is indeed a paradox. Customers, who practise self-service using net-banks rather than branch offices are much more profitable as the banks save all the staff costs in personal service. In addition the customers pay for the on-line time to the telephone company.

Therefore, the "smart" customer should ask for a discount instead of accepting a charge. But it underlines the elimination of effective market forces.

Is Lack of Differentiation a Possible Reason for Loyalty?

In retrospect, it is thought provoking that all retail banks have approximately the same strategic profile and image. No important player in the industry has chosen differentiation as the way to obtain sustainable competitive advantage. The legal constraints would be substantial if they did. Maybe this fact has had an important impact on consumer behaviour in the direction of loyalty.

When consumers do not see any differences between the money service suppliers, it is hard to imagine that you will get a better service or sharper prices by changing supplier. There is no reason to change. Maybe a one-time advantage can be obtained in a market contract negotiation, but as both you and the bank expect the market contract to be eliminated as soon as the customer has signed on, the non-relationship advantages will soon disappear again. To put it simply: The combination of deep customer loyalty (approx. 30% of the population uses more than one bank, however) and the look-alike of all retail banks are effective protections against dynamics.

All Invasion Attempts Have Failed

Throughout the history of modern banking there have been many attempts to defeat or shake our financial life companion by questioning the rationality of almost blind loyalty.

Niche banks have tried. Some with a discount concept, others by focusing on certain customer segments, typically called "high net worth individuals". Lately, independent net banks have tried hard to gain a foothold.

A decade ago the insurance industry entered the private customer market through acquisitions and established their own banks. All attempts have failed. Then there is the "embedded banking services" concept where the car loan plus the insurance as an element in a buying-selling transaction. The same packaging is seen in home buying. Most recently, mortgage institutes have started investing big money in retail banking positioning themselves as the no nonsense direct banking solution, where you get what you pay for and vice versa.

Almost none has succeeded. Not yet, at least. From different angles of legacy all invaders have presented attractive offers and often based on a range of services that does not challenge the "mother relationship". But the Danes have said no to courtesy, the marriage has resisted all temptations. Can a winning formula be developed at all?

The True Price Explains It All

Neither the literature nor practice has so far been able to explain our apparently irrational consumer behaviour. After a period in time, it became a widespread expectation that the fast penetration of electronic payment systems (Dankort), ATM's and the self-service on-line solutions, which have all reduced the level and frequency of personal contacts between customer and bank would finally erode loyalty. But this has not been the case.

Some observers conclude that the bank customer finds it complicated, painful and time consuming to either switch banks or become a single-product buyer using a group of suppliers. In addition the tearing apart of old ties leaves you with a sentiment like loosing an old friend. You know what you have got.

In other words, the bank customer would face very high transaction costs by switching or shopping around. From a customer's perspective, transaction costs are an integral part of the total price. Even a substantially better offer from the competitor means a price increase, when the true perceived transaction costs are included. Paying higher interests on loans and credits leads to the lowest overall price!

Our bank has succeeded in packaging products, services and financial/asset management so that the total relationship is perceived as convincing and secure. In fact, your banker knows more about your household's financial situation than you do yourself. The financial freedom has been voluntarily deposited with the bank.

Topics to Discuss:

1. Do you think Danish banks live up to the relationship marketing definition?
2. Discuss the plusses and minuses of the typical customer behaviour in a relationship economic sense.

3. Why is it that all retail banks stick to the same relationship marketing strategy?
4. Do you think that the upcoming digital value chains (net-banks etc) will gradually become a driving force threatening the bank-customer relationship?

11.11 The Danish Car Industry: www.bilsalg.dk

In 1999, after a period[11] of high sales records for new cars due to strong economic and market conditions, the car industry in Denmark went through a period of decreasing sales; actually sales fell by 50%. This was not the case however for second hand or used car market where the supply of used cars was still high due to the large inventories of the dealers. For the private buyer this meant that there were numerous options to buy in the market.

Due to the large inventories of used cars available at this time, there was pressure on dealers to lower prices. This combined with changes in the tax laws, forced dealers to bring down their inventories and put further pressure on prices, driving them down even further.

The customer who bought a used car without the need to trade in their existing car (80% of all private buyers have a trade-in) was in a good position. But the vast majority of potential buyers were at a disadvantage (as they did have a used car already) and since they could not get a sufficient price on their used they weren't able to buy and finance a new car.

This environment caused companies to focus on corporate car leasing where the car was part of wage packages for the employees. However, the market for company cars continued to grow primarily financed by leasing contracts.

These leasing companies are responsible either partly or completely for all the administration and maintenance of a company's fleet of cars. This type of leasing situation usually involves a contract situation with duration of on average three years.

Due to this focus on corporate leasing, many of these leased cars appeared on the used car market (primarily bought by private individuals) and this supply was therefore not dependent on economic situation of the private household sector.

During this period, the Internet also began to play a large role in the purchase of new and used cars. 60-70% of all car buyers in 2001 used the Internet

11. 1994-1998.

for information gathering purposes.[12] This is the double number of the one compared to 1999.

Another trend also showed it itself during the period following 1999. The Internet began to influence the transparency of the used car industry. Customers could compare prices and therefore get a clearer idea of what their cars were worth and how much they could expect whcn trading with dealers. This also made the profits earned by dealers on used cars transparent. This knowledge was the catalyst for a shift in this market as it created the private-to-private sale, in order to cut out the dealer's profit and make the selling and buying experience more profitable to both parties.

In 1999 the percentage of private-to-private used car transactions was only 25% of the total market and has shot up since then to 50% in 2001.[13]

The Basic Idea

In the spring of 1999, Avis Rental Car Company registered a fall in their sales of used cars to private buyers. In 1999, Avis was responsible for the sale of 2,500 used cars from their rental fleet combined with a partnership agreement with Axus leasing to sell their formerly leased cars. Yearly sales to private buyers fell from 250 cars in 1998 to 150 cars in 1999 and had a significant impact on Avis' financial result.

The reason for focusing on the private buyers is that profit on vehicles sold to these buyers were, and are an extra 12% net profit as compared to profits obtained from vehicles sold to used car dealers.[14]

Avis Rental Car company needed to make sure that the prices on their next wave (year 2000) of used vehicles didn't fall too much as that would have a great influence on their fiscal performance. The ambition was to regain a considerable no. of cars sold to private buyers; the goal was to reach 1,000 cars equal to an additional net profit of DKK 25 million.

With the dawn of the Internet, the physical location of the car became less important. This made it possible for huge savings in logistics when dealing cars. Cars could be rented and at the same time be put up for sale, which was a much more cost efficient use of the vehicle fleet than before.

---

12. Source: The Danish Auto Dealers Association.
13. Source: The Danish Auto Dealers Association.
14. A T Kearny report (2000) internal material AVIS. The figures correspond to figures in the UK (2000).

The alternative to selling cars to private buyers has been and is to sell the cars at auctions or to used car dealers. Selling cars at auctions or used car dealers creates lower profits than selling cars to private buyers.

The first version of the site

After a survey made in May of 1999, the management of Avis in Denmark decided on a new strategy that was based on using the Internet as a platform for the sale of their used cars directly to private buyers.

In the first phase of this project it was expected that the Internet would service the used car market selling cars entirely from Avis' rental fleet to private buyers. However, in the middle of the development of this project it became apparent that there were more opportunities than just used car sales or merely focusing on Avis' own cars. The Internet was also a potential platform for selling used leasing cars as well as selling used rental cars. These cars could come not only from Avis, but from other leasing and rental companies as well. In the fall of 1999, the existing website www.avis.dk was used to test the potential opportunities by using the Internet as a sales channel while at the same time developing an independent site that was just for used car sales only.

In December of 1999, www.bilsalg.dk was launched with the help of 4 web design company and the company Nordenconsult as the strategy consultant. This site was launched at the same time that the Internet was really being pushed and hyped, making the website a success from day one.

Right after the launch of this site, Avis implemented an off-line marketing campaign to increase the awareness of the website.

Existing barriers and results

It quickly became clear that other rental companies in this market didn't want to take part in www.bilsalg.dk due to the overwhelming presence Avis had on the site at that time.

The business model of www.bilsalg.dk was thus changed to be a media for selling and marketing used cars. The revenue model was then based a transaction fee paid by the participating companies. The fee structure was two-fold – one part paid per car appearing on the site and a fee for each vehicle sold.

Even after the concept was modified to an independent company owned by both Avis and a board of directors, it was not possible until the end of year 2000 that other Danish companies could participate. The reasons for this were insecurity about the effectiveness of the type of sales channel and emotional ties between the individuals involved.

In the middle of year 2000 an organisation was established which enabled the company to have all IT development taking place in-house and allowed it to be independent of external IT suppliers.

At the same time contractual relationships to suppliers and partners based on standard business agreements were established. Avis retained ownership and in fact both companies resided in the same building and the perception, internally and externally was that the two organisations were one.

It later became apparent the ownership status of Avis was not always an advantage. In retrospect, it probably would have been much easier to establish a network of suppliers if the site has been an independent entity. On the other hand, start-up costs were less. As always in business life a trade-off had to be made.

Relationships with both Customers and Suppliers

The concept of creating a new portal with the goal of filling the needs of all the players within the used car market has made www.bilsalg.dk one of the largest and most successful car sites in Denmark. This success is primarily due to the amount of information available on the site and the fact that the information is of interest to many car enthusiasts as well as sellers and buyers. Moreover, bilsalg.dk has created a car community that is unique in Denmark and this also accounts for the increase in website traffic.

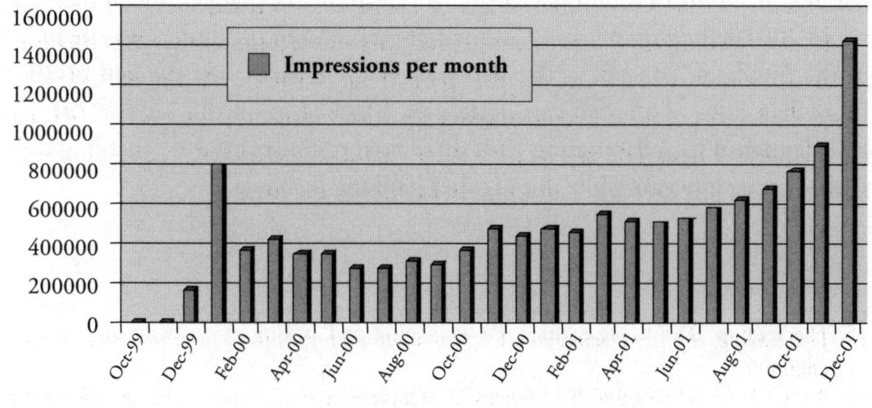

Figure 11-7: Number of page impressions per month on bilsalg.dk. Source: bilsalg.dk

The unique access to the used car market as well as the concepts that are behind Bilsalg.dk have both played role in Bilsalg.dk being nominated and elected as the best overall eCommerce solution in Denmark in year 2000. (Reboot 2000).[15] This site has been presented at two international conferences for eCommerce in the automotive sector: Cars Online 2000 in Brussels and Cars Online 2001 in London.

Relationships with both Customers and Suppliers, BtC and BtB

In order to serve not only private buyers (BtC) but also the larger market (BtB) bilsalg.dk established a special facility in which the individual used car dealer could access bilsalg.dk directly.

The reason for separating the BtC from the BtB market was, and is, that trading terms and conditions vary considerably.

As a result of this the largest leasing operator, Nordania with a market share of approximately 40% joined bilsalg.dk as Nordania only sells its cars to the BtB market. The concept has therefore changed to be a two-in-one.

A side effect of this was quite important as it meant that a potential channel conflict was avoided, as the used car dealers now could access the BtB part of bilsalg.dk, meaning that bilaslg.dk was a potential partner, not a competitor.

The Current Situation

The current situation is that bilsalg.dk has been developed with programmes that are oriented towards BtB, BtC as well as BtE(C)[16] markets and it therefore has developed into a solution that can be transferred to many different markets.

In 2001 selling used leasing and rental cars to used car dealers was included in the Bilsalg.dk concept as the BtB part of the business. At the end of 2001 more than 70% of all used cars dealers were locked in on this service. BtE has been launched in collaboration with three financial institutions[17] enabling their customers to buy cars while doing other banking business.

15. The leading Danish organisation for evaluating and pricing eCommerce and Internet solutions.
16. BtE(C) is an abbreviation for business to employees and customers – i.e. closed markets within large organisations accessible to employees and customers.
17. Nextbank, Lån&Spar Bank and Danske Bank.

The results have been encouraging and there is reason for hope for the future.

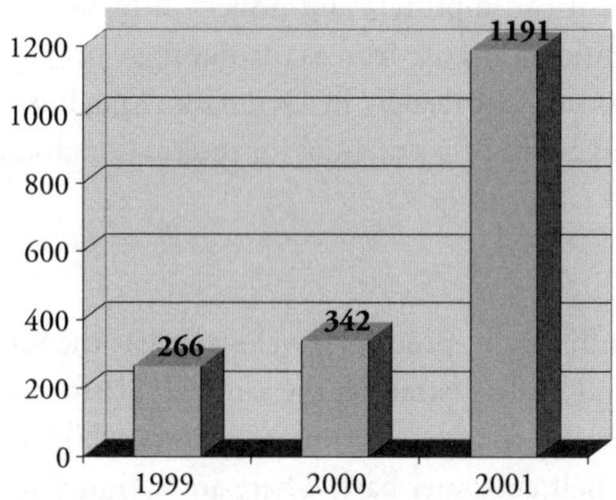

Figure 11-8: Number of cars sold to private buyers 1999-2001.
Source: Avis Bilsalg, Axus Bilsalg and bilsalg.dk

bilsalg.dk has manoeuvred itself into a very strong position because of its first mover advantage and its low start-up costs and promotional expenses.

> However, the market potential for bilsalg.dk within Denmark is quite small and therefore the revenue potential is equally limited. Currently Bilsalg.dk is also being negatively influenced by the many car sale websites that don't charge for their services, severely limiting bilsalg.dk's ability to generate revenues. The result is that bilsalg.dk will need to investigate alternative business models or choose to focus on expansion in other geographical markets.

Current and Future Challenges

The technology that has been developed and tested over the last 2 years combined with the concept that has been developing over time has naturally created opportunities to expand into international markets as well the potential of developing similar web solutions for other customers.

The business model implemented in bilsalg.dk suffers from a limit to success as it is directly linked to the number of cars sold from leasing and rental companies in Denmark (approximately 10% of all used cars) – therefore an alternative business model has been invented – the potential for selling ASP solutions.

This means that the software used in bilsalg.dk has been packaged and offered to independent car importers and dealers in Denmark. This represents a much higher potential in license fees, as the numbers of potential buyers are 29 importers and 900 new car dealers in Denmark. This business opportunity is very promising and could be a potential for internationalisation as well.

ASP Solutions:

The most recent offering in product development is the sale of ASP solutions to car importers and dealers based on the same IT platform that was developed for bilsalg.dk. Thereby sharing development costs while at the time substantially broadening their customer base. There are 29 importers and 900 new car dealers in Denmark. This business opportunity is very promising and could be a potential for internationalisation as well.

Internationalisation

There have been enquiries from various companies outside Denmark but due to the general decline in the dot.com industry as a whole, it has been extremely difficult to gain any ground without a show-case proving positive ROI. bilsalg.dk's strategy is therefore based on obtaining success in Denmark, operationally as well as financially. After that international expansion may be possible.

Contacts have already been established to potential international partners due to the presentations at international conferences and will naturally be maintained.

The concept has changed from an internally focused BtC business model to an integration of all sales channels into one software based marketplace – dynamics have been high and ongoing adaption a key to success.

Benefits are the key – not the deliverables.

Topics to Discuss:

1. How would you describe the business model of bilsalg.dk?
2. Discuss the relationship dependency between bilsalg.dk and the used car dealers, and do the same for private buyers.
3. Identify the strengths and weaknesses of the relationships between bilsalg.dk and the partners.

References

Dibb, S. and Simkin, L. (2001) *The Marketing Casebook – Cases and Concepts*, Thomson Learning.

Financial Times (2001) May-June 2001.10.19

Finansrådet (1994) *Bankerhvervets omdømme 1990-1994*,Vilstrup Research.

Heddaa L. (1998) *Flybonus: Verdens mest succesrige loyalitetsprogram*, Markedsføring.

Hougaard, S. (1995) *Relationstankegang som virksomhedsfilosofi i fremtidens pengeinstitut*, Handelshøjskolen i København.

Lynch, J. L. (1996) *Psychology of Relationship Banking*, Gresham.

McKinsey Quarterly (2001), vol. 3.

Nordiska Bankmannunion (1994) *Hvordan skal de nordiske banker overleve?*.

Normann, R. and Ramirez, R. (1983) *From Value Chain to Value Constelation: Designing Interactive Strategy*, Harvard Business Review.

Quelch, J., Kashami, K. and Vandermerve, S. (1994) *European Cases in Marketing Management*, Irwin.

Abbreviations

BtB	business to business
BtC	business to consumer
BtE	business to employees
BTO	built to order
CLC	customer life cycle
CRM	customer relationship management
CRS	computer reservation system
DPP	Direct Product Profitability
EDI	electronic data interchange
FBP	flight bonus program
FMCG	Fast Moving Comsumer Goods
HRM	human resources management
JIT	just in time
OEM	original equipment manufacturer
OTC	over the counter
PLC	product life cycle
ROI	return on investment
SCM	Supply Chain Management
SEC	Securities Exchange Commission
SWOT	strengths weaknesses opportunities threats
USP	unique selling proposition
VAM	value adding model

Index of subjects